Story and Art by Arina Tanemura

SAKURA HIME

The Legend of Princess Sakura

Characters

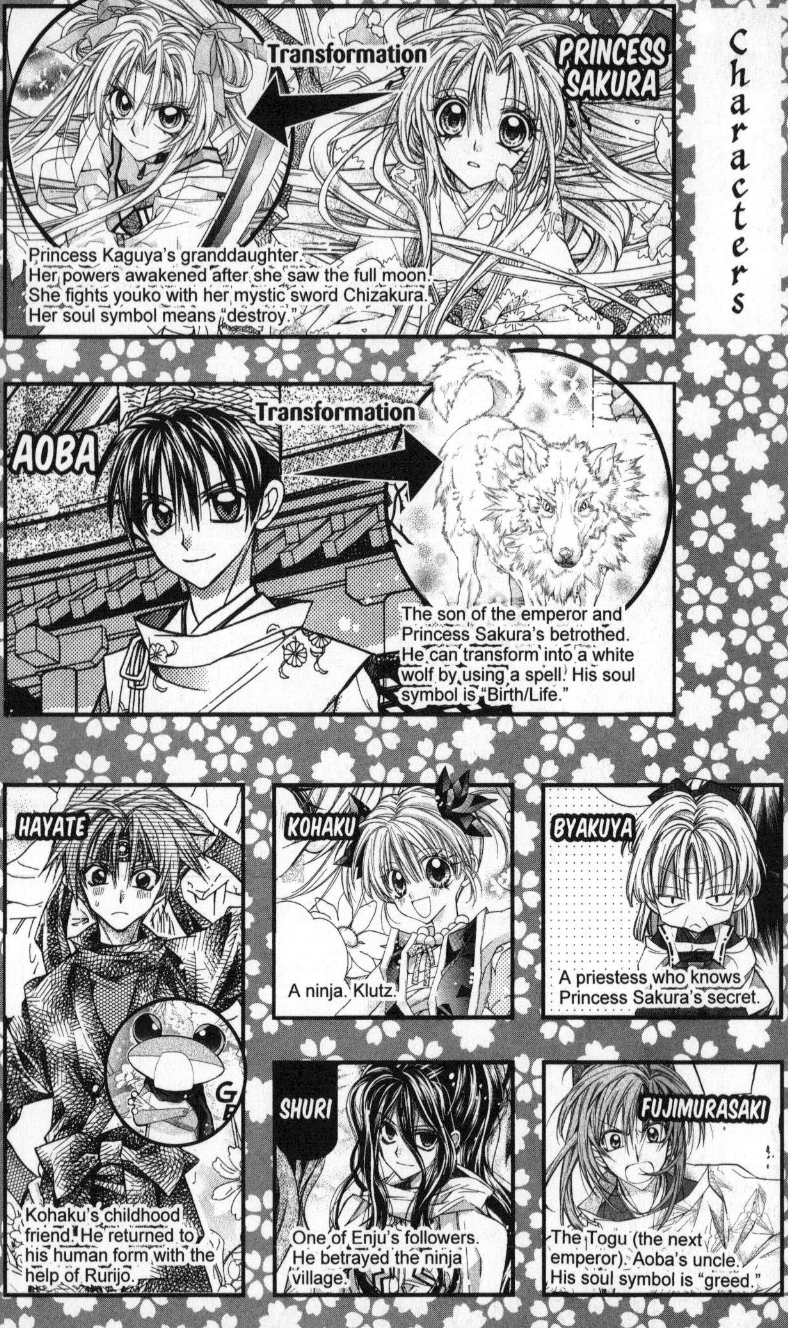

PRINCESS SAKURA
Transformation
Princess Kaguya's granddaughter. Her powers awakened after she saw the full moon. She fights youko with her mystic sword Chizakura. Her soul symbol means "destroy."
AOBA
Transformation
The son of the emperor and Princess Sakura's betrothed. He can transform into a white wolf by using a spell. His soul symbol is "Birth/Life."
BYAKUYA
A priestess who knows Princess Sakura's secret.
KOHAKU
A ninja. Klutz.
FUJIMURASAKI
The Togu (the next emperor). Aoba's uncle. His soul symbol is "greed."
SHURI
One of Enju's followers. He betrayed the ninja village.
HAYATE
GE
Kohaku's childhood friend. He returned to his human form with the help of Rurijo.

ENJU

Princess Sakura's older brother. He used to be kind, but he hates humans now and hopes to reinstate the moon kingdom.

ASAGIRI

A snow spirit. Her body is unusually small from taking the blood of a one-inch spirit. She lives together with Princess Sakura.

RURIJO

Enju's follower. She hates Princess Sakura.

SAKURA HIME
The Legend of Princess Sakura

Story Thus Far

Heian era. Princess Sakura, granddaughter to Princess Kaguya, has the power to wield the mystic sword Chizakura. Under orders from the Emperor, she must hunt down youko with Aoba, her betrothed.

Enju, whom she thought dead, kidnaps her and takes her to Shura Yugenden. While under Enju's control, Sakura kills Ukyo with her sword Chizakura. Sakura also learns of Enju's plans to resurrect Princess Kaguya and decides to part ways with him. She escapes Shura Yugenden with the help of Aoba, Fujimurasaki, and her other allies who came to save her.

Sakura and Aoba return to their daily lives, but Sakura discovers that Aoba will have a life cut short, just like Asagiri. Sakura is determined to take responsibility for his fate and begins her search for Enju once again.

Sakura is given the opportunity to meet the emperor, but she is attacked and tossed into the water chamber. Enju appears and murders the emperor to save Sakura, but he also steals Sakura's and Aoba's soul symbols. Meanwhile, Maimai meet with Princess Yuri under Enju's orders, but he is shocked to find she's the sister he was separated from as a child. Maimai decides to protect her from Enju, and they leave the capital together...

SAKURA HIME
The Legend of Princess Sakura

....

CONTENTS

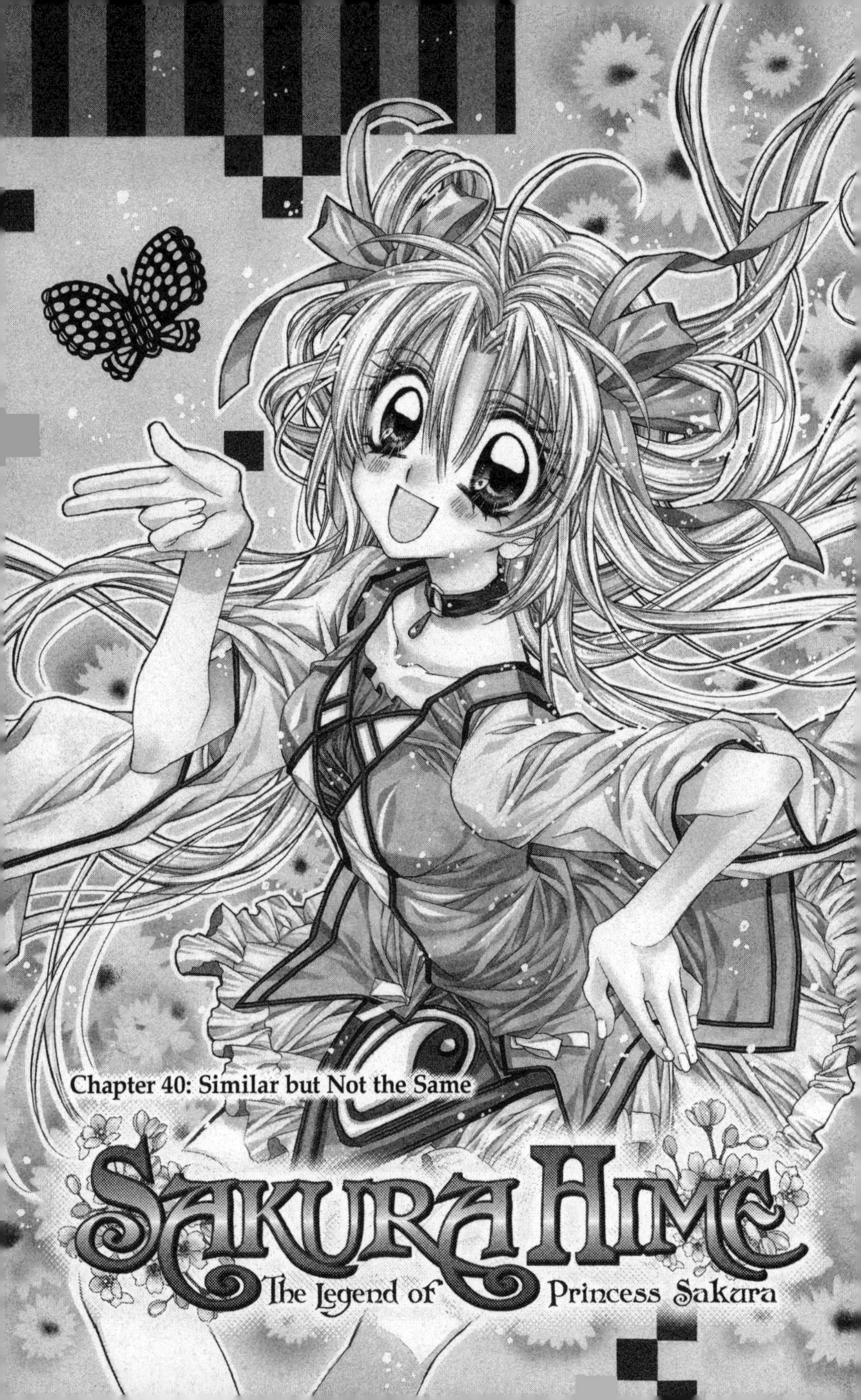
Chapter 40: Similar but Not the Same
SAKURA HIME
The Legend of Princess Sakura

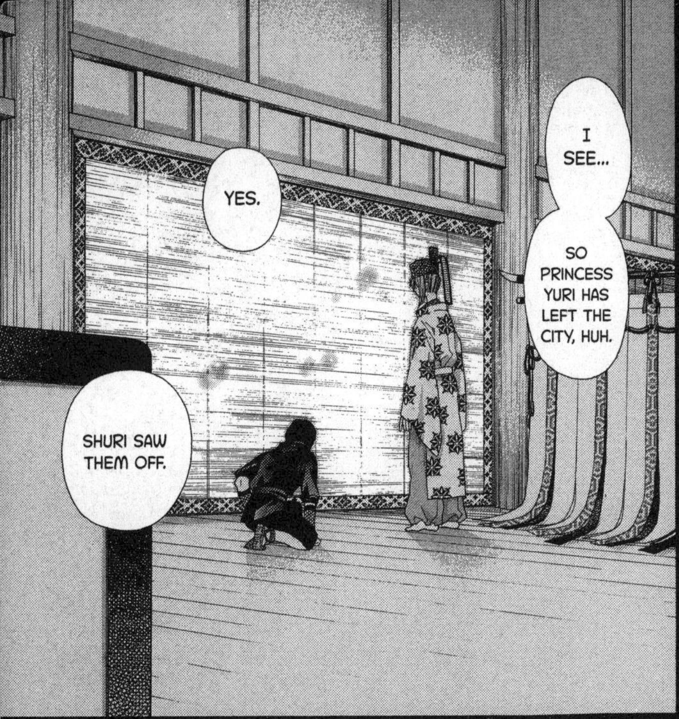
I SEE...
SO PRINCESS YURI HAS LEFT THE CITY, HUH.
YES.
SHURI SAW THEM OFF.

Chapter 40: Similar but Not the Same

(※ I'm giving away the story.)

The chapter title refers to Sakura and Rurijo of course. The two look similar, but they are very different... Hayate and Aoba know that—Enju is the only one who doesn't seem to realize it. But Enju treats Rurijo differently. If it had been Sakura, Enju wouldn't have gotten so angry. He couldn't forgive because Rujiro was the one who did it. He probably sees her as a "woman," I think. Anyhow, Enju is clueless when it comes to romantic relationships... (Maybe that is his weakness...?) I enjoy drawing Rurijo and Hayate. They're so heartwarming to watch. Hayate is in a romantic mood, but both Rurijo and I see him as a good friend. I think that's the reason the story doesn't get too heavy and depressing.

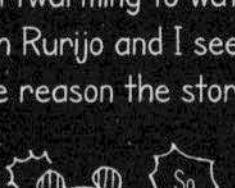
So mean!

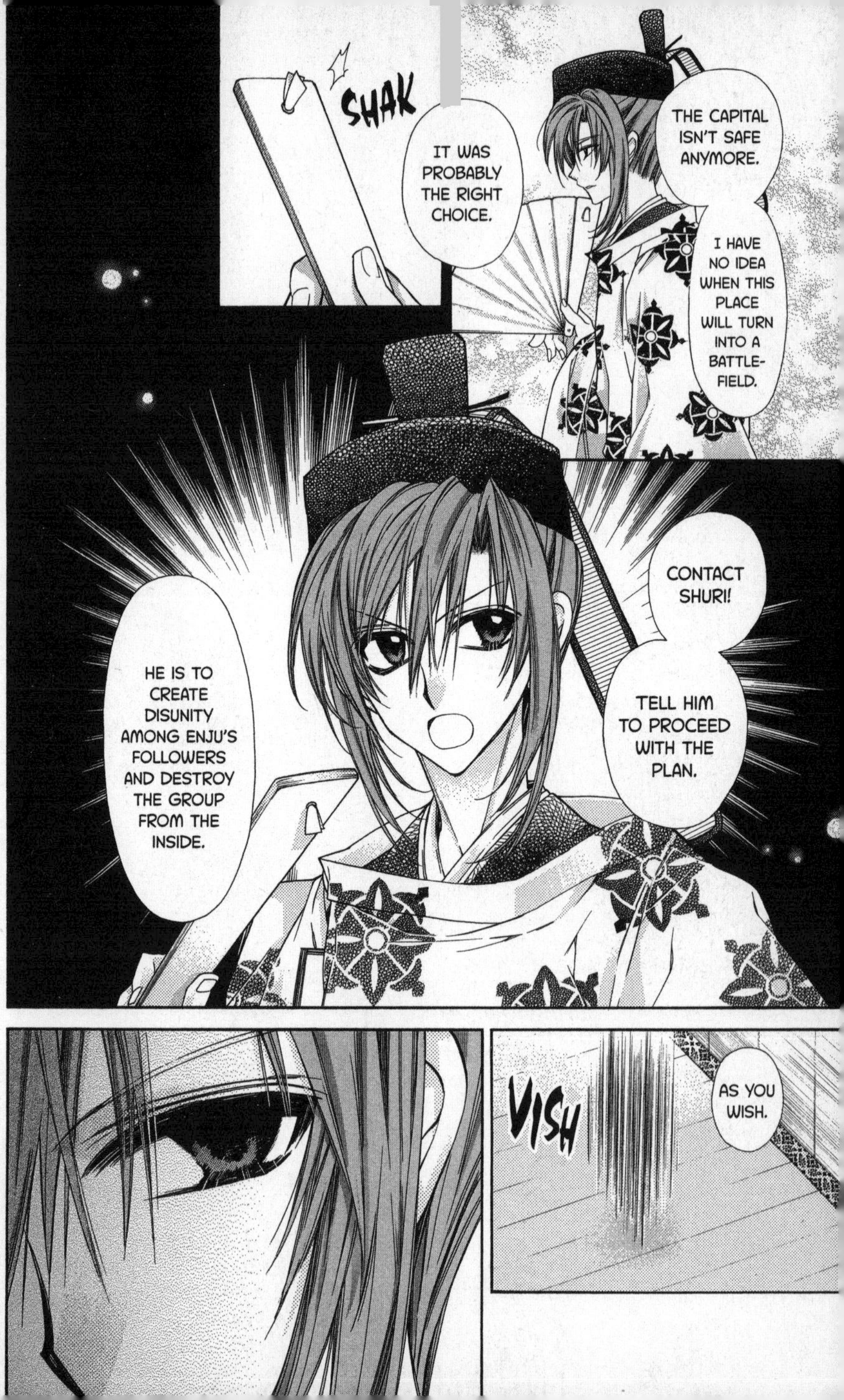
THE CAPITAL ISN'T SAFE ANYMORE.
I HAVE NO IDEA WHEN THIS PLACE WILL TURN INTO A BATTLE-FIELD.
SHAK
IT WAS PROBABLY THE RIGHT CHOICE.
CONTACT SHURI!
TELL HIM TO PROCEED WITH THE PLAN.
HE IS TO CREATE DISUNITY AMONG ENJU'S FOLLOWERS AND DESTROY THE GROUP FROM THE INSIDE.
AS YOU WISH.
VISH

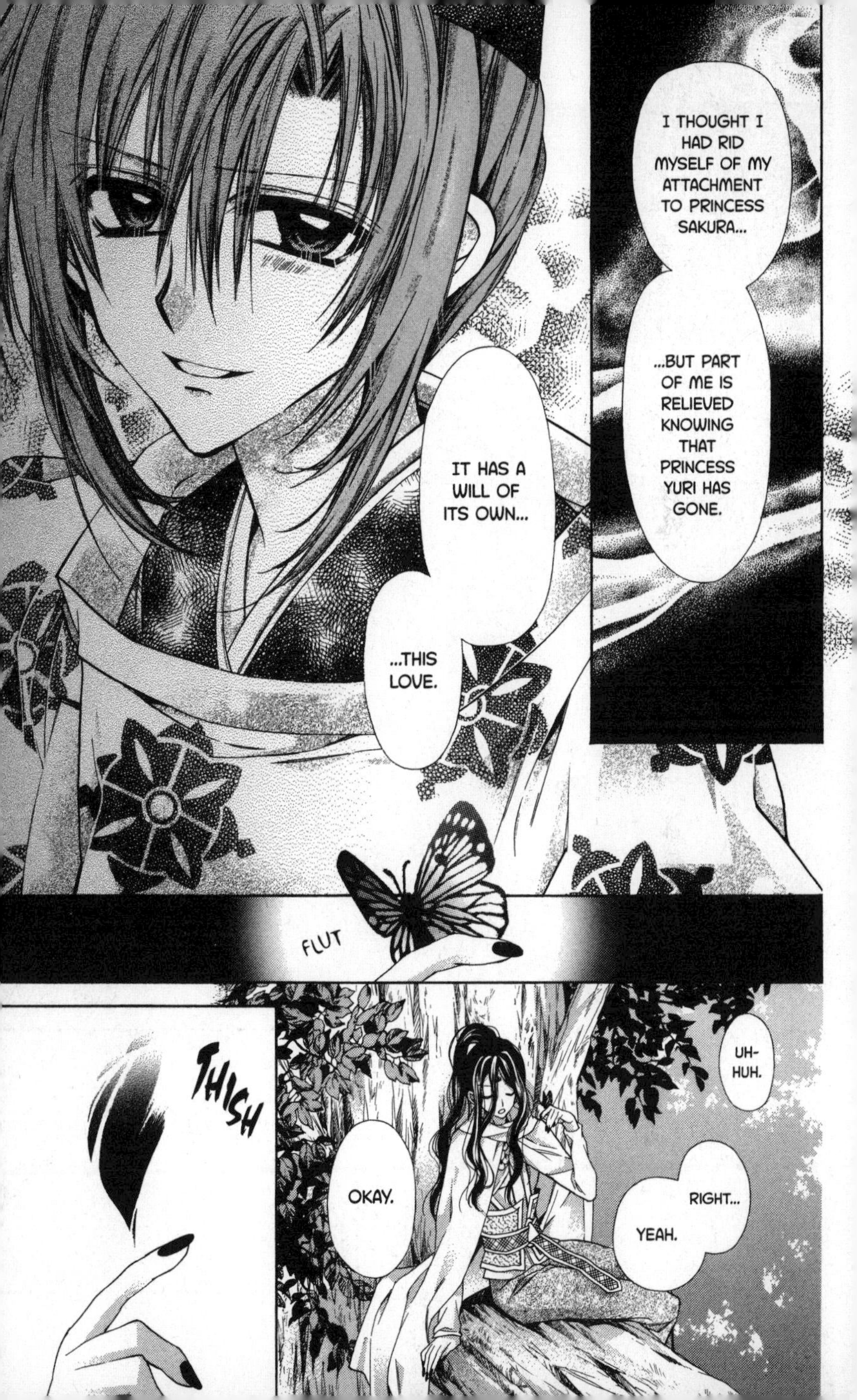
I THOUGHT I HAD RID MYSELF OF MY ATTACHMENT TO PRINCESS SAKURA...
...BUT PART OF ME IS RELIEVED KNOWING THAT PRINCESS YURI HAS GONE.
IT HAS A WILL OF ITS OWN...
...THIS LOVE.
FLUT
UH-HUH.
RIGHT...
YEAH.
OKAY.
THISH

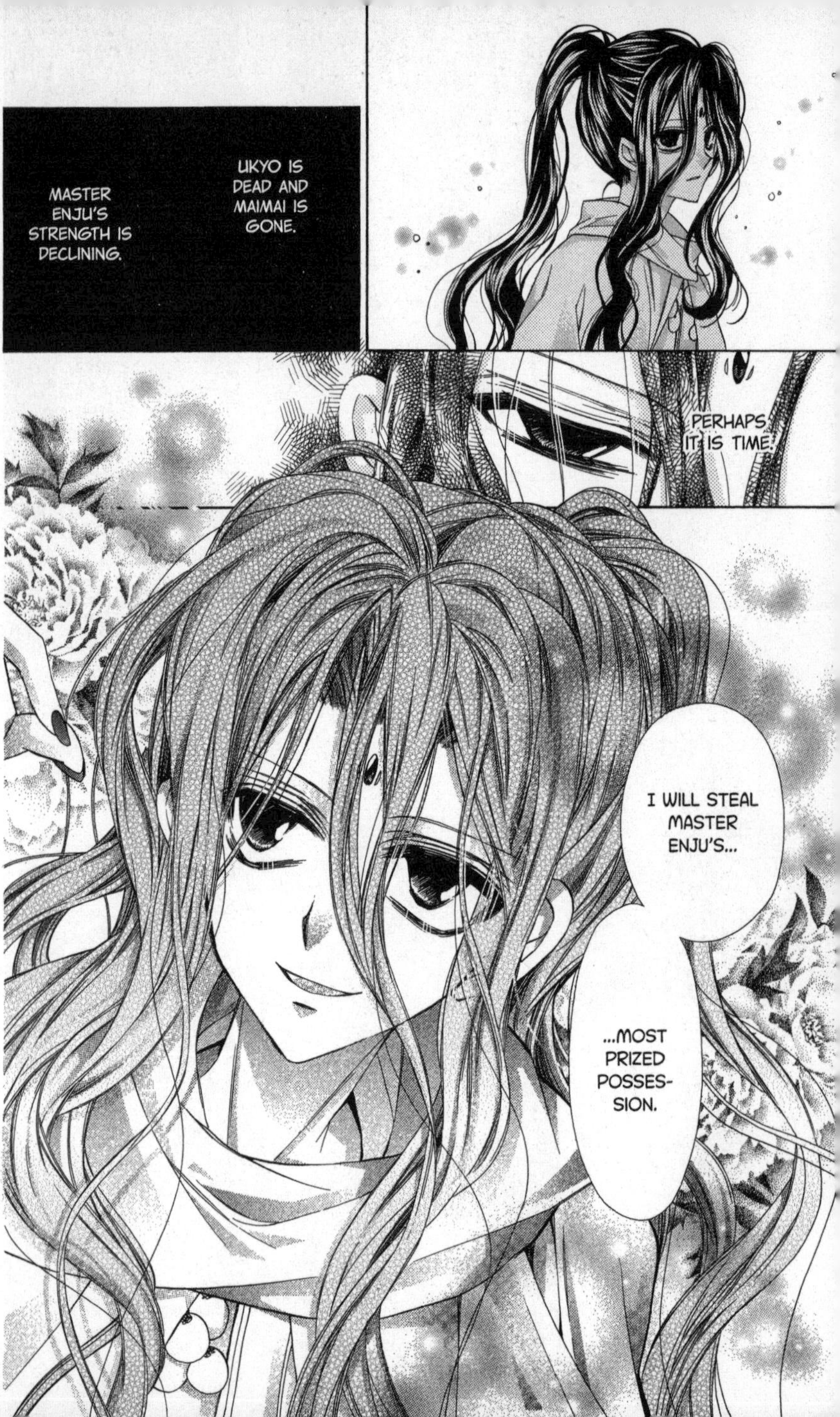
UKYO IS DEAD AND MAIMAI IS GONE.
MASTER ENJU'S STRENGTH IS DECLINING.
PERHAPS IT IS TIME.
I WILL STEAL MASTER ENJU'S...
...MOST PRIZED POSSESSION.

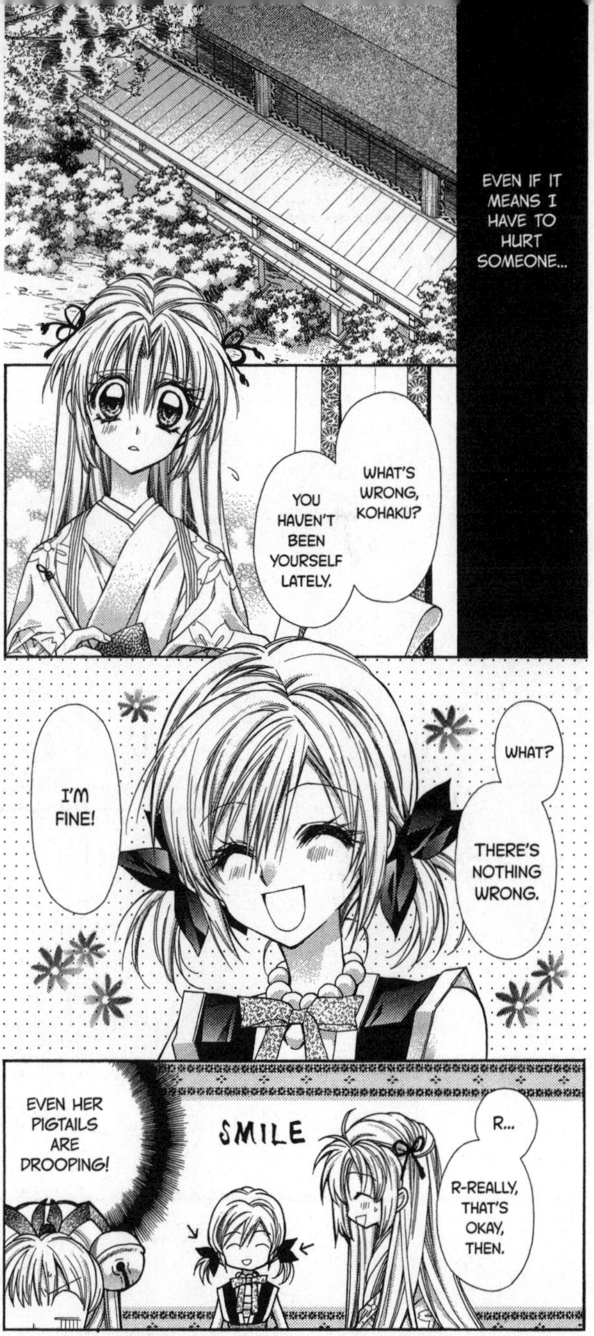
EVEN IF IT MEANS I HAVE TO HURT SOMEONE...
WHAT'S WRONG, KOHAKU?
YOU HAVEN'T BEEN YOURSELF LATELY.
WHAT?
THERE'S NOTHING WRONG.
I'M FINE!
R...
R-REALLY, THAT'S OKAY, THEN.
SMILE
EVEN HER PIGTAILS ARE DROOPING!

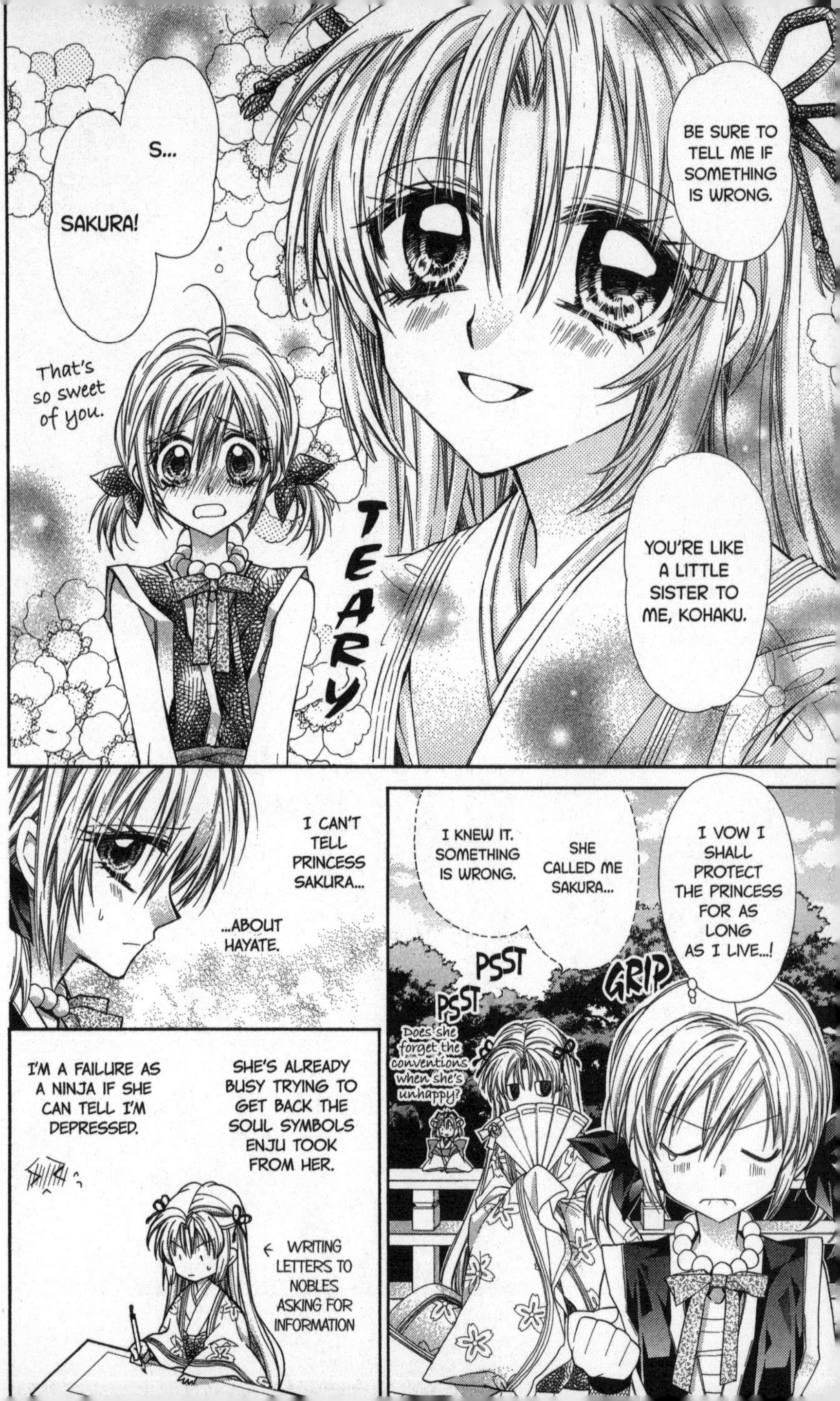
BE SURE TO TELL ME IF SOMETHING IS WRONG.
YOU'RE LIKE A LITTLE SISTER TO ME, KOHAKU.
S...
SAKURA!
That's so sweet of you.
TEARY
I VOW I SHALL PROTECT THE PRINCESS FOR AS LONG AS I LIVE...!
GRIP
SHE CALLED ME SAKURA...
I KNEW IT. SOMETHING IS WRONG.
PSST
PSST
Does she forget the conventions when she's unhappy?
I CAN'T TELL PRINCESS SAKURA...
...ABOUT HAYATE.
SHE'S ALREADY BUSY TRYING TO GET BACK THE SOUL SYMBOLS ENJU TOOK FROM HER.
I'M A FAILURE AS A NINJA IF SHE CAN TELL I'M DEPRESSED.
WRITING LETTERS TO NOBLES ASKING FOR INFORMATION

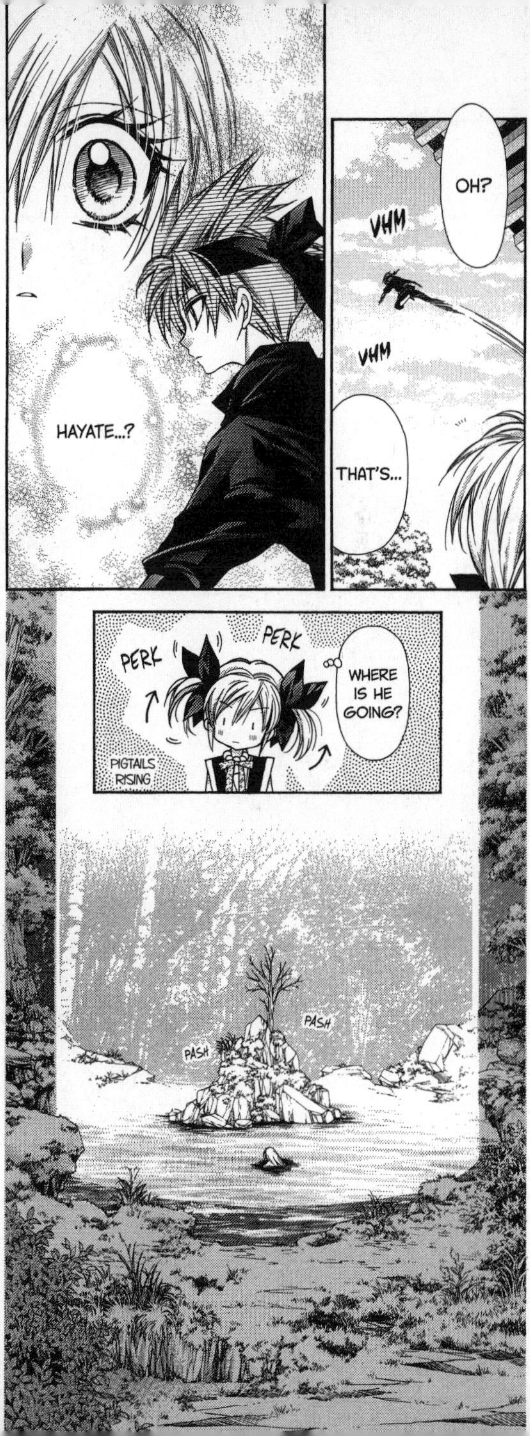

OH?
VHM
VHM
THAT'S...
HAYATE...?
PERK
PERK
WHERE IS HE GOING?
PIGTAILS RISING
PASH
PASH

Halloo

Hello! Arina Tanemura here! I bring to you volume 11 of *Sakura Hime: The Legend of Princess Sakura.* ♪

The cover illustration for this volume is of Sakura and Rurijo. They were naked last time they were on the cover, so this time I dressed them up nicely. ♥ The color (background) is black! I've always wanted to give that a try. And so, let's begin volume 11 in which Sakura and Rurijo take center stage!

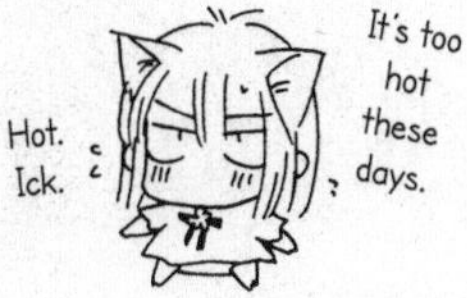

Hot. Ick.
It's too hot these days.

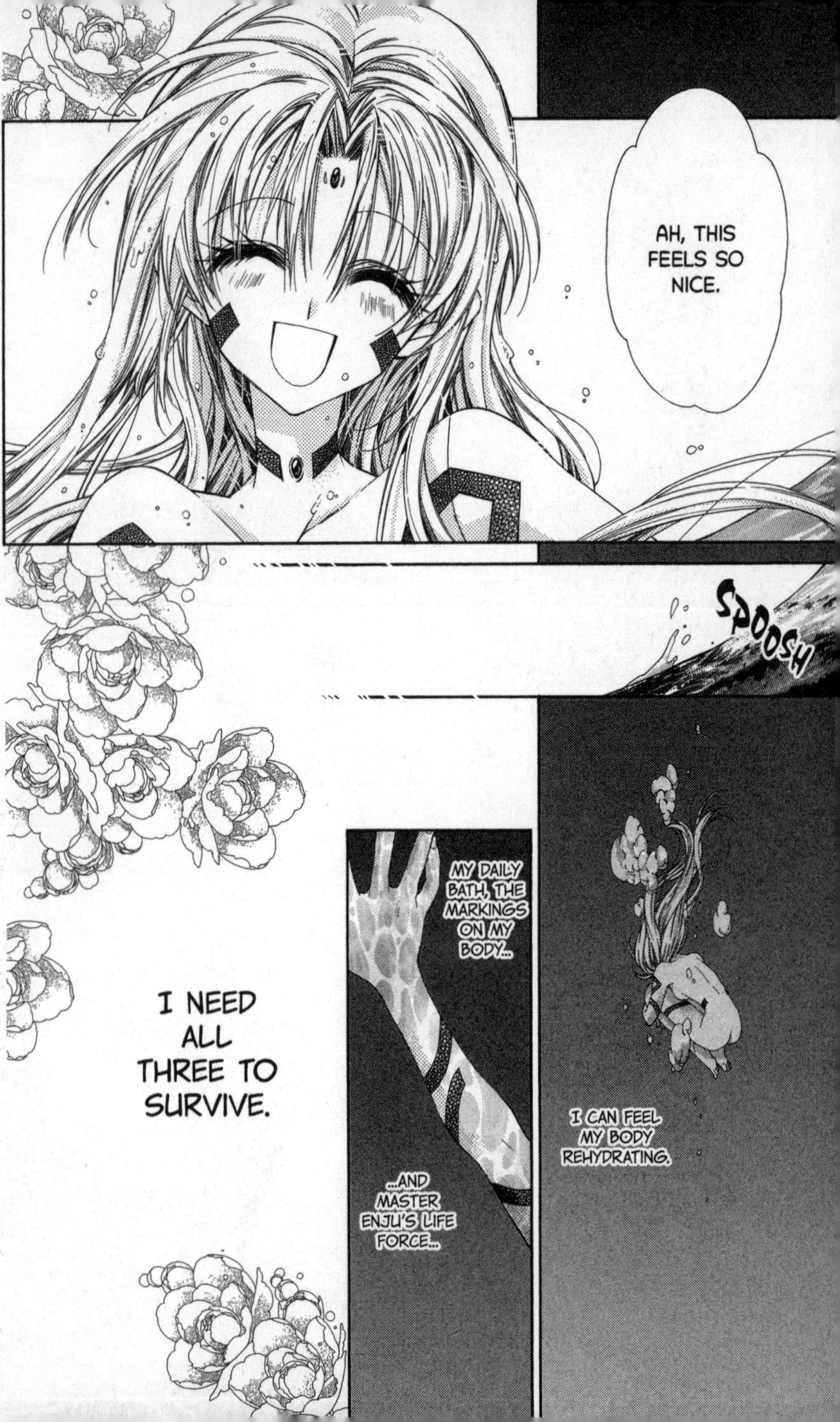
AH, THIS FEELS SO NICE.
SPOOSH
I CAN FEEL MY BODY REHYDRATING.
MY DAILY BATH, THE MARKINGS ON MY BODY...
...AND MASTER ENJU'S LIFE FORCE...
I NEED ALL THREE TO SURVIVE.

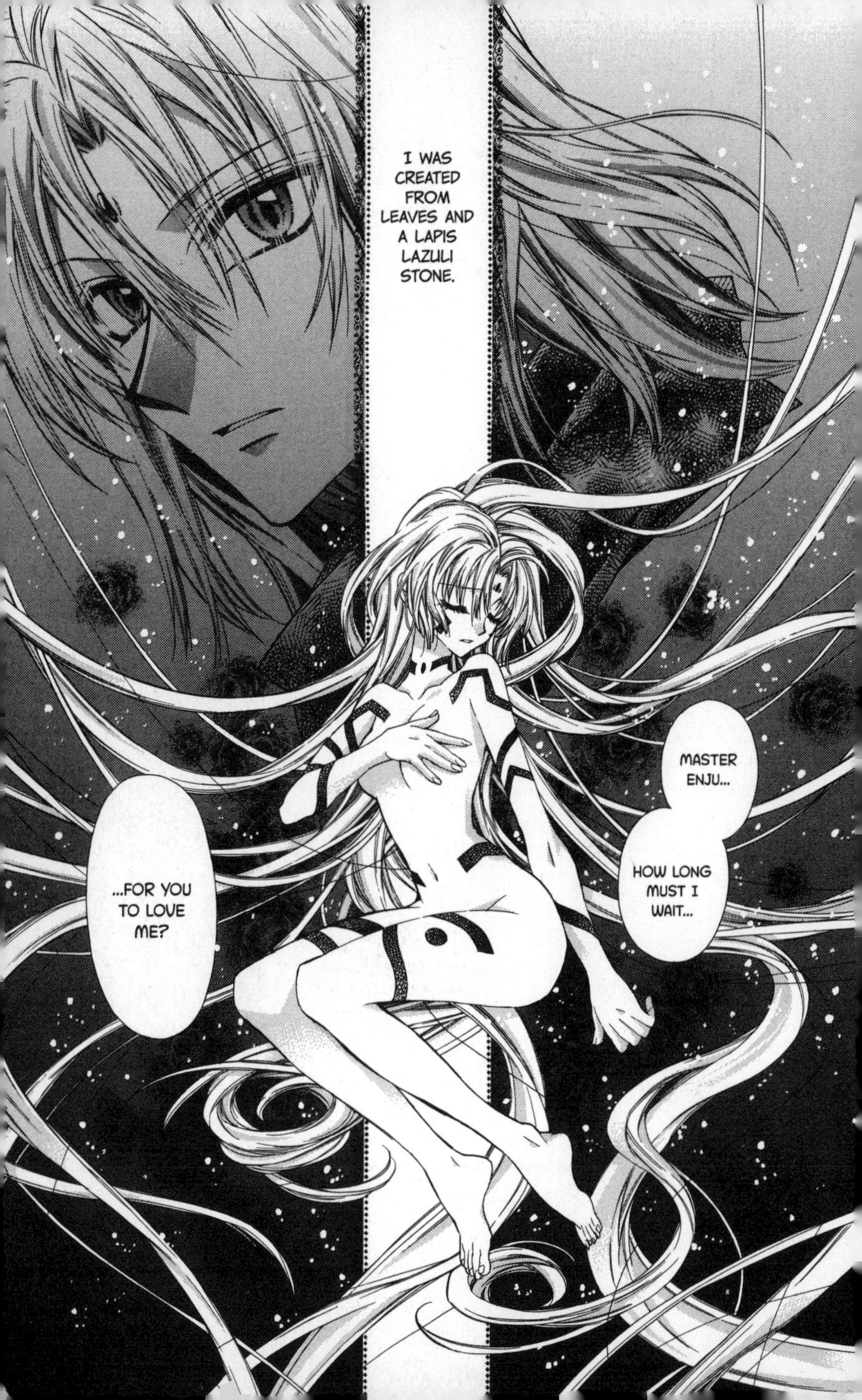
I WAS CREATED FROM LEAVES AND A LAPIS LAZULI STONE.
MASTER ENJU...
HOW LONG MUST I WAIT...
...FOR YOU TO LOVE ME?

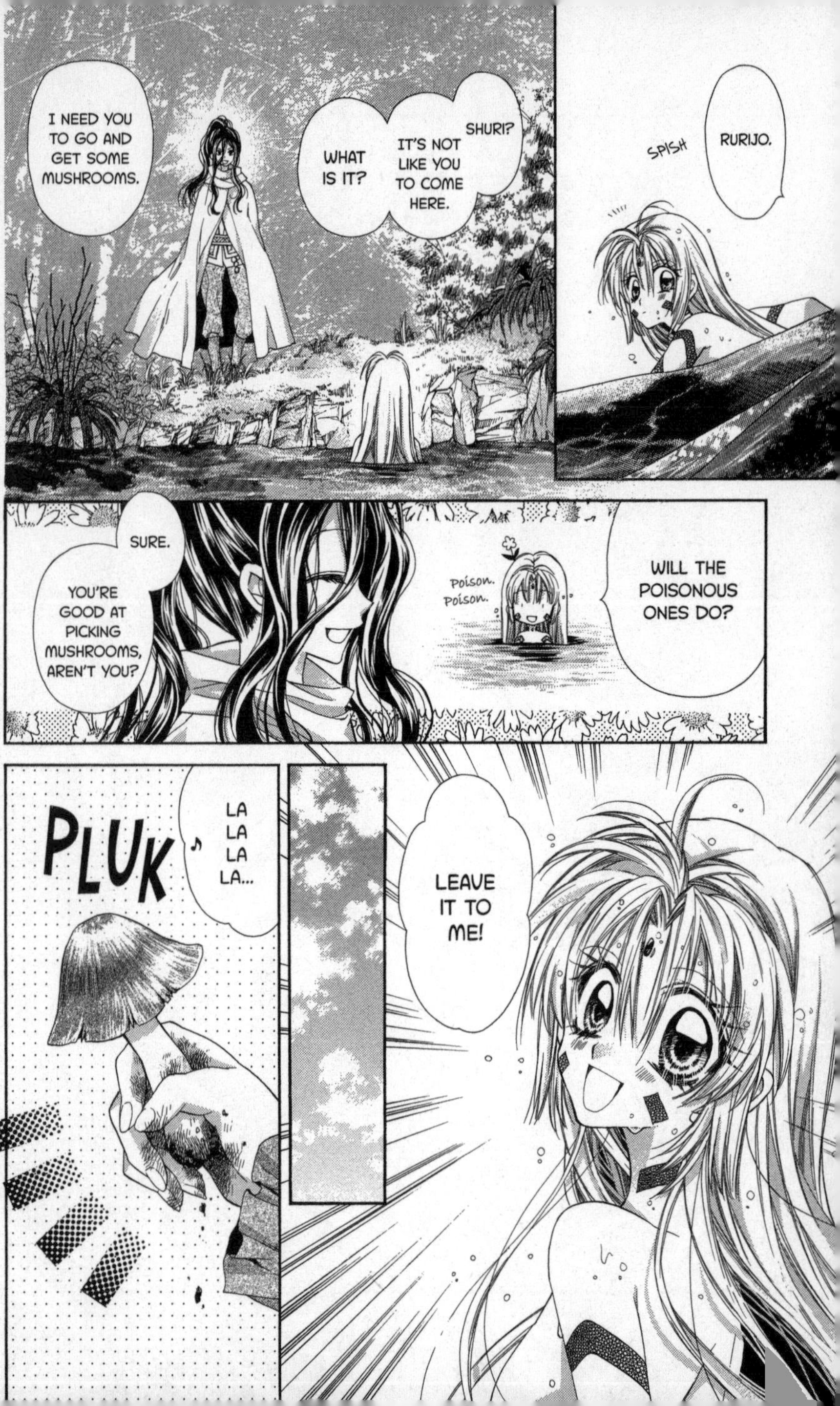
SPISH
RURIJO.
SHURI? IT'S NOT LIKE YOU TO COME HERE.
WHAT IS IT?
I NEED YOU TO GO AND GET SOME MUSHROOMS.
WILL THE POISONOUS ONES DO?
Poison. Poison.
SURE.
YOU'RE GOOD AT PICKING MUSHROOMS, AREN'T YOU?
LEAVE IT TO ME!
LA LA LA LA...
PLUK

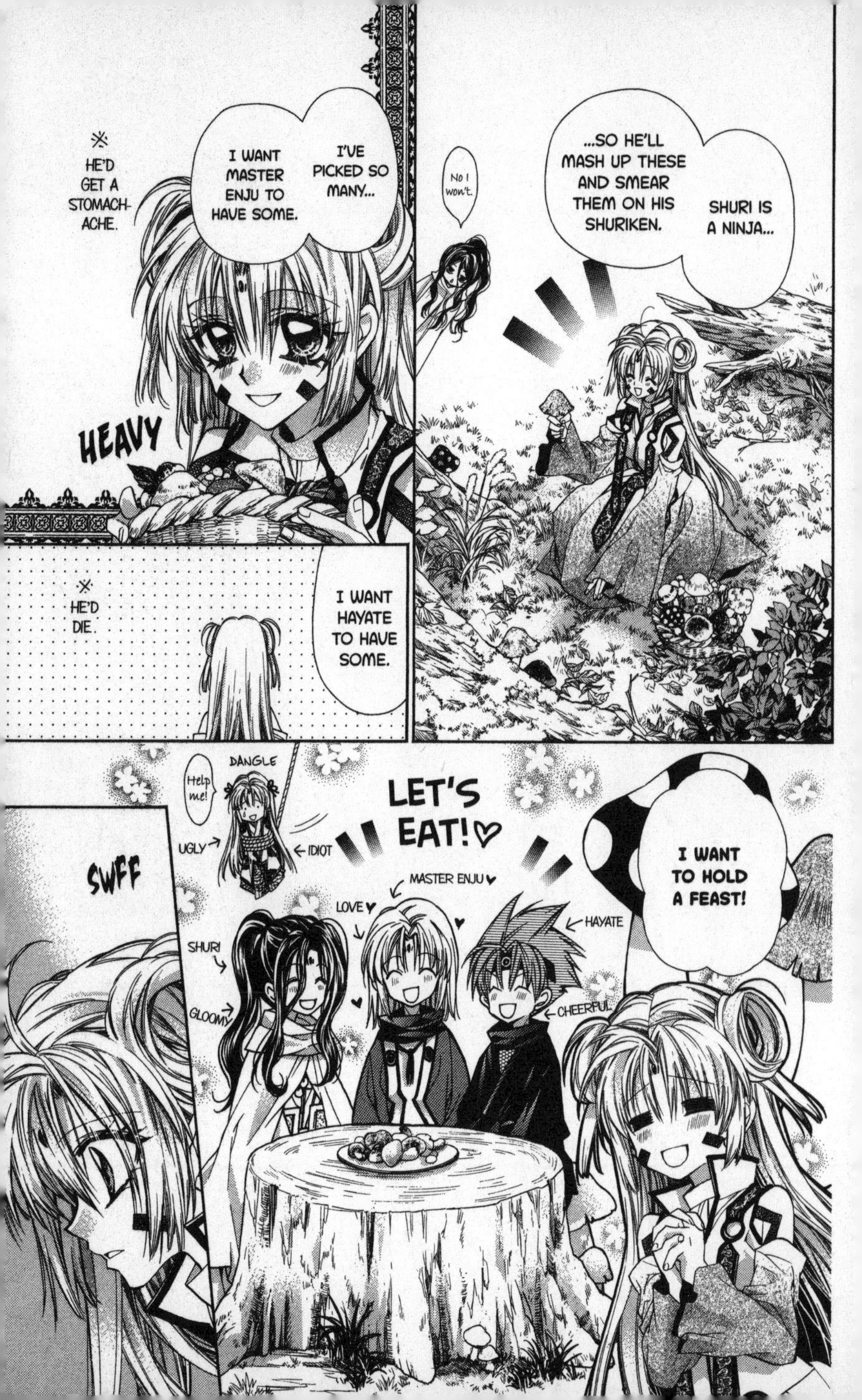
SHURI IS A NINJA...
...SO HE'LL MASH UP THESE AND SMEAR THEM ON HIS SHURIKEN.
No! Won't.
I'VE PICKED SO MANY...
I WANT MASTER ENJU TO HAVE SOME.
※ HE'D GET A STOMACHACHE.
HEAVY
I WANT HAYATE TO HAVE SOME.
※ HE'D DIE.
I WANT TO HOLD A FEAST!
LET'S EAT!♡
HAYATE
CHEERFUL
MASTER ENJU♥
LOVE♥
DANGLE
Help me!
IDIOT
UGLY
SHURI
GLOOMY
SWFF

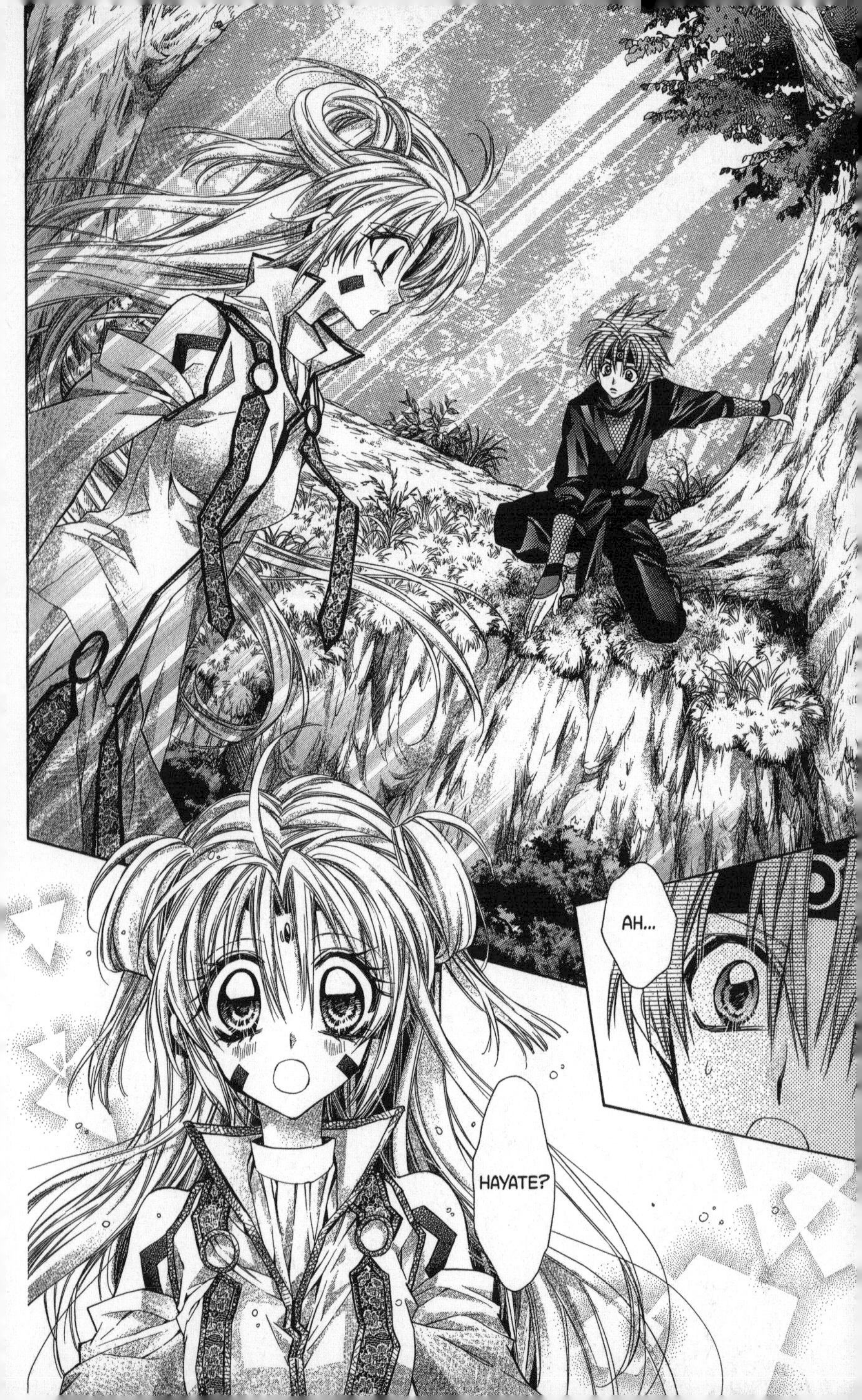
AH...
HAYATE?

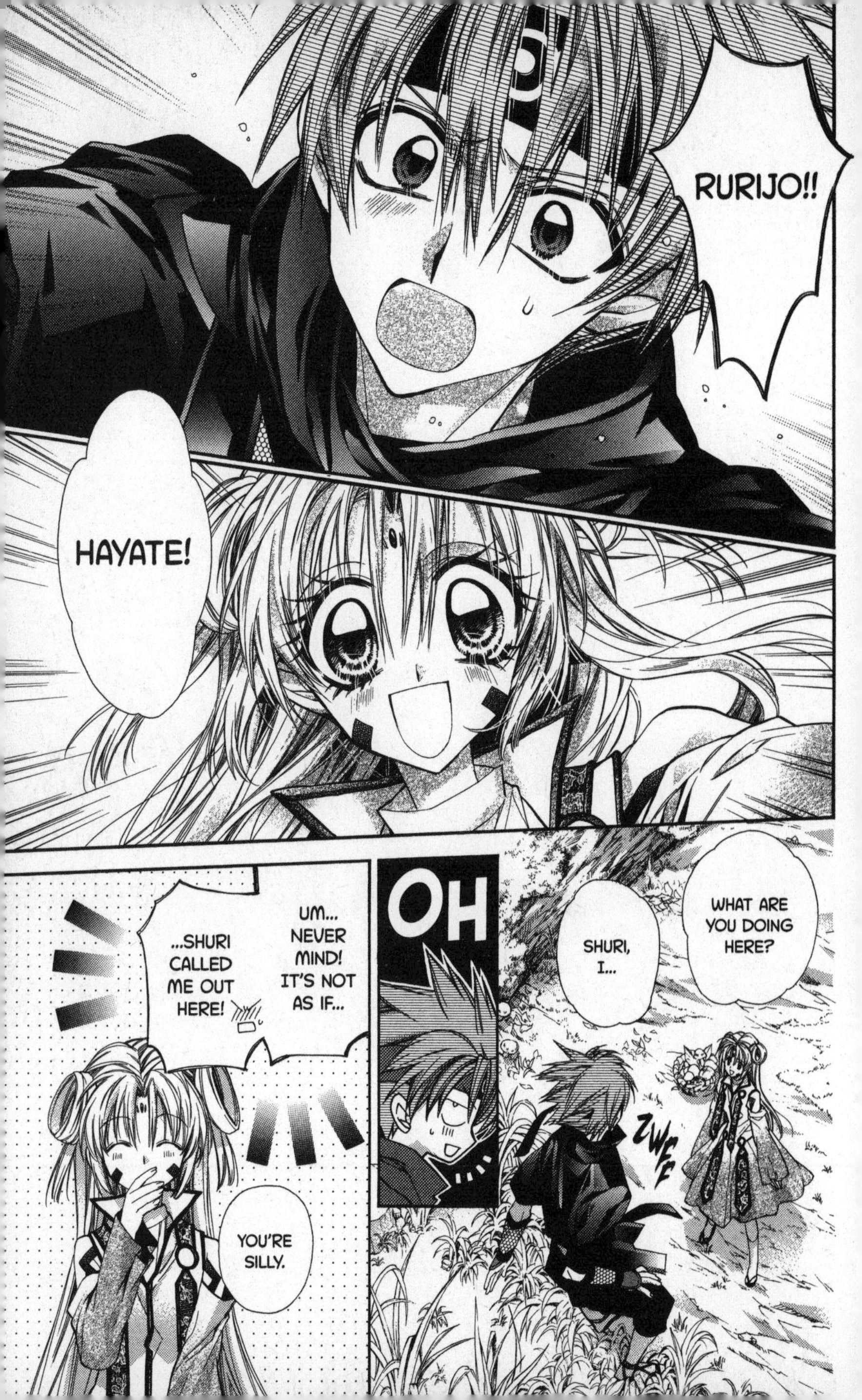
RURIJO!!
HAYATE!
WHAT ARE YOU DOING HERE?
SHURI, I...
OH
UM... NEVER MIND! IT'S NOT AS IF...
...SHURI CALLED ME OUT HERE!
YOU'RE SILLY.

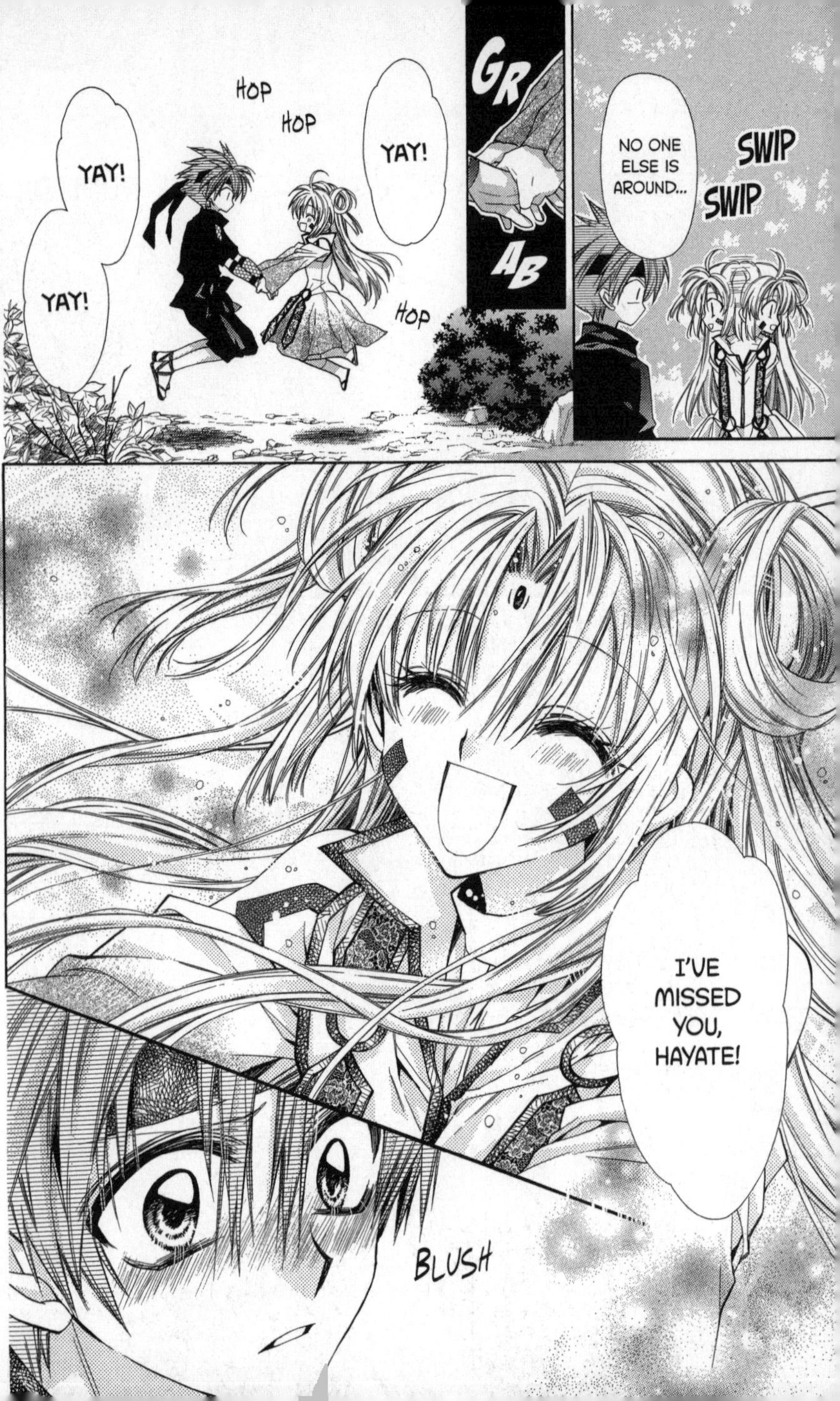
NO ONE ELSE IS AROUND...
SWIP
SWIP
GRAB
YAY!
HOP
HOP
YAY!
YAY!
HOP
I'VE MISSED YOU, HAYATE!
BLUSH

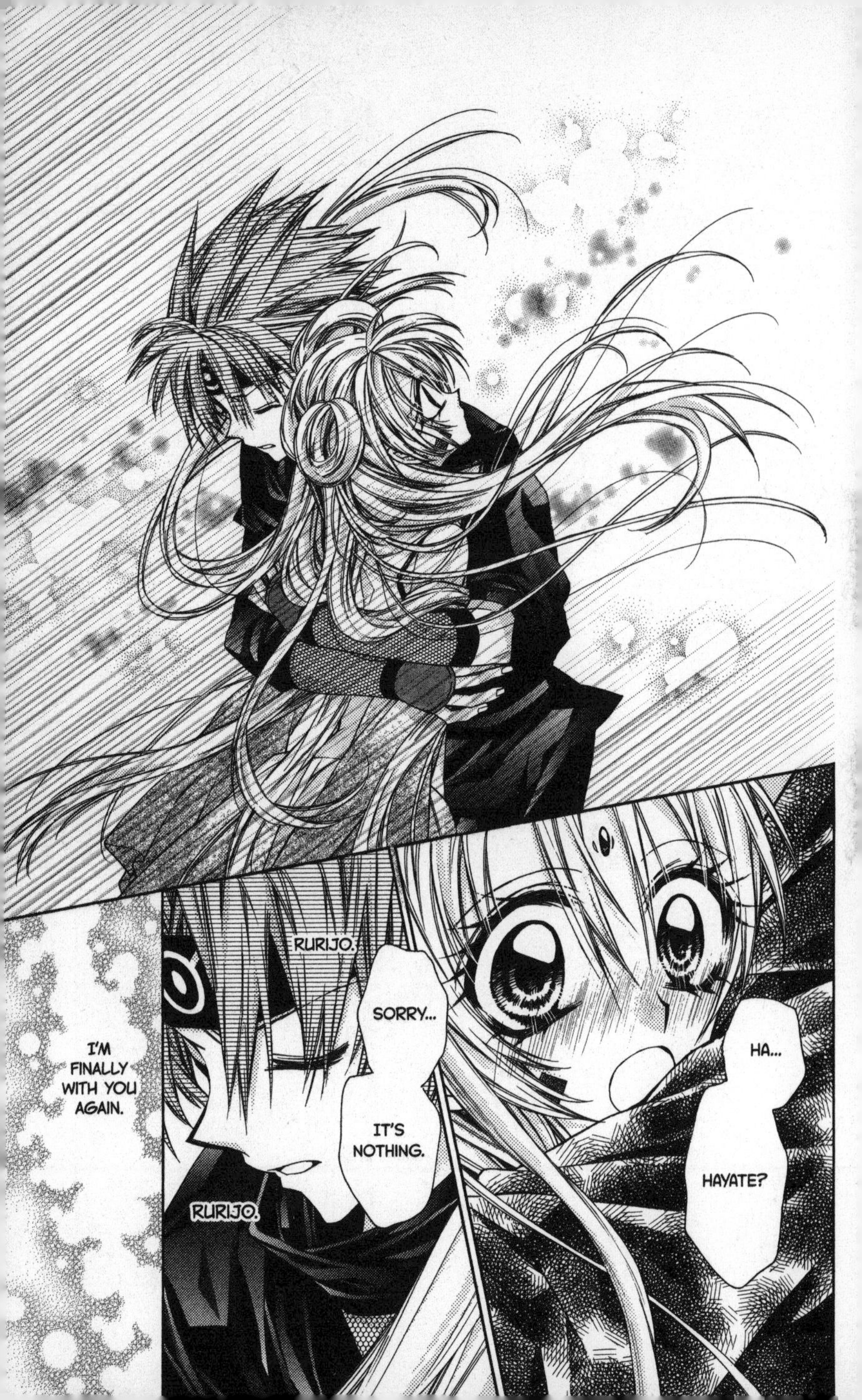
HA...
HAYATE?
RURIJO.
SORRY...
IT'S NOTHING.
RURIJO.
I'M FINALLY WITH YOU AGAIN.

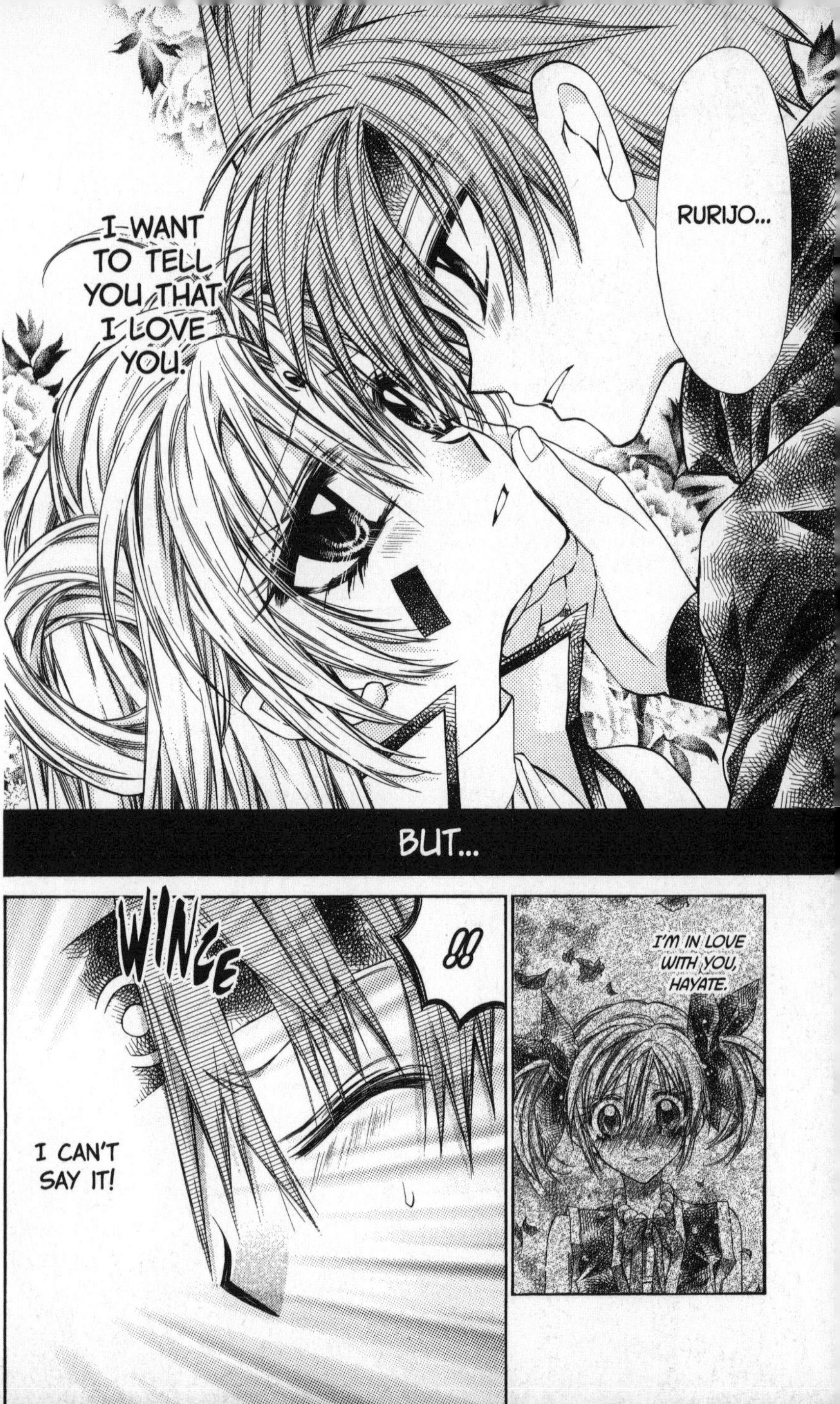
RURIJO...
I WANT TO TELL YOU THAT I LOVE YOU.
BUT...
I'M IN LOVE WITH YOU, HAYATE.
!!
WINCE
I CAN'T SAY IT!

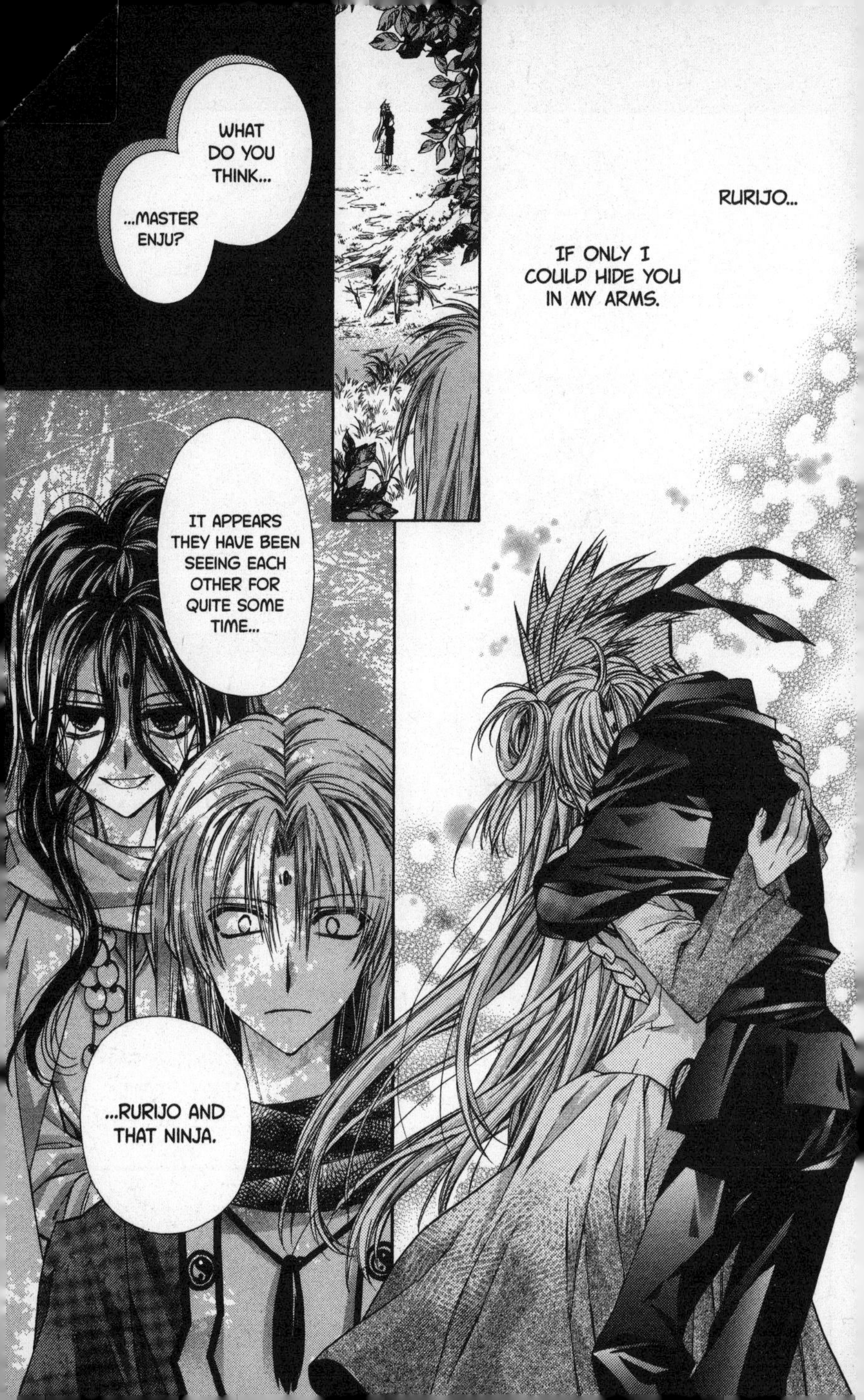
RURIJO...
IF ONLY I COULD HIDE YOU IN MY ARMS.
WHAT DO YOU THINK...
...MASTER ENJU?
IT APPEARS THEY HAVE BEEN SEEING EACH OTHER FOR QUITE SOME TIME...
...RURIJO AND THAT NINJA.

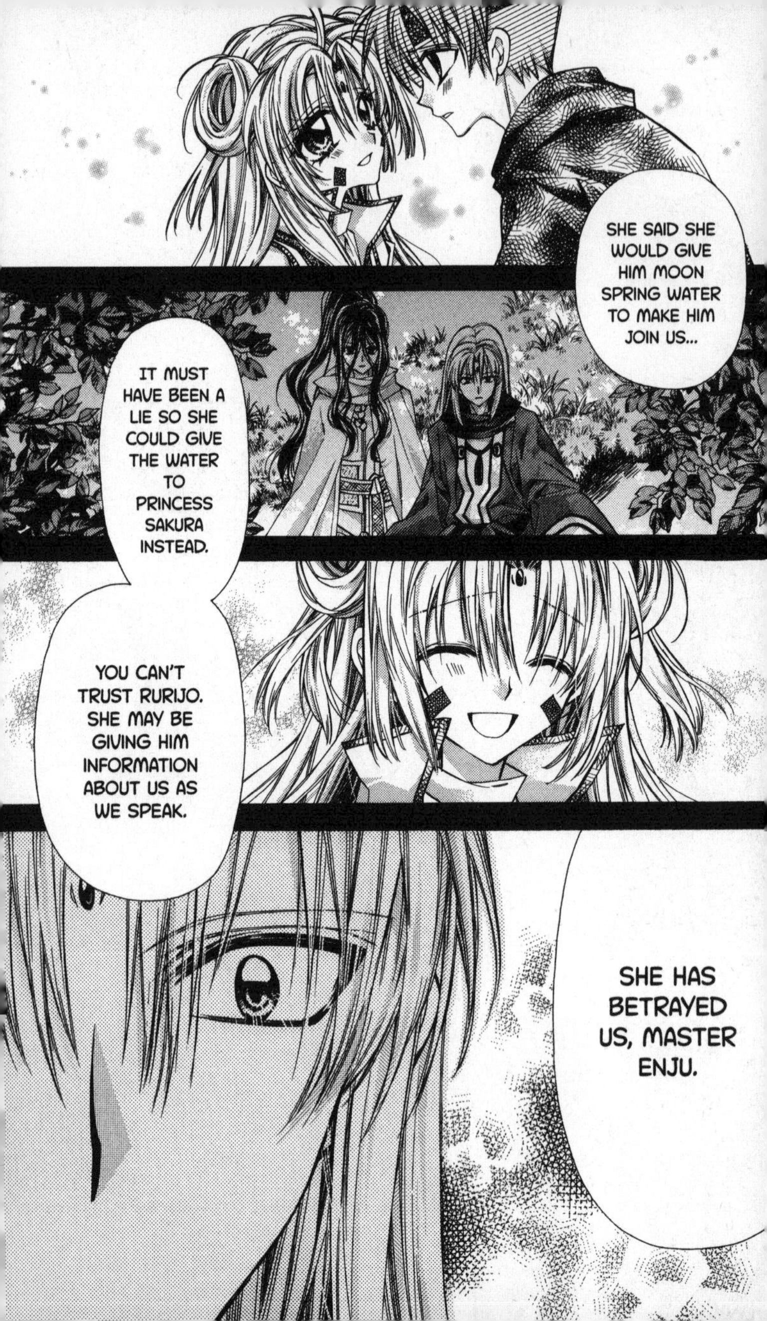
SHE SAID SHE WOULD GIVE HIM MOON SPRING WATER TO MAKE HIM JOIN US...
IT MUST HAVE BEEN A LIE SO SHE COULD GIVE THE WATER TO PRINCESS SAKURA INSTEAD.
YOU CAN'T TRUST RURIJO. SHE MAY BE GIVING HIM INFORMATION ABOUT US AS WE SPEAK.
SHE HAS BETRAYED US, MASTER ENJU.

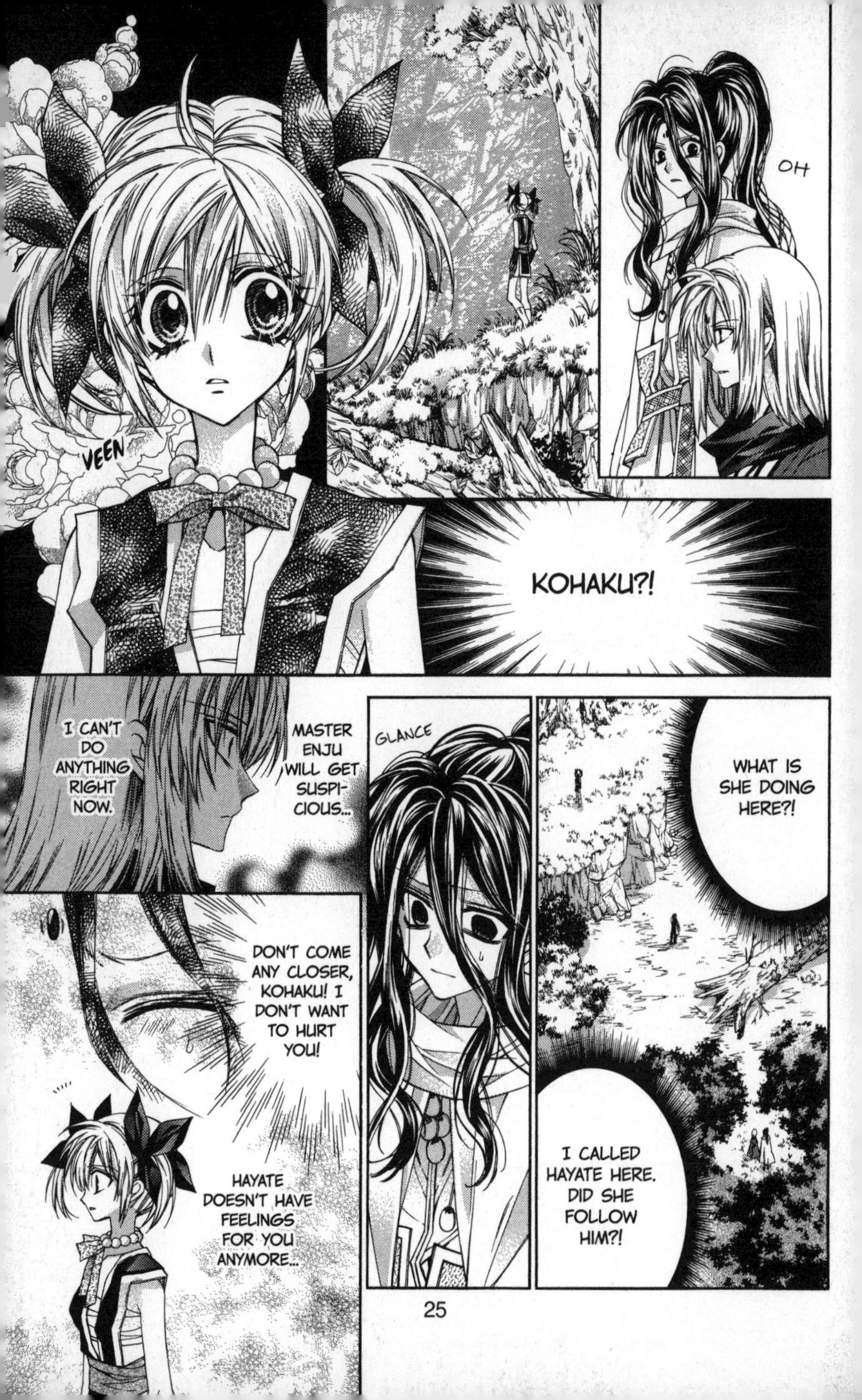
OH
KOHAKU?!
VEEN
WHAT IS SHE DOING HERE?!
I CALLED HAYATE HERE. DID SHE FOLLOW HIM?!
GLANCE
MASTER ENJU WILL GET SUSPICIOUS...
I CAN'T DO ANYTHING RIGHT NOW.
DON'T COME ANY CLOSER, KOHAKU! I DON'T WANT TO HURT YOU!
HAYATE DOESN'T HAVE FEELINGS FOR YOU ANYMORE...

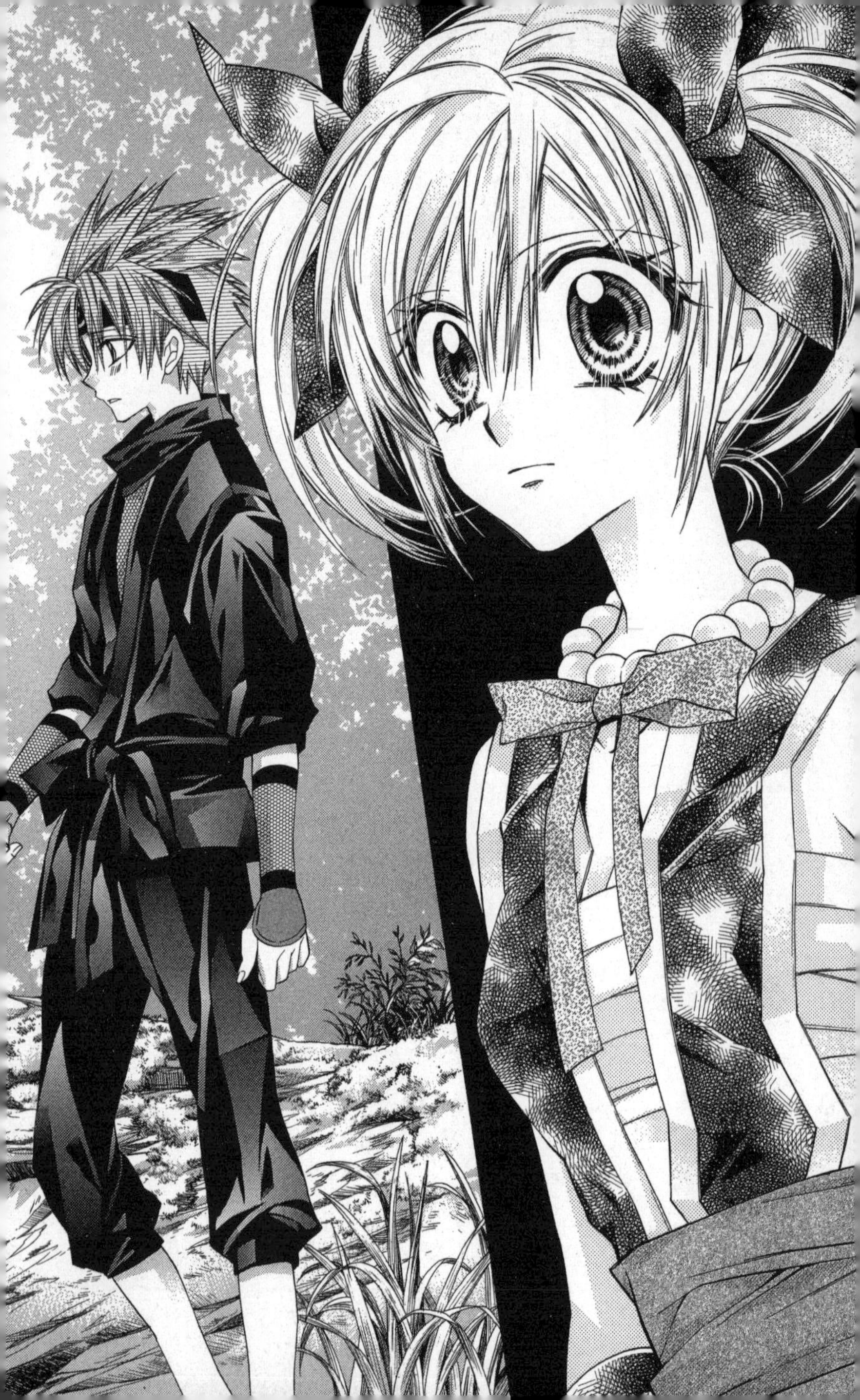

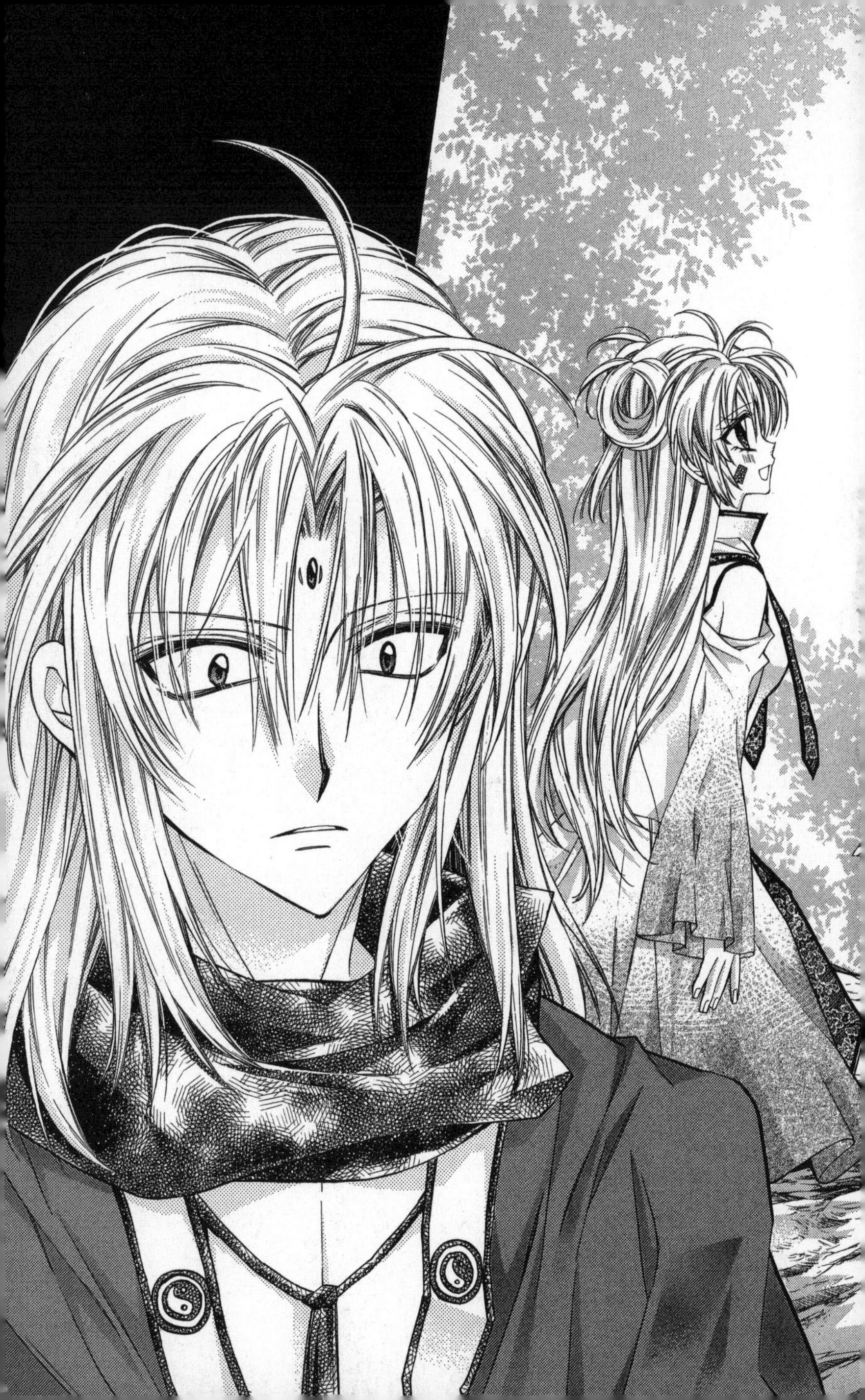

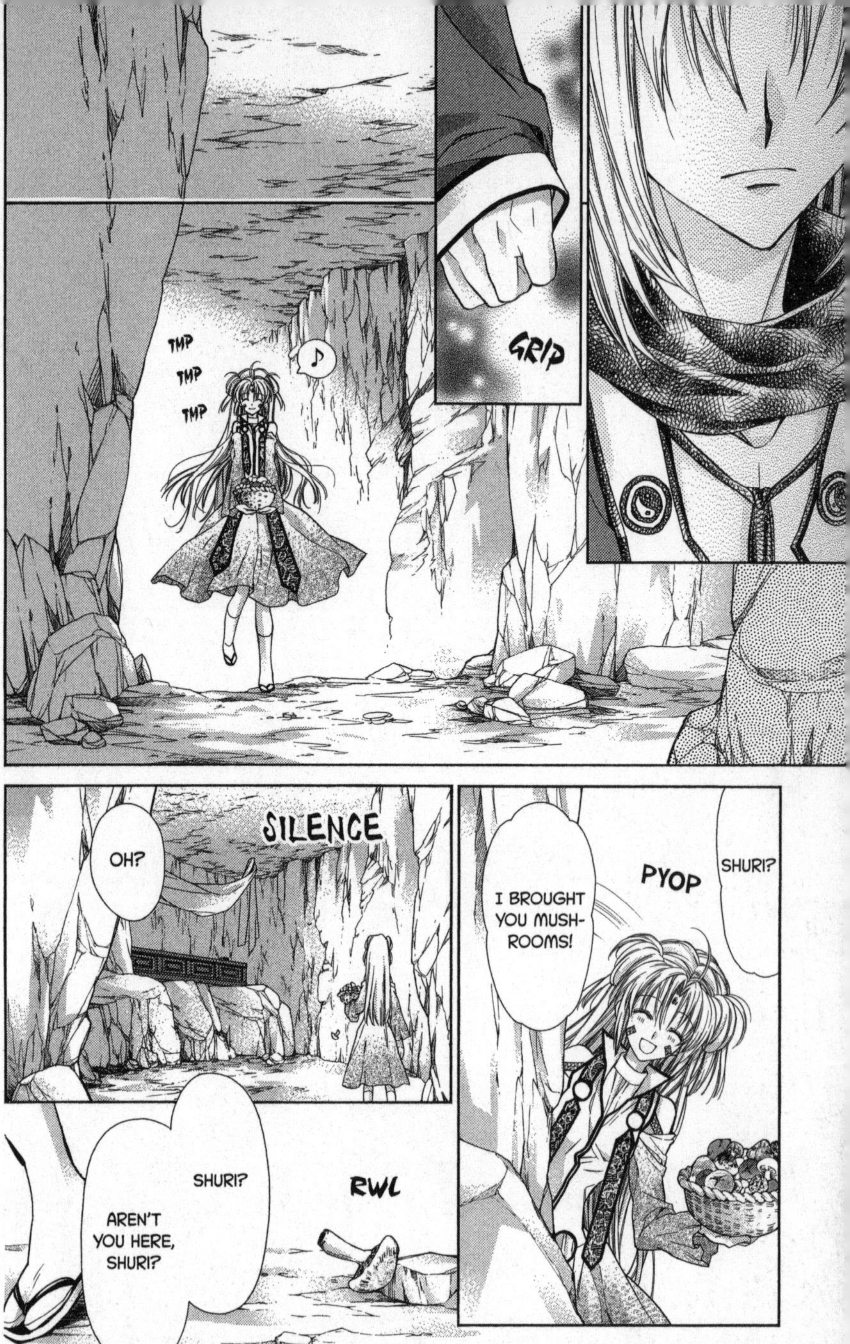
GRIP
TMP
TMP
TMP
♪
SHURI?
PYOP
I BROUGHT YOU MUSH-ROOMS!
SILENCE
OH?
SHURI?
AREN'T YOU HERE, SHURI?
RWL

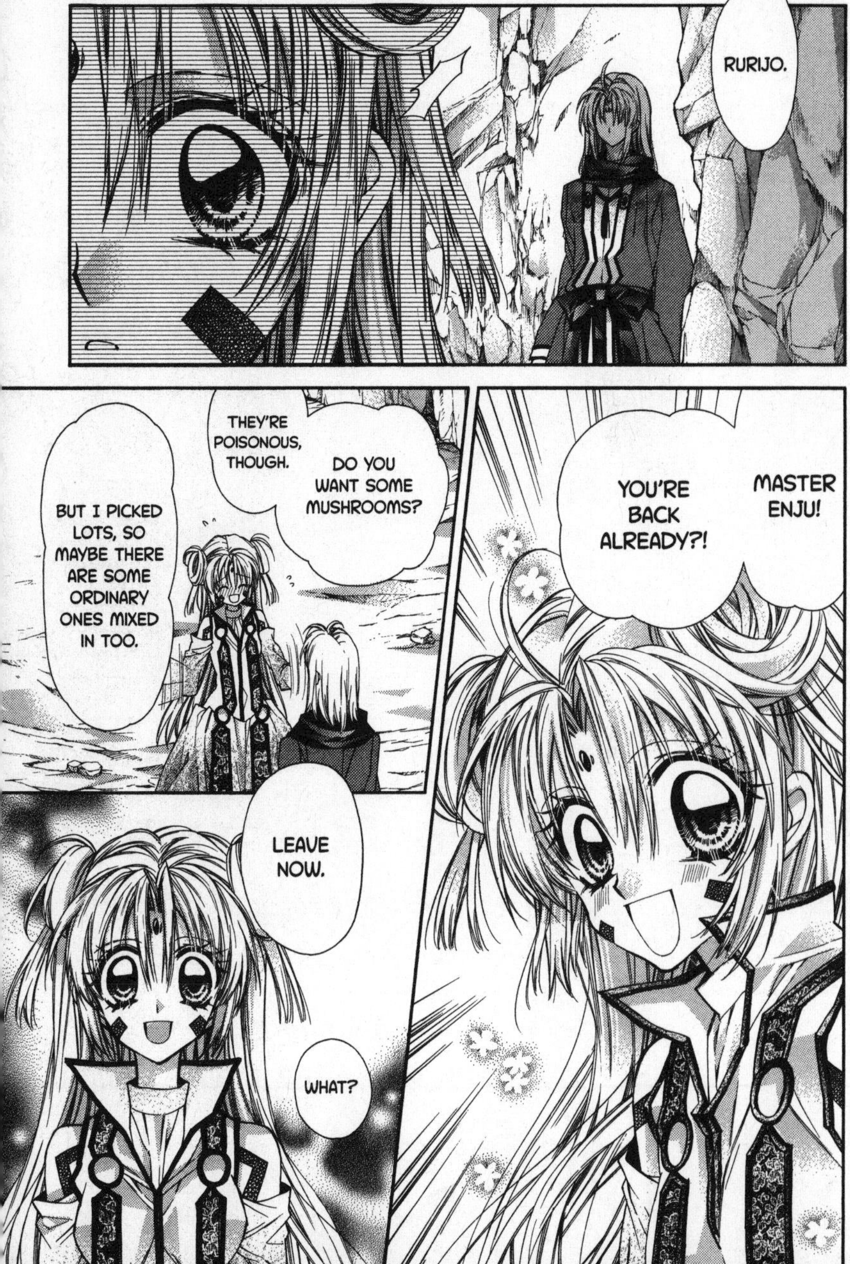
RURIJO.
MASTER ENJU!
YOU'RE BACK ALREADY?!
DO YOU WANT SOME MUSHROOMS?
THEY'RE POISONOUS, THOUGH.
BUT I PICKED LOTS, SO MAYBE THERE ARE SOME ORDINARY ONES MIXED IN TOO.
LEAVE NOW.
WHAT?

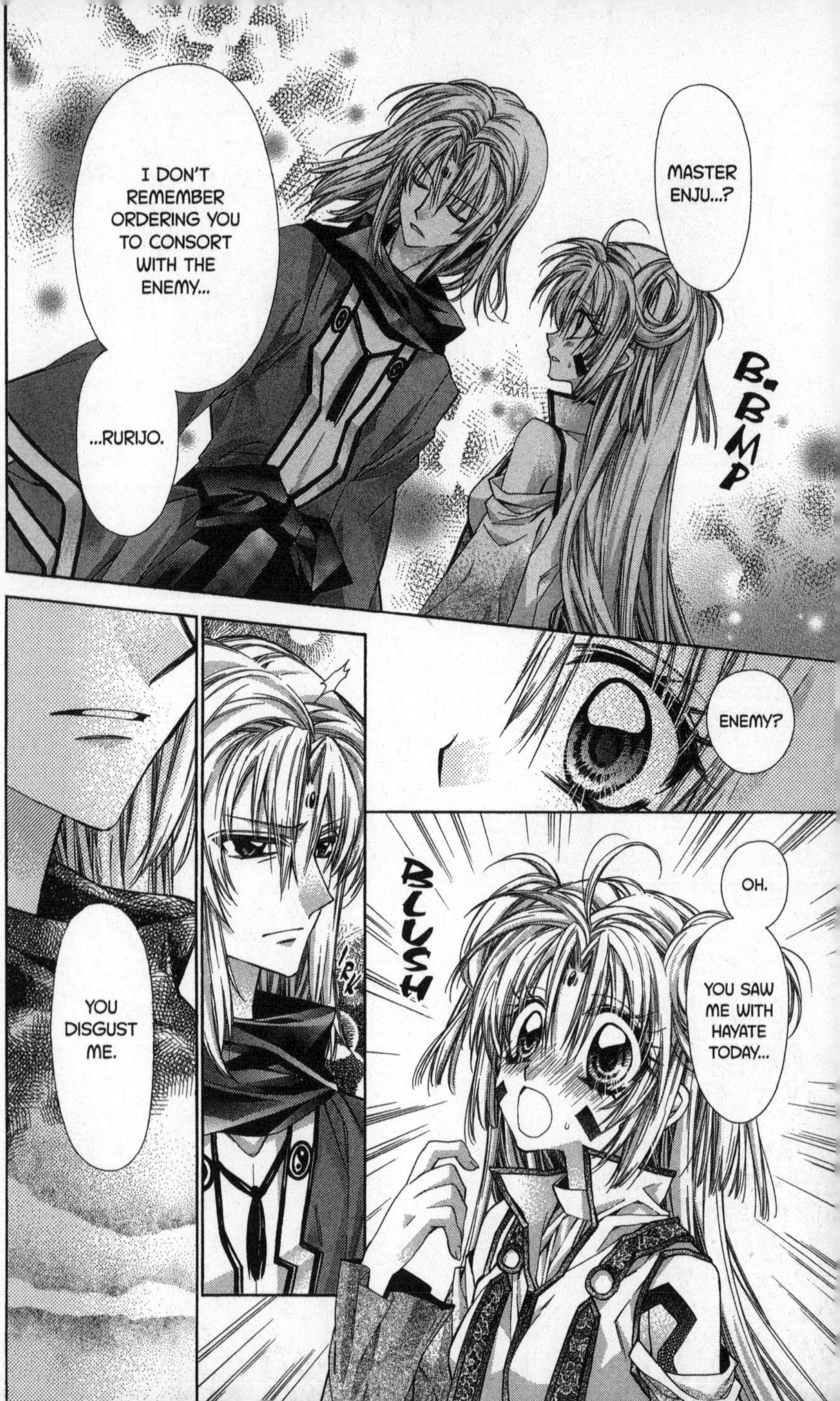
MASTER ENJU...?
B-BMP
I DON'T REMEMBER ORDERING YOU TO CONSORT WITH THE ENEMY...
...RURIJO.
ENEMY?
BLUSH
OH.
YOU SAW ME WITH HAYATE TODAY...
IRK
YOU DISGUST ME.

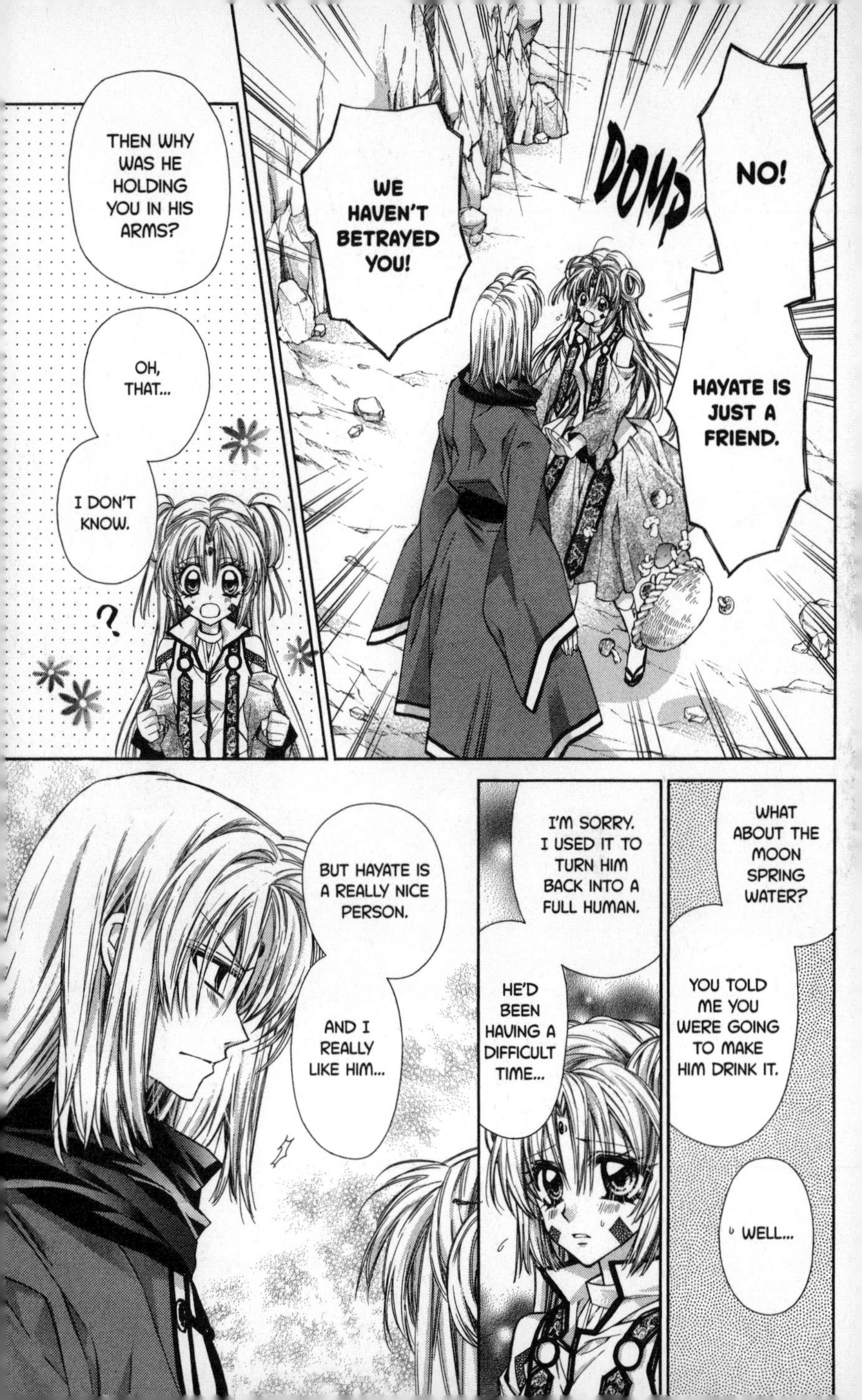
NO!
HAYATE IS JUST A FRIEND.
DOMP
WE HAVEN'T BETRAYED YOU!
THEN WHY WAS HE HOLDING YOU IN HIS ARMS?
OH, THAT...
I DON'T KNOW.
?
WHAT ABOUT THE MOON SPRING WATER?
YOU TOLD ME YOU WERE GOING TO MAKE HIM DRINK IT.
WELL...
I'M SORRY. I USED IT TO TURN HIM BACK INTO A FULL HUMAN.
HE'D BEEN HAVING A DIFFICULT TIME...
BUT HAYATE IS A REALLY NICE PERSON.
AND I REALLY LIKE HIM...

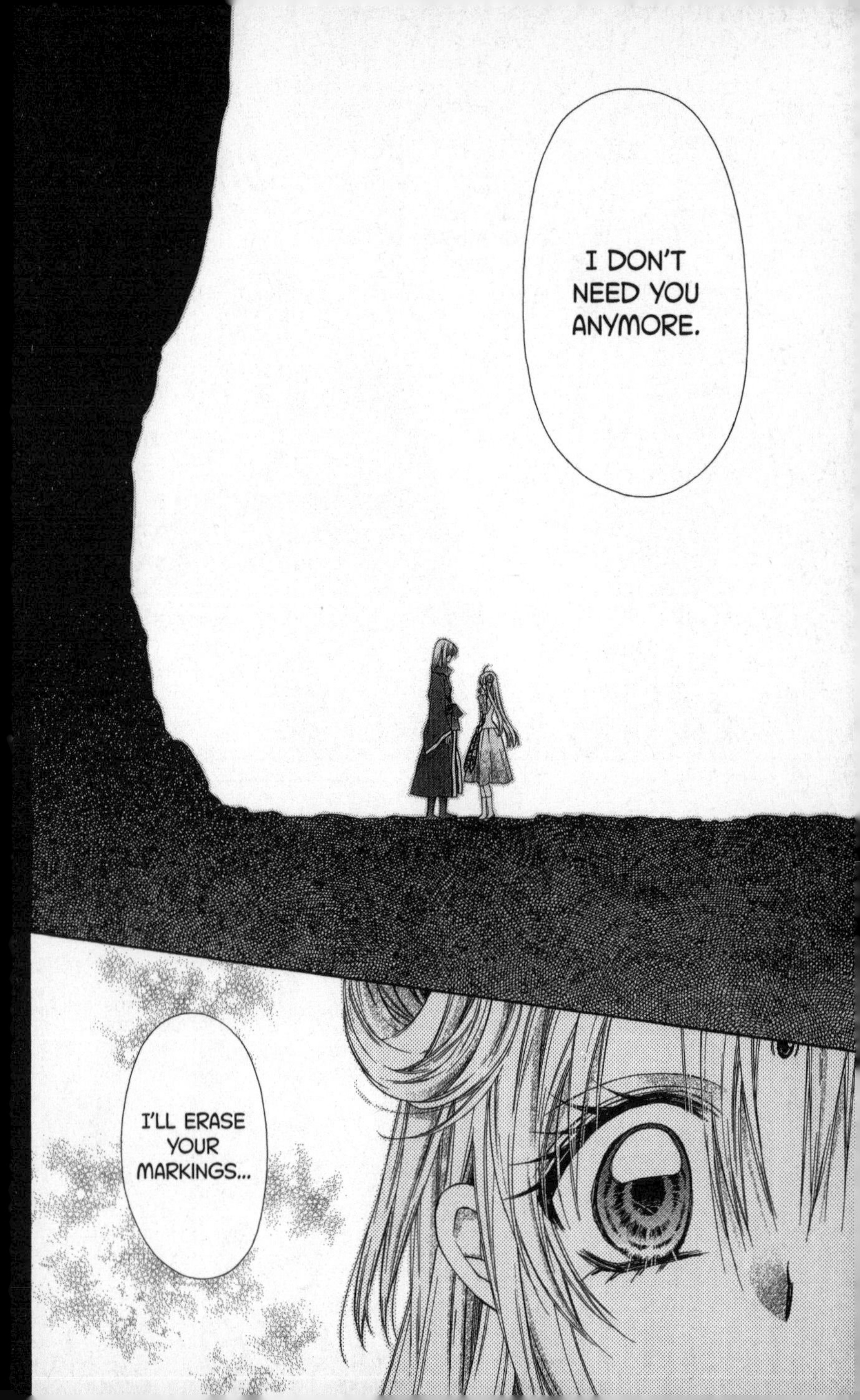
I DON'T NEED YOU ANYMORE.
I'LL ERASE YOUR MARKINGS...

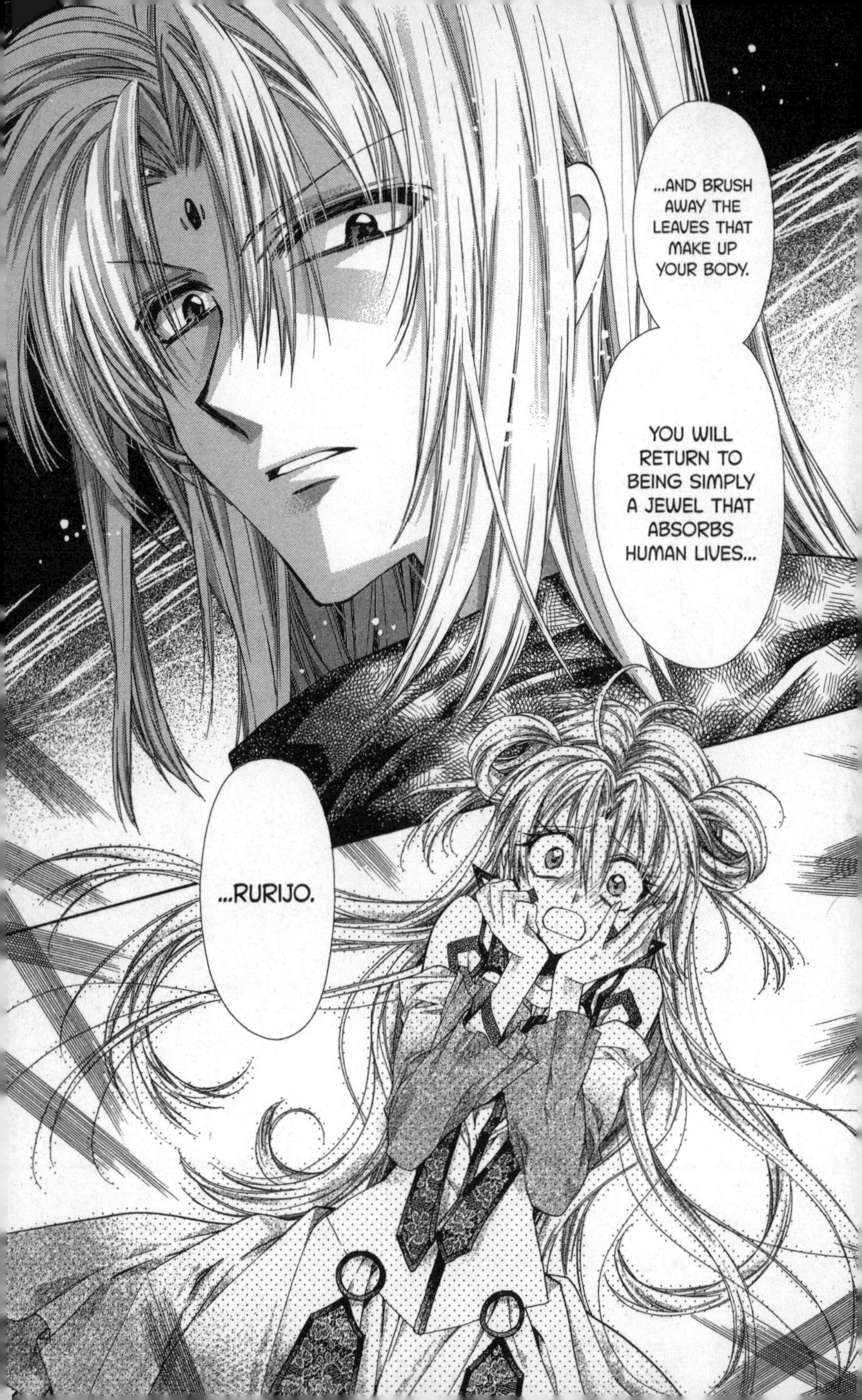
...AND BRUSH AWAY THE LEAVES THAT MAKE UP YOUR BODY.
YOU WILL RETURN TO BEING SIMPLY A JEWEL THAT ABSORBS HUMAN LIVES...
...RURIJO.

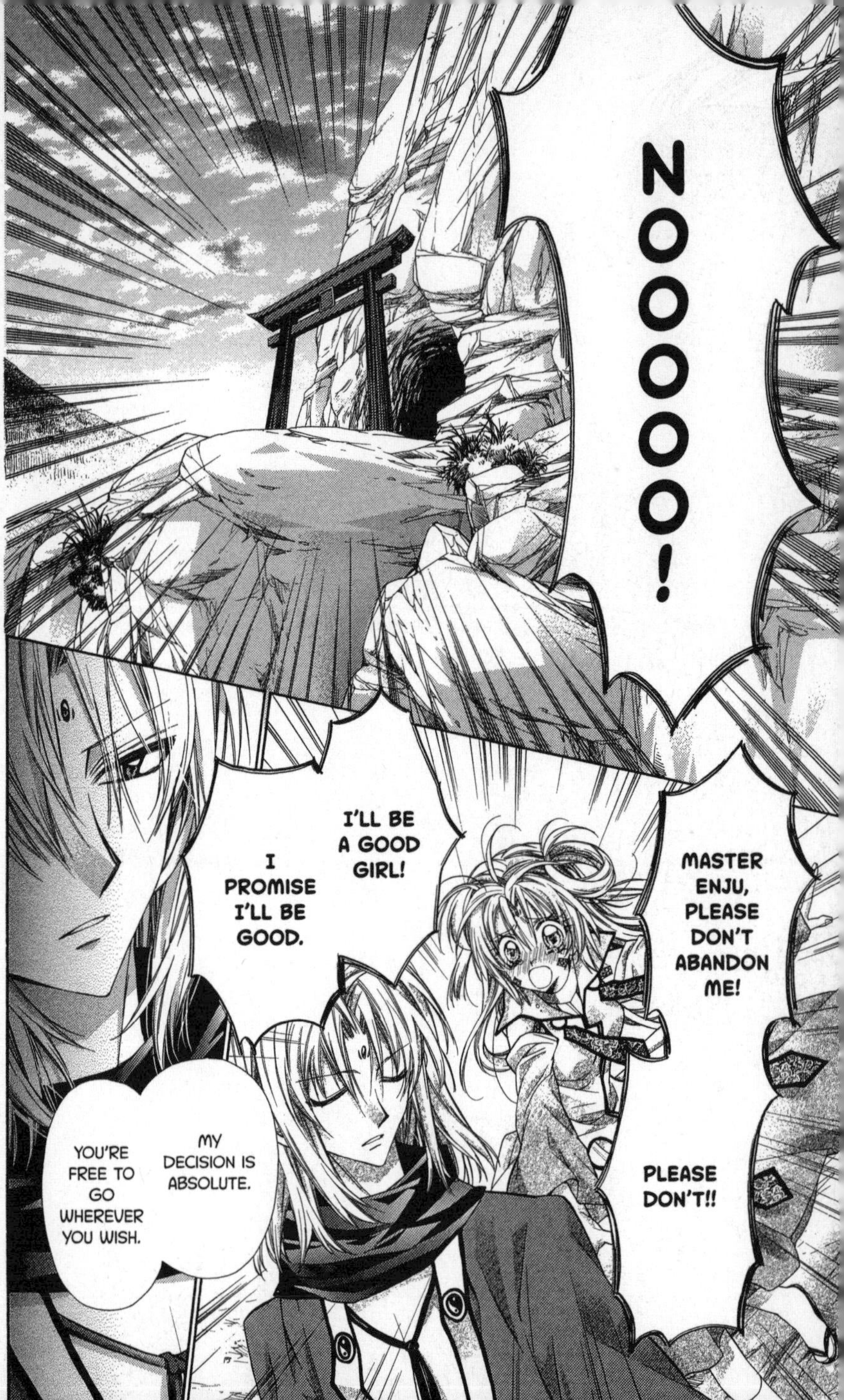
NOOOOO!
MASTER ENJU, PLEASE DON'T ABANDON ME!
I'LL BE A GOOD GIRL!
I PROMISE I'LL BE GOOD.
PLEASE DON'T!!
MY DECISION IS ABSOLUTE.
YOU'RE FREE TO GO WHEREVER YOU WISH.

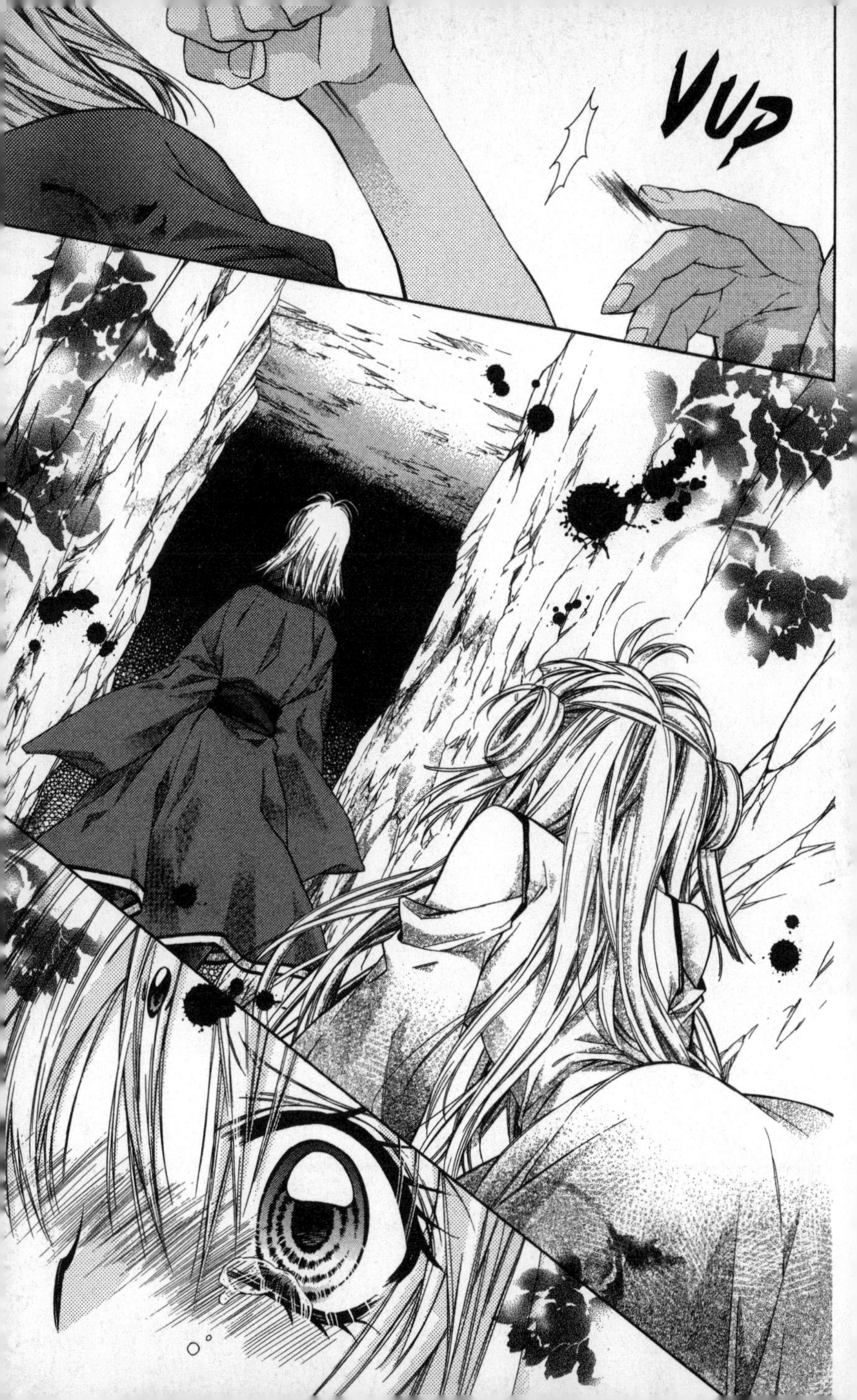
VUP

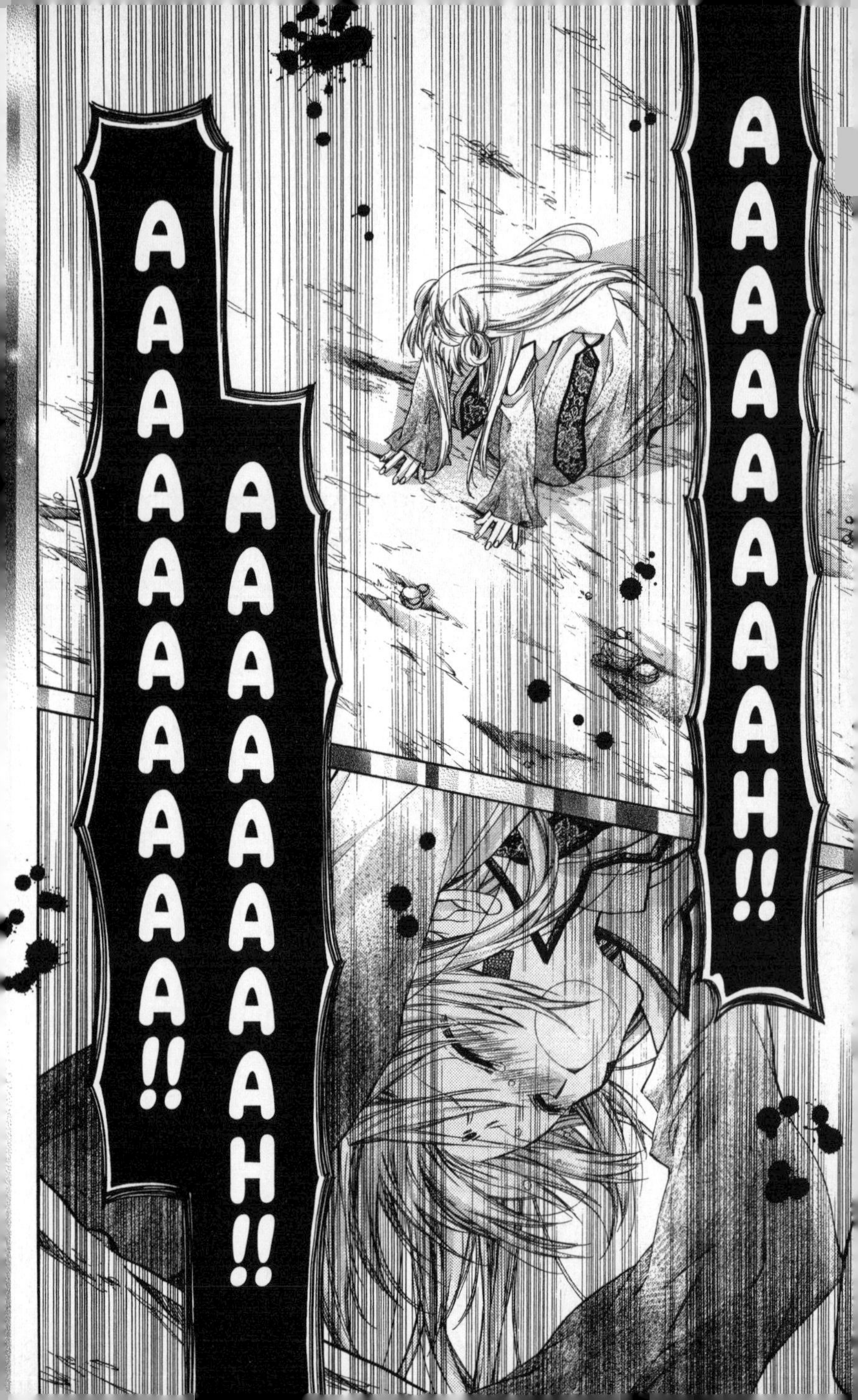
AAAAAAAAH!!
AAAAAAAAH!!
AAAAAAAAAA!!

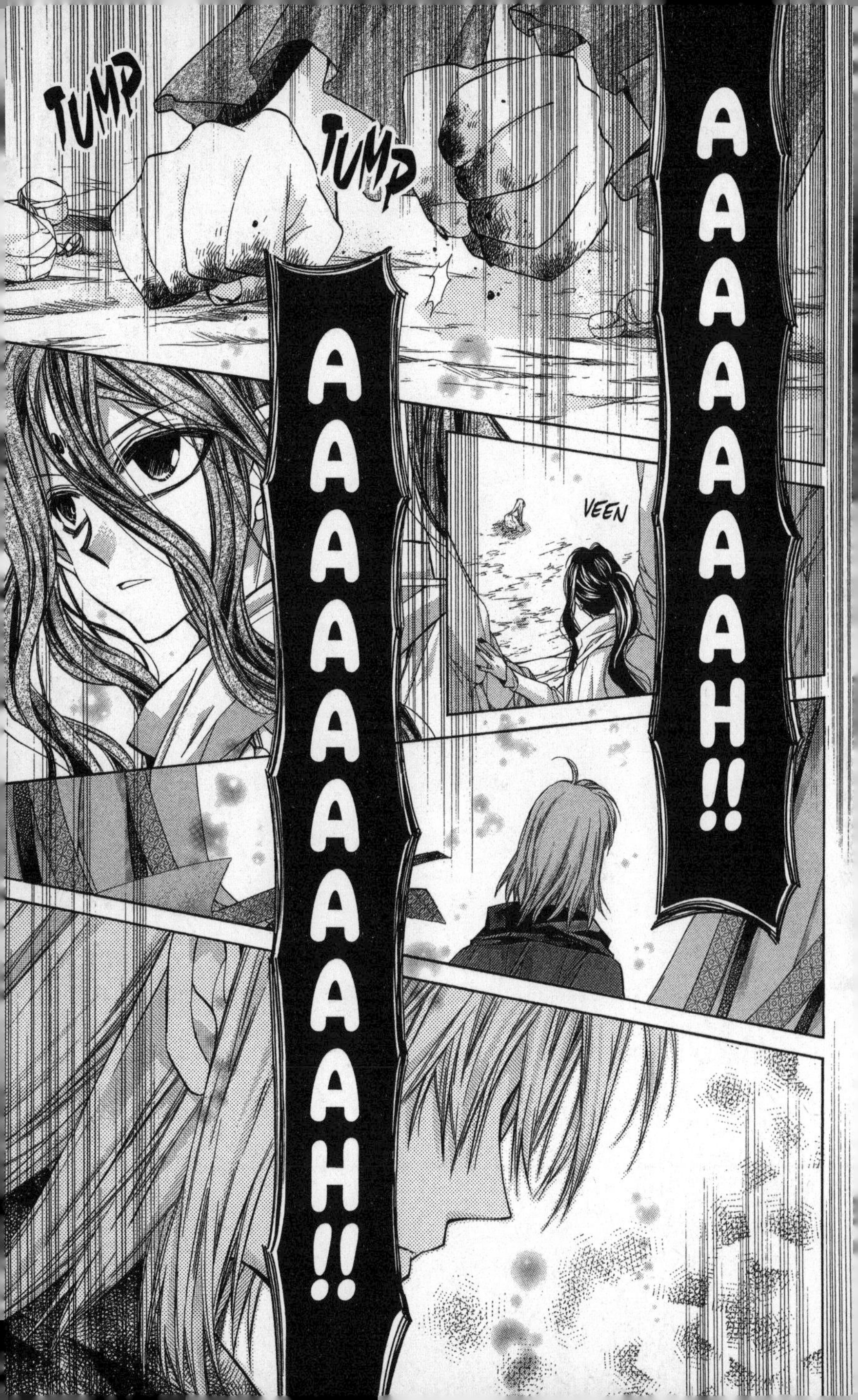

TUMP
TUMP
AAAAAAAH!!
VEEN
AAAAAAAAAH!!

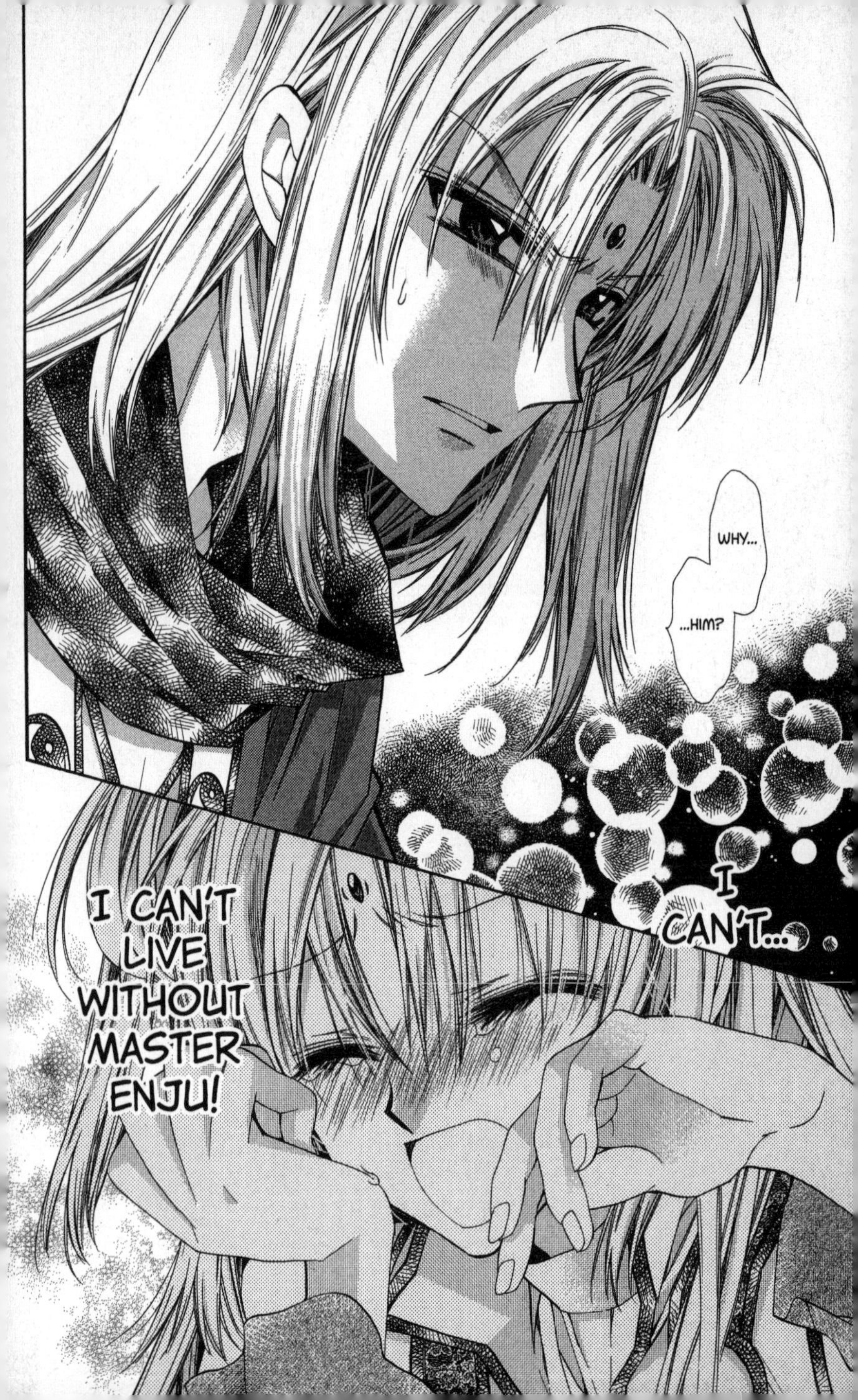
WHY...
...HIM?
I CAN'T...
I CAN'T LIVE WITHOUT MASTER ENJU!

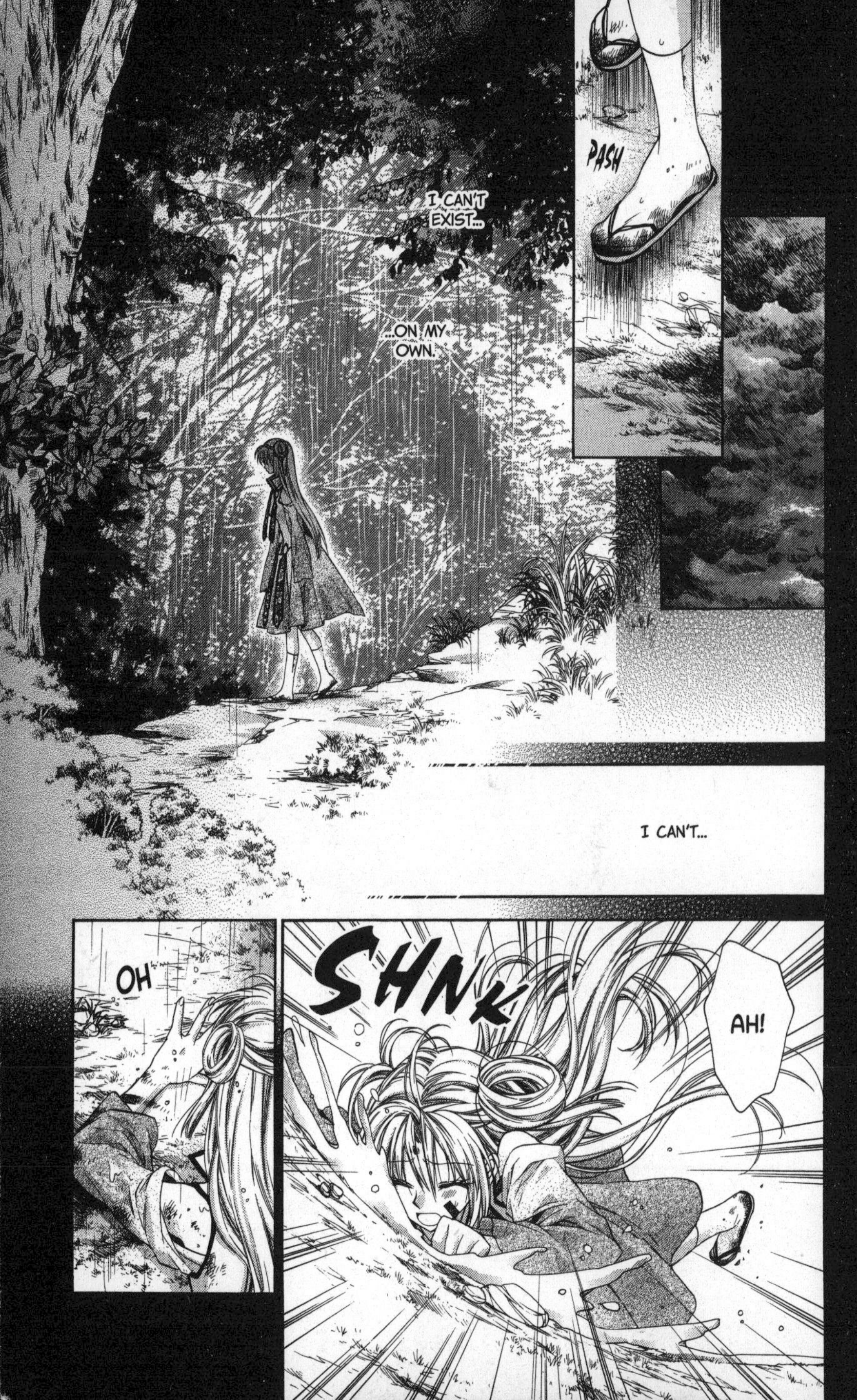
PASH
I CAN'T EXIST...
...ON MY OWN.
I CAN'T...
SHNK
AH!
OH

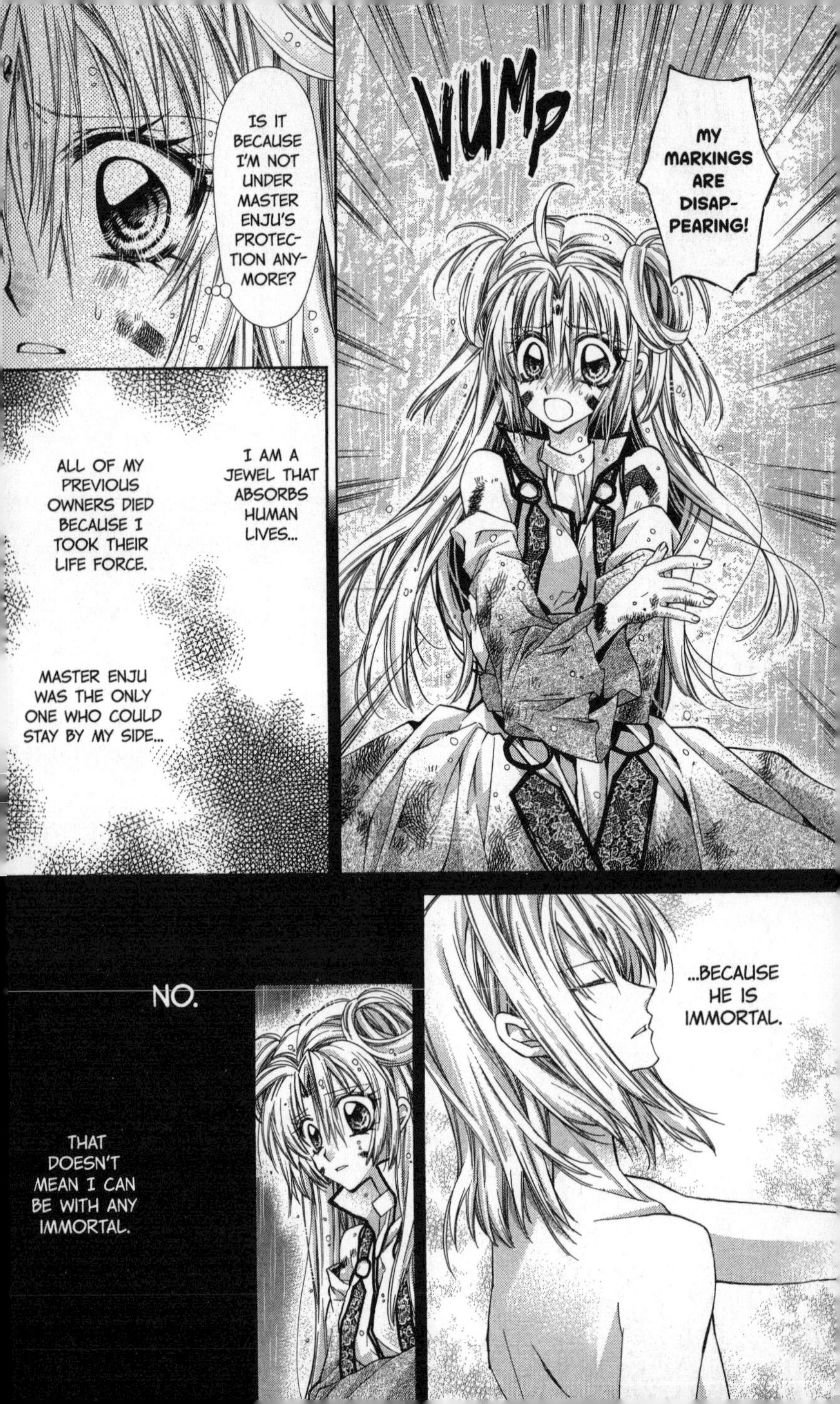
VUMP
MY MARKINGS ARE DISAP-PEARING!
IS IT BECAUSE I'M NOT UNDER MASTER ENJU'S PROTEC-TION ANY-MORE?
I AM A JEWEL THAT ABSORBS HUMAN LIVES...
ALL OF MY PREVIOUS OWNERS DIED BECAUSE I TOOK THEIR LIFE FORCE.
MASTER ENJU WAS THE ONLY ONE WHO COULD STAY BY MY SIDE...
...BECAUSE HE IS IMMORTAL.
NO.
THAT DOESN'T MEAN I CAN BE WITH ANY IMMORTAL.

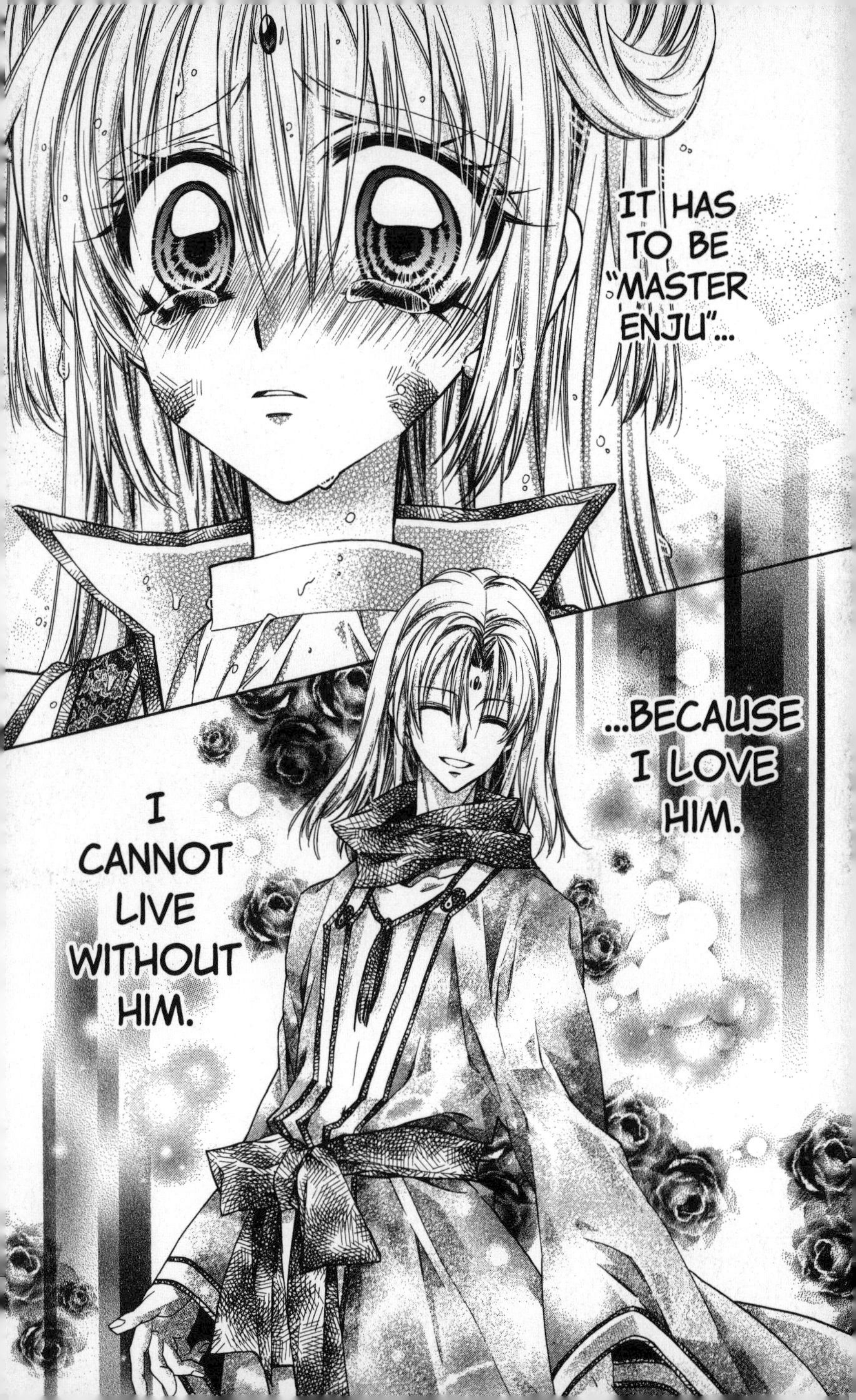
IT HAS TO BE "MASTER ENJU"...
...BECAUSE I LOVE HIM.
I CANNOT LIVE WITHOUT HIM.

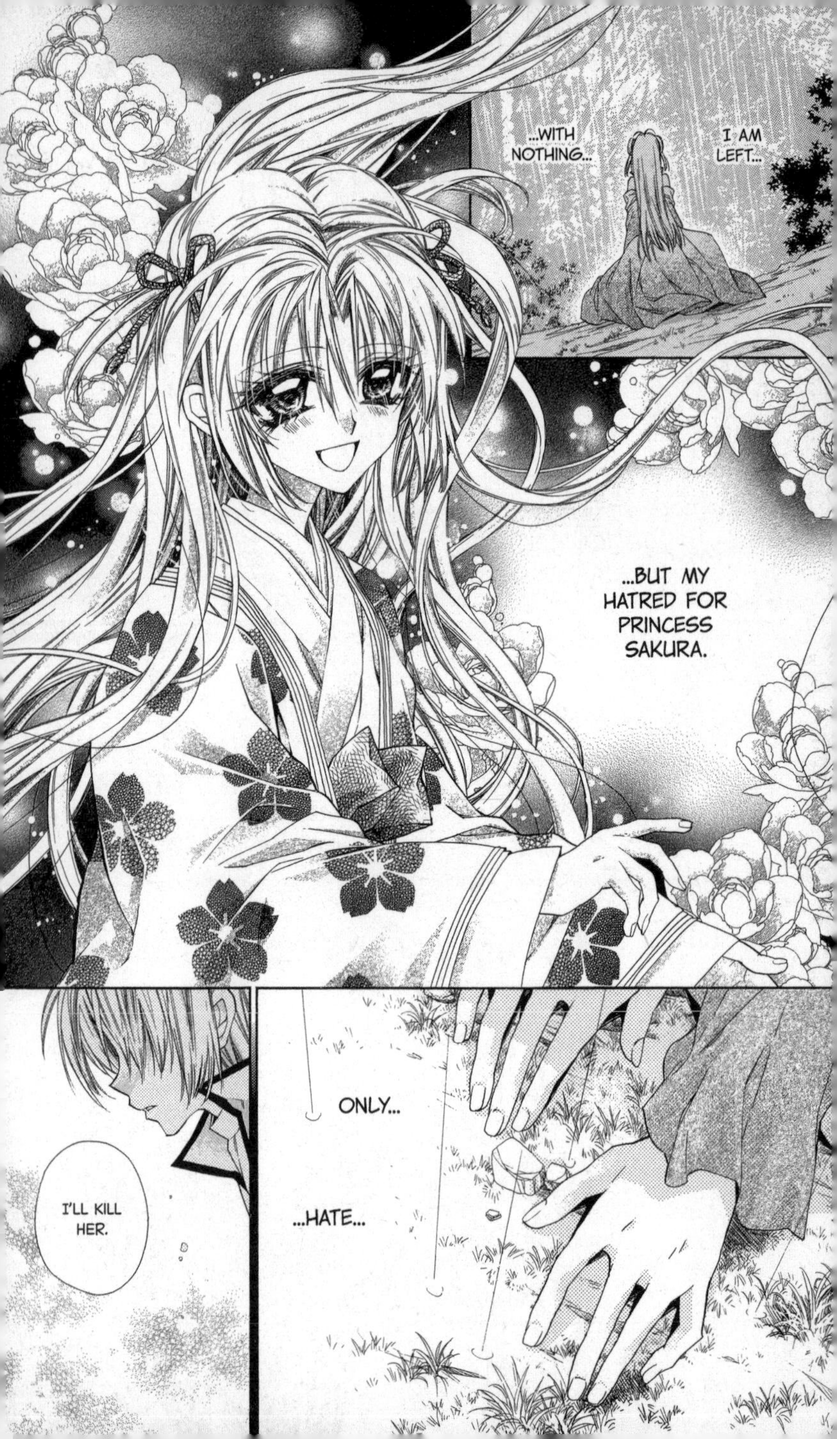
I AM LEFT...
...WITH NOTHING...
...BUT MY HATRED FOR PRINCESS SAKURA.
ONLY...
...HATE...
I'LL KILL HER.

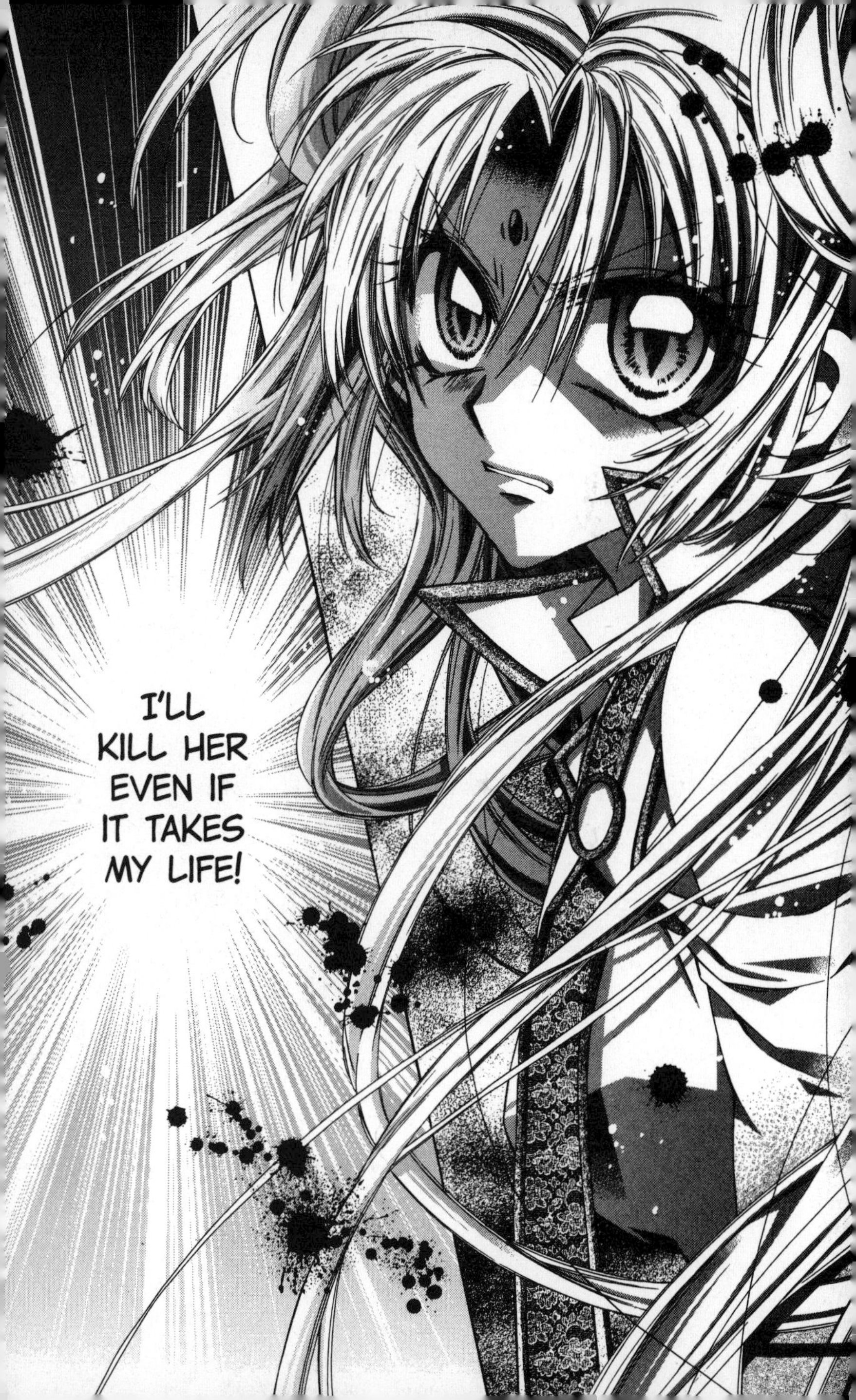
I'LL KILL HER EVEN IF IT TAKES MY LIFE!

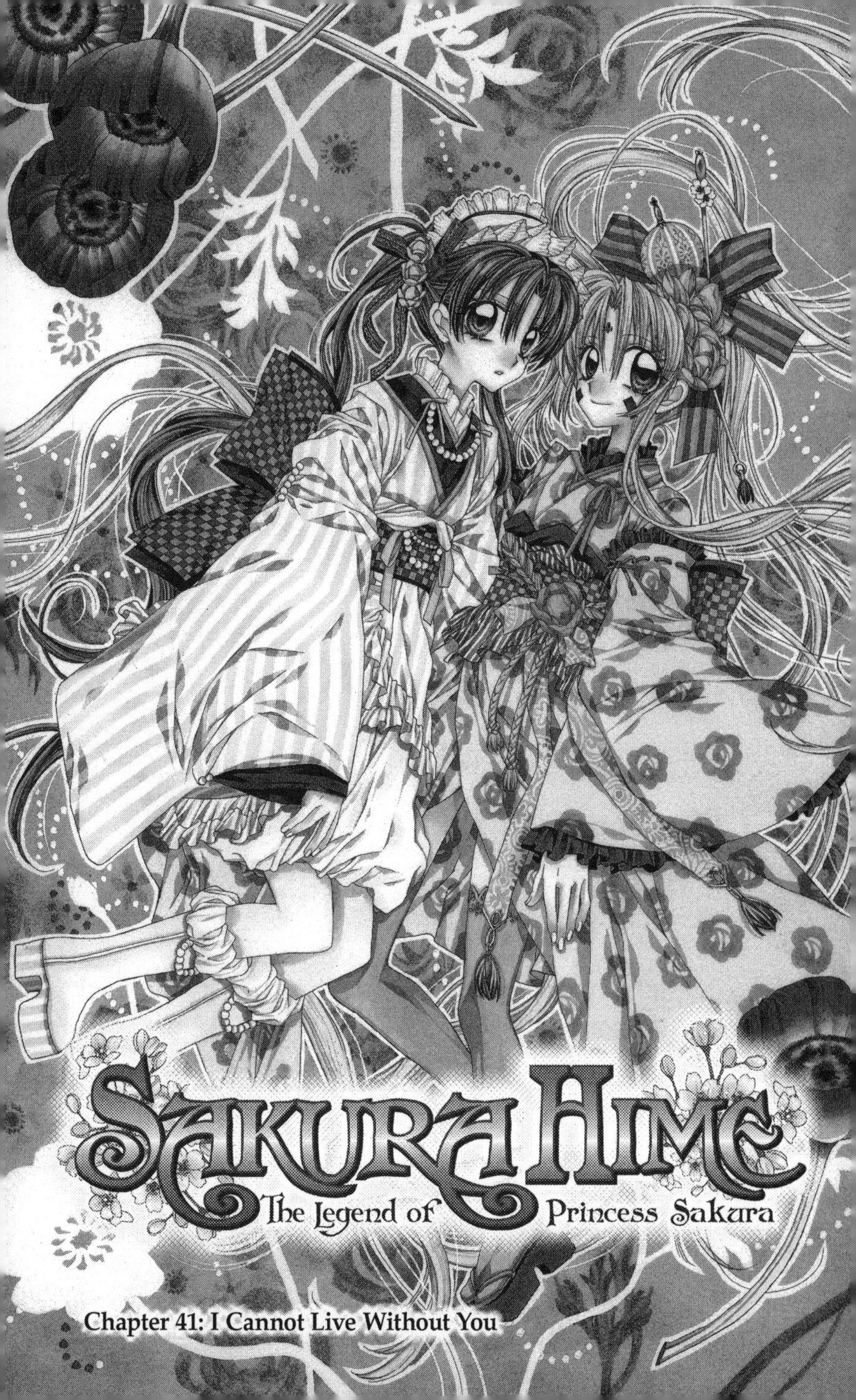
SAKURA HIME
The Legend of Princess Sakura
Chapter 41: I Cannot Live Without You

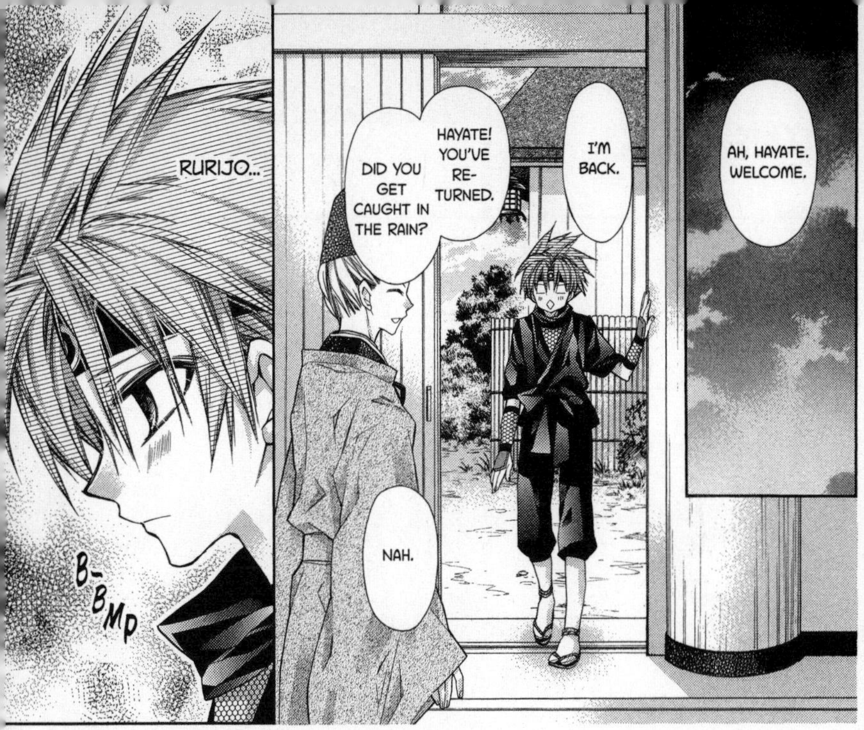
AH, HAYATE. WELCOME.
I'M BACK.
HAYATE! YOU'VE RE-TURNED.
DID YOU GET CAUGHT IN THE RAIN?
NAH.
RURIJO...
B-BMP

Chapter 41: I Cannot Live Without You

(※ I'm giving away the story.)

In this chapter Sakura faces Rurijo one-on-one. I guess Rurijo's downside is that once she starts running she won't stop until she crashes into something... (´‿`) She's ignorant, so she believes she has no way out. That's why she's being rather suicidal. I've been longing to write this story, and it made me feel really alive while I was working on it. I think it's Rurijo's "innocence" that makes her an attractive character... I decided to draw a "crying image" that I had been avoiding up until now—to have the character raise her voice while crying (to include a crying sound in the dialogue bubble to be precise). This is just my personal opinion, but I've avoided drawing that because I've always thought it looked a bit distasteful. But when I thought about the scene, the situation, and Rurijo's personality, this was the only way I could depict it. And it turned out to be my favorite scene in this chapter. Maybe I'd been biased without ever trying it?

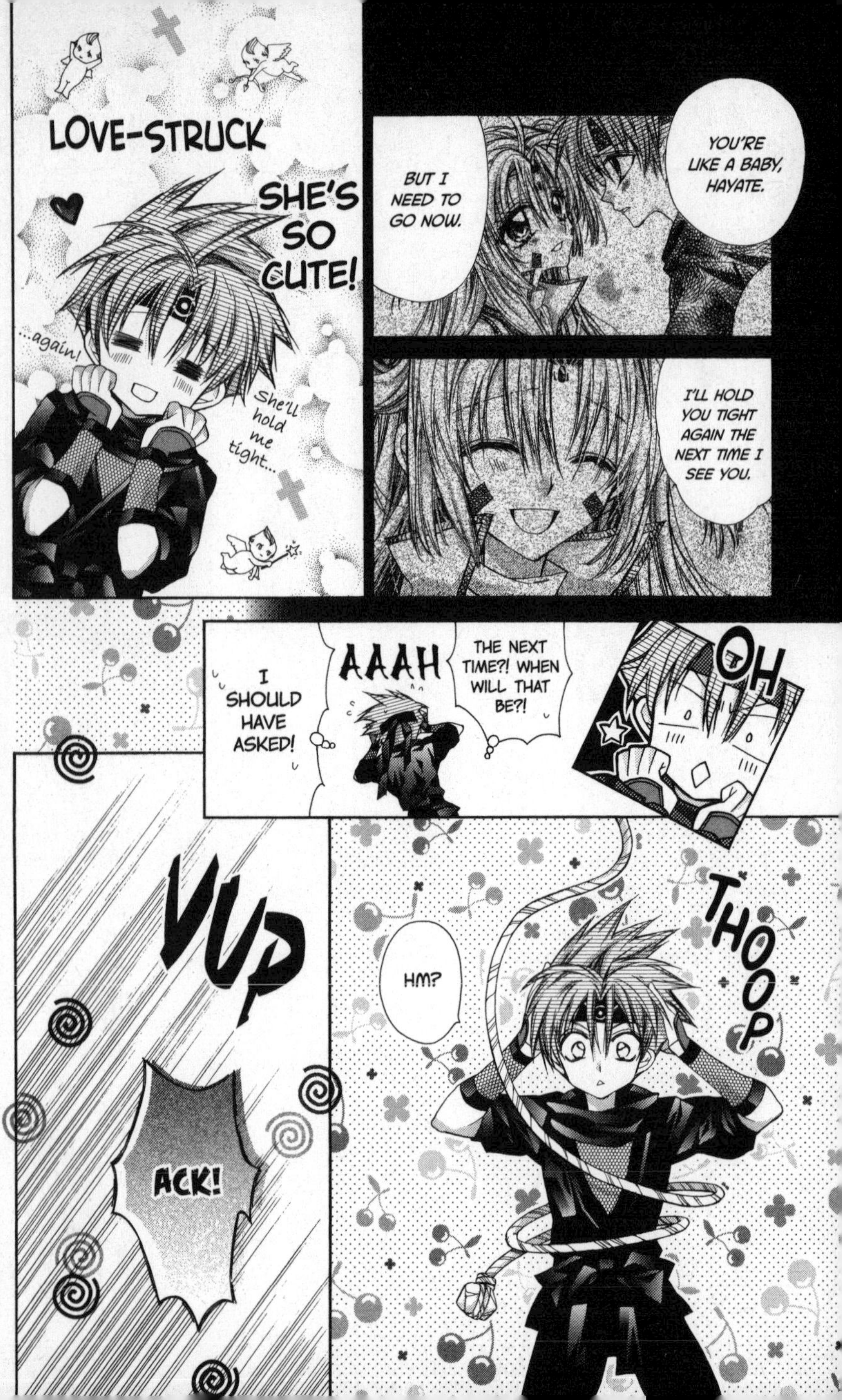
YOU'RE LIKE A BABY, HAYATE.
BUT I NEED TO GO NOW.
I'LL HOLD YOU TIGHT AGAIN THE NEXT TIME I SEE YOU.
LOVE-STRUCK
SHE'S SO CUTE!
She'll hold me tight...
...again!
OH
THE NEXT TIME?! WHEN WILL THAT BE?!
AAAH
I SHOULD HAVE ASKED!
THOOP
HM?
VUP
ACK!

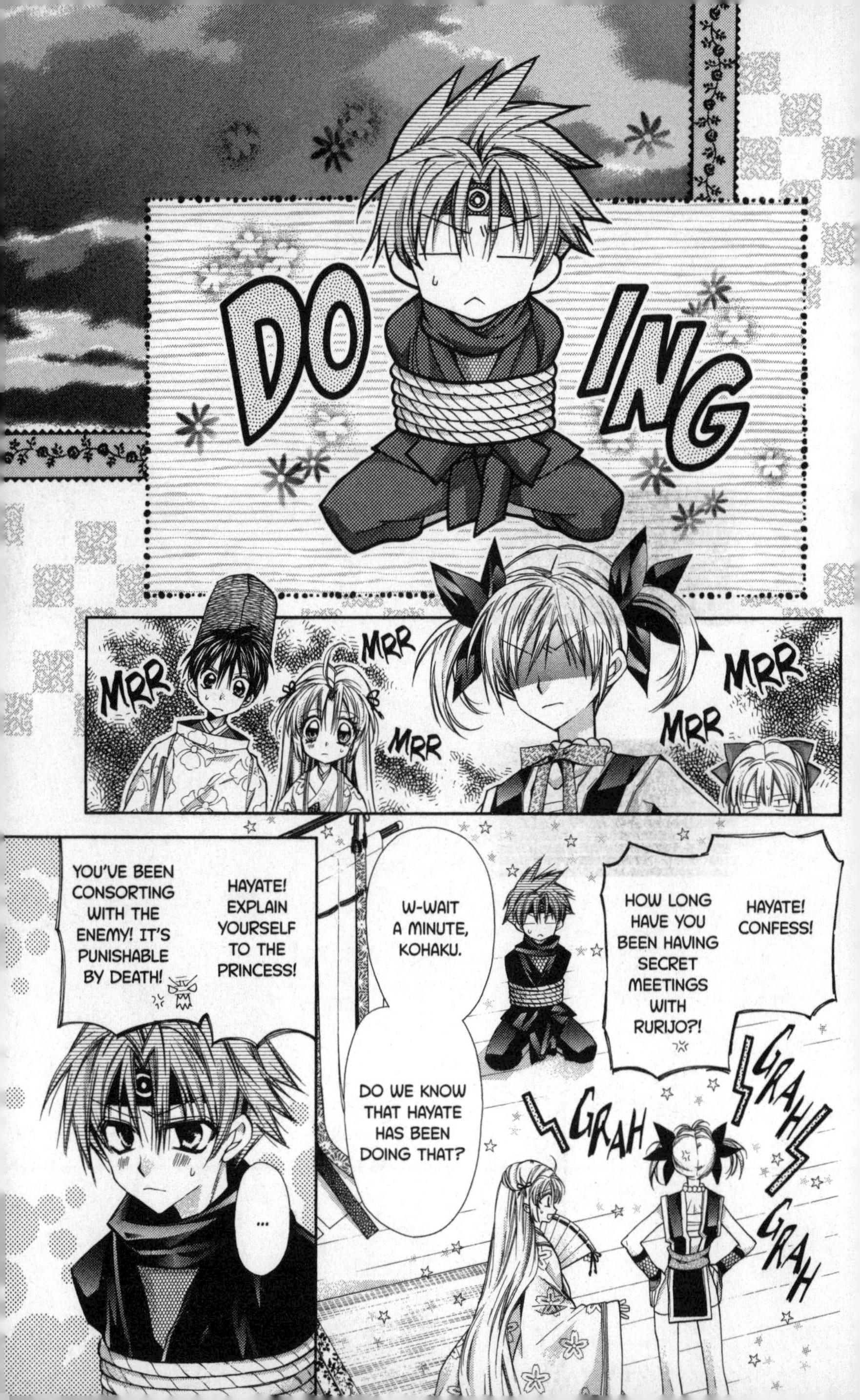
DOING
MRR
MRR
MRR
MRR
MRR
HAYATE! CONFESS!
HOW LONG HAVE YOU BEEN HAVING SECRET MEETINGS WITH RURIJO?!
GRAH
GRAH
GRAH
W-WAIT A MINUTE, KOHAKU.
DO WE KNOW THAT HAYATE HAS BEEN DOING THAT?
HAYATE! EXPLAIN YOURSELF TO THE PRINCESS!
YOU'VE BEEN CONSORTING WITH THE ENEMY! IT'S PUNISHABLE BY DEATH!
...

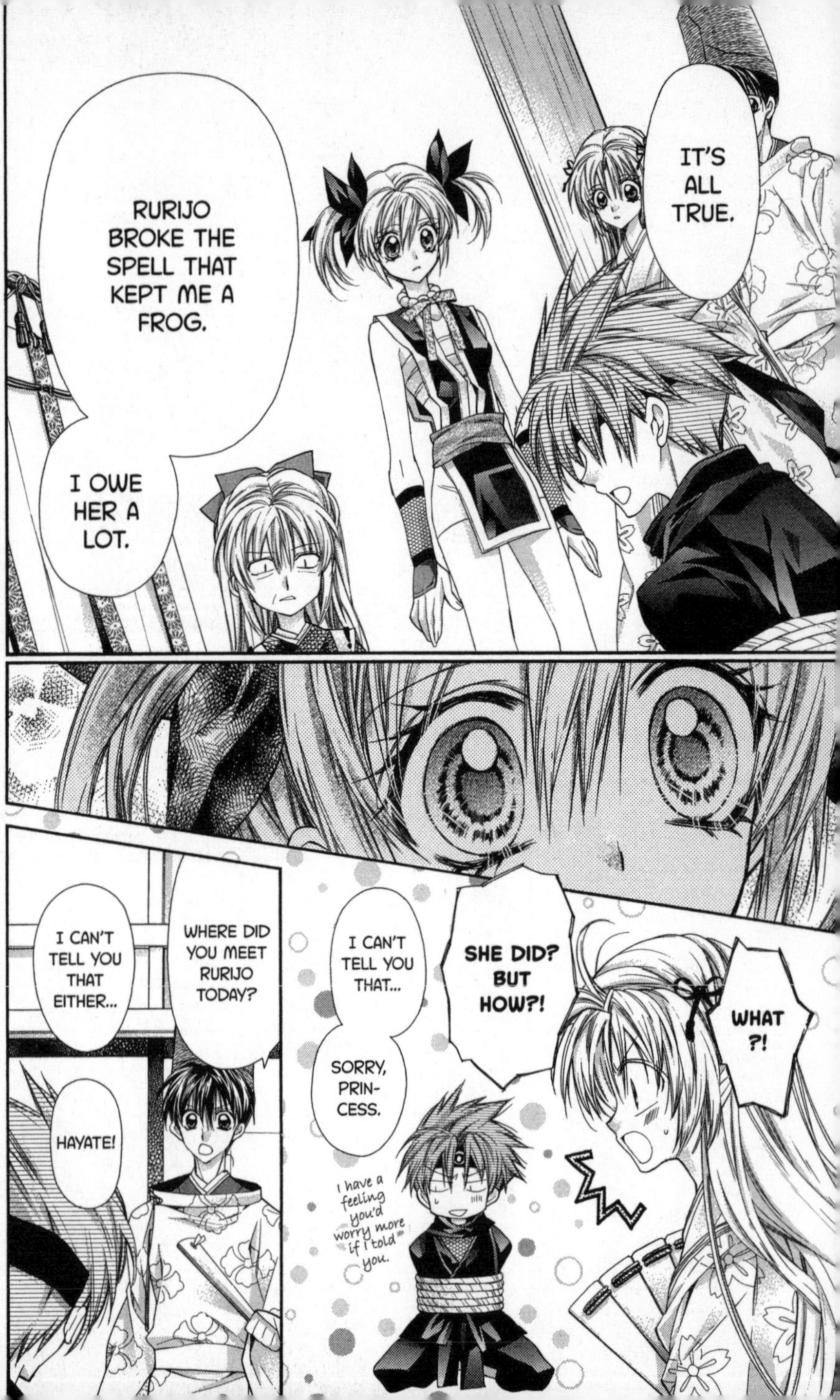
IT'S ALL TRUE.
RURIJO BROKE THE SPELL THAT KEPT ME A FROG.
I OWE HER A LOT.
WHAT?!
SHE DID? BUT HOW?!
I CAN'T TELL YOU THAT...
SORRY, PRINCESS.
I have a feeling you'd worry more if I told you.
WHERE DID YOU MEET RURIJO TODAY?
I CAN'T TELL YOU THAT EITHER...
HAYATE!

To Kyoto

The other day I went on a three-day trip to Kyoto with Kyan-chi aka Chiaki Kyan (from Nakano Fujo Sisters)! I decided to go on the trip suddenly the day before, but I really enjoyed it.♥

It was raining cats and dogs on the day we left. We had planned to go to Kyushu, but the flight was canceled due to bad weather. We decided to go to Kyoto because we could get there on the bullet train. But when we got to Kyoto, we couldn't disembark for 40 minutes. (There were six bullet trains at the platform and our train could not enter the station.) When we did arrive, we took another train for 20 minutes → to get to Arashiyama!

We arrived at Arashiyama at 9 o'clock at night... We took a bath and ate dinner, and that was it for the day. (laugh) This area is famous for the Hozu River Cruise, so we talked about how we'd like to do that. But the river was flooded and the cruise had been canceled. I wondered if we could take part in the cruise before we had to leave?!

The next day, we went sightseeing around Arashiyama! We checked the map for places we wanted to see, and we went to Togetsu Bridge first. There were lots of foreign tourists there. From what I heard, the temperature in Arashiyama is lower than in the city of Kyoto. The cherry blossoms weren't yet in bloom, but the place was swarming with people because the Kyoto area is so popular with tourists. There were many places to get a bite to eat around the bridge too! We both had the famous tofu croquette. (They were freshly fried! Both Kyan-chi and I love deep-fried food.) After that, we took a rickshaw on the bridge and went around Arashiyama.

Continues →

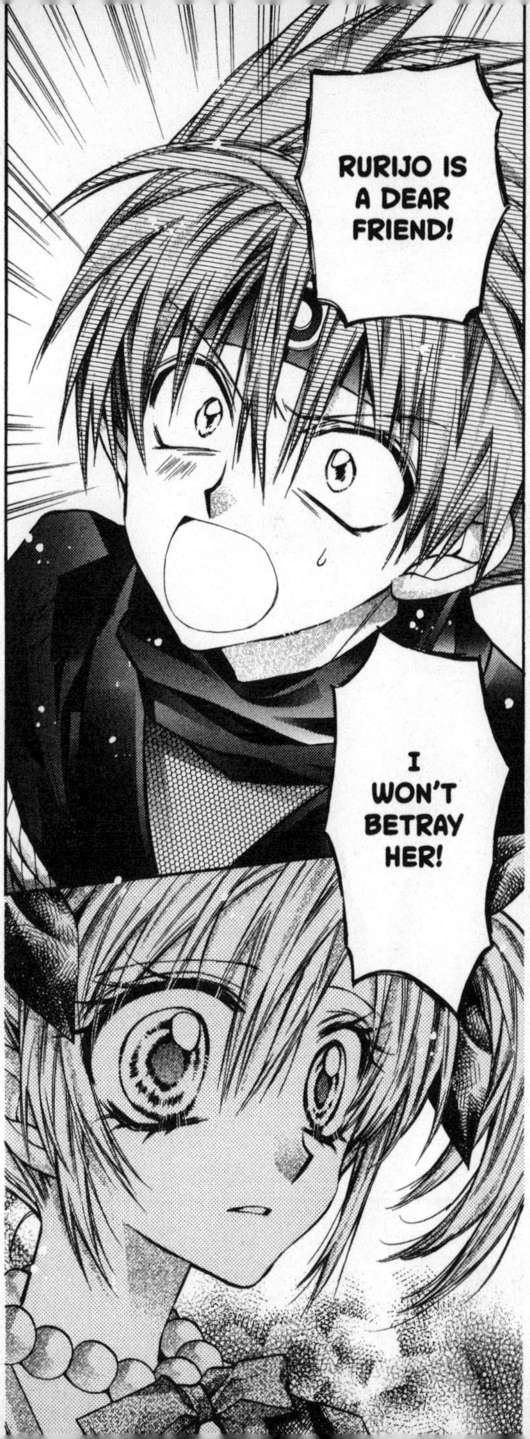
RURIJO IS A DEAR FRIEND!
I WON'T BETRAY HER!

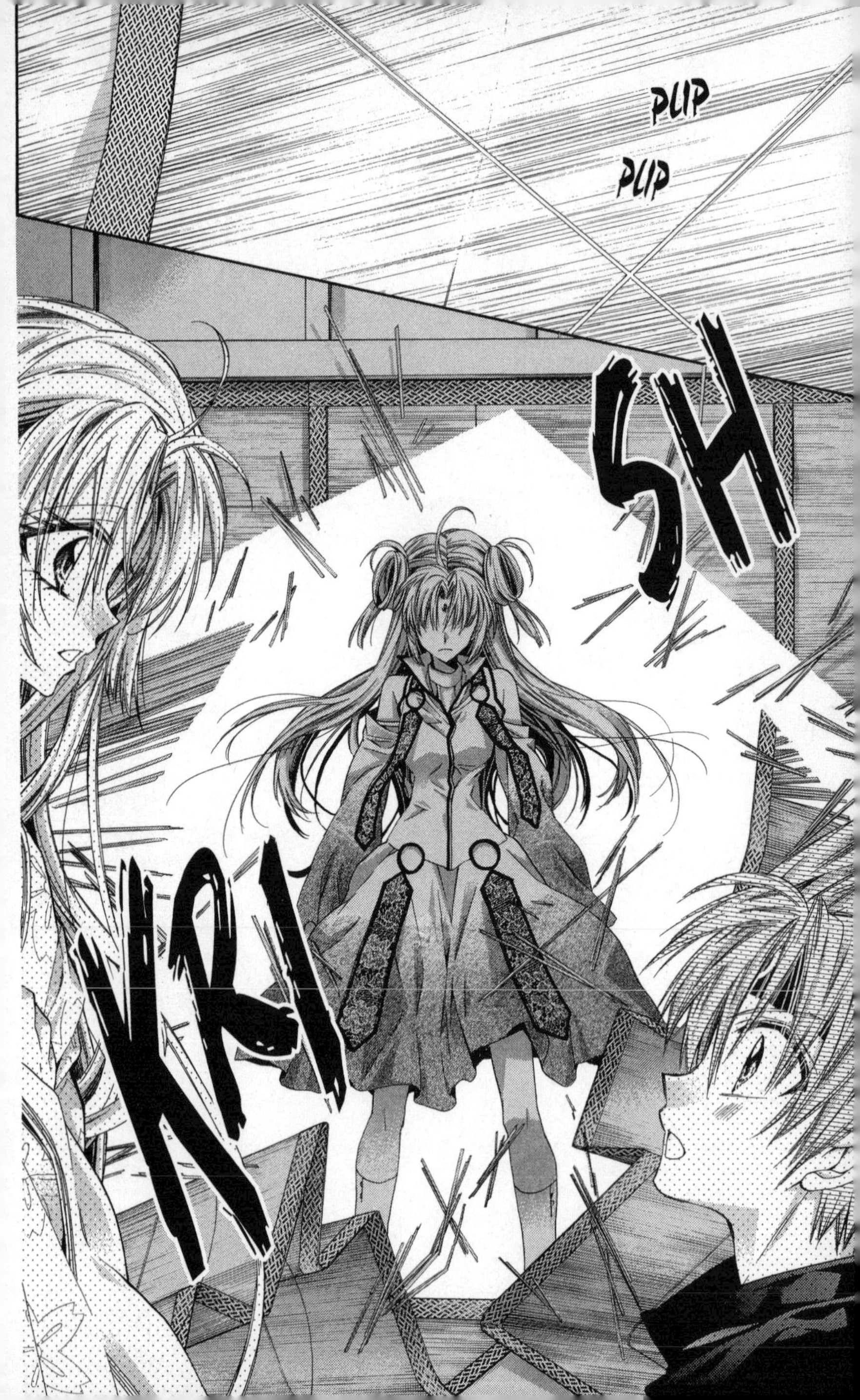
PLIP
PLIP
SH
KRI

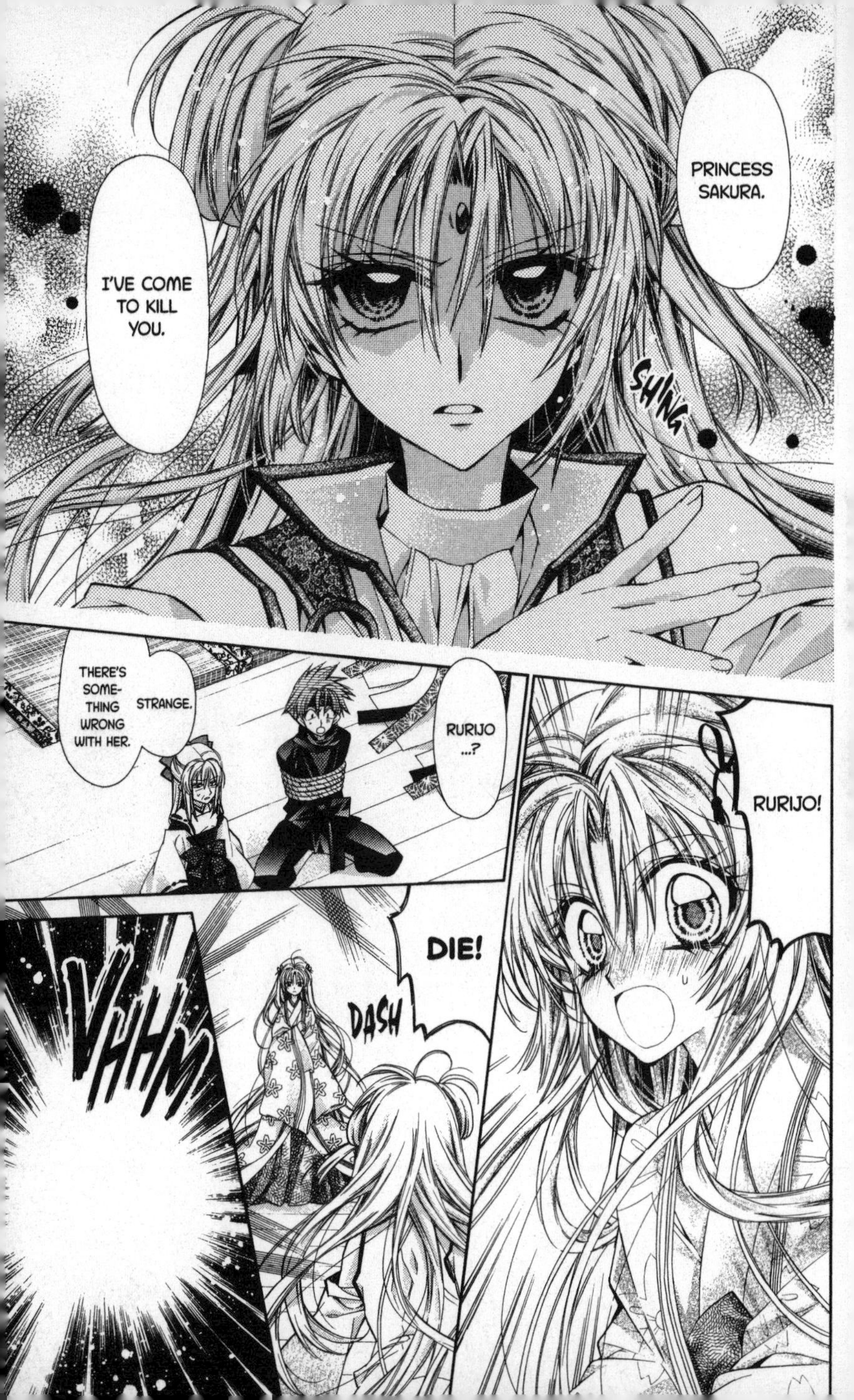
PRINCESS SAKURA.
I'VE COME TO KILL YOU.
SHING
RURIJO!
RURIJO ...?
STRANGE.
THERE'S SOME-THING WRONG WITH HER.
DIE!
DASH
VHM

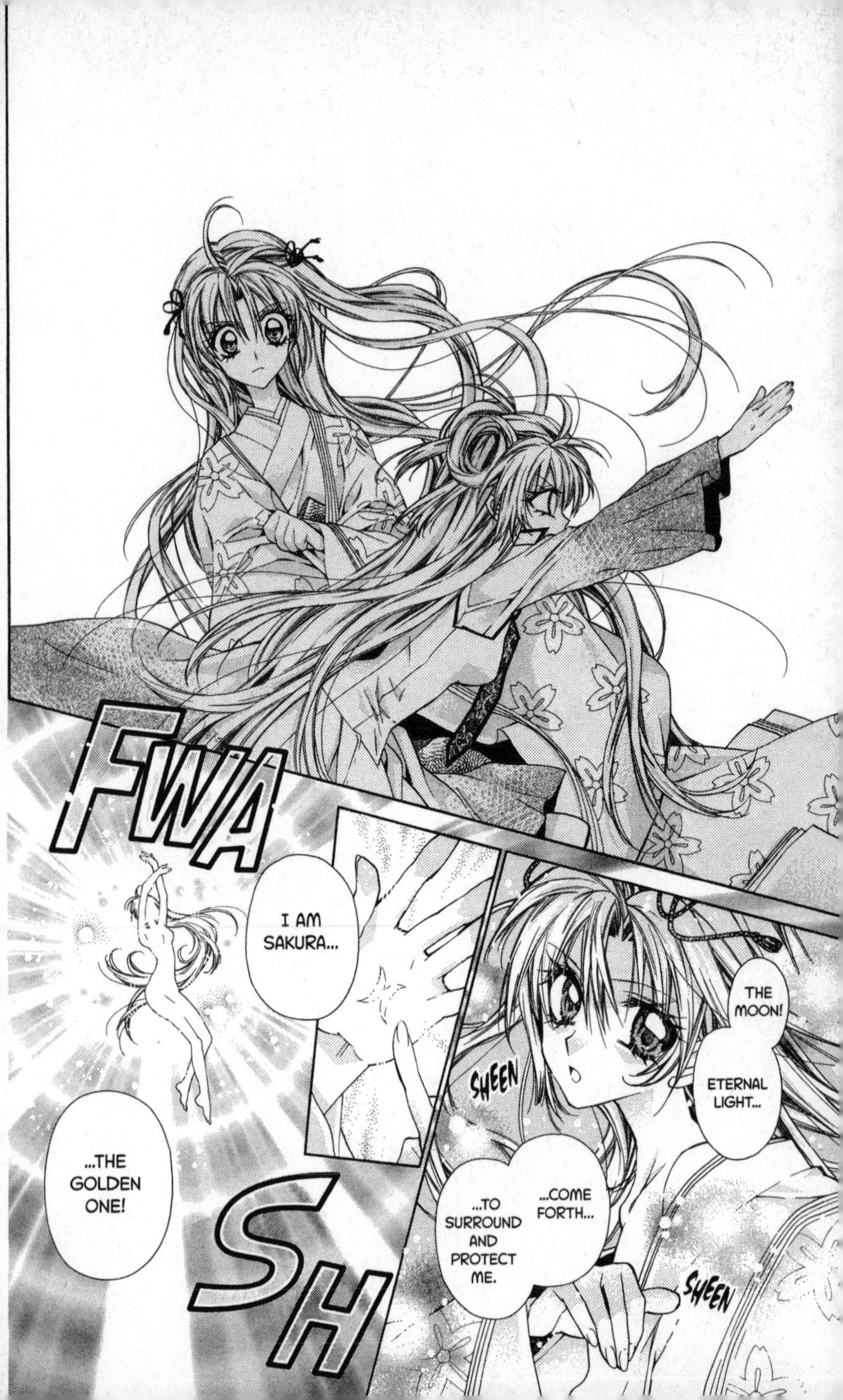
THE MOON!
ETERNAL LIGHT...
SHEEN
...COME FORTH...
...TO SURROUND AND PROTECT ME.
SHEEN
I AM SAKURA...
FWA
...THE GOLDEN ONE!
SH

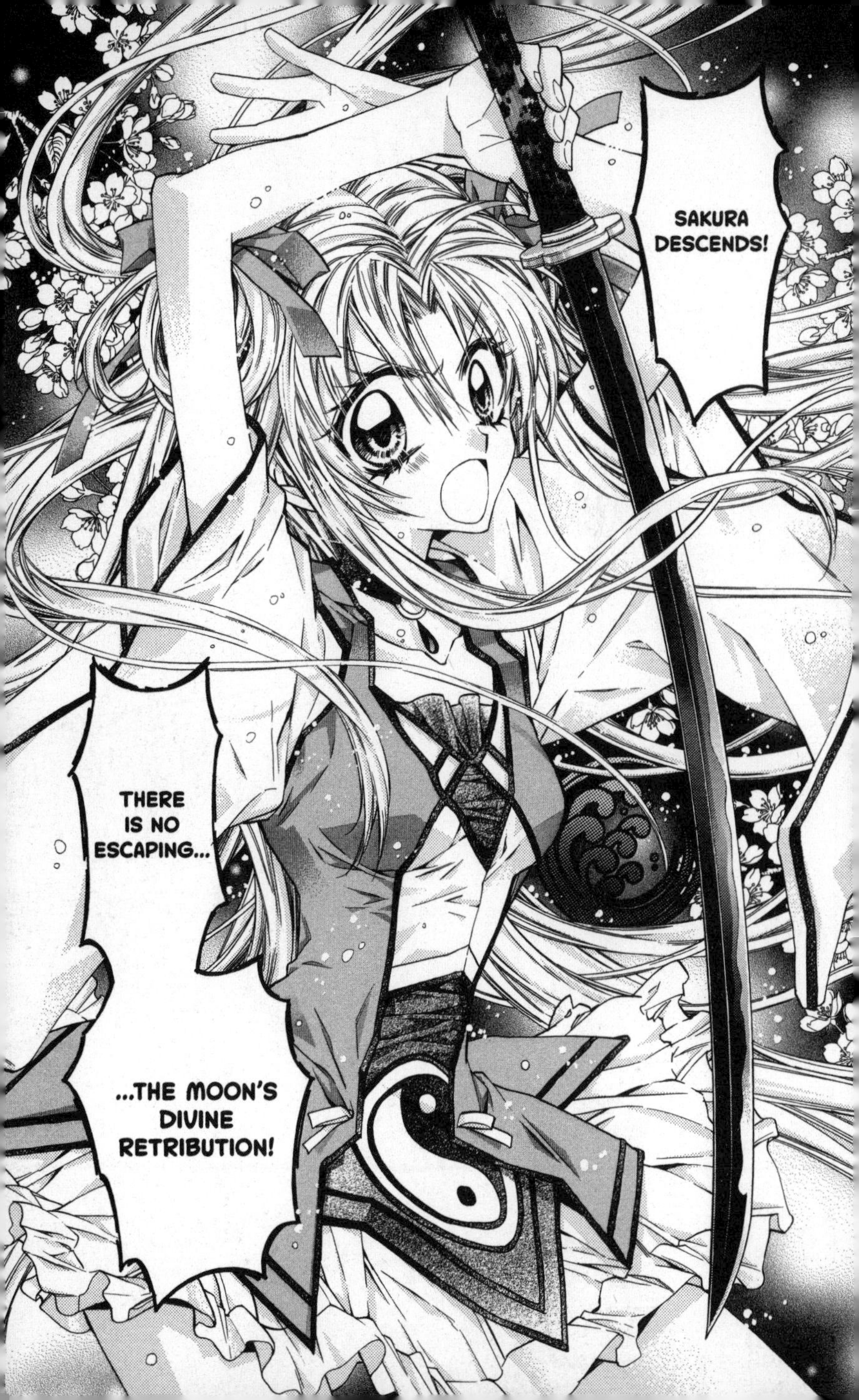
SAKURA DESCENDS!
THERE IS NO ESCAPING...
...THE MOON'S DIVINE RETRIBUTION!

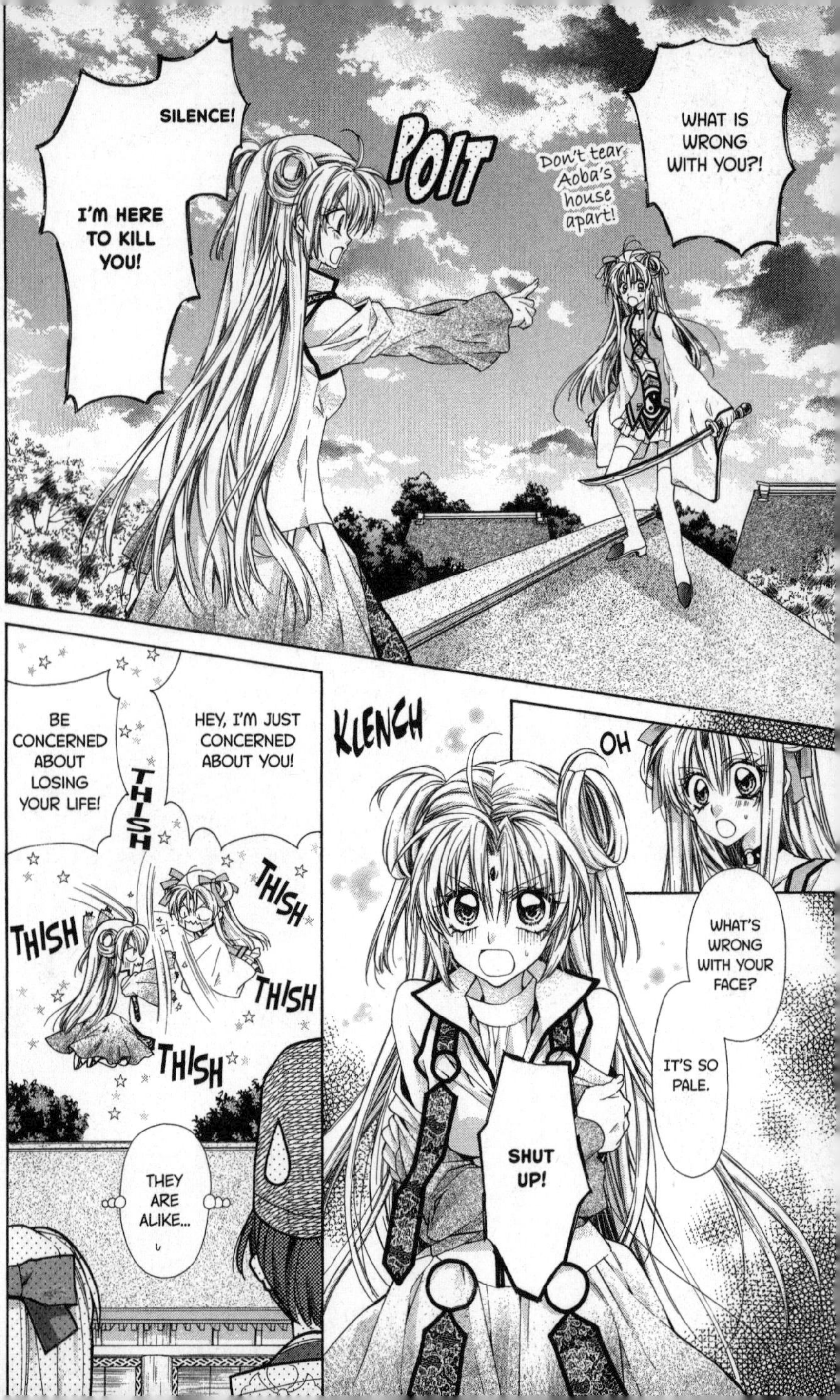
WHAT IS WRONG WITH YOU?!
Don't tear Aoba's house apart!
POIT
SILENCE!
I'M HERE TO KILL YOU!
OH
KLENCH
WHAT'S WRONG WITH YOUR FACE?
IT'S SO PALE.
SHUT UP!
HEY, I'M JUST CONCERNED ABOUT YOU!
BE CONCERNED ABOUT LOSING YOUR LIFE!
THISH
THISH
THISH
THISH
THISH
THEY ARE ALIKE...

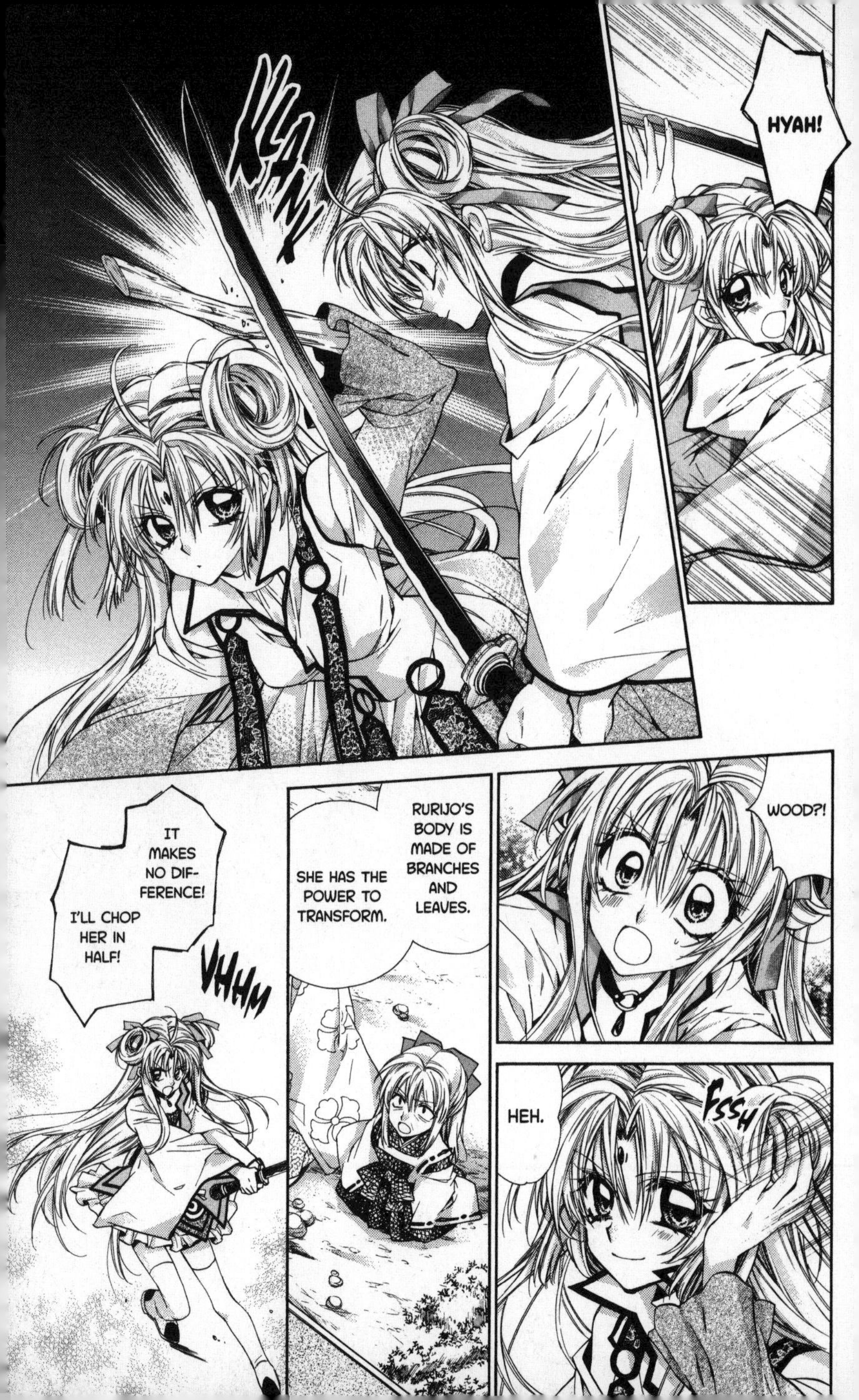
HYAH!
WOOD?!
HEH.
FSSH
RURIJO'S BODY IS MADE OF BRANCHES AND LEAVES.
SHE HAS THE POWER TO TRANSFORM.
IT MAKES NO DIF- FERENCE!
I'LL CHOP HER IN HALF!
VHHM

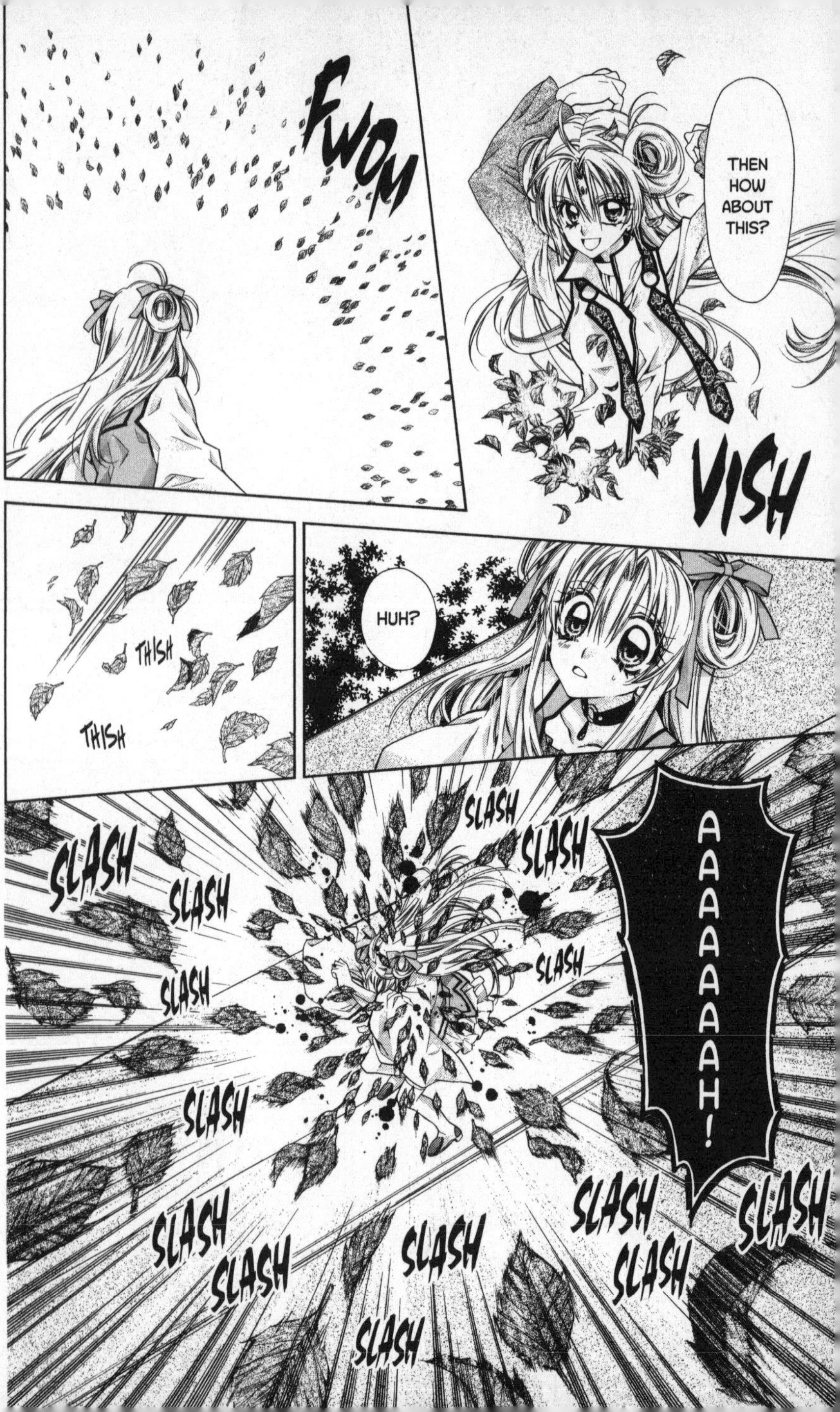
THEN HOW ABOUT THIS?
VISH
FWOM
HUH?
THISH
THISH
AAAAAAAH!
SLASH
SLASH
SLASH
SLASH
SLASH
SLASH
SLASH
SLASH
SLASH
SLASH
SLASH
SLASH
SLASH
SLASH

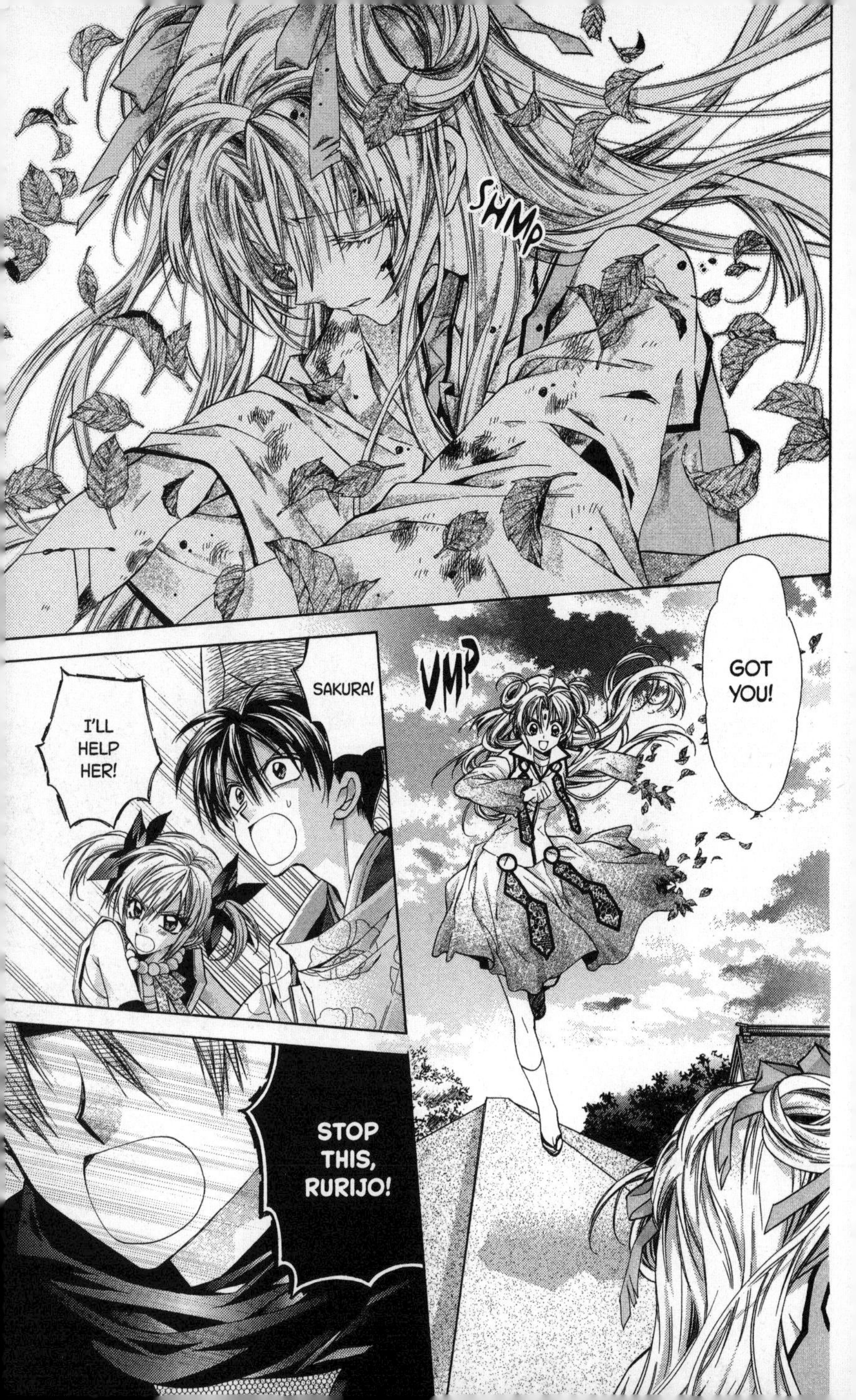
SHMP
GOT YOU!
VMP
SAKURA!
I'LL HELP HER!
STOP THIS, RURIJO!

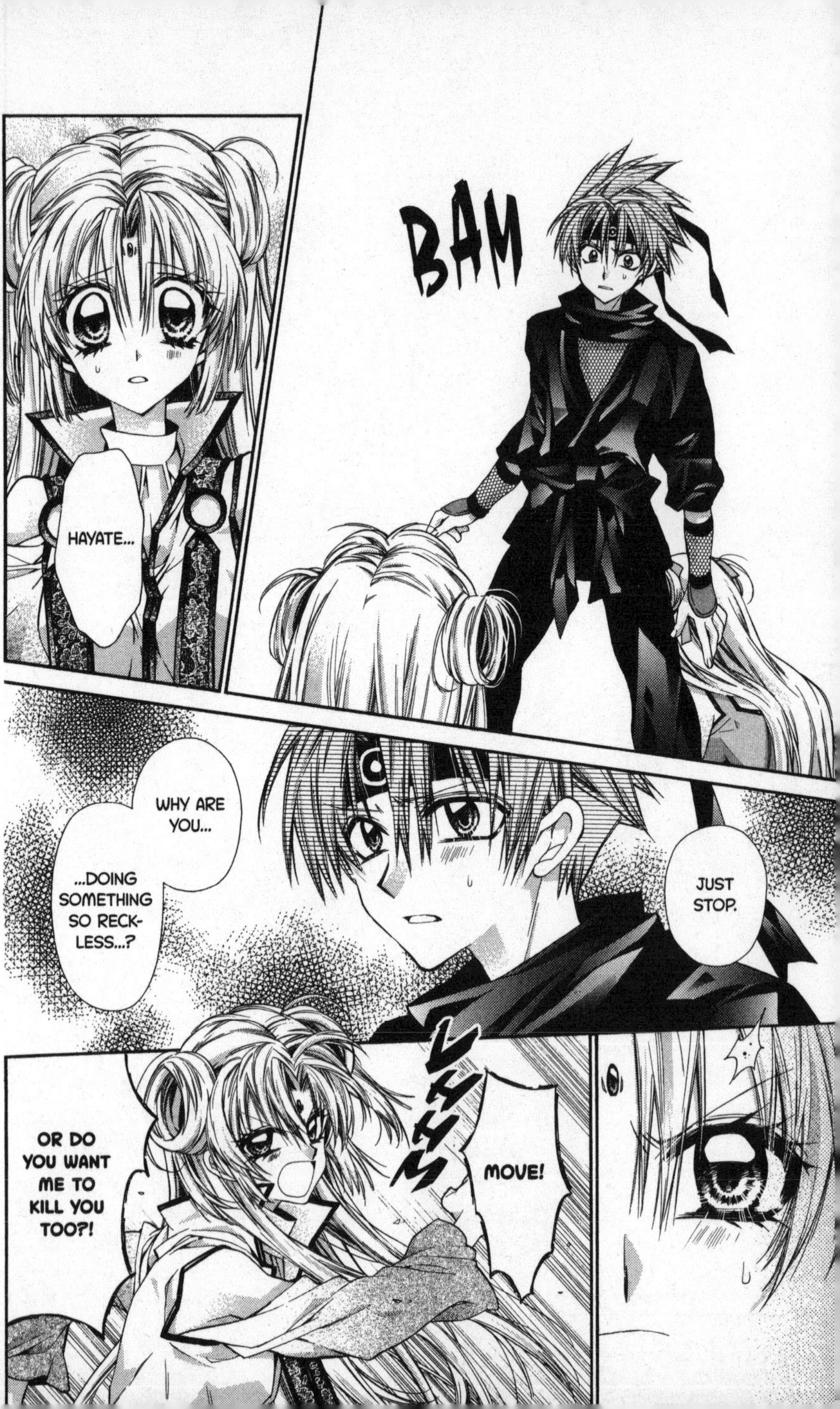
BAM
HAYATE...
WHY ARE YOU...
...DOING SOMETHING SO RECK-LESS...?
JUST STOP.
VHHM
MOVE!
OR DO YOU WANT ME TO KILL YOU TOO?!

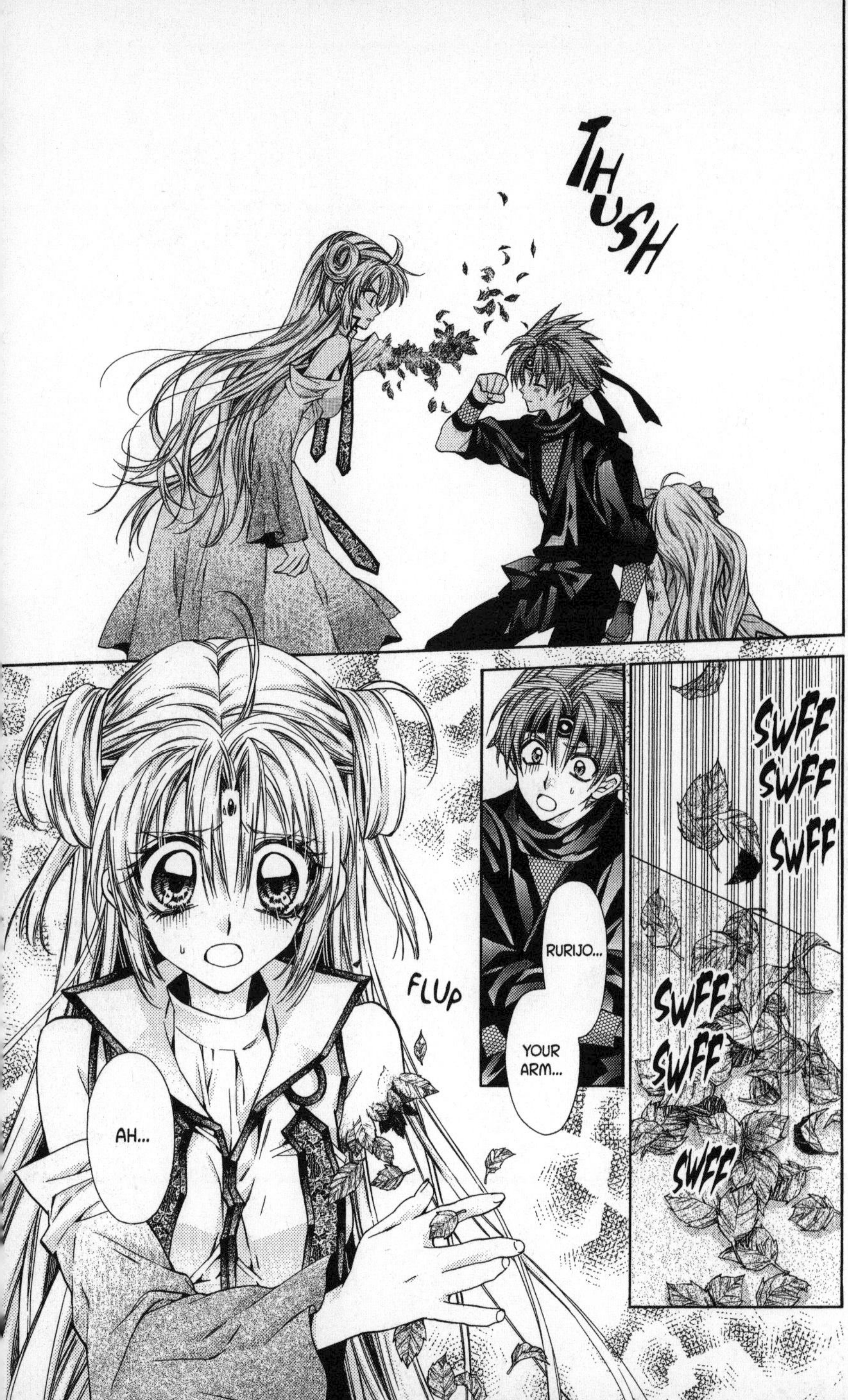
THUSH
SWFF SWFF SWFF
SWFF SWFF
SWFF
RURIJO...
YOUR ARM...
FLUP
AH...

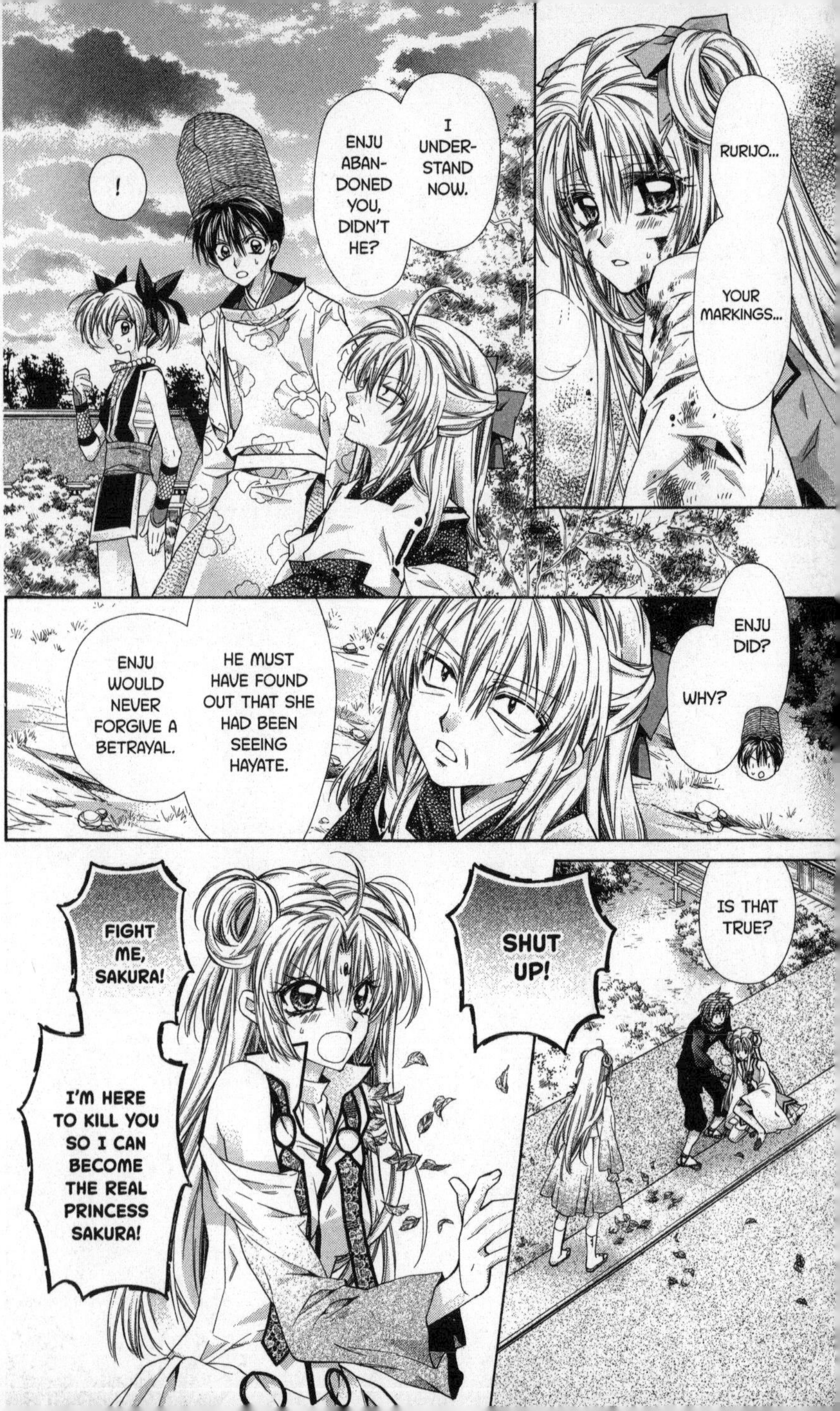
RURIJO...
YOUR MARKINGS...
I UNDER-STAND NOW.
ENJU ABAN-DONED YOU, DIDN'T HE?
!
ENJU DID?
WHY?
HE MUST HAVE FOUND OUT THAT SHE HAD BEEN SEEING HAYATE.
ENJU WOULD NEVER FORGIVE A BETRAYAL.
IS THAT TRUE?
SHUT UP!
FIGHT ME, SAKURA!
I'M HERE TO KILL YOU SO I CAN BECOME THE REAL PRINCESS SAKURA!

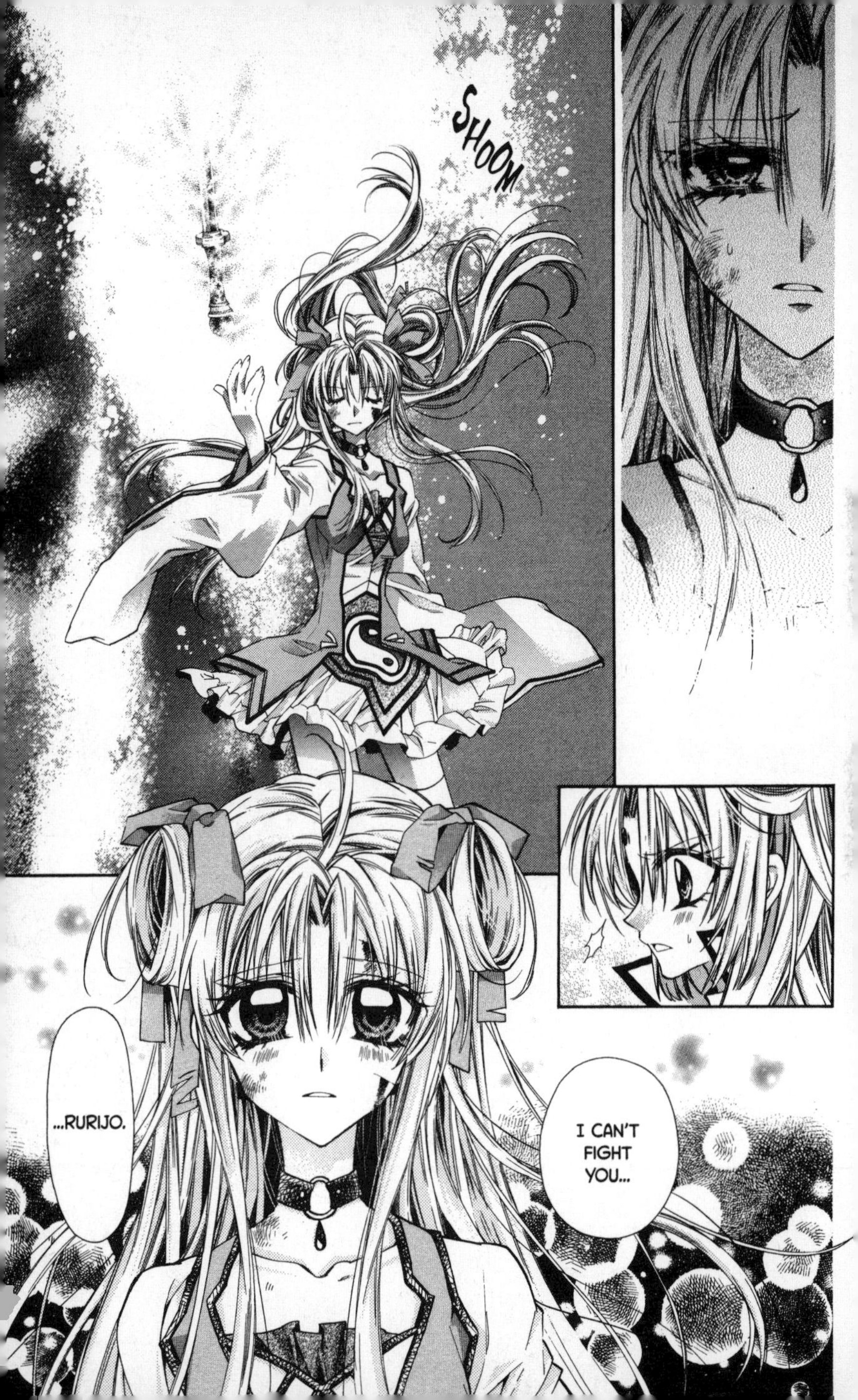
SHOOM
I CAN'T FIGHT YOU...
...RURIJO.

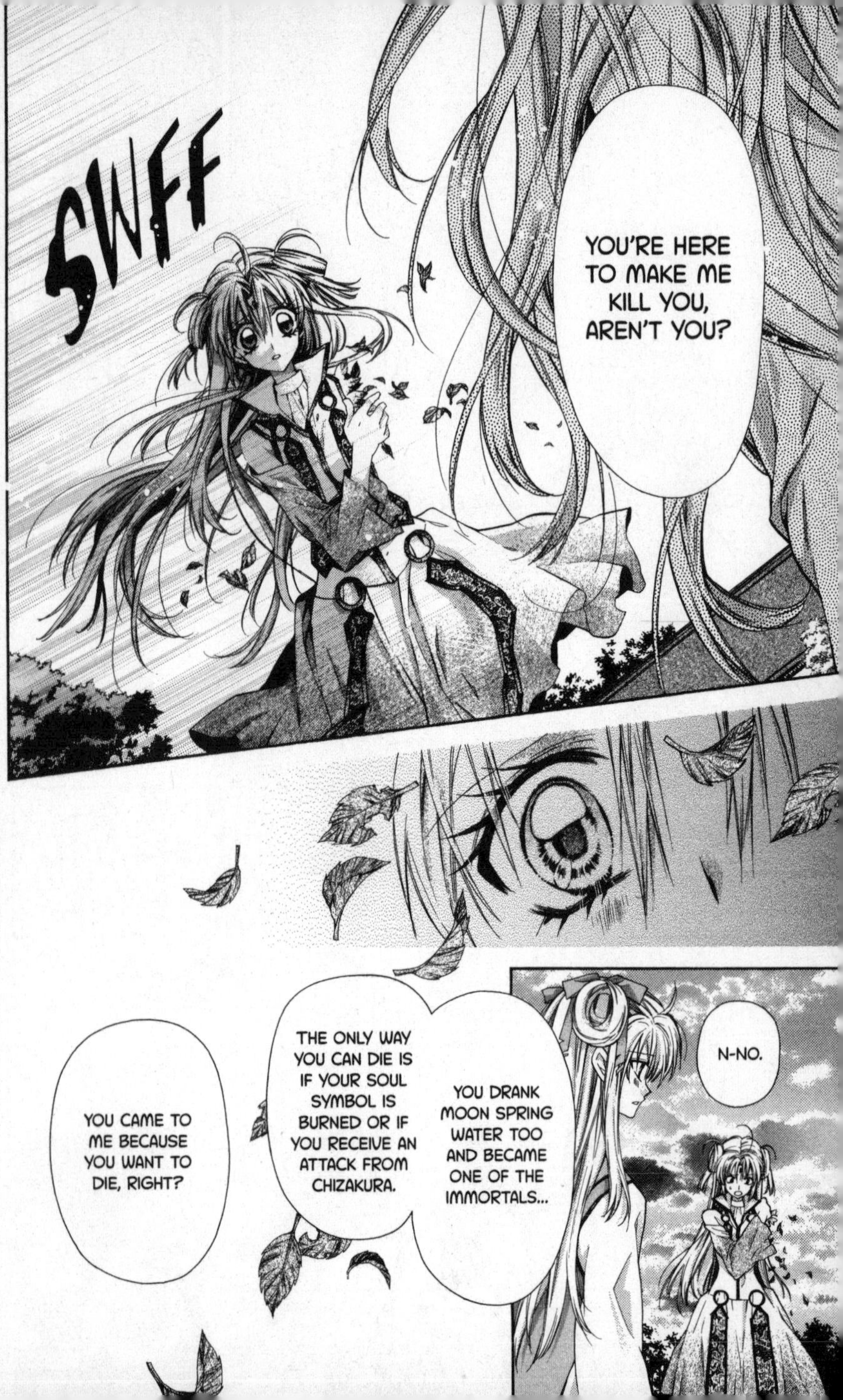
YOU'RE HERE TO MAKE ME KILL YOU, AREN'T YOU?
SWFF
N-NO.
YOU DRANK MOON SPRING WATER TOO AND BECAME ONE OF THE IMMORTALS...
THE ONLY WAY YOU CAN DIE IS IF YOUR SOUL SYMBOL IS BURNED OR IF YOU RECEIVE AN ATTACK FROM CHIZAKURA.
YOU CAME TO ME BECAUSE YOU WANT TO DIE, RIGHT?

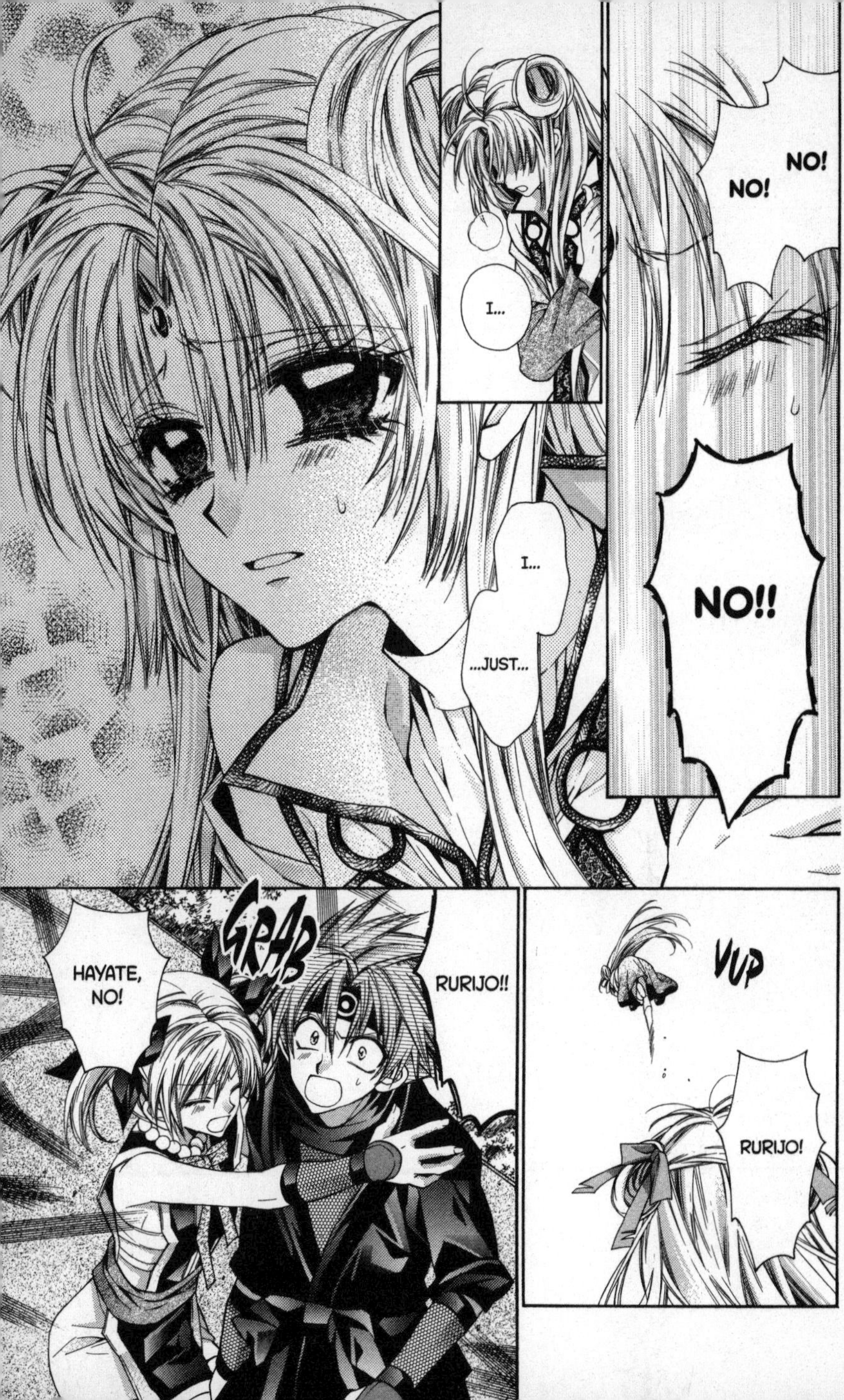
NO!
NO!
NO!!
I...
I...
...JUST...
VUP
RURIJO!
RURIJO!!
GRAB
HAYATE, NO!

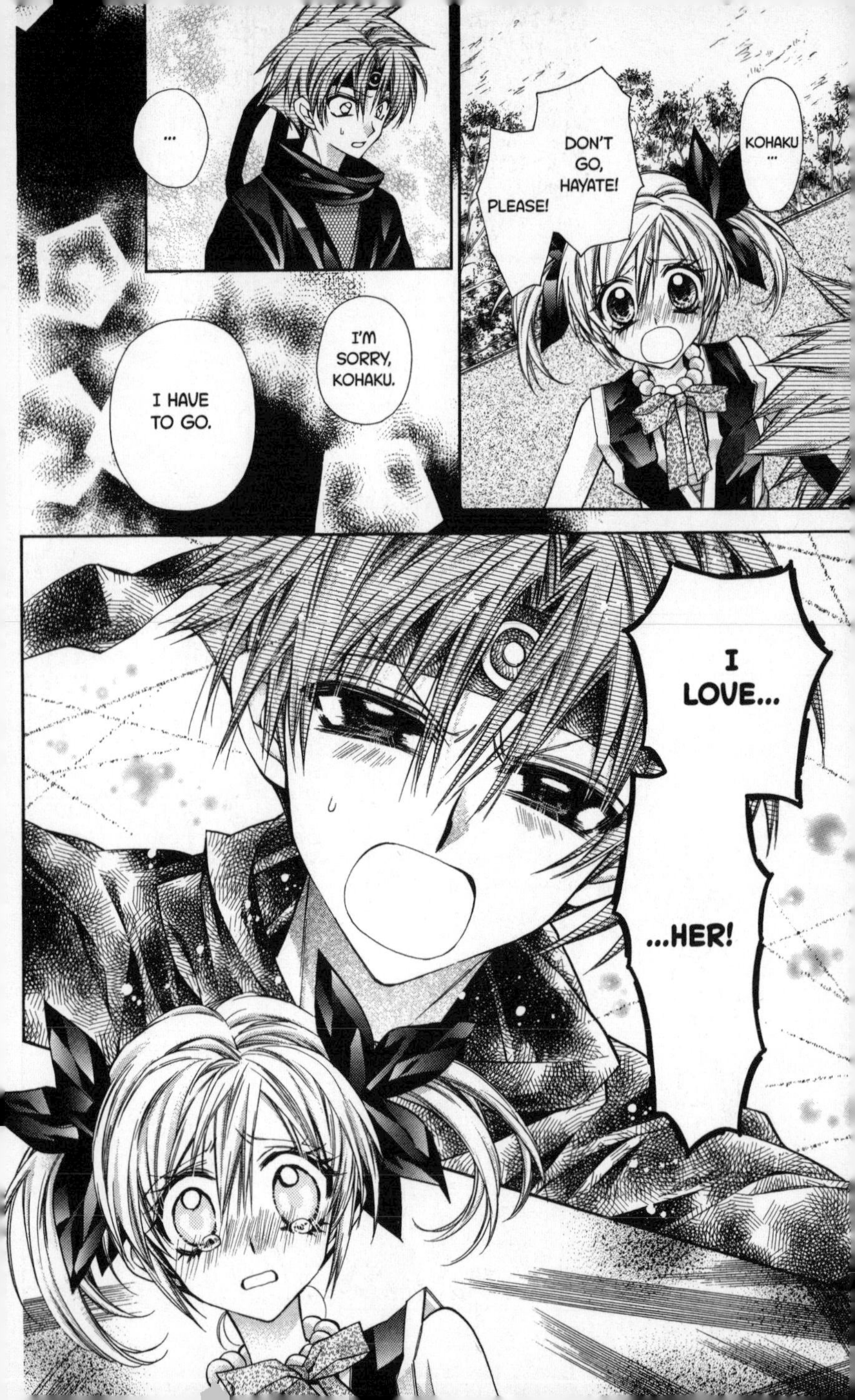
KOHAKU...
DON'T GO, HAYATE! PLEASE!
...
I'M SORRY, KOHAKU.
I HAVE TO GO.
I LOVE...
...HER!

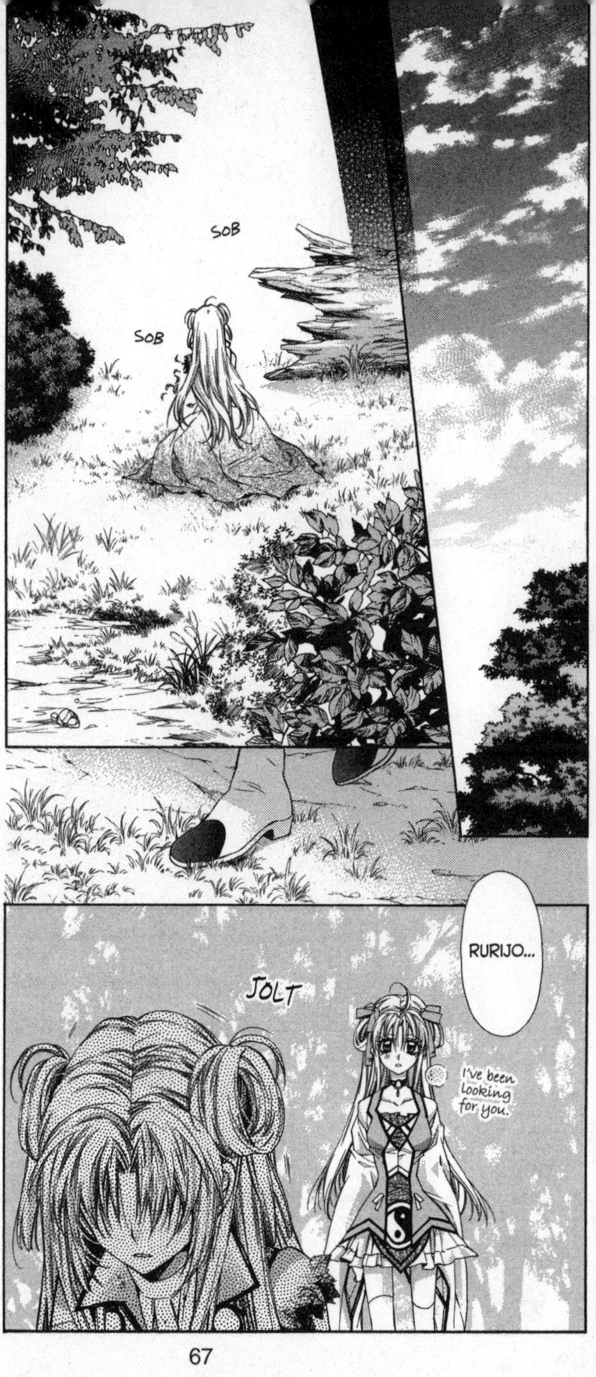
SOB
SOB
RURIJO...
I've been looking for you.
JOLT

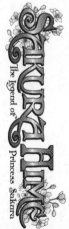

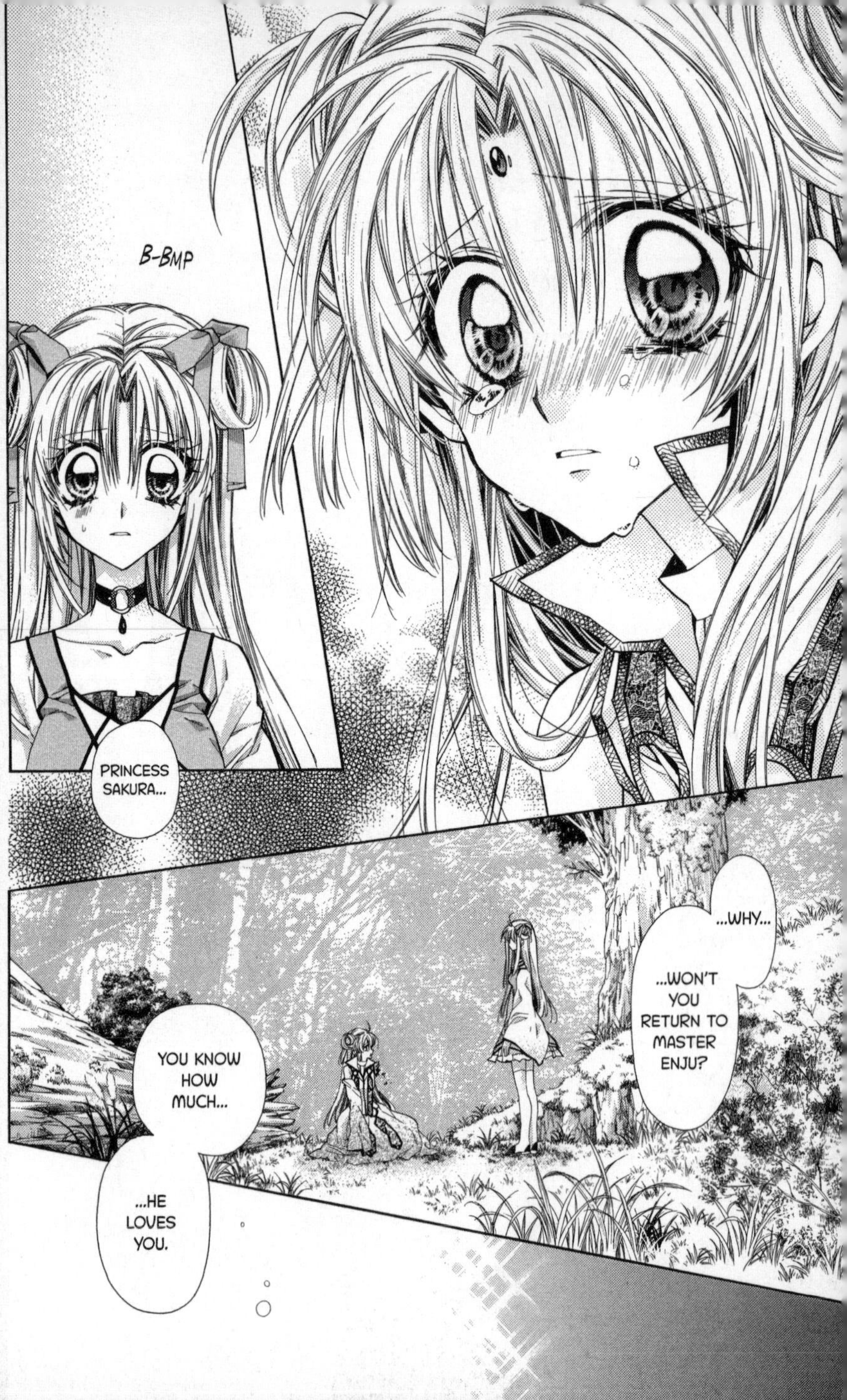
B-BMP
PRINCESS SAKURA...
...WHY...
...WON'T YOU RETURN TO MASTER ENJU?
YOU KNOW HOW MUCH...
...HE LOVES YOU.

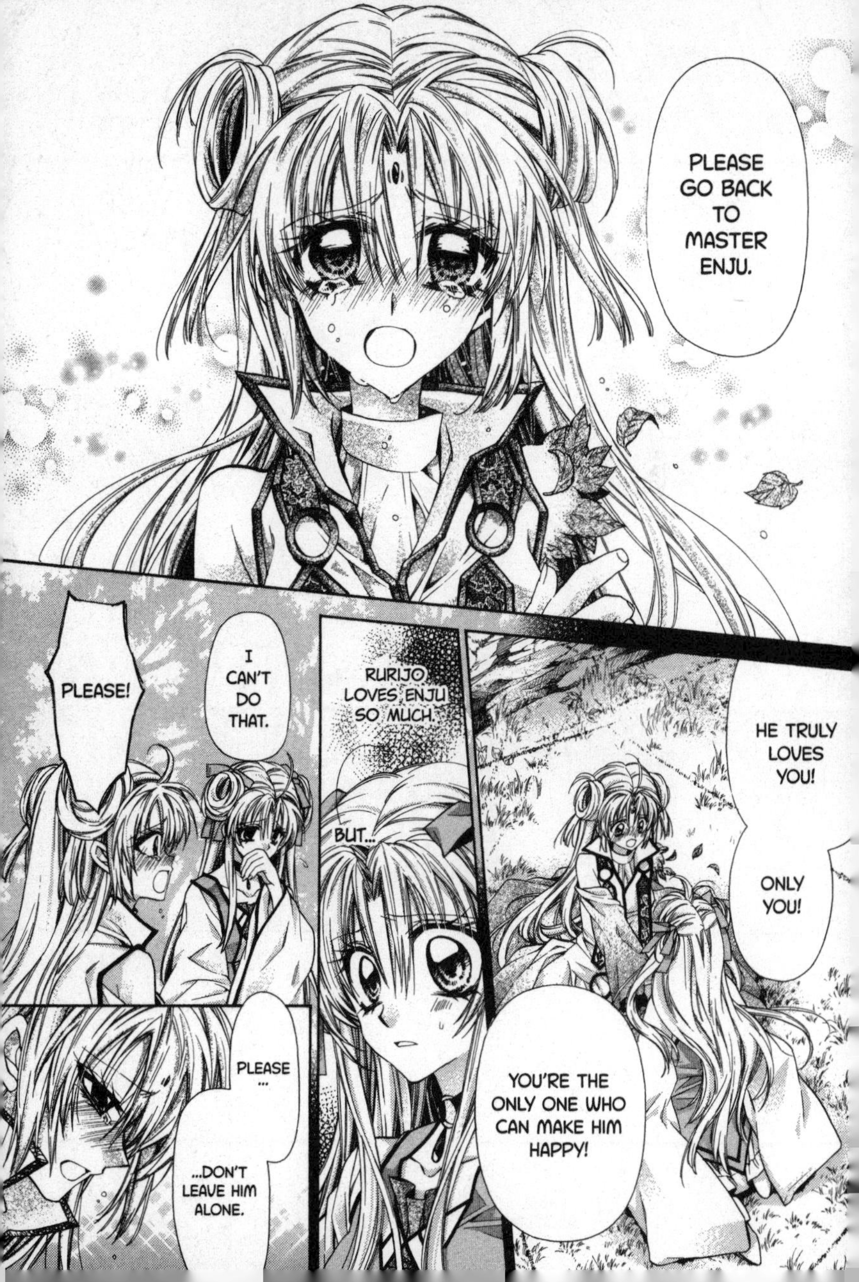
PLEASE GO BACK TO MASTER ENJU.
HE TRULY LOVES YOU!
ONLY YOU!
YOU'RE THE ONLY ONE WHO CAN MAKE HIM HAPPY!
RURIJO LOVES ENJU SO MUCH.
BUT...
I CAN'T DO THAT.
PLEASE!
PLEASE...
...DON'T LEAVE HIM ALONE.

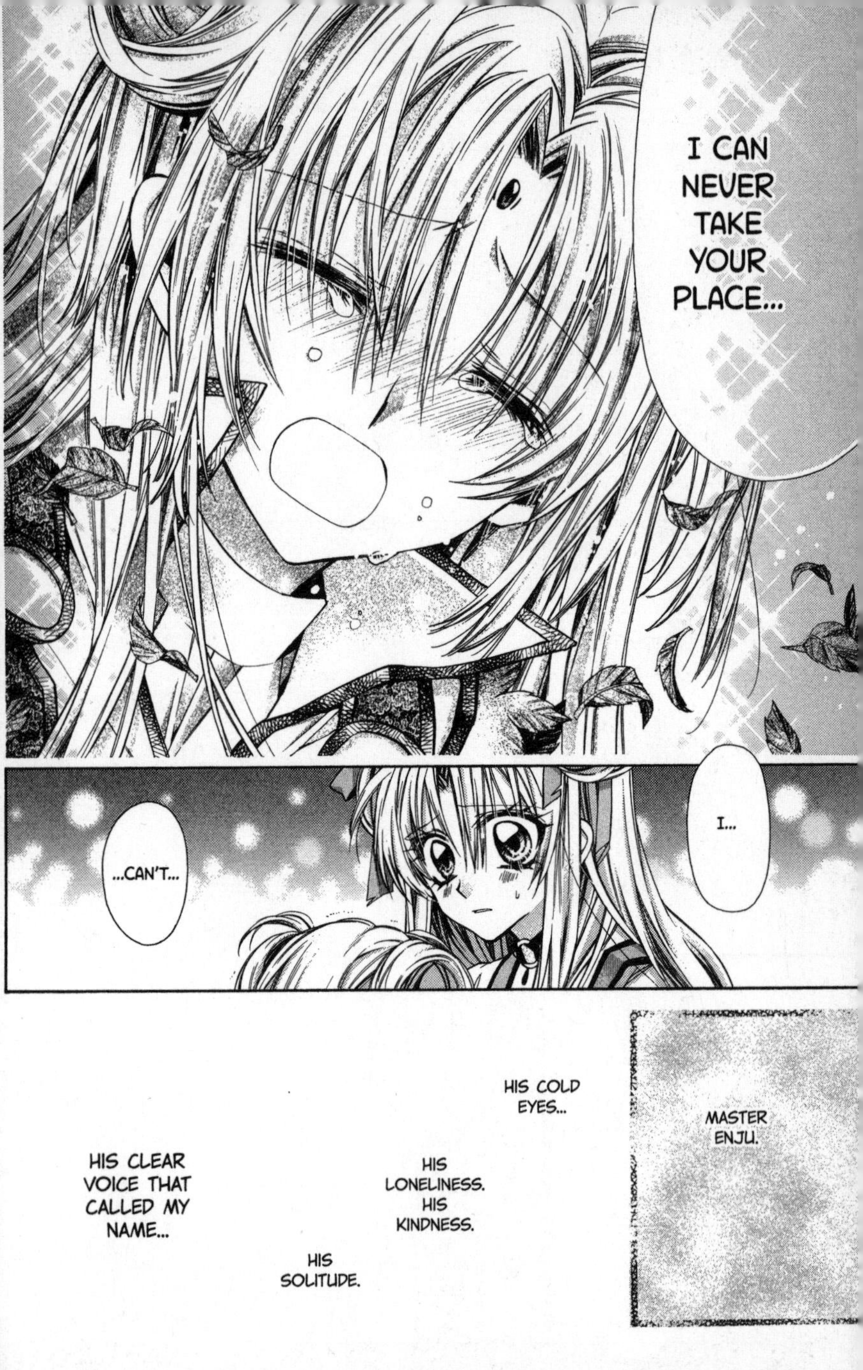
I CAN NEVER TAKE YOUR PLACE...
I...
...CAN'T...
MASTER ENJU.
HIS COLD EYES...
HIS LONELINESS. HIS KINDNESS.
HIS SOLITUDE.
HIS CLEAR VOICE THAT CALLED MY NAME...

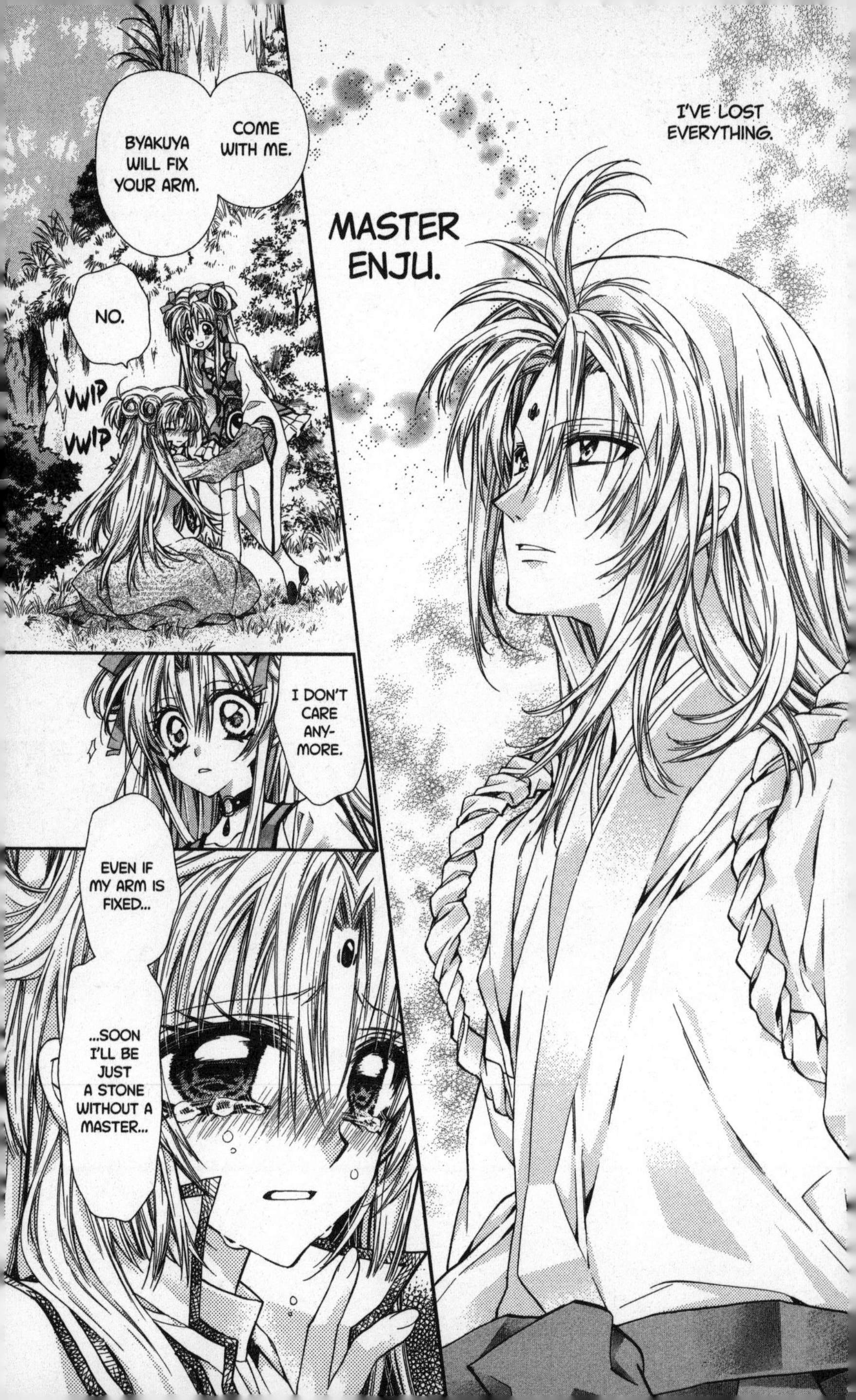
I'VE LOST EVERYTHING.
MASTER ENJU.
COME WITH ME.
BYAKUYA WILL FIX YOUR ARM.
NO.
VWIP VWIP
I DON'T CARE ANY-MORE.
EVEN IF MY ARM IS FIXED...
...SOON I'LL BE JUST A STONE WITHOUT A MASTER...

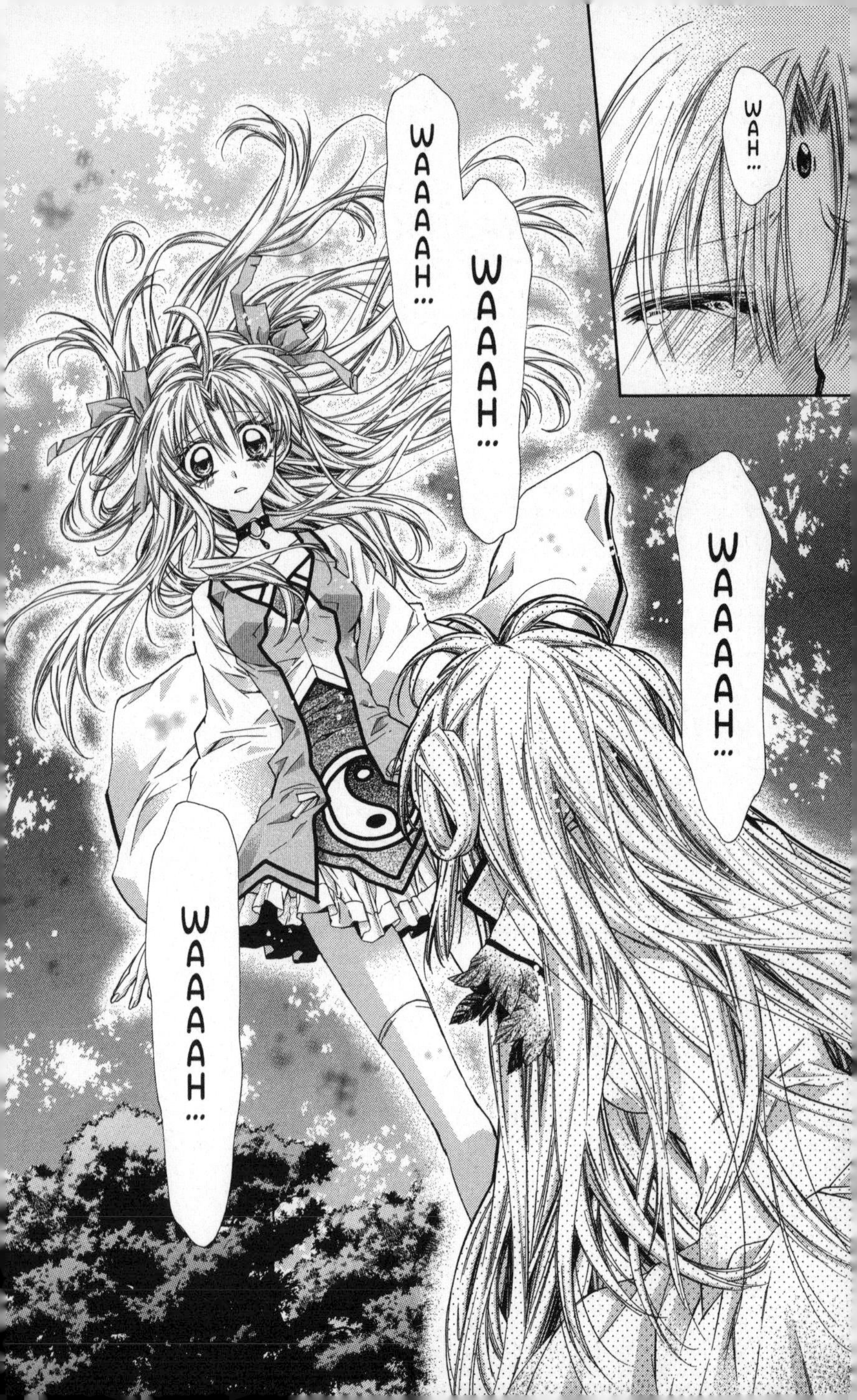
WAH...
WAAAAAH...
WAAAAAH...
WAAAAH...
WAAAAAH...

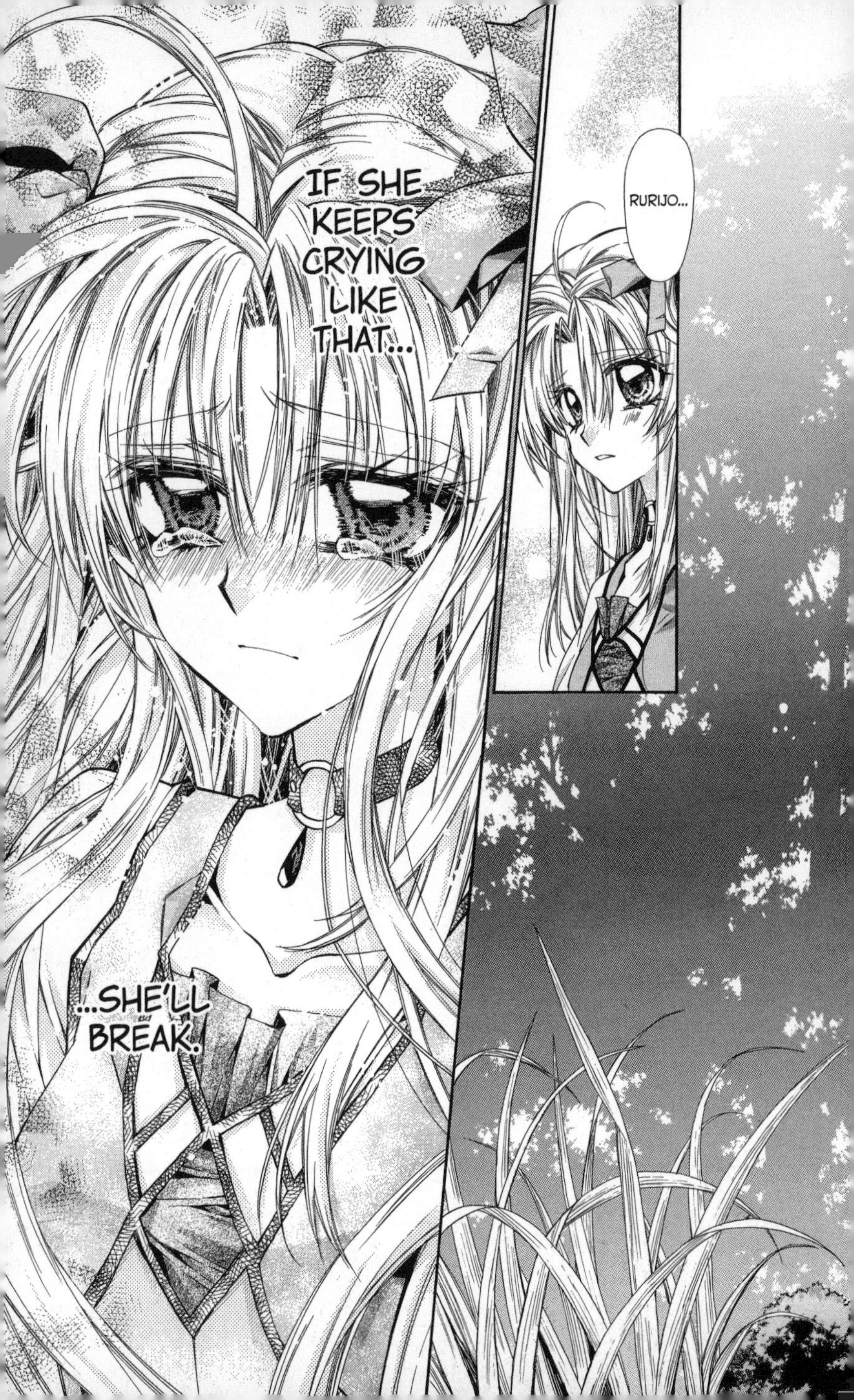
RURIJO...
IF SHE KEEPS CRYING LIKE THAT...
...SHE'LL BREAK.

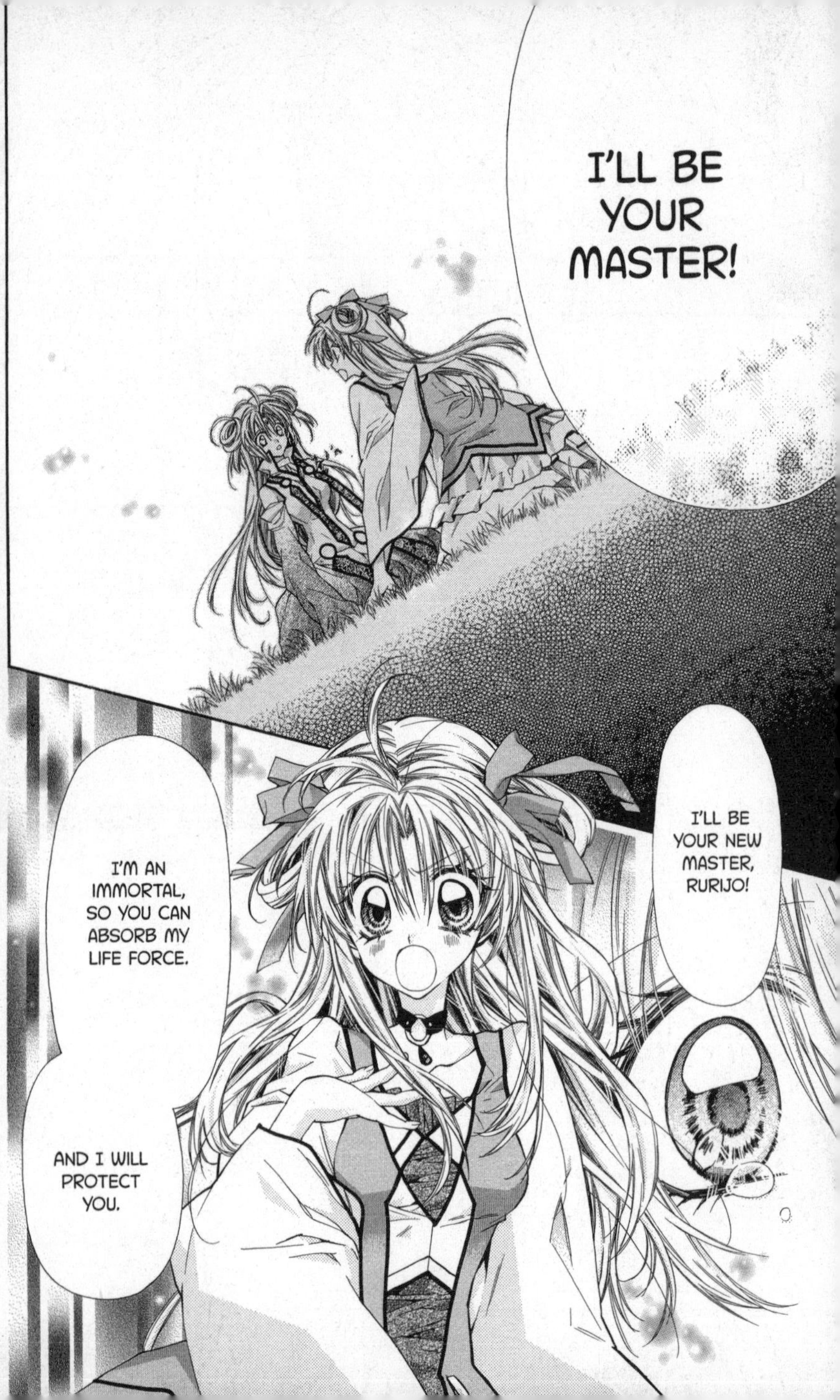
I'LL BE YOUR MASTER!
I'LL BE YOUR NEW MASTER, RURIJO!
I'M AN IMMORTAL, SO YOU CAN ABSORB MY LIFE FORCE.
AND I WILL PROTECT YOU.

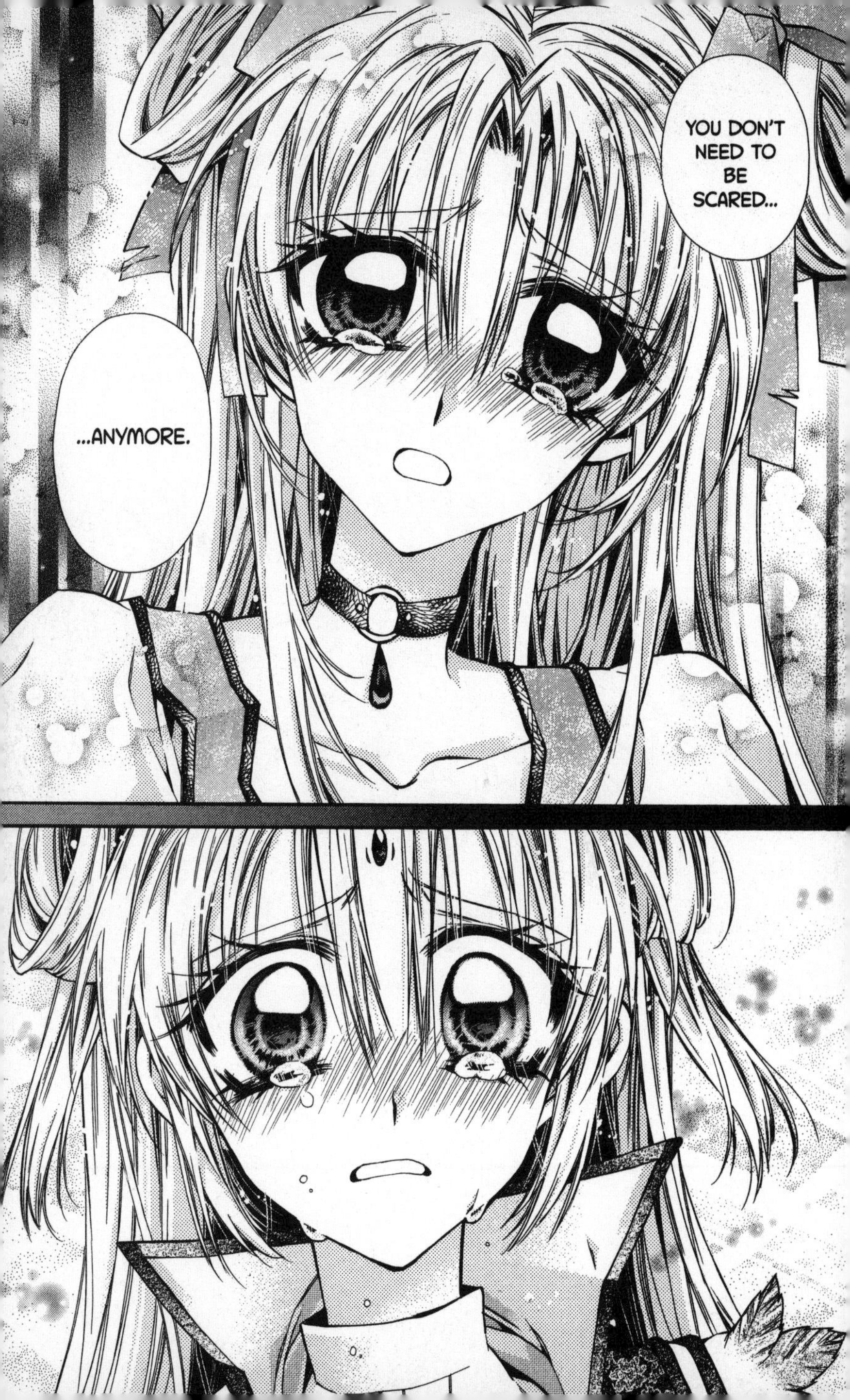
YOU DON'T NEED TO BE SCARED...
...ANYMORE.

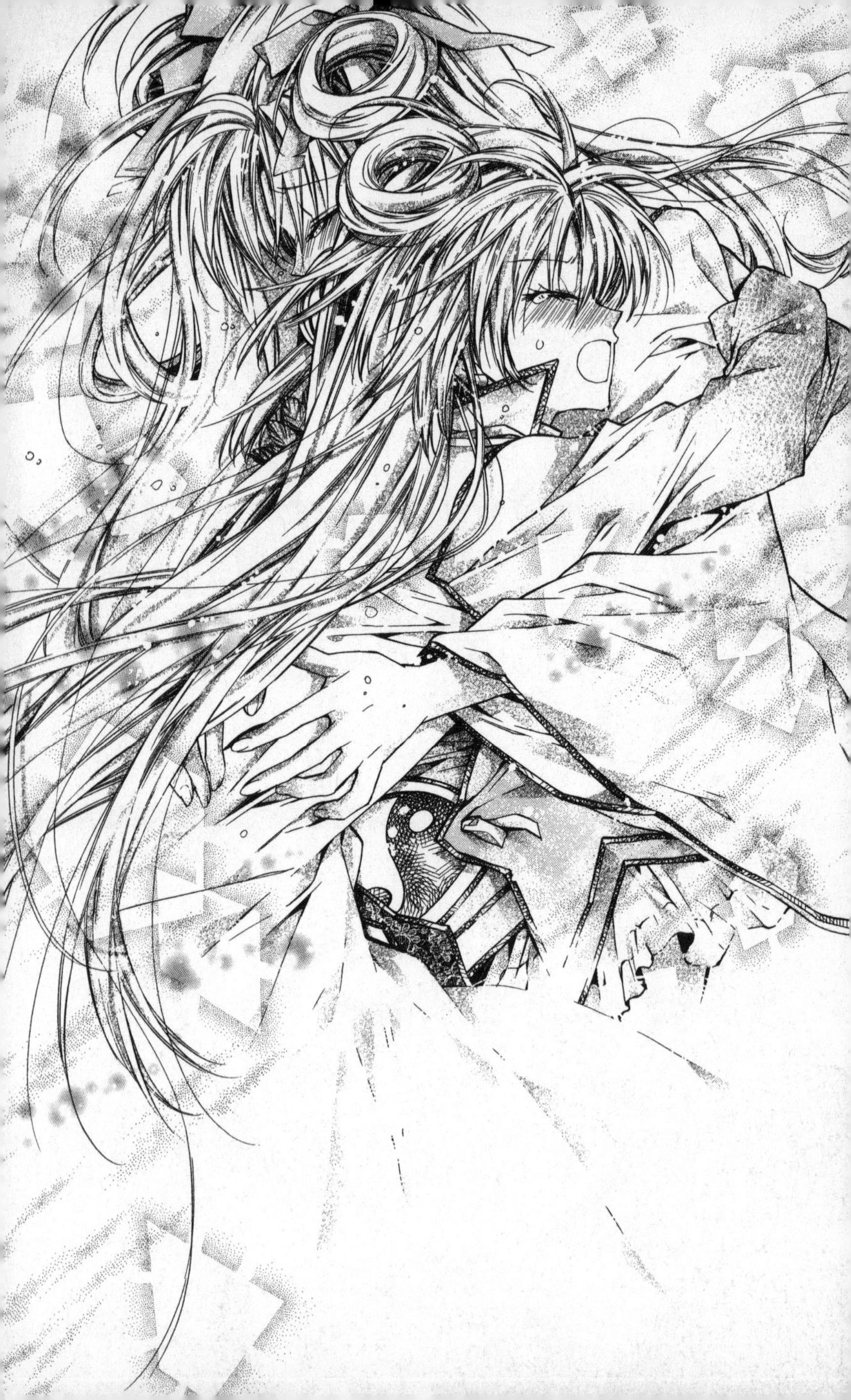

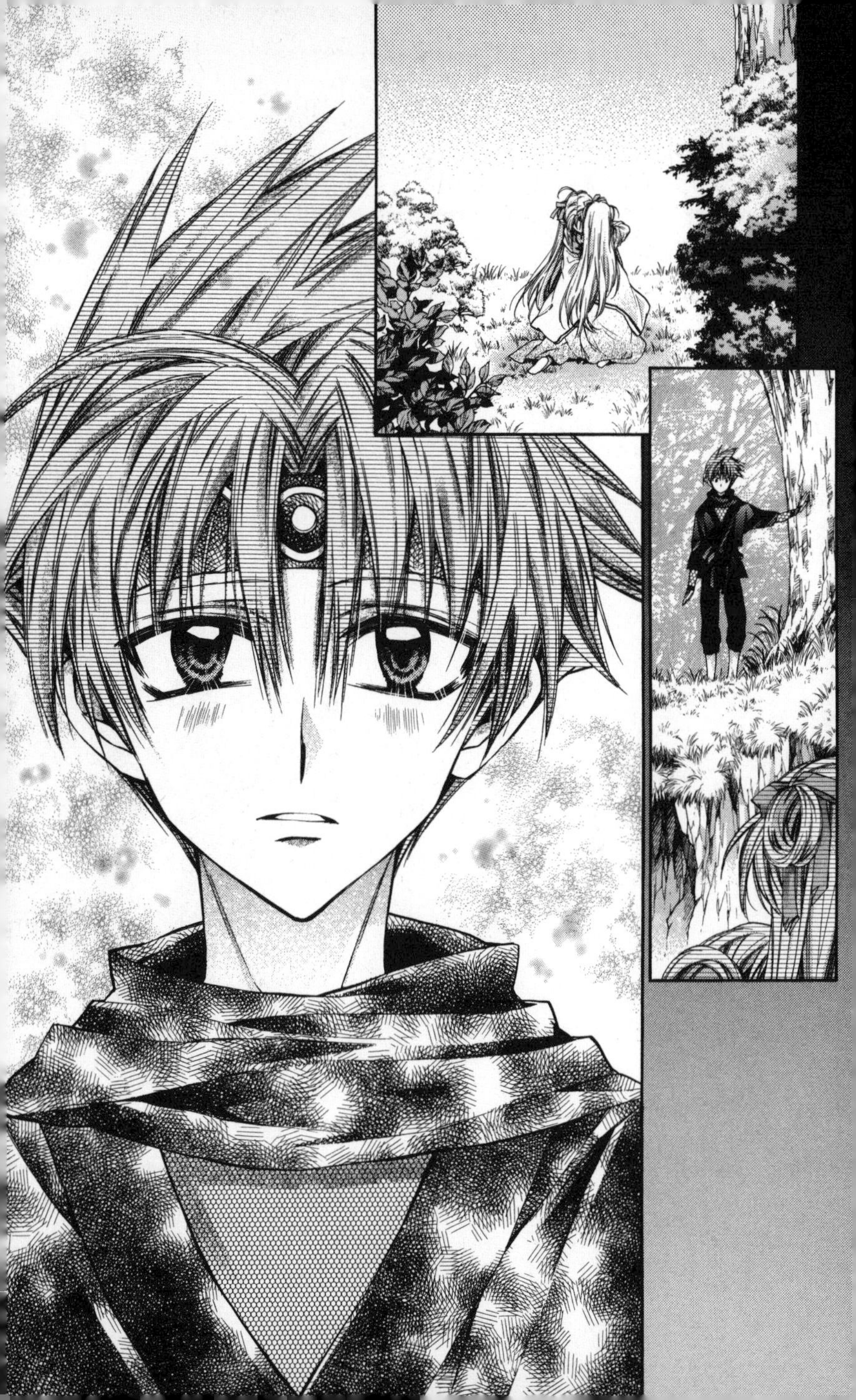

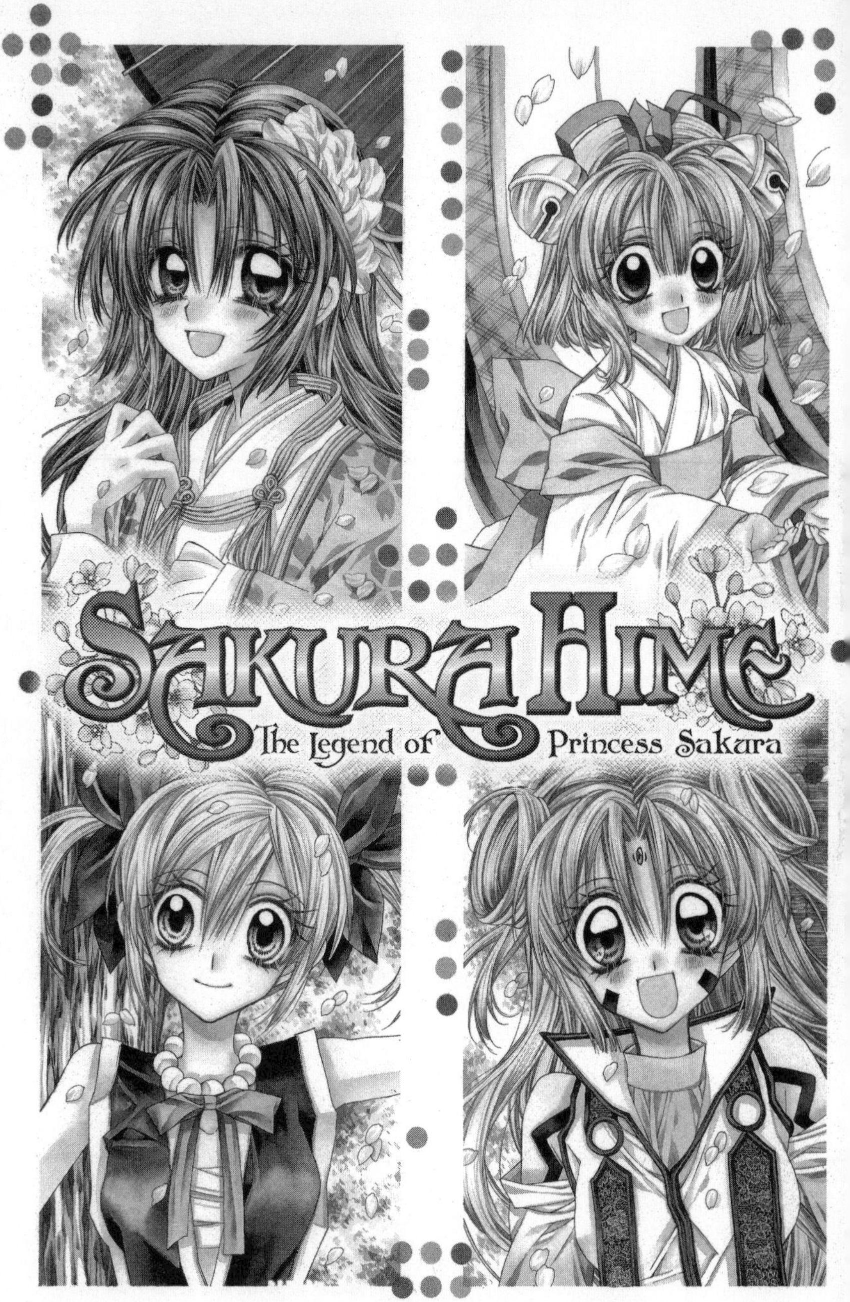
Sakura Hime
The Legend of Princess Sakura

Chapter 42: Fall in Love, Girls, Fall in Love with the Flower of Light

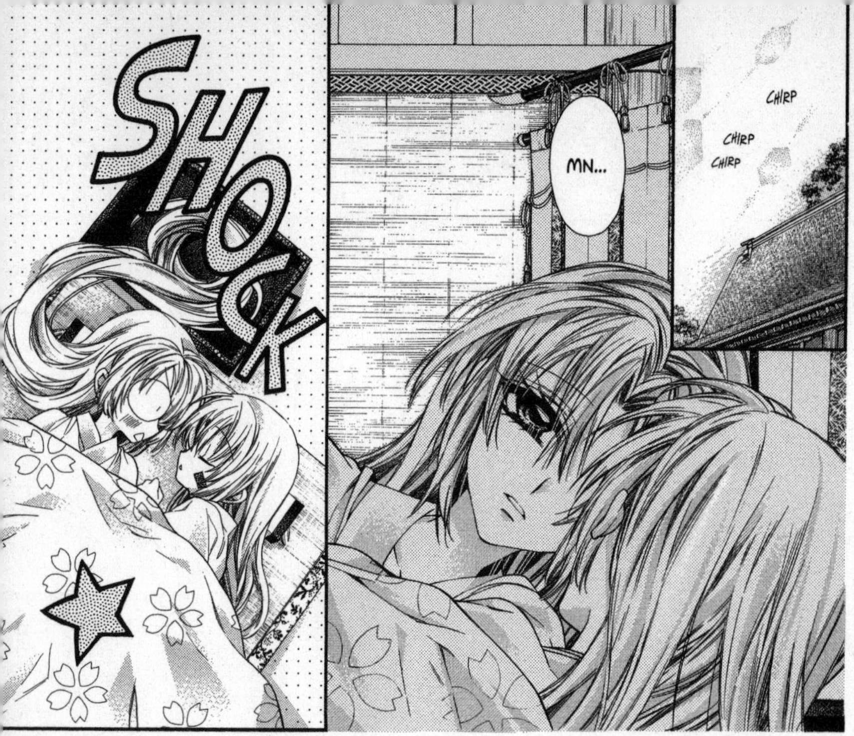
CHIRP
CHIRP
CHIRP
MN...
SHOCK

Chapter 42: Fall in Love, Girls, Fall in Love with the Flower of Light

(※ I'm giving away the story.)

This! This is it!! This is the chapter I've been looking forward to drawing so very much! Sakura and Rurijo are like twin sisters... They get along with each other and shine brightly like two high school girls... The image in my head was having the two be happy and cheerful, but it didn't turn out exactly as I had envisioned. (I never know how it'll turn out until I actually draw it.)

The reason is probably because Rurijo hasn't completely gotten over what happened. She still has some hesitations when interacting with Sakura. Rurijo seemed more adult than Sakura when they first met, but now Sakura is like the older sister.

The one I truly feel sorry for is Kohaku. I'm really sorry. I never thought Hayate would get so serious about Rurijo, and I don't know what's going to happen now.

And at the end of the chapter you will see Asagiri versus Enju... These two are the most incompatible of all the characters in *Sakura Hime*. Eeek.

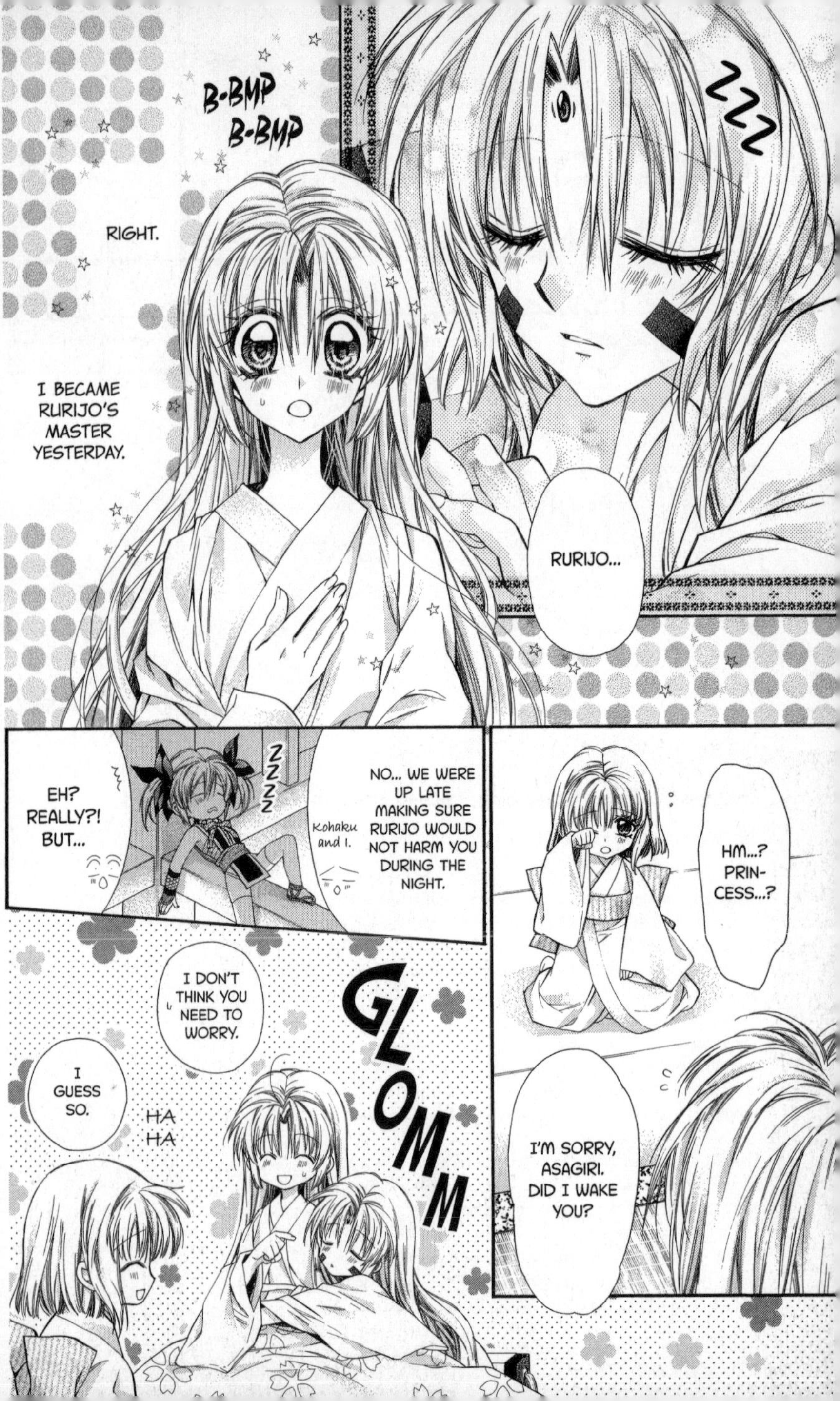
ZZZ
RURIJO...
B-BMP B-BMP
RIGHT.
I BECAME RURIJO'S MASTER YESTERDAY.
HM...? PRIN-CESS...?
I'M SORRY, ASAGIRI. DID I WAKE YOU?
NO... WE WERE UP LATE MAKING SURE RURIJO WOULD NOT HARM YOU DURING THE NIGHT.
Kohaku and I.
ZZZZ
EH? REALLY?! BUT...
GLOMM
I DON'T THINK YOU NEED TO WORRY.
I GUESS SO.
HA HA

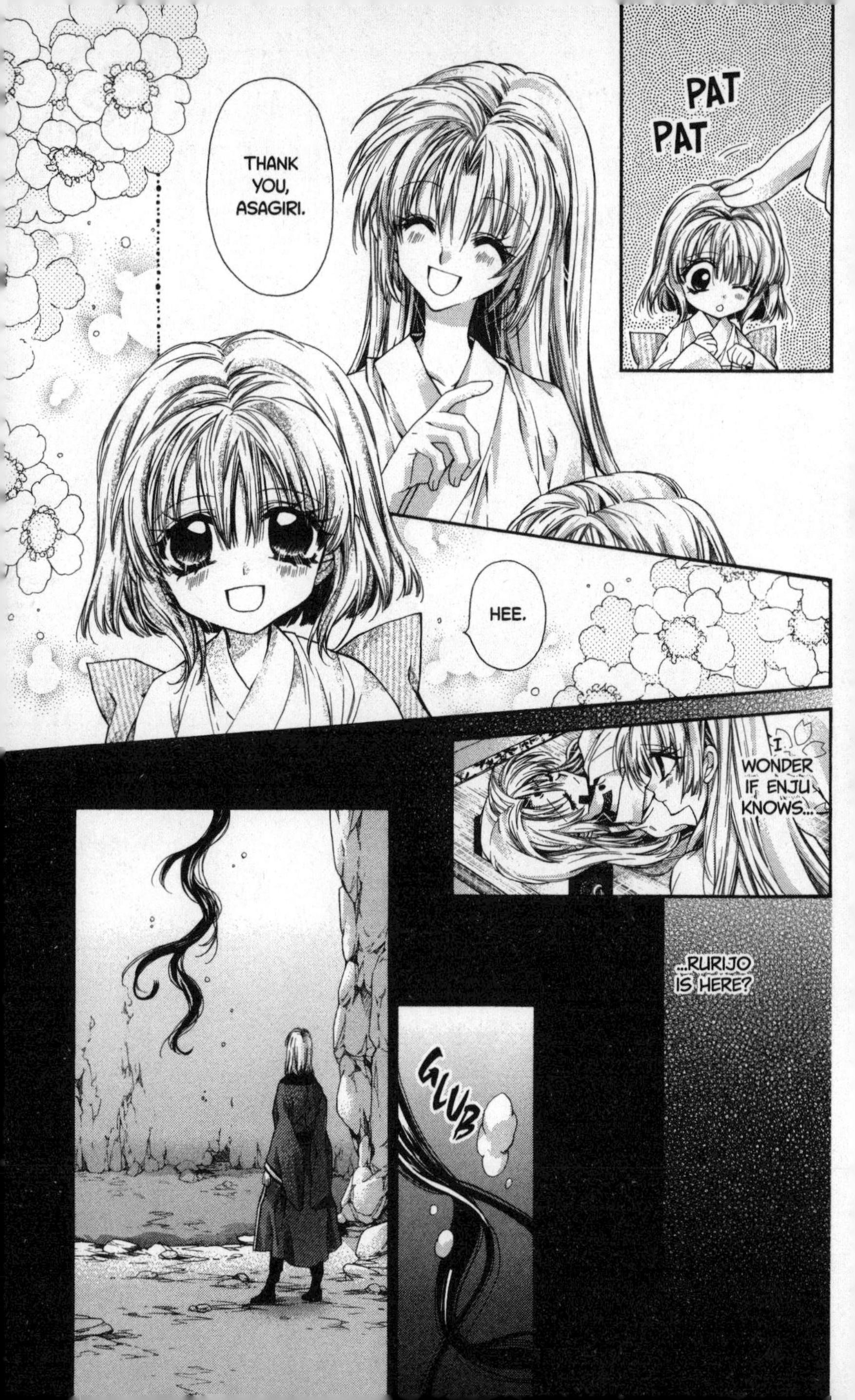
PAT
PAT
THANK YOU, ASAGIRI.
HEE.
I WONDER IF ENJU KNOWS...
...RURIJO IS HERE?
GLUB

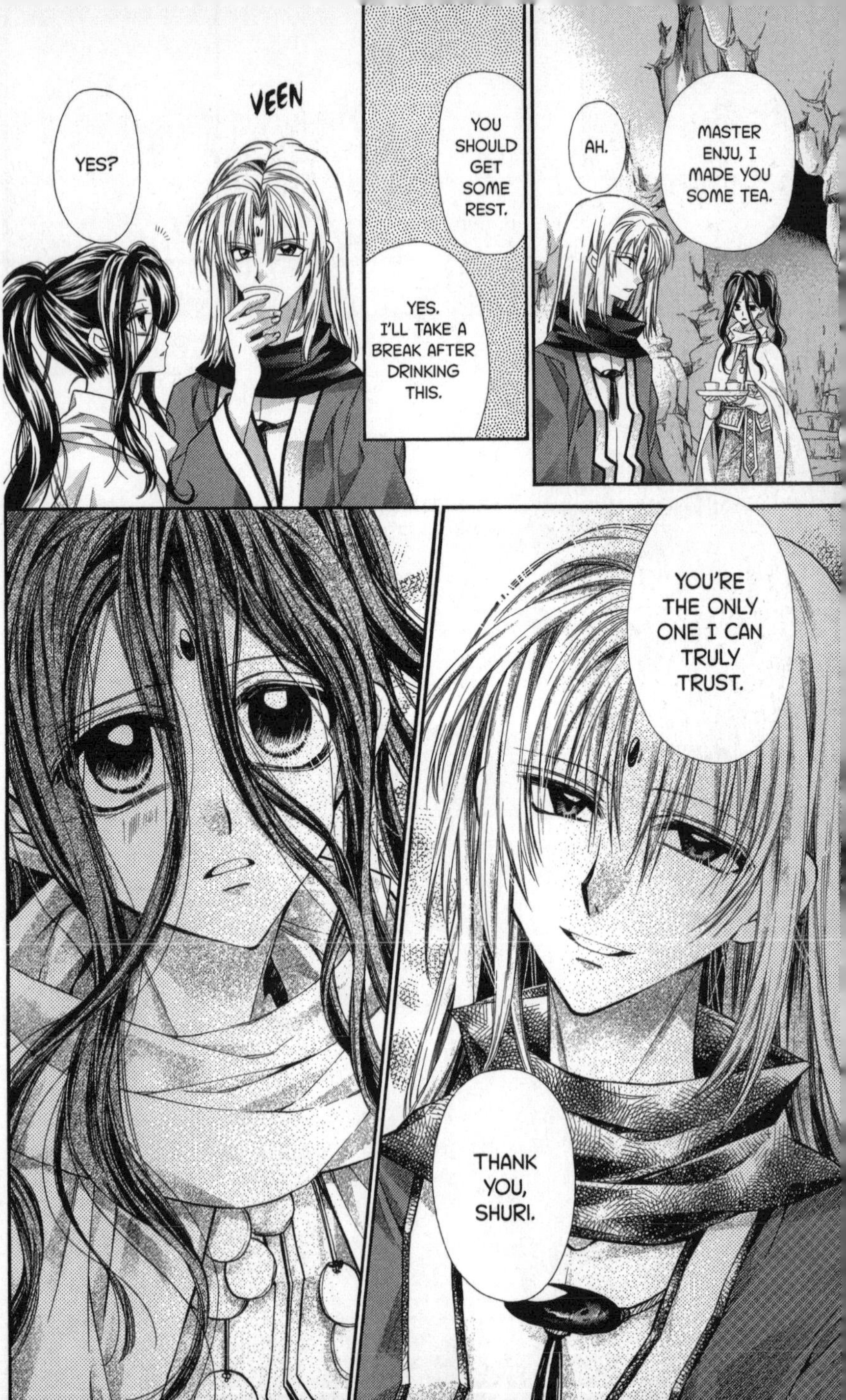
MASTER ENJU, I MADE YOU SOME TEA.
AH.
YOU SHOULD GET SOME REST.
YES. I'LL TAKE A BREAK AFTER DRINKING THIS.
VEEN
YES?
YOU'RE THE ONLY ONE I CAN TRULY TRUST.
THANK YOU, SHURI.

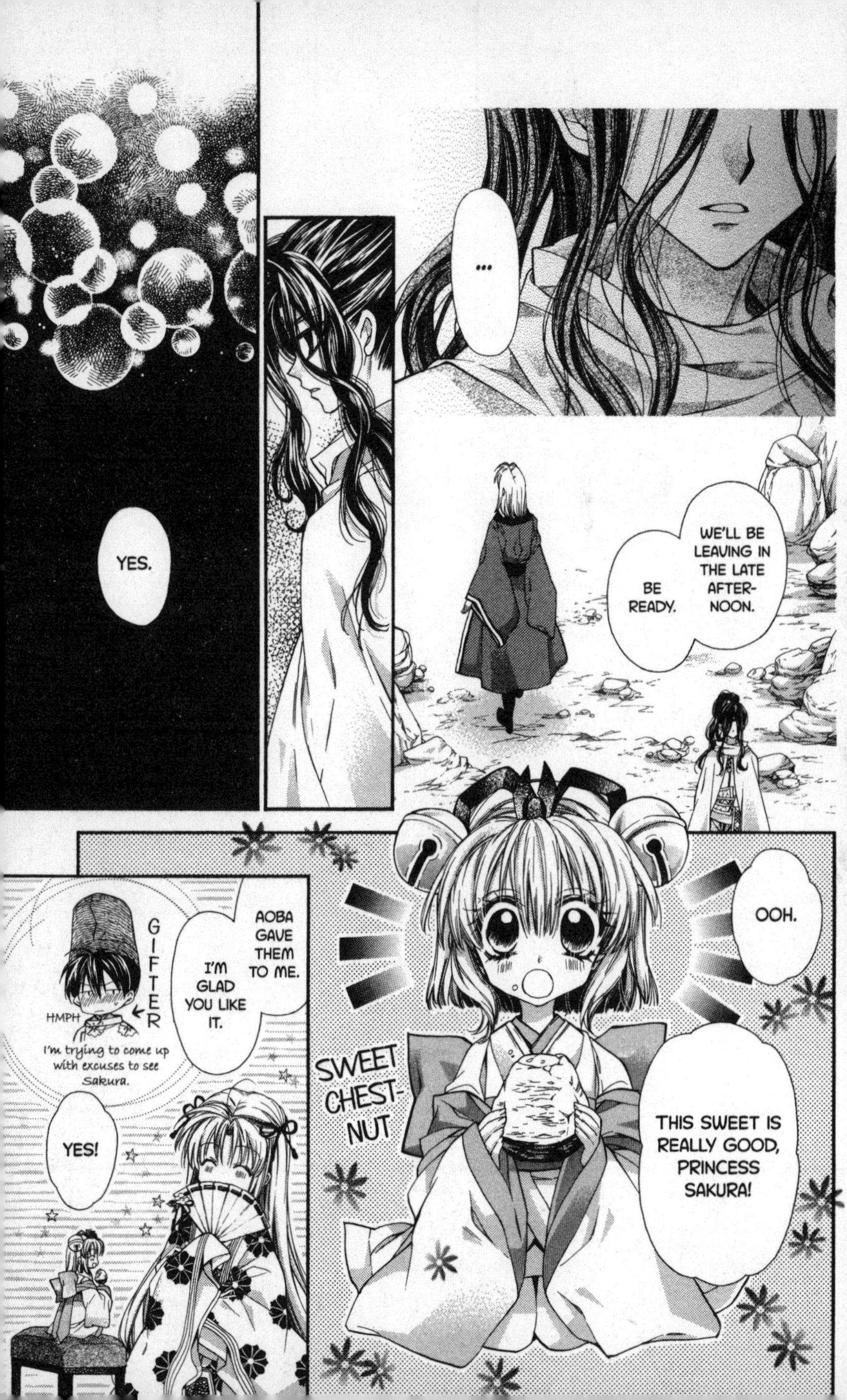
...
WE'LL BE LEAVING IN THE LATE AFTERNOON.
BE READY.
YES.
OOH.
THIS SWEET IS REALLY GOOD, PRINCESS SAKURA!
SWEET CHESTNUT
AOBA GAVE THEM TO ME.
I'M GLAD YOU LIKE IT.
GIFTER
HMPH
I'm trying to come up with excuses to see Sakura.
YES!

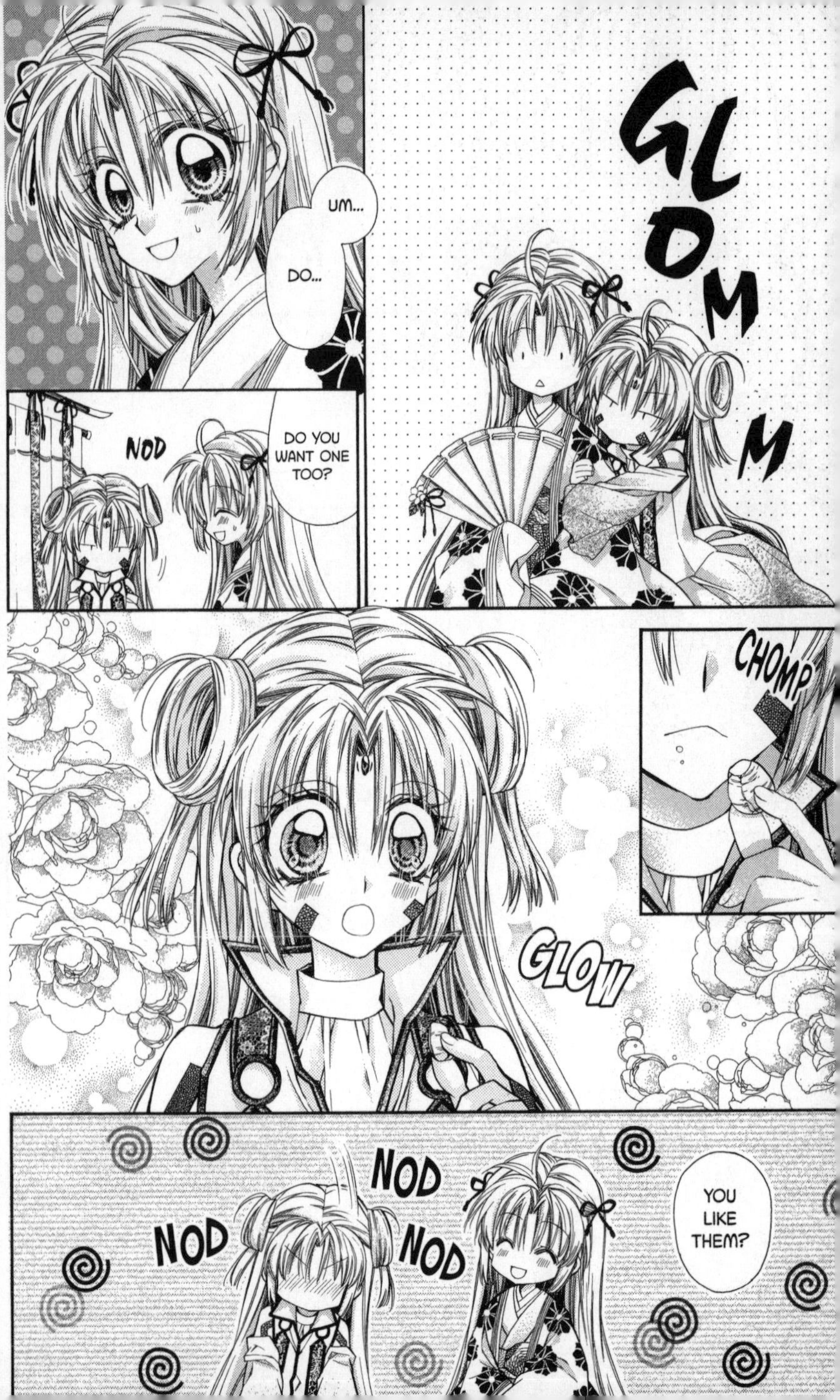
GLOMM
UM...
DO...
DO YOU WANT ONE TOO?
NOD
CHOMP
GLOW
YOU LIKE THEM?
NOD
NOD
NOD

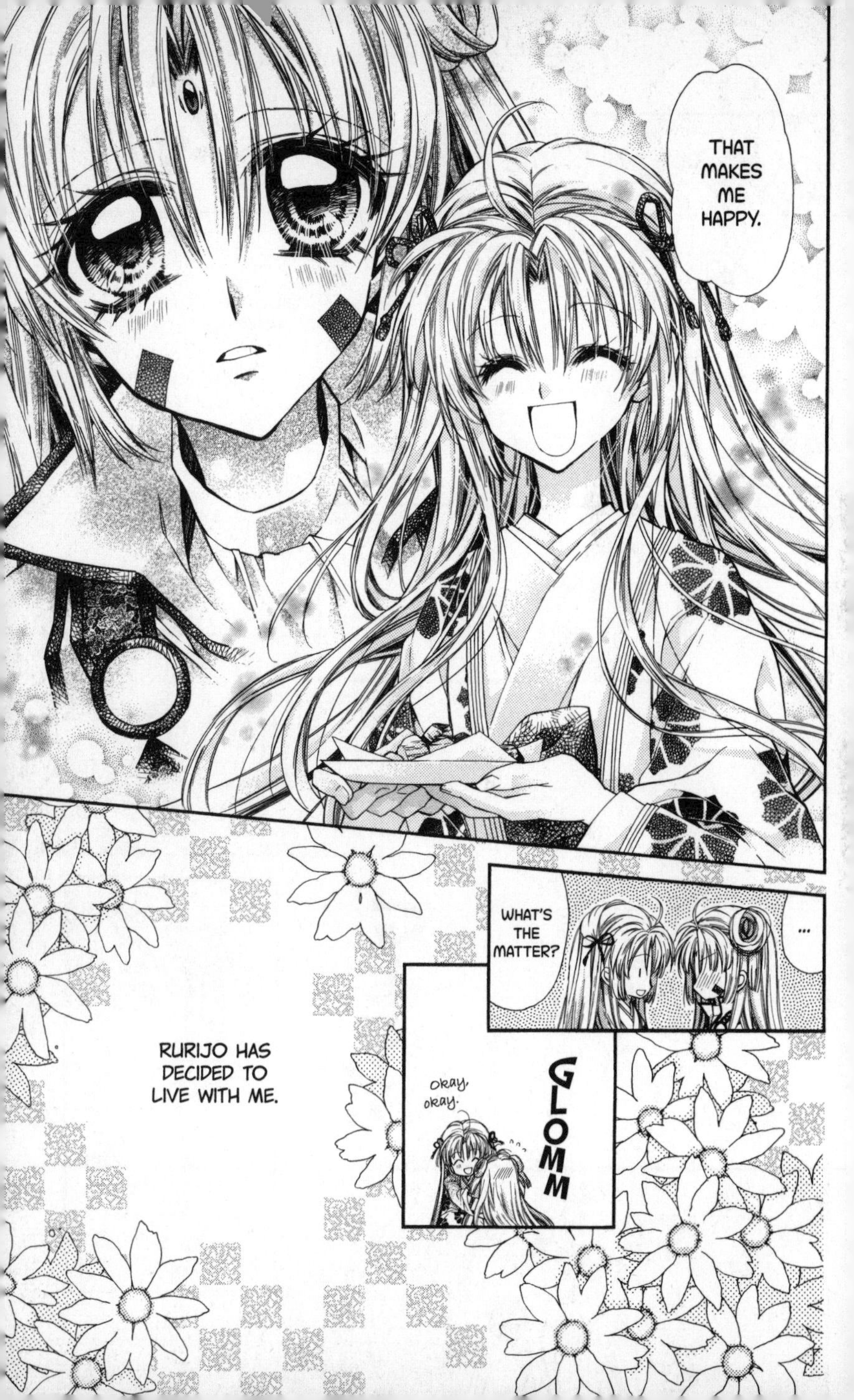
THAT MAKES ME HAPPY.
...
WHAT'S THE MATTER?
GLOMM
okay, okay.
RURIJO HAS DECIDED TO LIVE WITH ME.

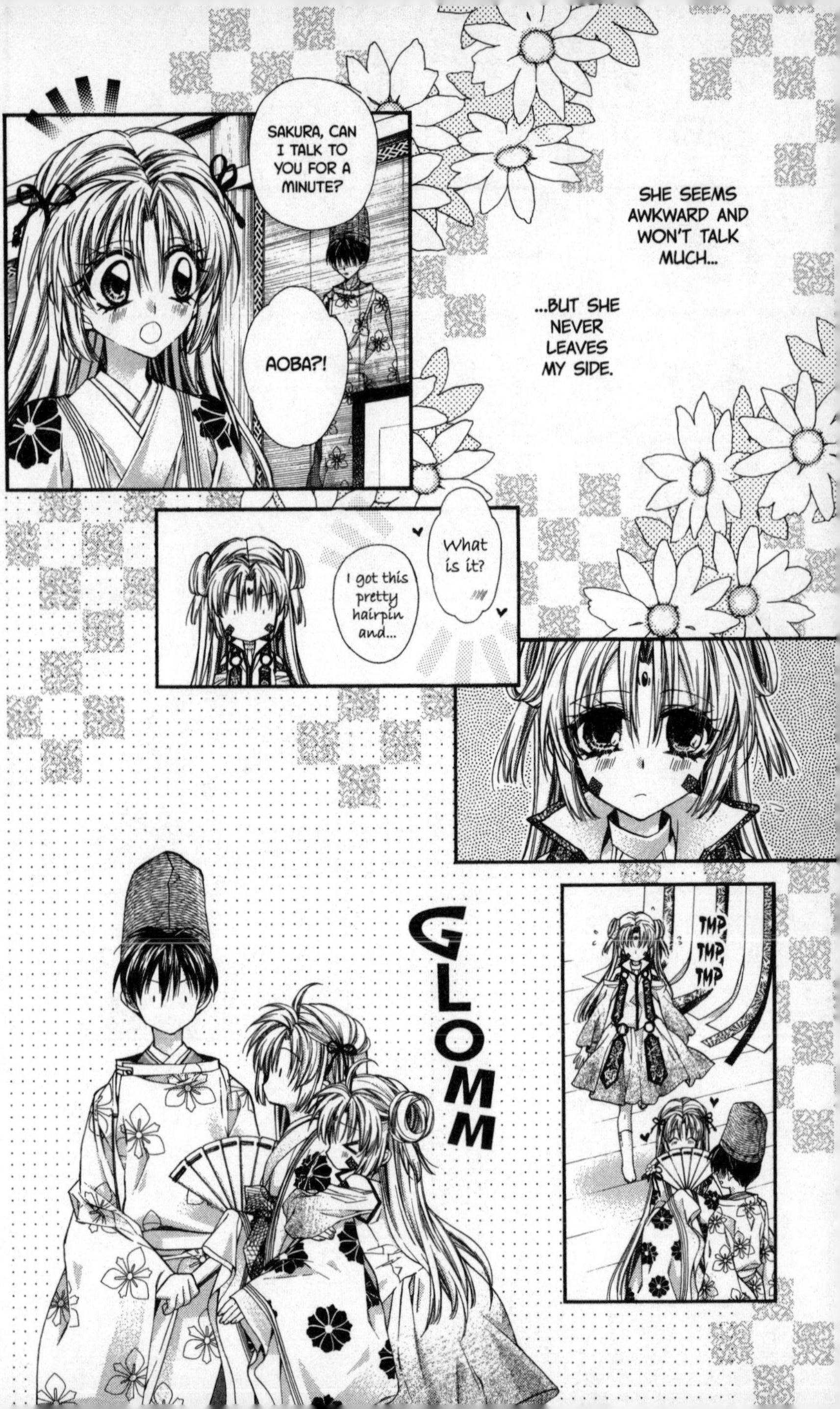

SHE SEEMS AWKWARD AND WON'T TALK MUCH...
...BUT SHE NEVER LEAVES MY SIDE.
SAKURA, CAN I TALK TO YOU FOR A MINUTE?
AOBA?!
What is it?
I got this pretty hairpin and...
TMP, TMP, TMP
GLOMM

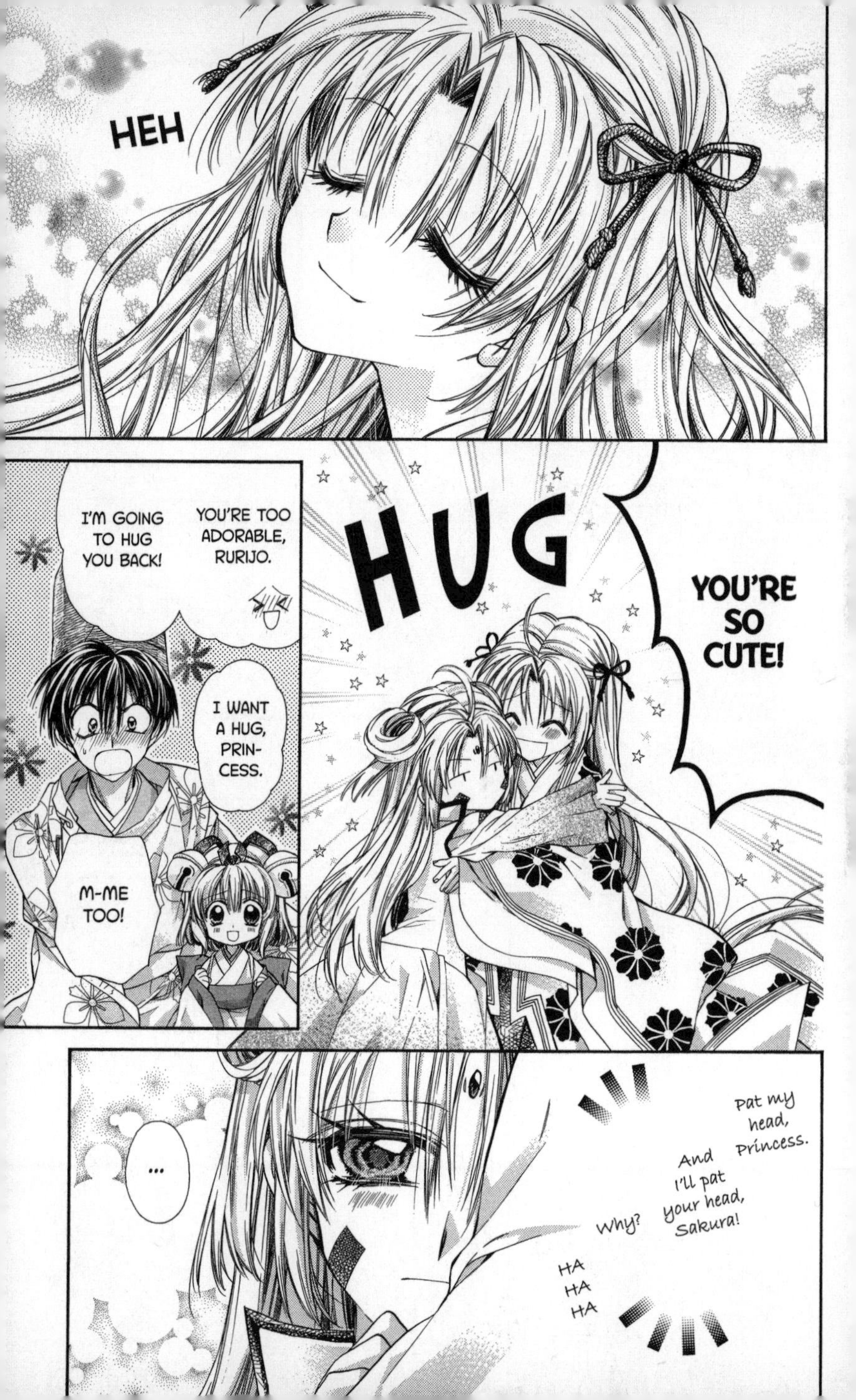
HEH
YOU'RE SO CUTE!
HUG
YOU'RE TOO ADORABLE, RURIJO.
I'M GOING TO HUG YOU BACK!
I WANT A HUG, PRINCESS.
M-ME TOO!
Pat my head, Princess.
And I'll pat your head, Sakura!
Why?
...
HA HA HA

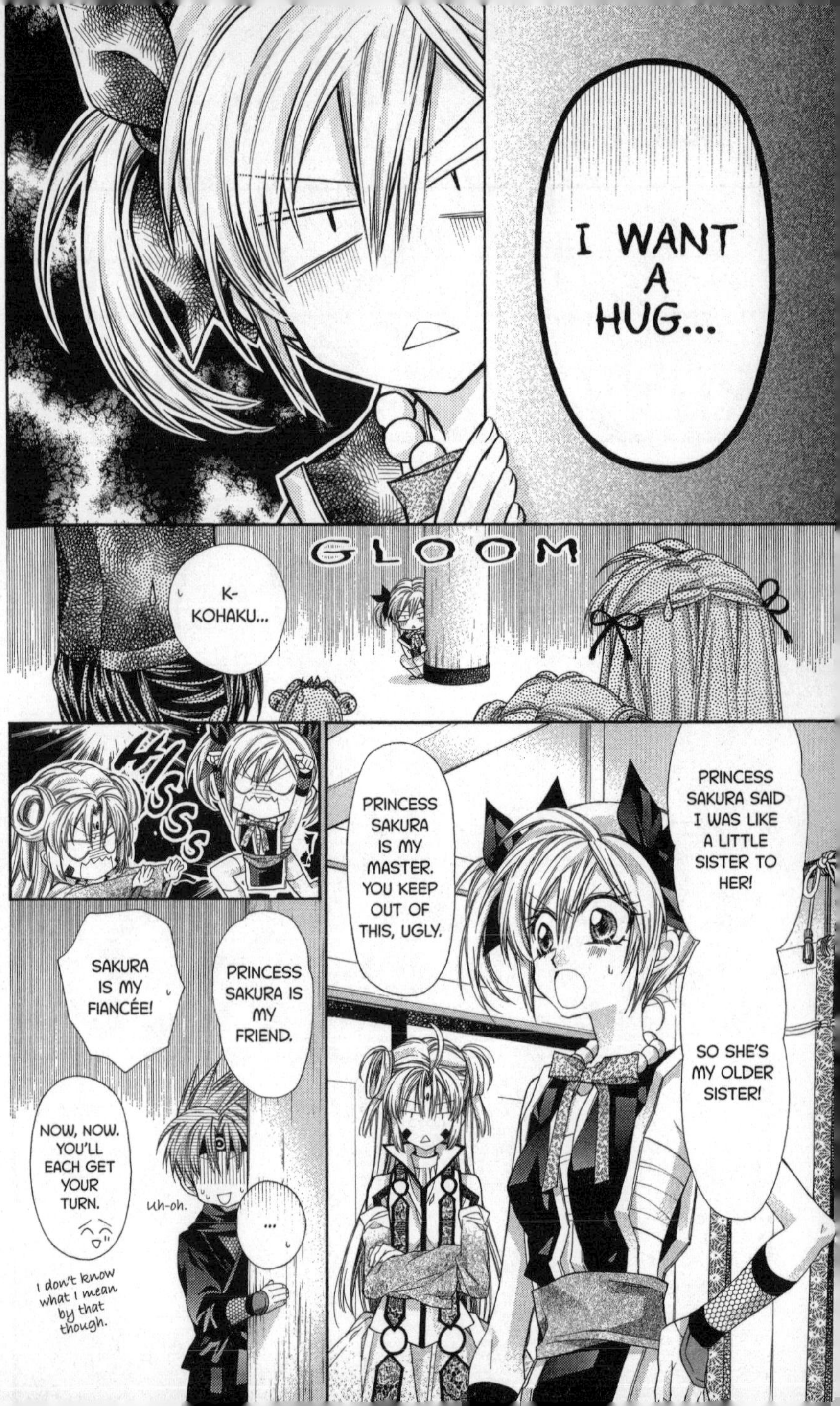
I WANT A HUG...
GLOOM
K-KOHAKU...
PRINCESS SAKURA SAID I WAS LIKE A LITTLE SISTER TO HER!
SO SHE'S MY OLDER SISTER!
PRINCESS SAKURA IS MY MASTER. YOU KEEP OUT OF THIS, UGLY.
HISSS
PRINCESS SAKURA IS MY FRIEND.
SAKURA IS MY FIANCÉE!
...
Uh-oh.
NOW, NOW. YOU'LL EACH GET YOUR TURN.
I don't know what I mean by that though.

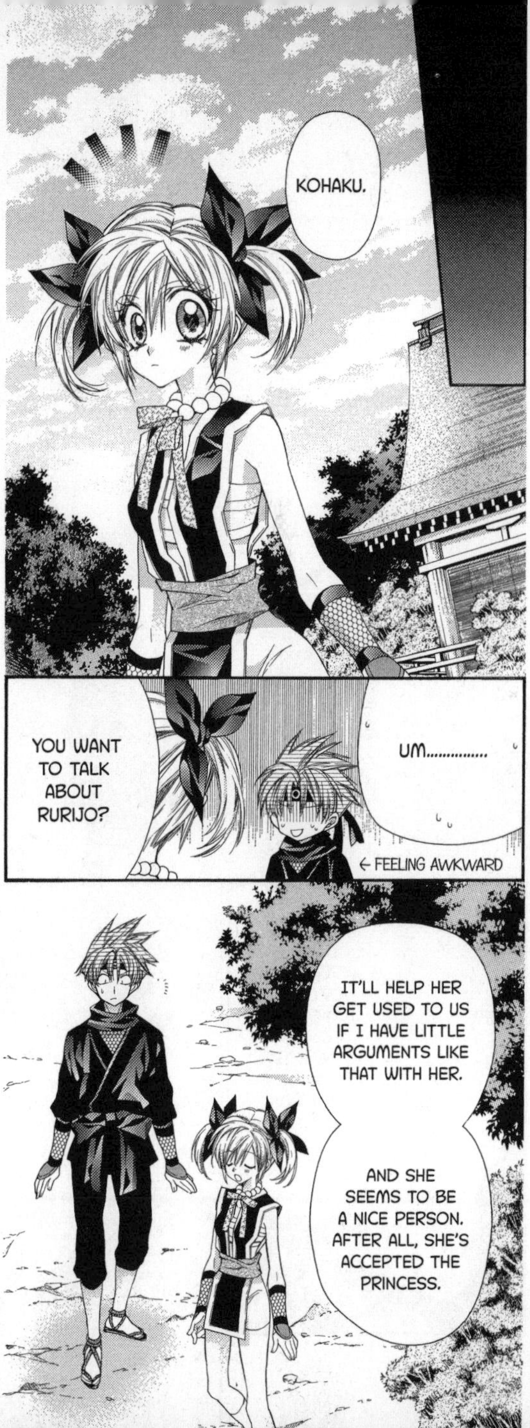
KOHAKU.
UM..............
YOU WANT TO TALK ABOUT RURIJO?
← FEELING AWKWARD
IT'LL HELP HER GET USED TO US IF I HAVE LITTLE ARGUMENTS LIKE THAT WITH HER.
AND SHE SEEMS TO BE A NICE PERSON. AFTER ALL, SHE'S ACCEPTED THE PRINCESS.

Continued→Kyoto②

This was my first experience of riding a rickshaw. It was nothing like I had imagined! First of all...

- ✿ It's expensive!! It's $100 for two people to ride for 30 minutes... Maybe it's a little cheaper if you only went a block or so.
- ✿ Comfy!! It was a very comfortable ride, and the rickshaw-puller provided us with two layers of red rugs to put over our legs to keep warm. Plus it was fast and the atmosphere was great.
- ✿ They give tours too. I thought the rickshaw-puller was just going to take us around, but he'd give us a little explanation of each tourist spot, and let us get off whenever we wanted to. He was a wonderful tour guide.

Consequently...✧ I thought we made the right decision to ride in one!! It was a wonderful experience. ♪ Many foreign tourists kept asking Kyan-chi if they could get a photo of her because she was so cute.

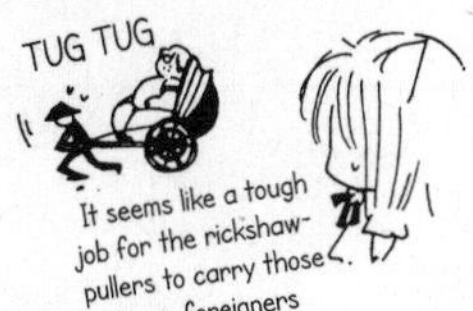
TUG TUG
It seems like a tough job for the rickshaw-pullers to carry those large foreigners around.

We went to Giouji Temple on the rickshaw too. This is the temple where two Shirabyoshi dancers, Giou and Hotokegozen, who were loved by Taira-no-Kiyomori, entered priesthood. I've always loved the story about those three. It's so romantic. Giou had always been Kiyomori's favorite. He was head-over-heels in love with her until he met a Shirabyoshi dancer named Hotokegozen and saw her dance...♥

Continues→

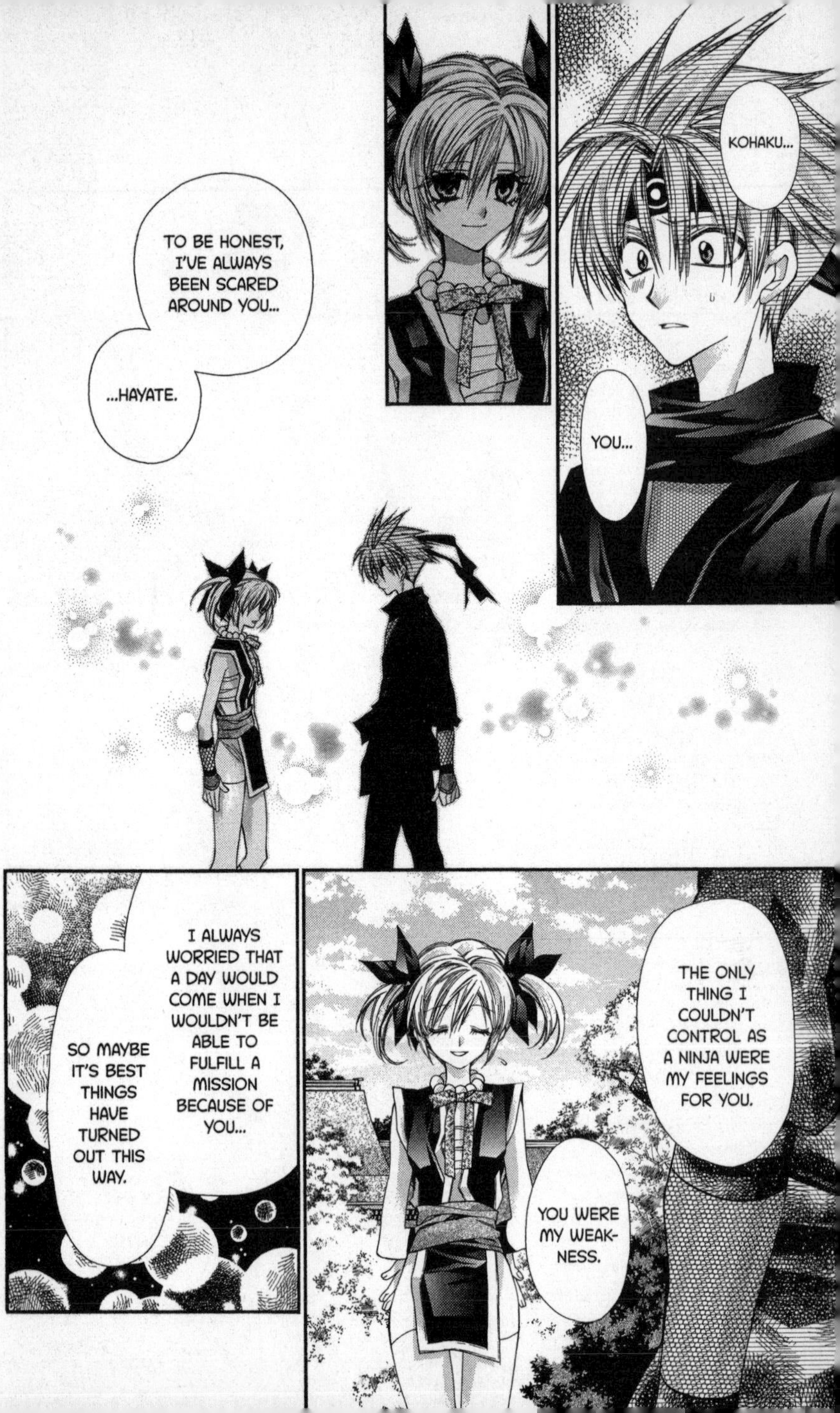
KOHAKU...
YOU...
TO BE HONEST, I'VE ALWAYS BEEN SCARED AROUND YOU...
...HAYATE.
THE ONLY THING I COULDN'T CONTROL AS A NINJA WERE MY FEELINGS FOR YOU.
YOU WERE MY WEAK-NESS.
I ALWAYS WORRIED THAT A DAY WOULD COME WHEN I WOULDN'T BE ABLE TO FULFILL A MISSION BECAUSE OF YOU...
SO MAYBE IT'S BEST THINGS HAVE TURNED OUT THIS WAY.

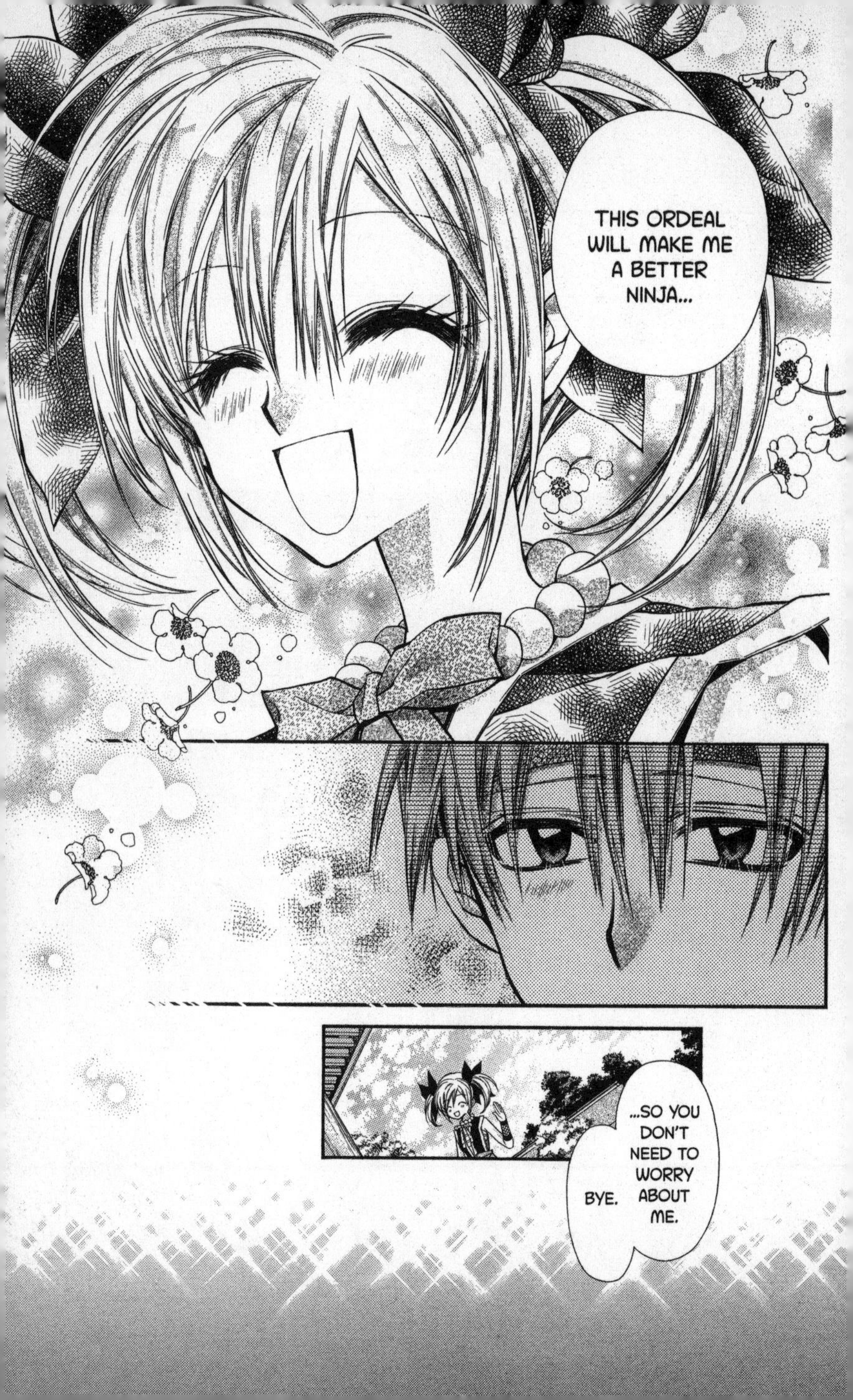
THIS ORDEAL WILL MAKE ME A BETTER NINJA...
...SO YOU DON'T NEED TO WORRY ABOUT ME.
BYE.

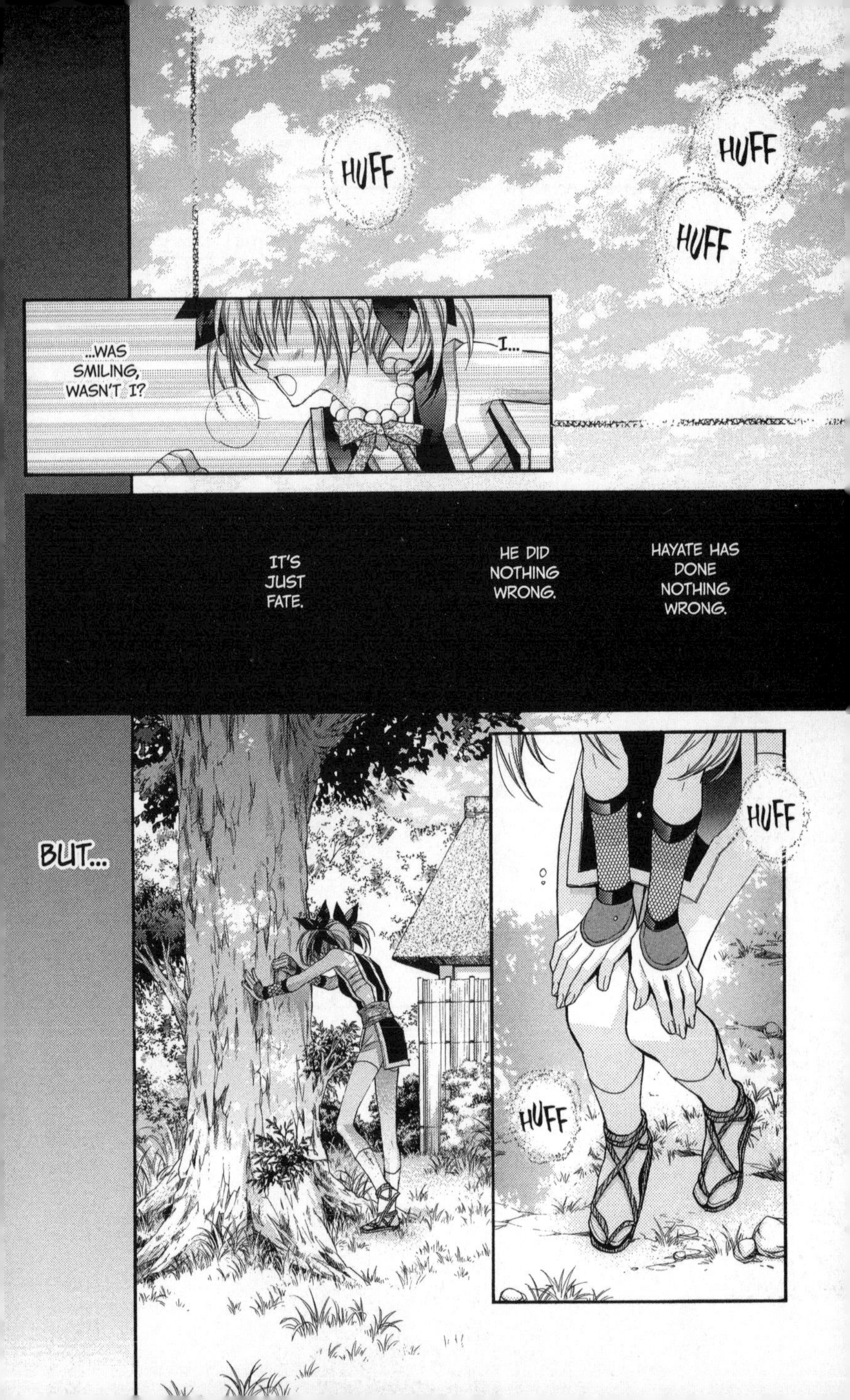
HUFF
HUFF
HUFF
I...
...WAS SMILING, WASN'T I?
HAYATE HAS DONE NOTHING WRONG.
HE DID NOTHING WRONG.
IT'S JUST FATE.
HUFF
HUFF
BUT...

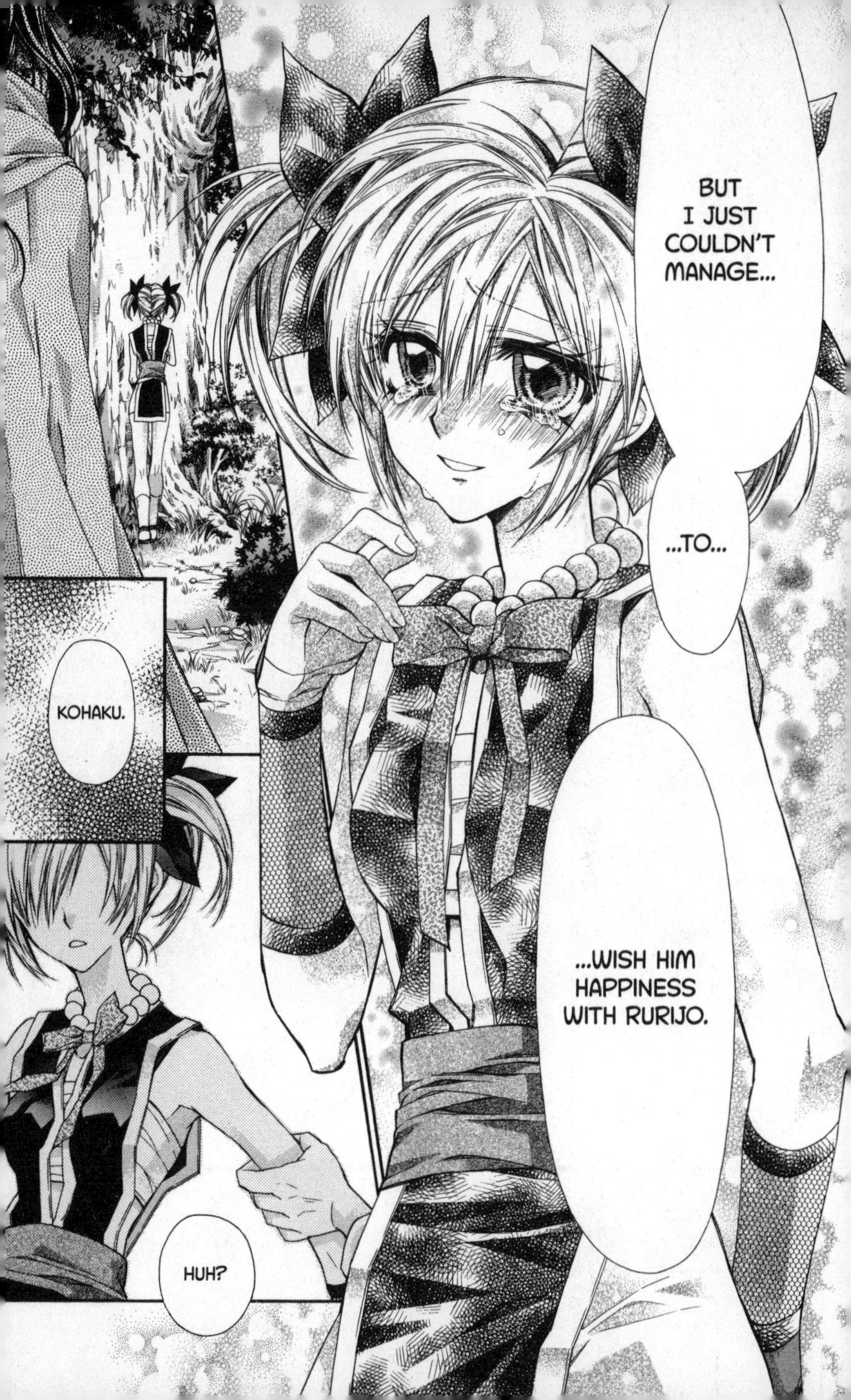
BUT I JUST COULDN'T MANAGE...
...TO...
...WISH HIM HAPPINESS WITH RURIJO.
KOHAKU.
HUH?

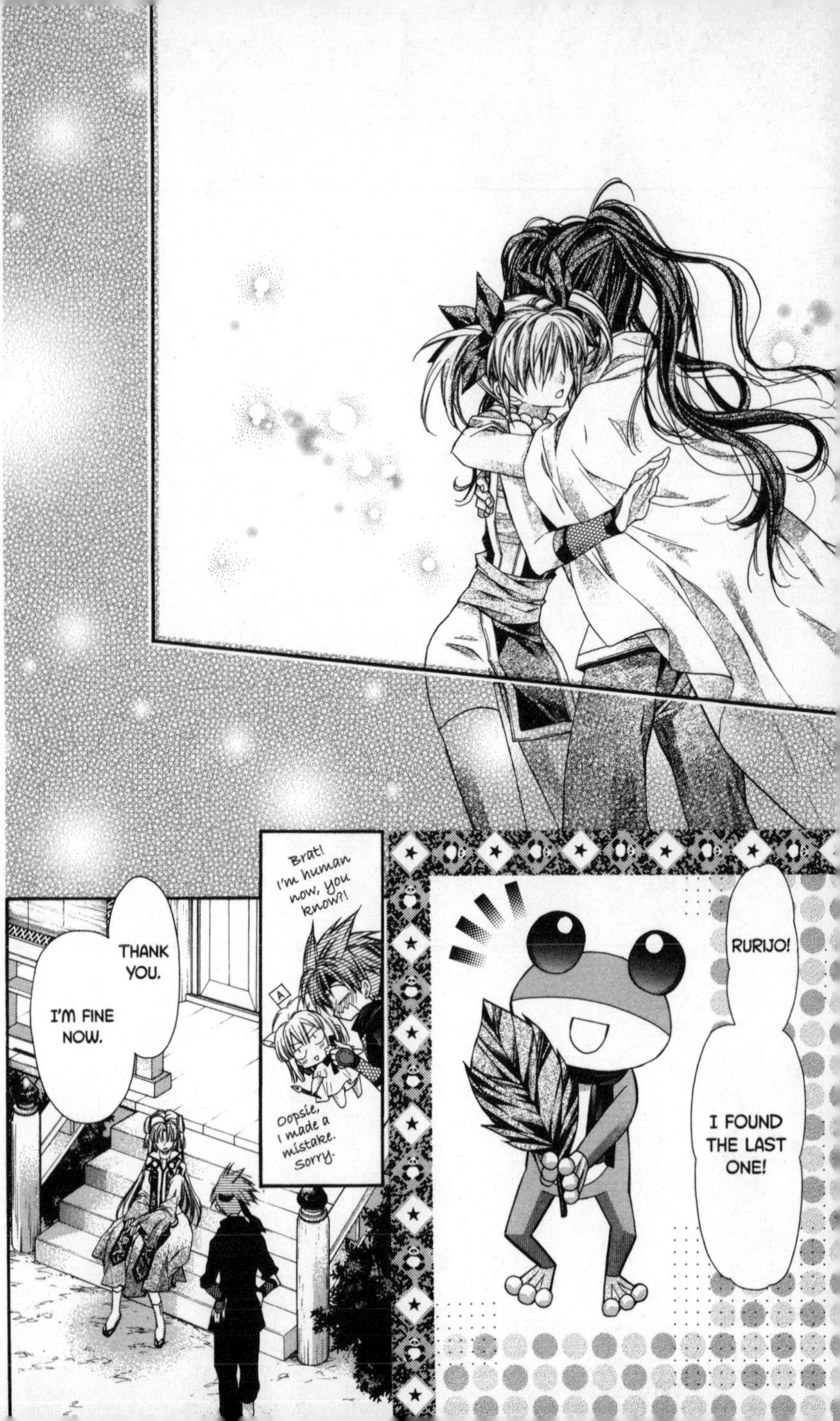
RURIJO!
I FOUND THE LAST ONE!
Brat! I'm human now, you know?!
Oopsie, I made a mistake. Sorry.
THANK YOU.
I'M FINE NOW.

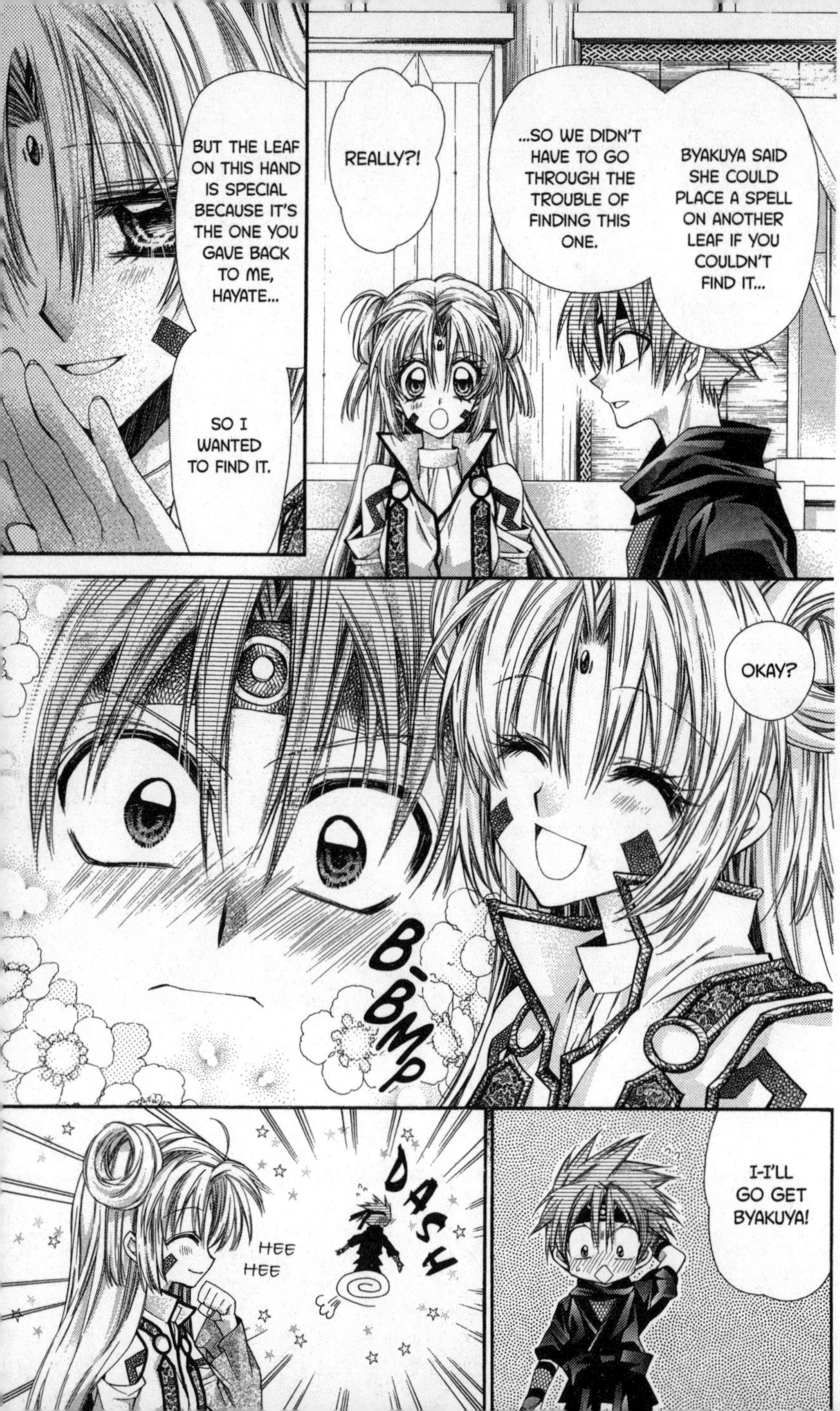
BYAKUYA SAID SHE COULD PLACE A SPELL ON ANOTHER LEAF IF YOU COULDN'T FIND IT...
...SO WE DIDN'T HAVE TO GO THROUGH THE TROUBLE OF FINDING THIS ONE.
REALLY?!
BUT THE LEAF ON THIS HAND IS SPECIAL BECAUSE IT'S THE ONE YOU GAVE BACK TO ME, HAYATE...
SO I WANTED TO FIND IT.
OKAY?
B-BMP
I-I'LL GO GET BYAKUYA!
DASH
HEE HEE

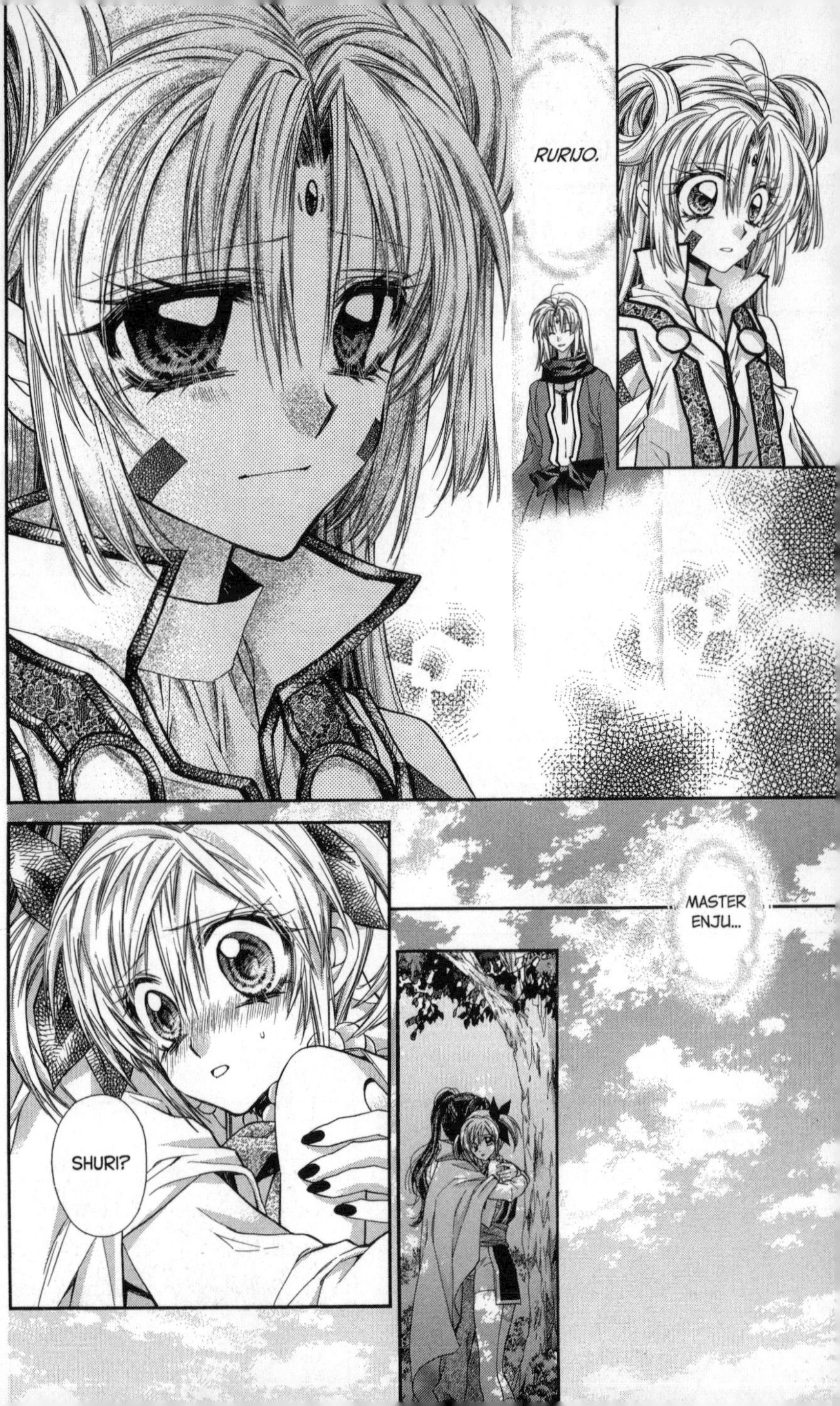
RURIJO.
MASTER ENJU...
SHURI?

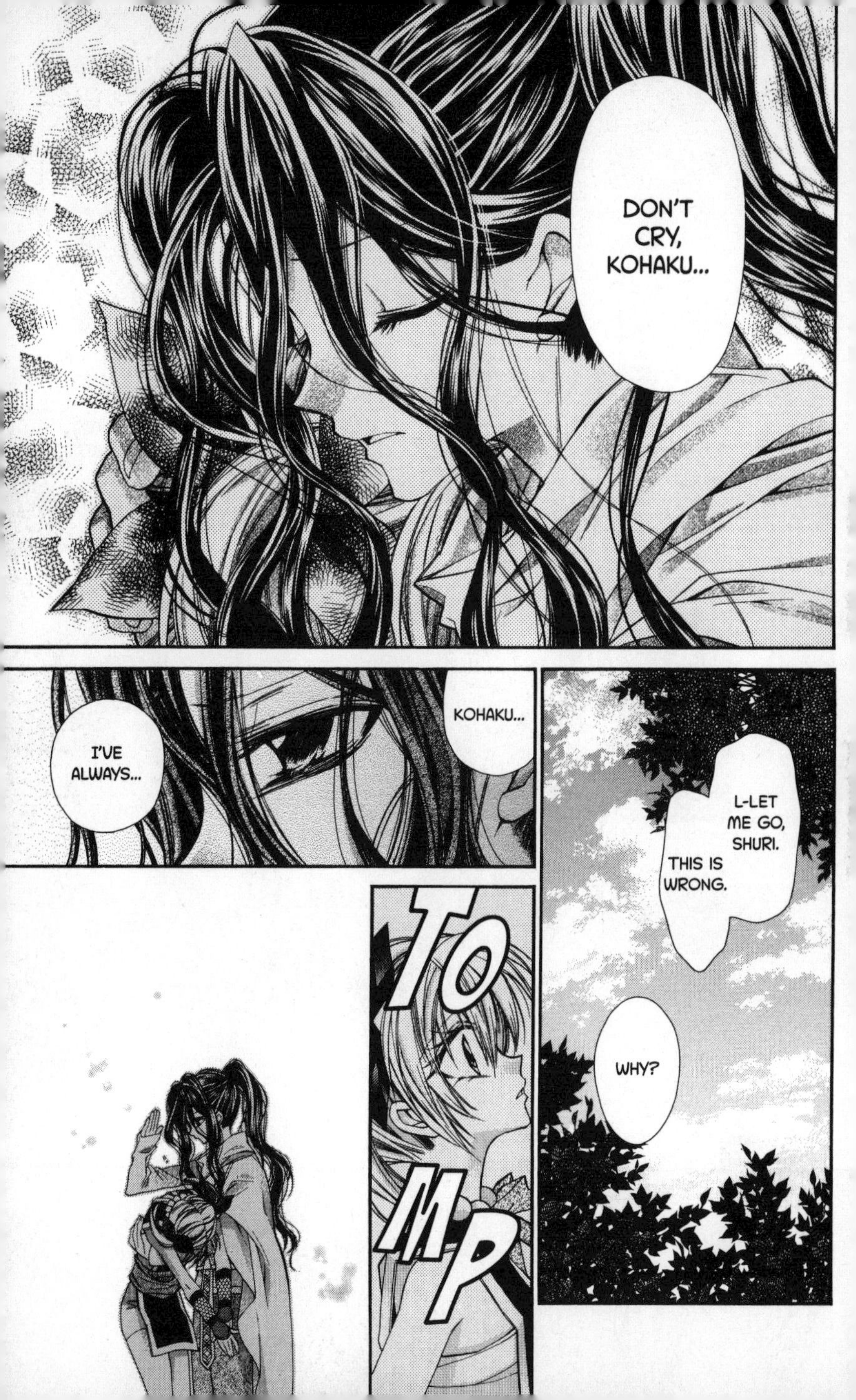
DON'T CRY, KOHAKU...
L-LET ME GO, SHURI.
THIS IS WRONG.
WHY?
KOHAKU...
I'VE ALWAYS...
TOMP

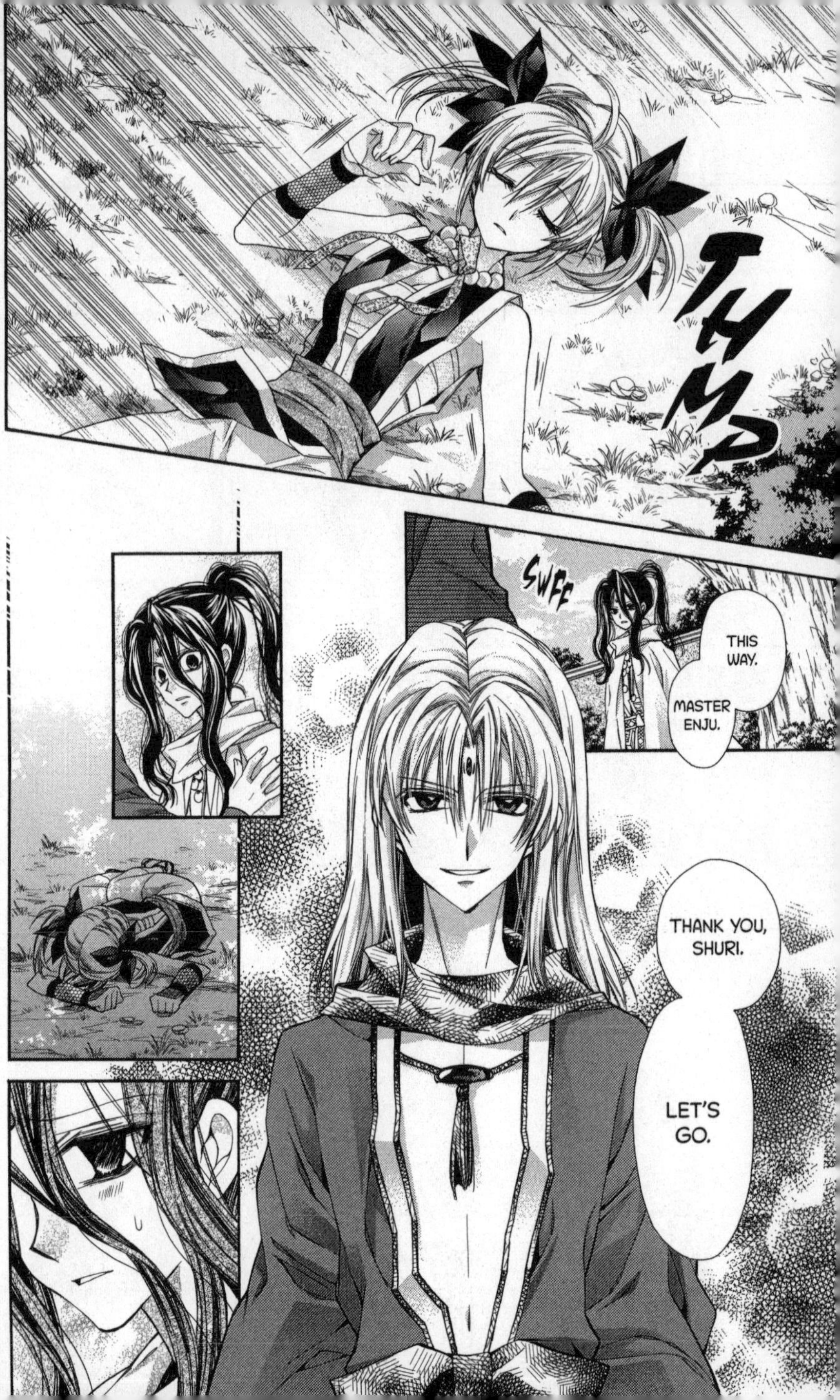
THMP
SWFF
THIS WAY.
MASTER ENJU.
THANK YOU, SHURI.
LET'S GO.

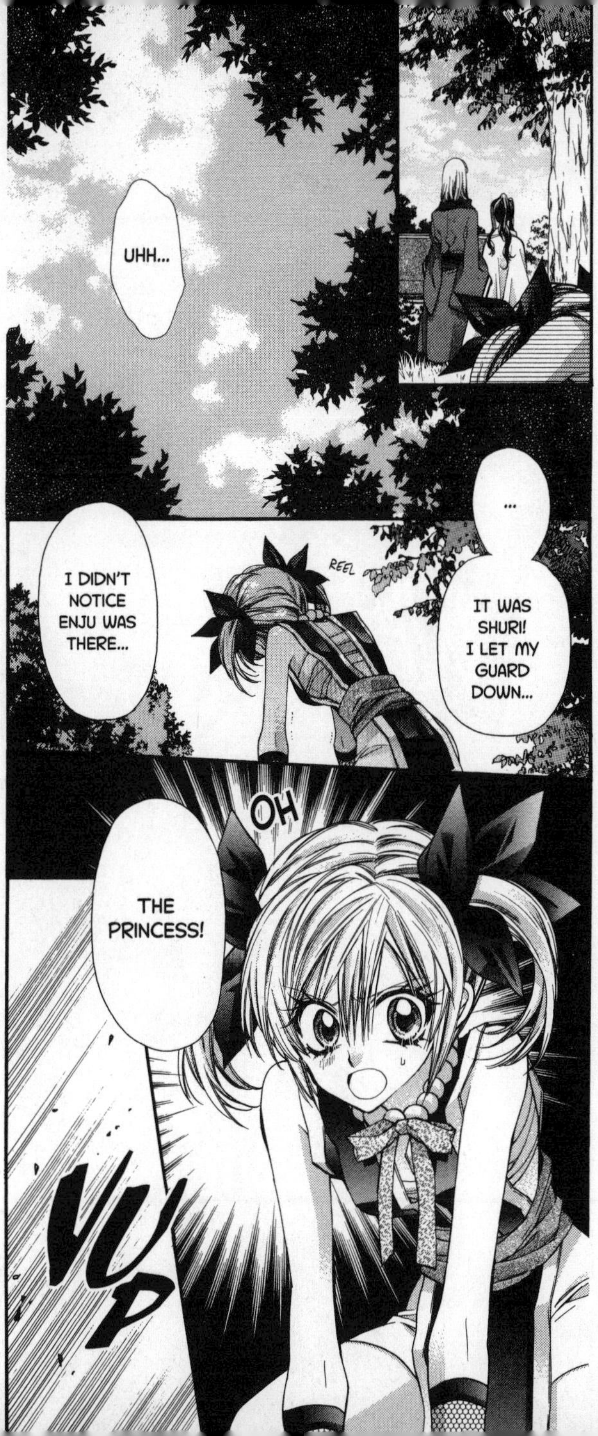
UHH...
...
IT WAS SHURI! I LET MY GUARD DOWN...
REEL
I DIDN'T NOTICE ENJU WAS THERE...
OH
THE PRINCESS!
VUP

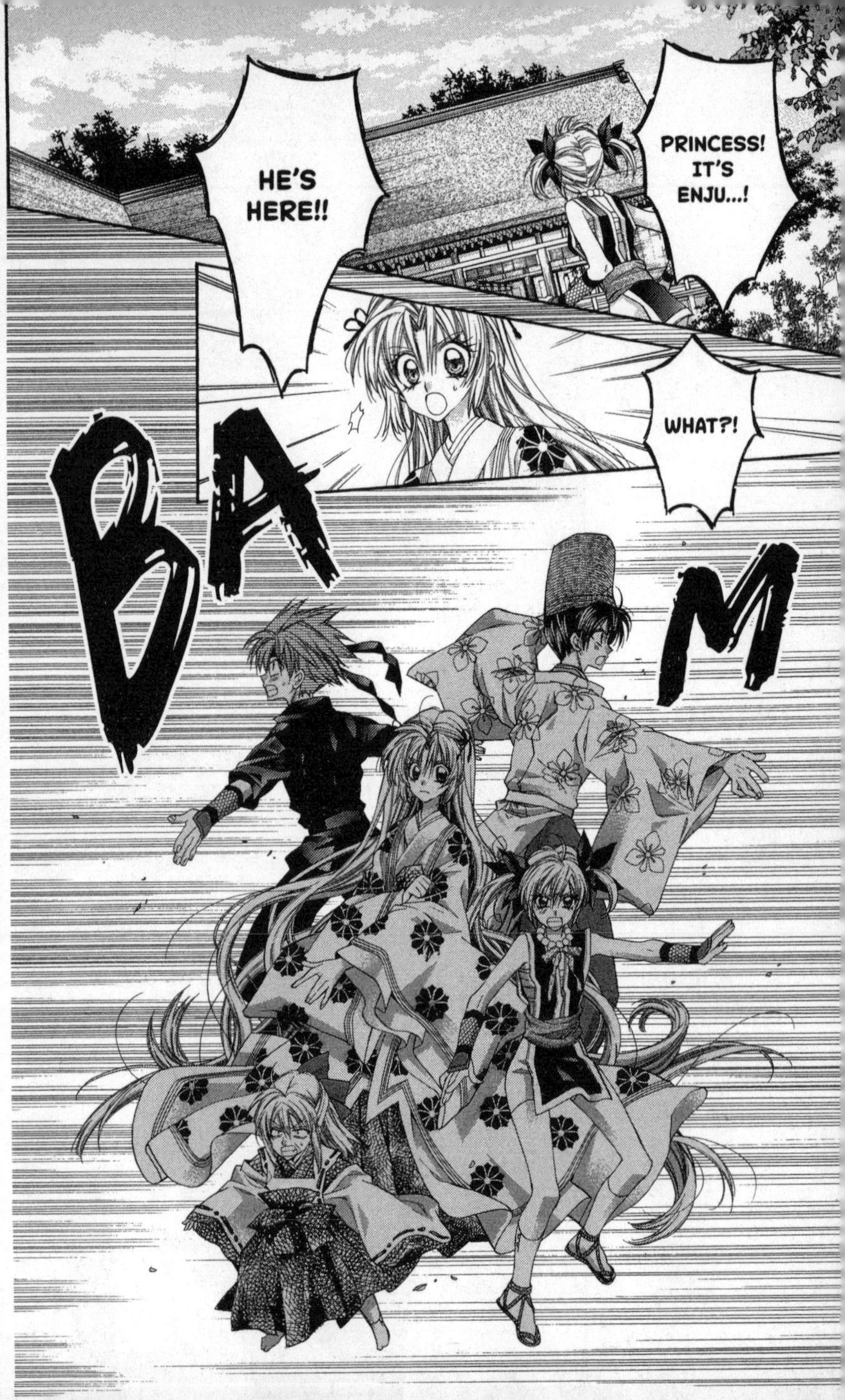
PRINCESS! IT'S ENJU...!
HE'S HERE!!
WHAT?!
BAM

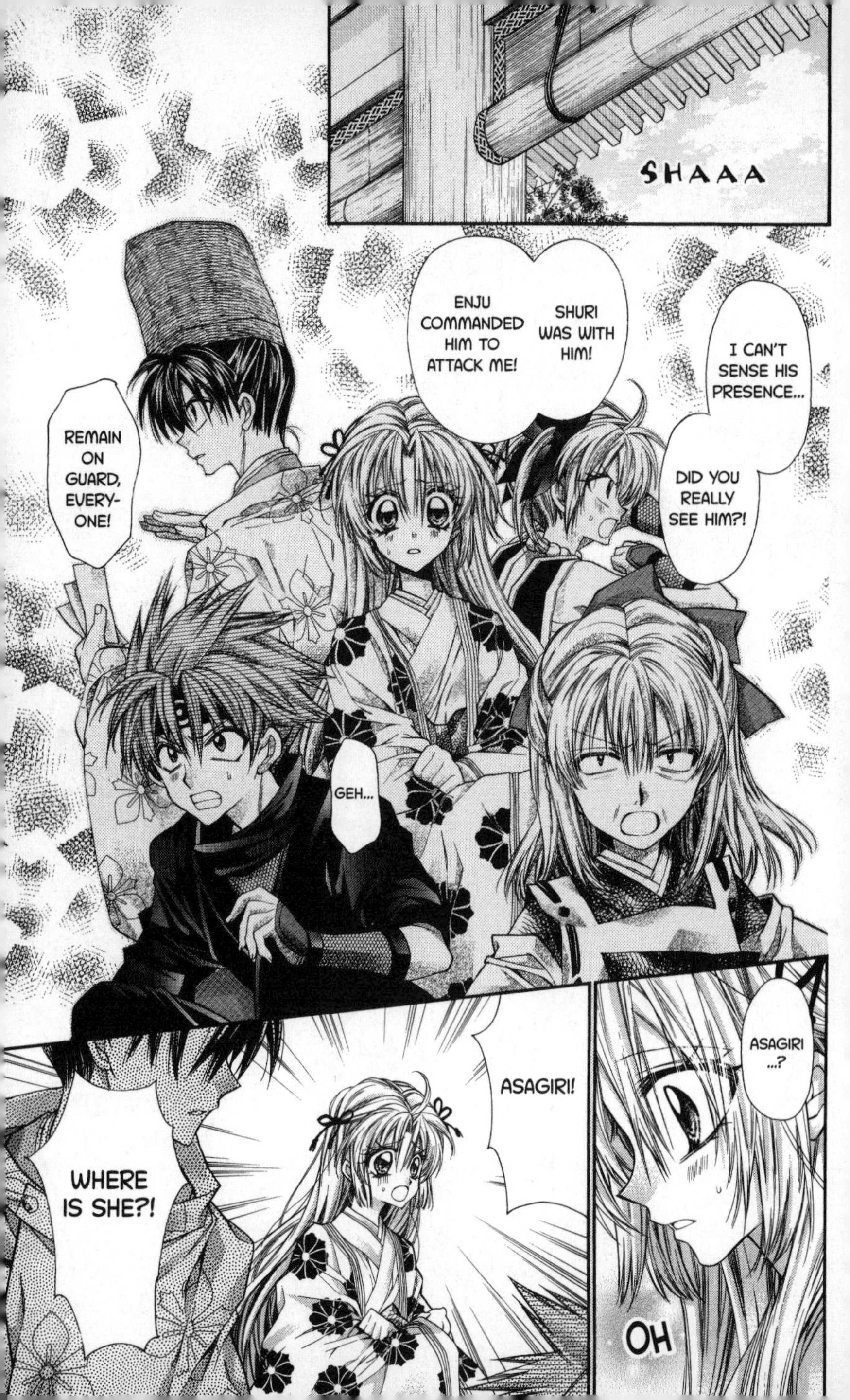
SHAAA
I CAN'T SENSE HIS PRESENCE...
DID YOU REALLY SEE HIM?!
SHURI WAS WITH HIM!
ENJU COMMANDED HIM TO ATTACK ME!
REMAIN ON GUARD, EVERY-ONE!
GEH...
ASAGIRI ...?
OH
ASAGIRI!
WHERE IS SHE?!

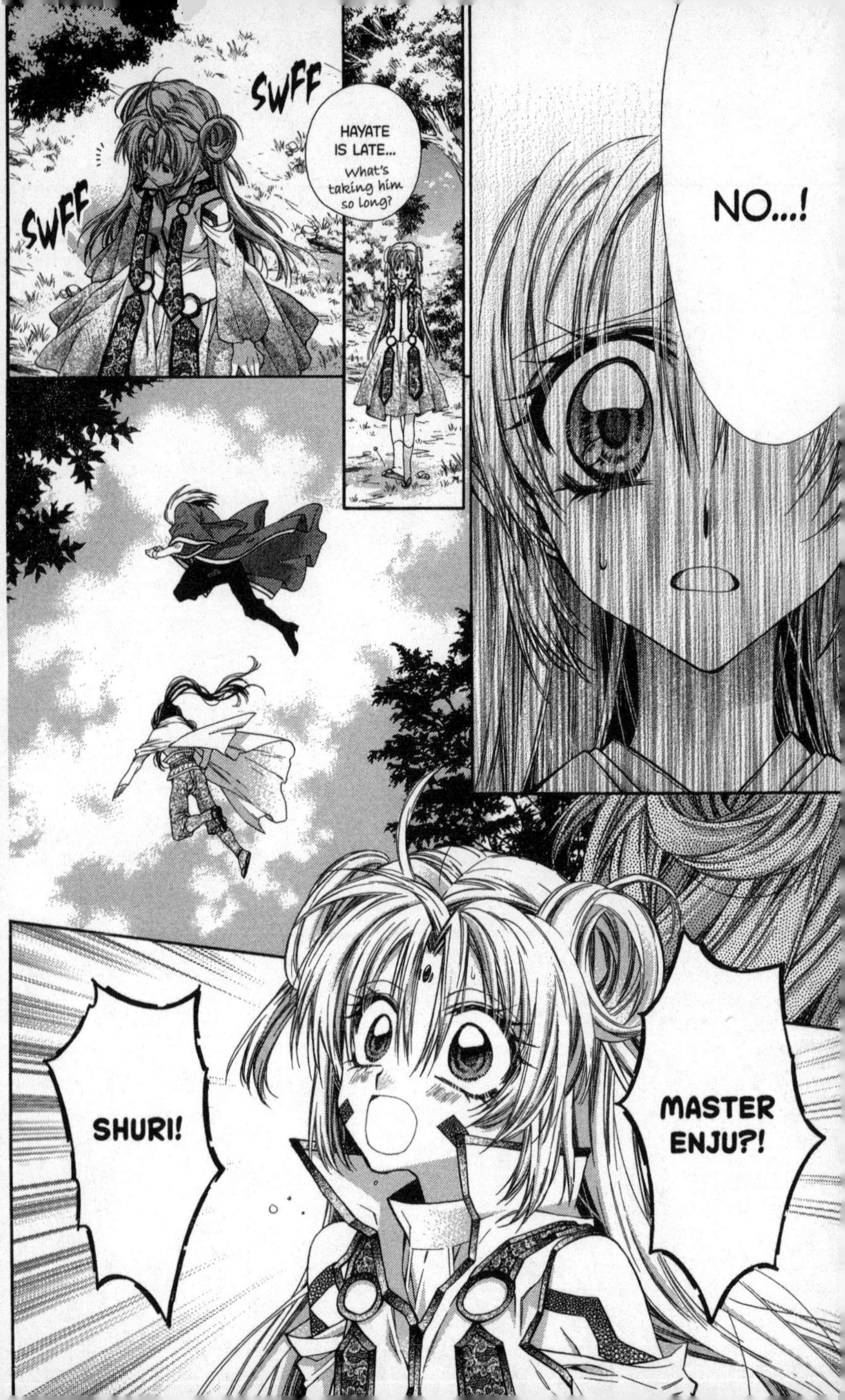
NO...!
HAYATE IS LATE... What's taking him so long?
SWFF
SWFF
MASTER ENJU?!
SHURI!

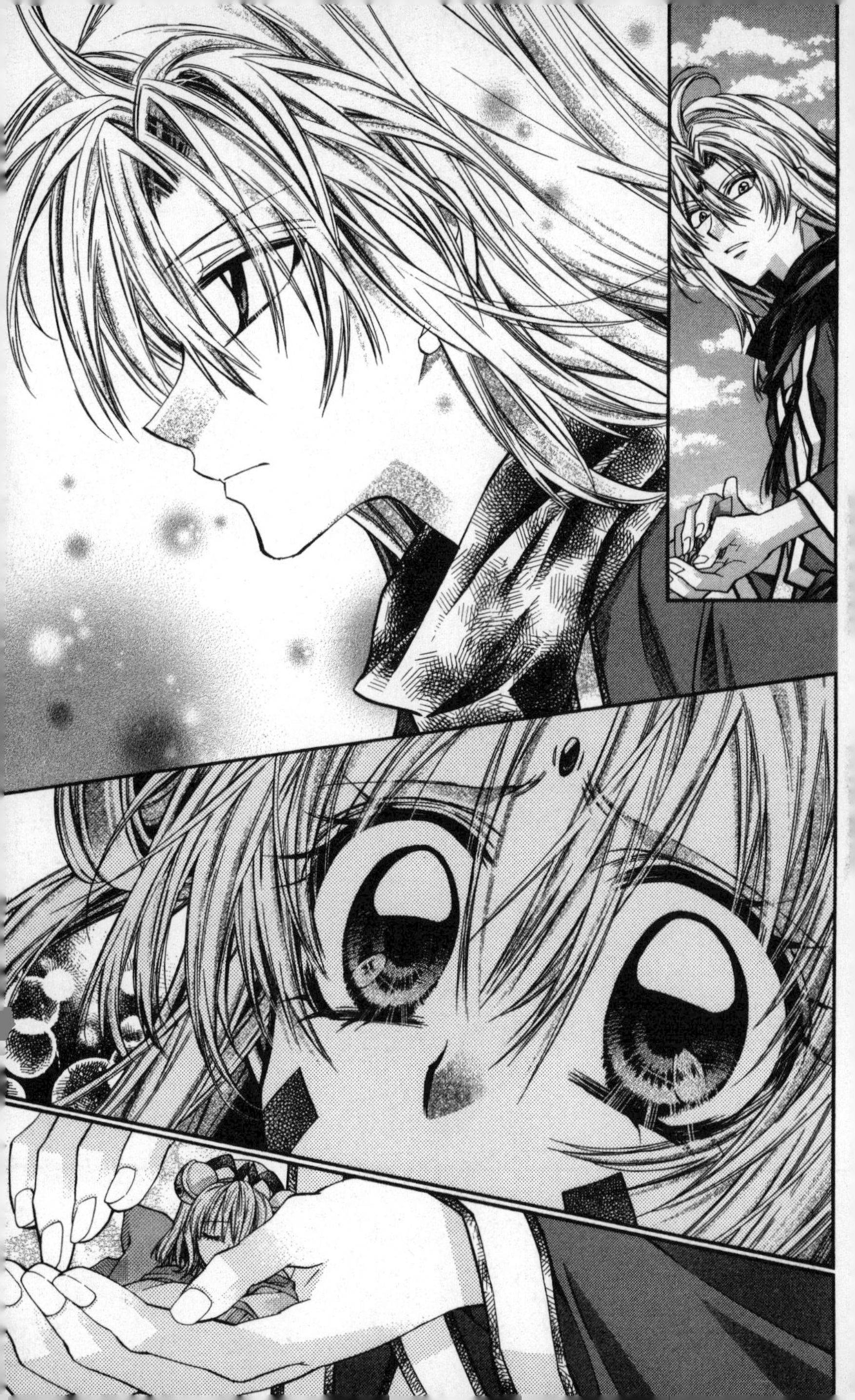

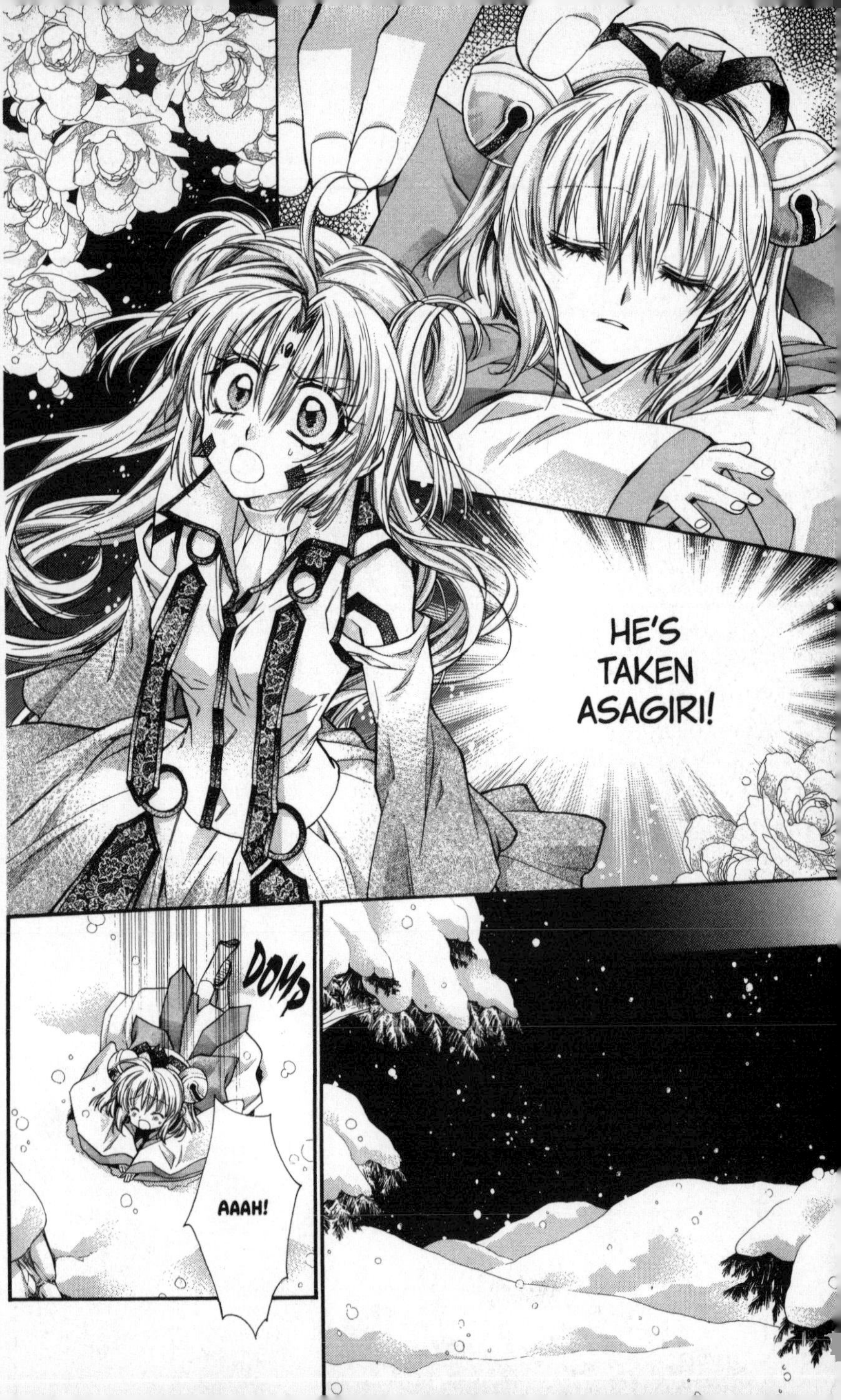
HE'S TAKEN ASAGIRI!
DOMP
AAAH!

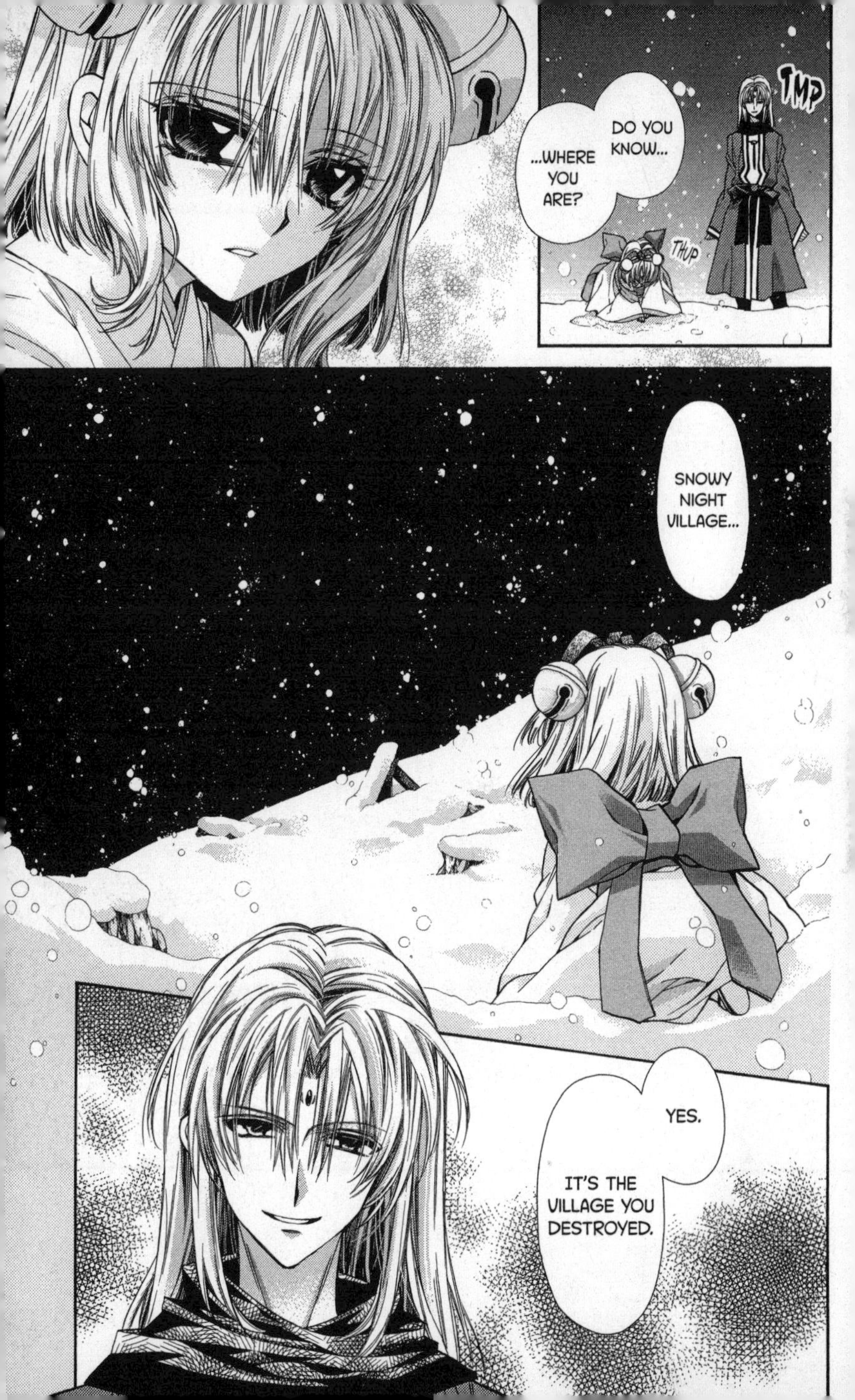
TMP
DO YOU KNOW...
...WHERE YOU ARE?
THUP
SNOWY NIGHT VILLAGE...
YES.
IT'S THE VILLAGE YOU DESTROYED.

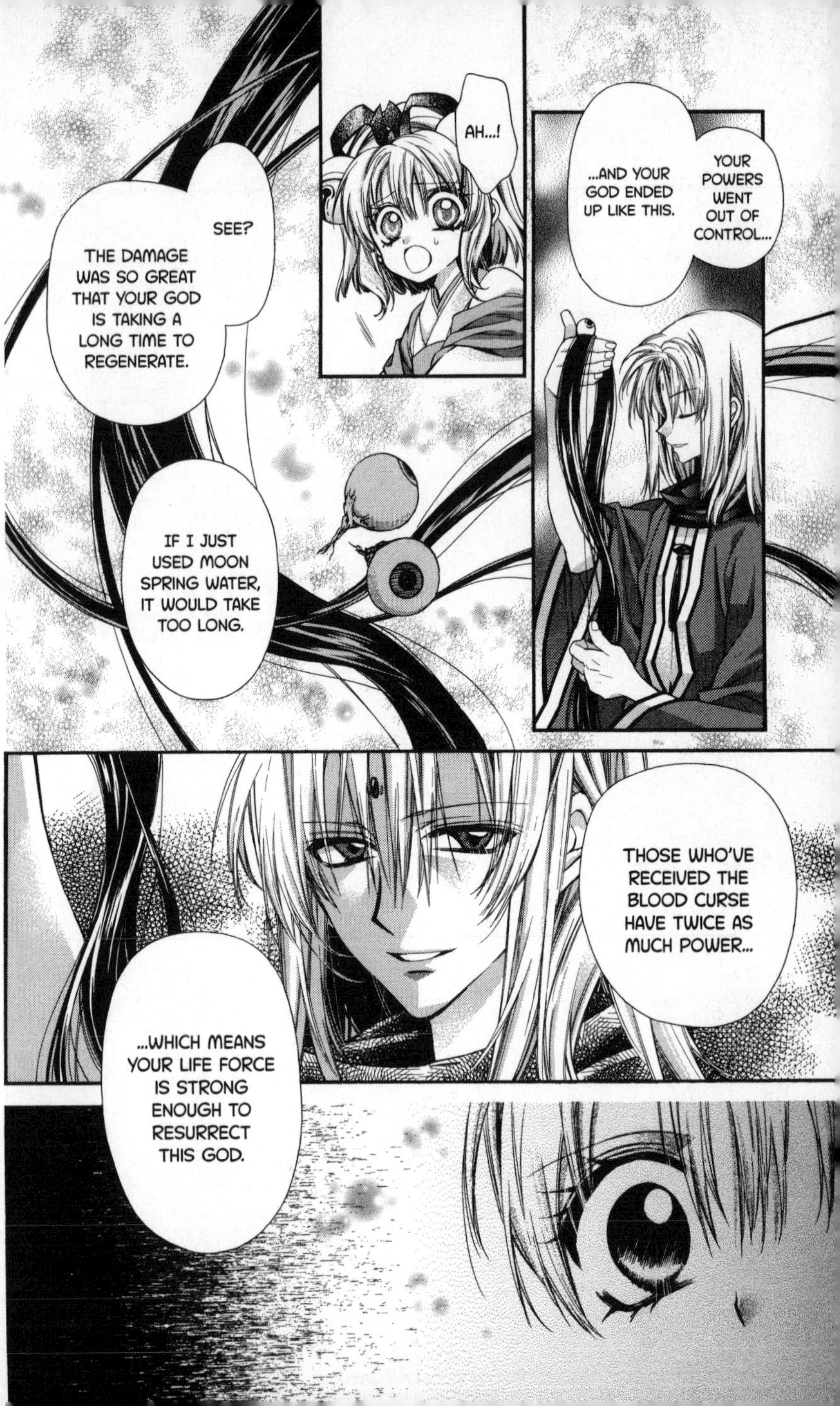
YOUR POWERS WENT OUT OF CONTROL...
...AND YOUR GOD ENDED UP LIKE THIS.
AH...!
SEE?
THE DAMAGE WAS SO GREAT THAT YOUR GOD IS TAKING A LONG TIME TO REGENERATE.
IF I JUST USED MOON SPRING WATER, IT WOULD TAKE TOO LONG.
THOSE WHO'VE RECEIVED THE BLOOD CURSE HAVE TWICE AS MUCH POWER...
...WHICH MEANS YOUR LIFE FORCE IS STRONG ENOUGH TO RESURRECT THIS GOD.

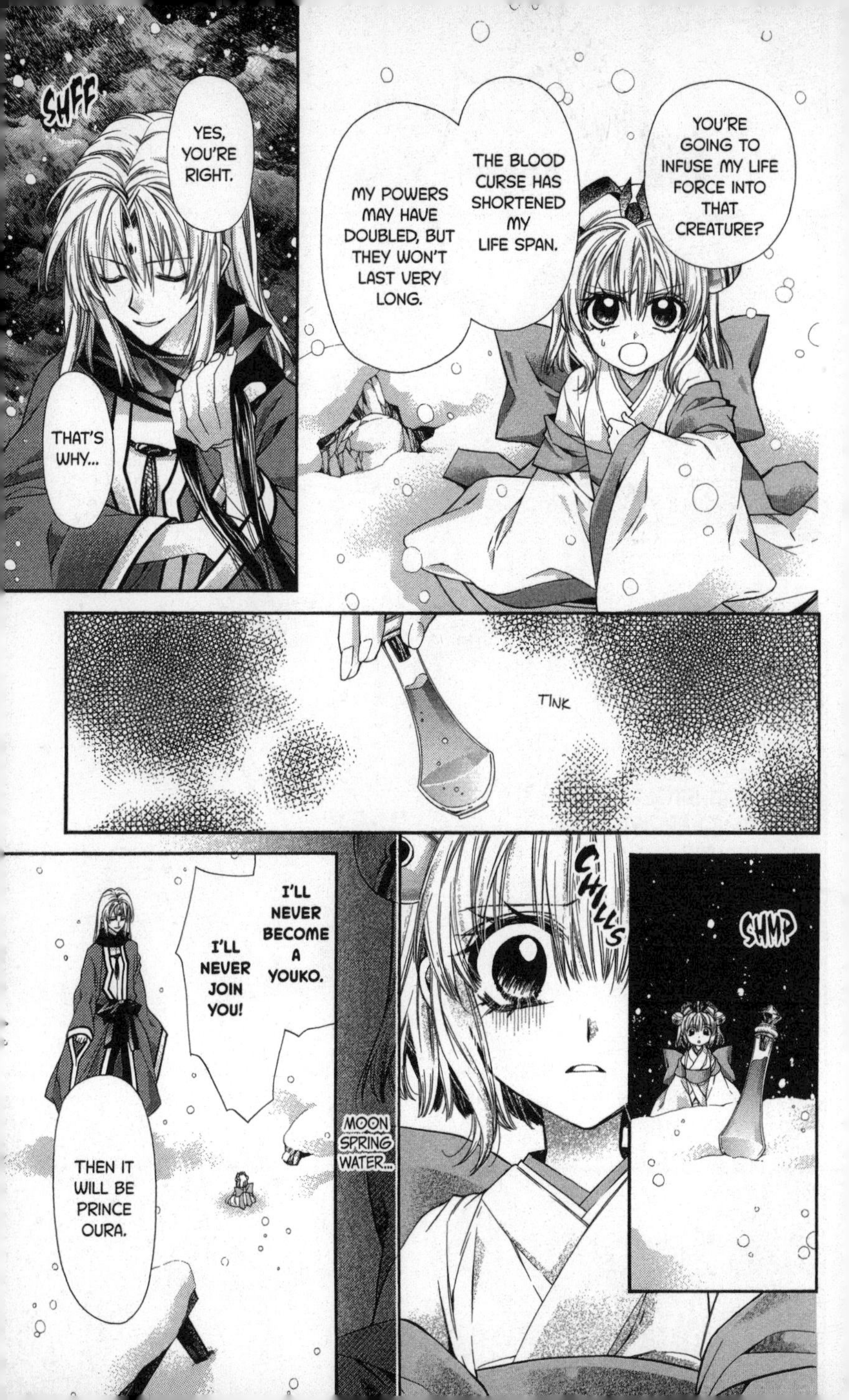
YOU'RE GOING TO INFUSE MY LIFE FORCE INTO THAT CREATURE?
THE BLOOD CURSE HAS SHORTENED MY LIFE SPAN.
MY POWERS MAY HAVE DOUBLED, BUT THEY WON'T LAST VERY LONG.
SHFF
YES, YOU'RE RIGHT.
THAT'S WHY...
TINK
SHMP
CHILLS
MOON SPRING WATER...
I'LL NEVER BECOME A YOUKO.
I'LL NEVER JOIN YOU!
THEN IT WILL BE PRINCE OURA.

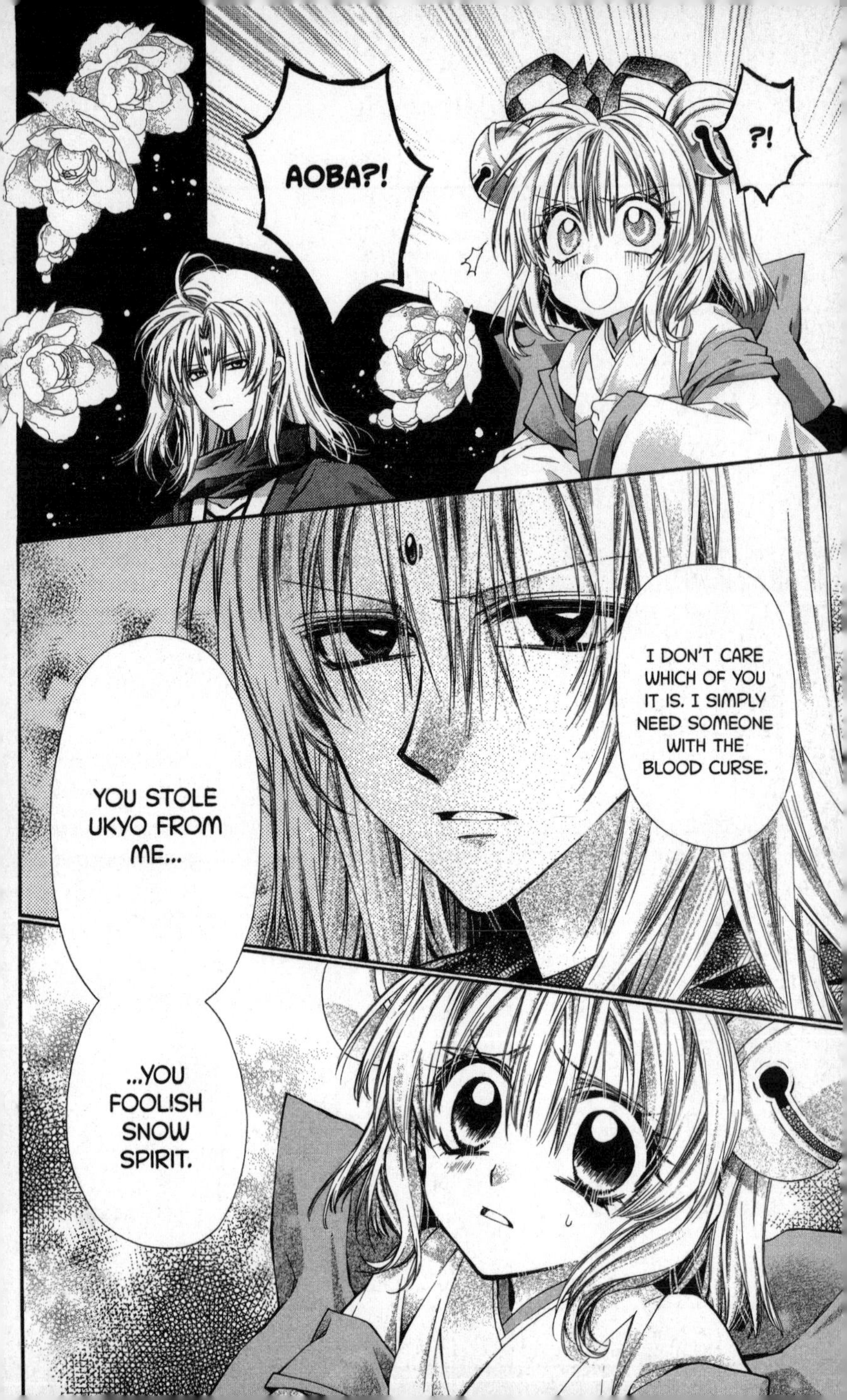
?!
AOBA?!
I DON'T CARE WHICH OF YOU IT IS. I SIMPLY NEED SOMEONE WITH THE BLOOD CURSE.
YOU STOLE UKYO FROM ME...
...YOU FOOLISH SNOW SPIRIT.

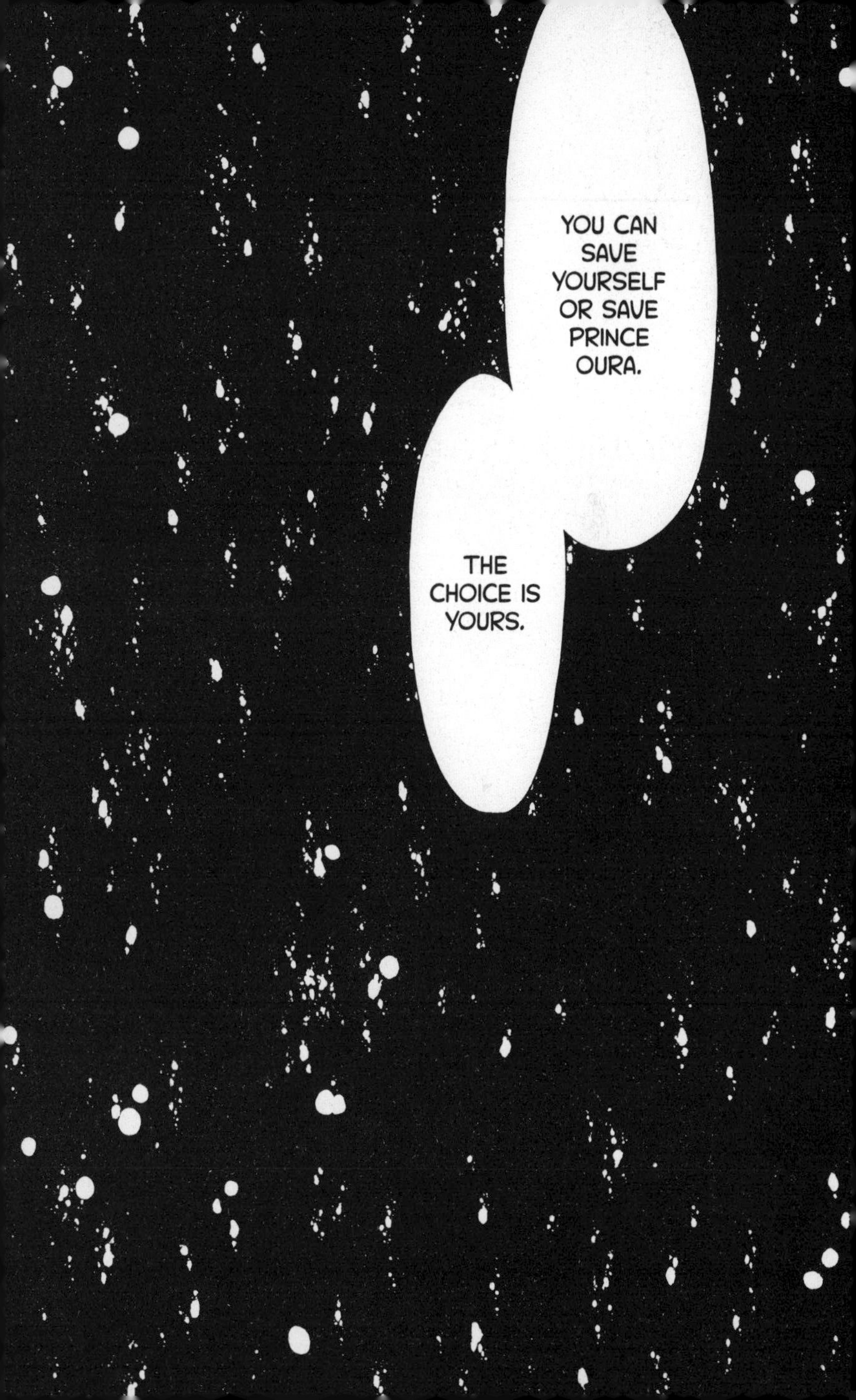
YOU CAN SAVE YOURSELF OR SAVE PRINCE OURA.
THE CHOICE IS YOURS.

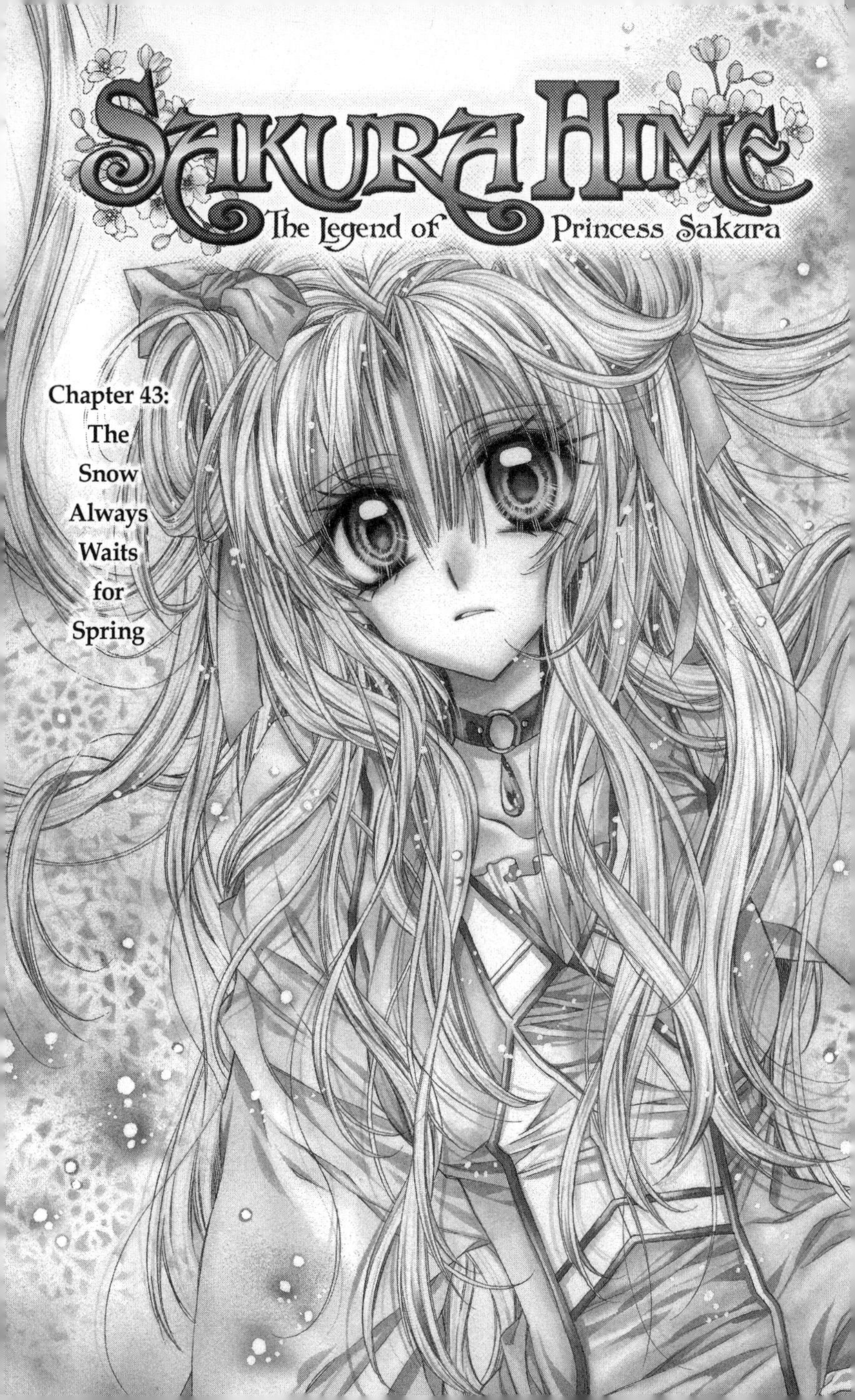
Sakura Hime
The Legend of Princess Sakura
Chapter 43: The Snow Always Waits for Spring

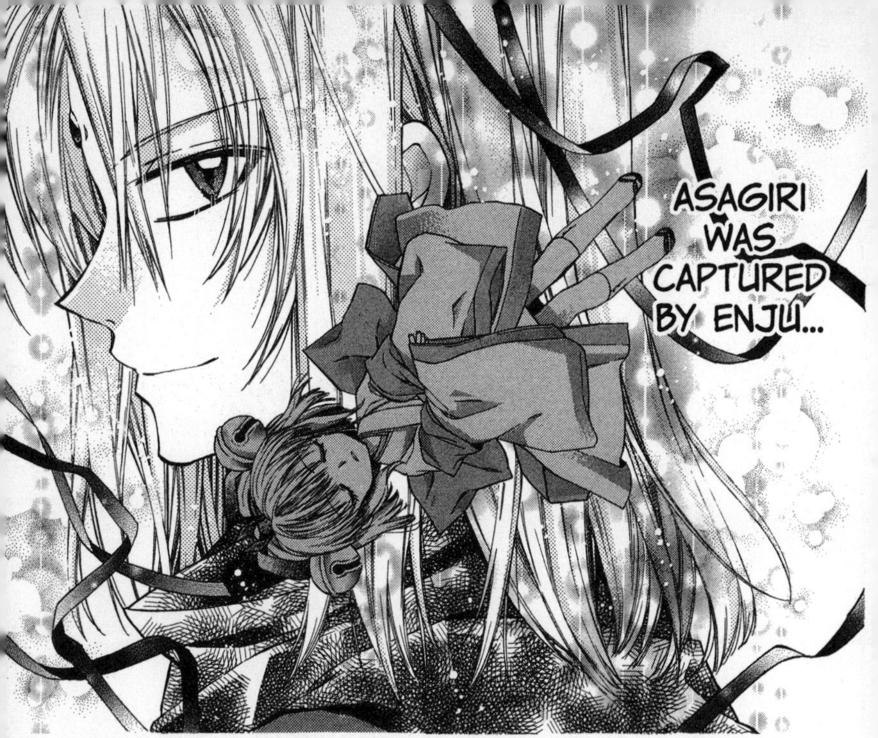
ASAGIRI WAS CAPTURED BY ENJU...

Chapter 43: The Snow Always Waits for Spring

(✶ I'm giving away the story.)

Well then, I wrote in chapter 42 that Asagiri and Enju are the most incompatible, but maybe it's more like they have the most animosity towards each other. Sakura is so strong that their love for her is one-sided... Aoba will always be the most important person to Sakura. So no matter how much they love her, she will never love them equally in return. In that sense, I think Asagiri and Enju are victims of a one-sided, unrequited love. I included the scene of Sakura and Rurijo switching places at the spur of the moment when I was drawing this. I thought it would be a good idea. By the way, Asagiri is a character who shines in tragic scenes... (Hey!) And we see some progress in the love triangle involving Rurijo, Hayate, and Kohaku. Hmm, but Rurijo can't stop thinking about Enju when she's alone, so I think it'll always be Rurijo ♥→ Enju. (I feel so sorry for Rurijo... This is all Enju's fault for being so dense.)

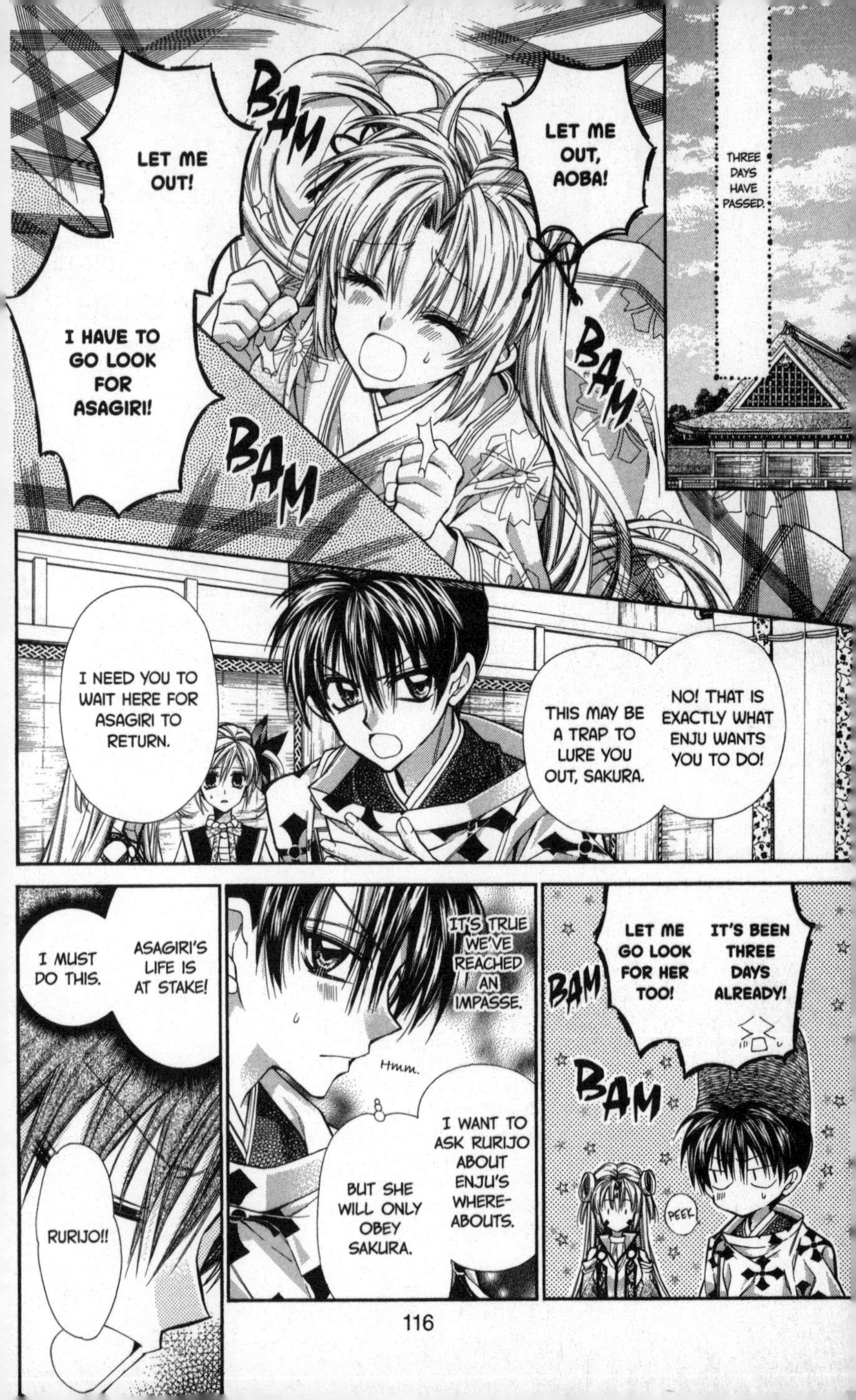
THREE DAYS HAVE PASSED.
LET ME OUT, AOBA!
BAM
BAM
LET ME OUT!
I HAVE TO GO LOOK FOR ASAGIRI!
BAM
NO! THAT IS EXACTLY WHAT ENJU WANTS YOU TO DO!
THIS MAY BE A TRAP TO LURE YOU OUT, SAKURA.
I NEED YOU TO WAIT HERE FOR ASAGIRI TO RETURN.
IT'S BEEN THREE DAYS ALREADY!
LET ME GO LOOK FOR HER TOO!
BAM
BAM
PEEK
IT'S TRUE WE'VE REACHED AN IMPASSE.
Hmm.
I WANT TO ASK RURIJO ABOUT ENJU'S WHEREABOUTS.
BUT SHE WILL ONLY OBEY SAKURA.
ASAGIRI'S LIFE IS AT STAKE!
I MUST DO THIS.
RURIJO!!

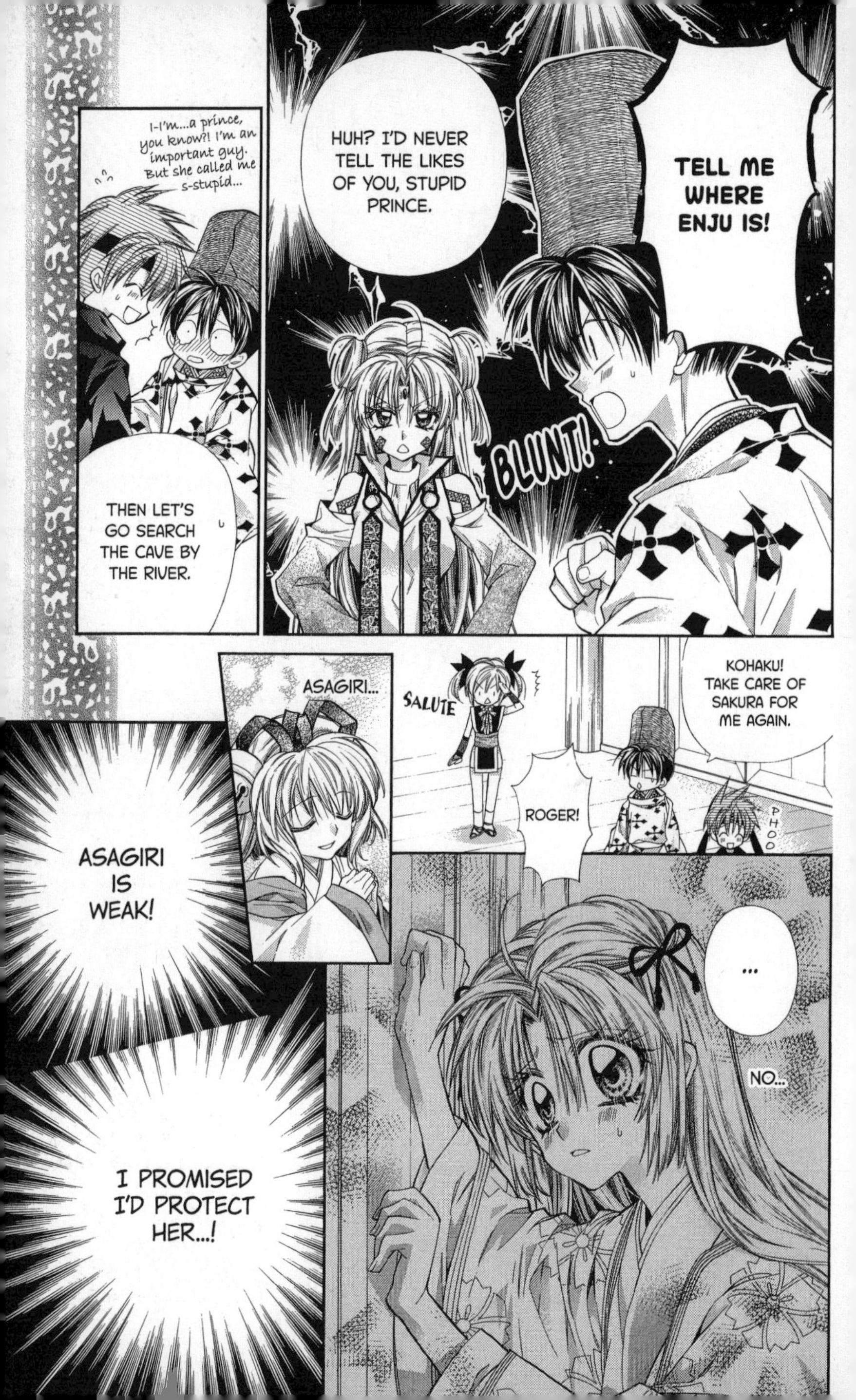
TELL ME WHERE ENJU IS!
HUH? I'D NEVER TELL THE LIKES OF YOU, STUPID PRINCE.
BLUNT!
I-I'm...a prince, you know?! I'm an important guy. But she called me s-stupid...
THEN LET'S GO SEARCH THE CAVE BY THE RIVER.
KOHAKU! TAKE CARE OF SAKURA FOR ME AGAIN.
SALUTE
ROGER!
PHOO
ASAGIRI...
...
NO...
ASAGIRI IS WEAK!
I PROMISED I'D PROTECT HER...!

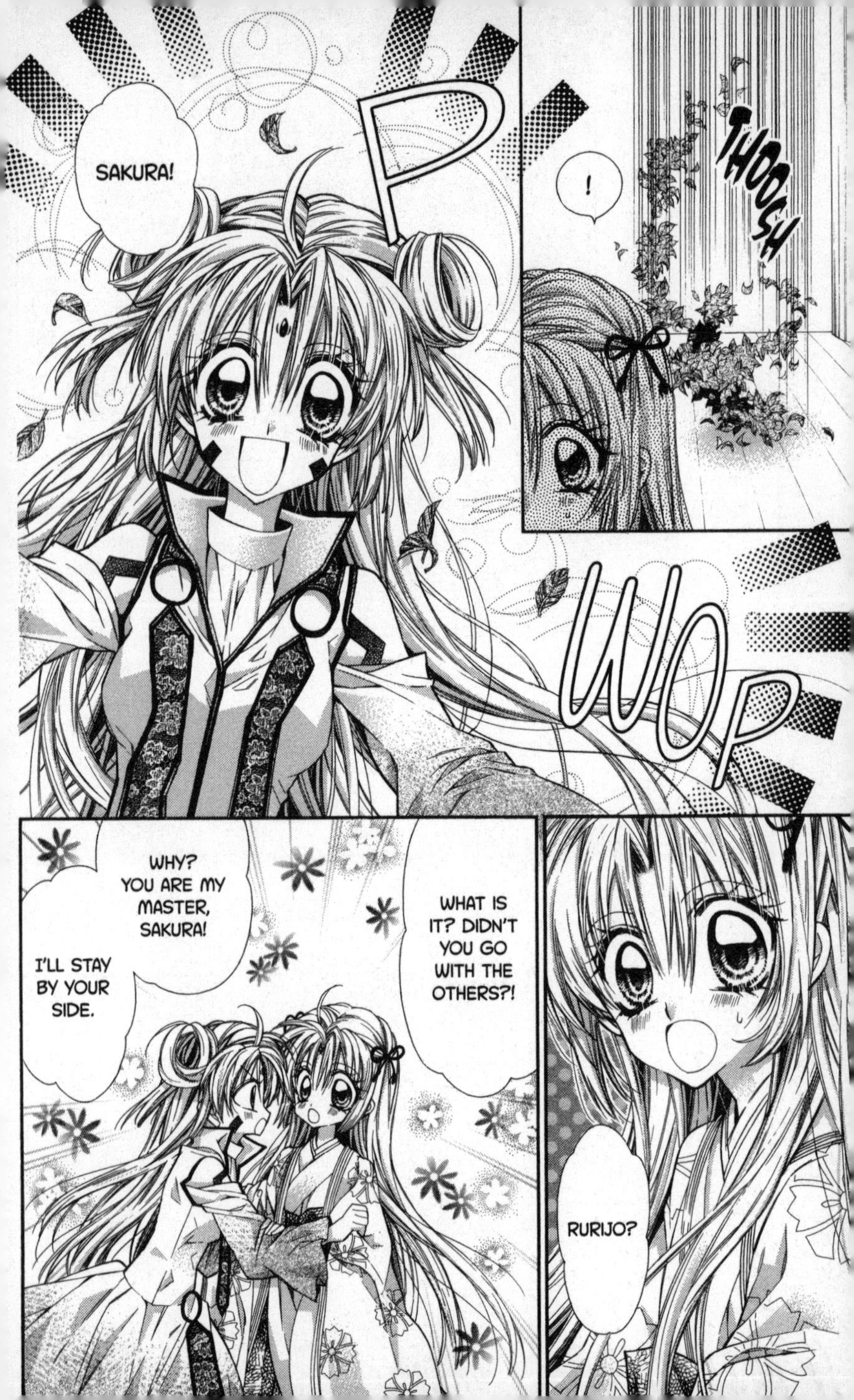
THOOSH
!
P
SAKURA!
WOP
RURIJO?
WHAT IS IT? DIDN'T YOU GO WITH THE OTHERS?!
WHY? YOU ARE MY MASTER, SAKURA!
I'LL STAY BY YOUR SIDE.

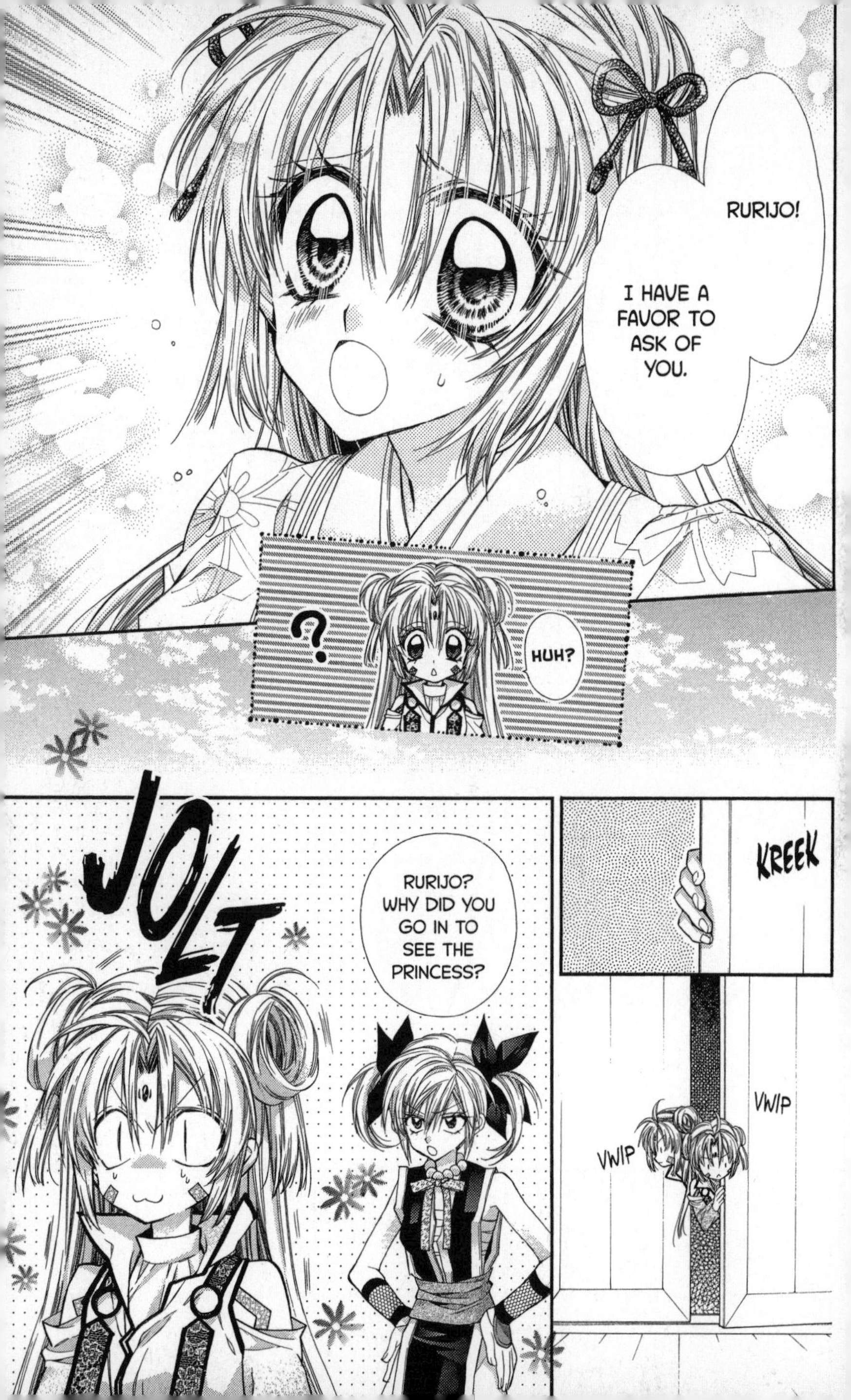
RURIJO!
I HAVE A FAVOR TO ASK OF YOU.
HUH?
KREEK
VWIP
VWIP
RURIJO? WHY DID YOU GO IN TO SEE THE PRINCESS?
JOLT

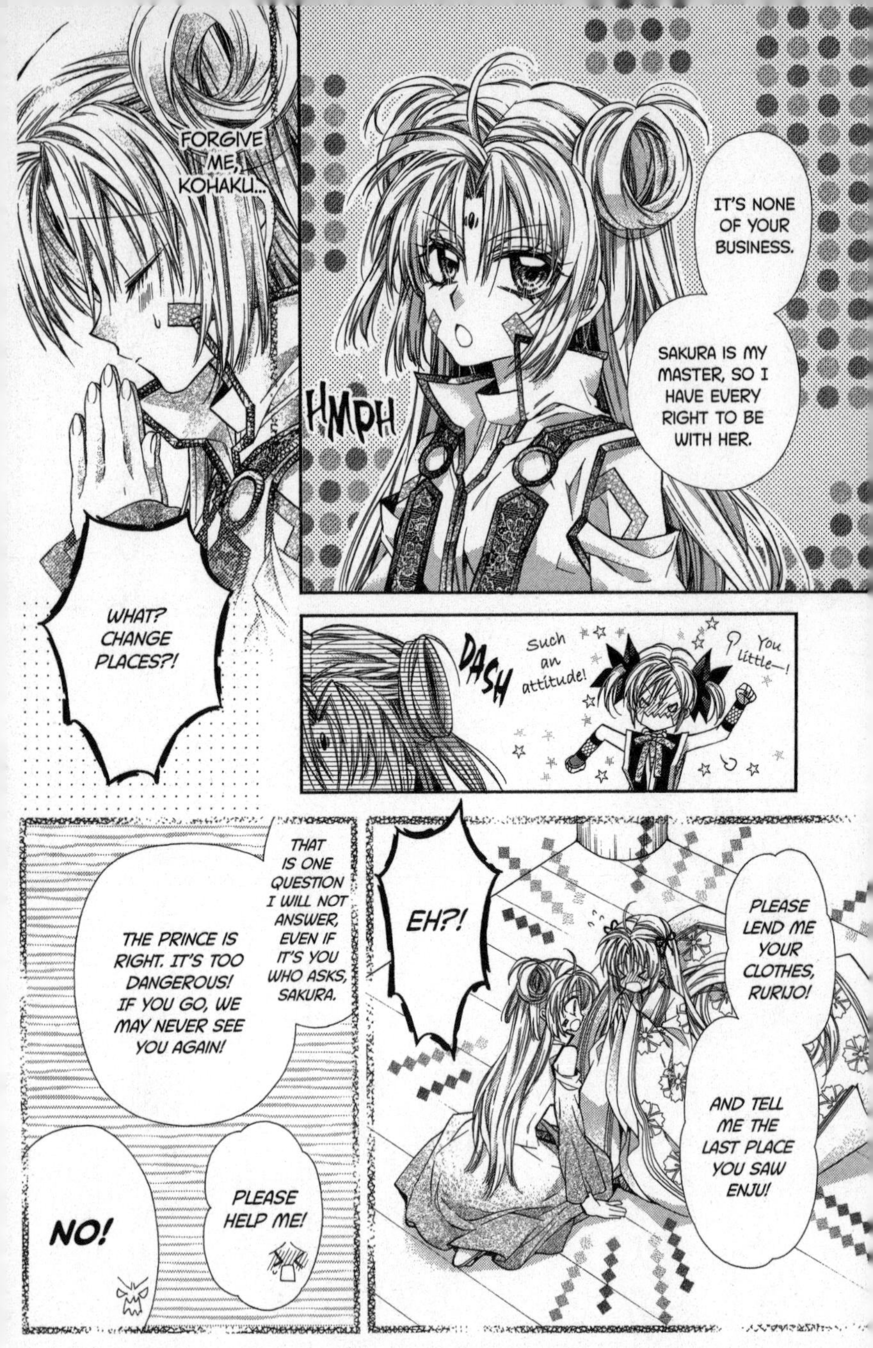
IT'S NONE OF YOUR BUSINESS.
SAKURA IS MY MASTER, SO I HAVE EVERY RIGHT TO BE WITH HER.
HMPH
You little—!
Such an attitude!
DASH
FORGIVE ME, KOHAKU...
WHAT? CHANGE PLACES?!
PLEASE LEND ME YOUR CLOTHES, RURIJO!
EH?!
AND TELL ME THE LAST PLACE YOU SAW ENJU!
THAT IS ONE QUESTION I WILL NOT ANSWER, EVEN IF IT'S YOU WHO ASKS, SAKURA.
THE PRINCE IS RIGHT. IT'S TOO DANGEROUS! IF YOU GO, WE MAY NEVER SEE YOU AGAIN!
PLEASE HELP ME!
NO!

Continued → ③

At first, Kiyomori rejects her by saying, "I have Giou, so I won't watch you dance." But Giou lends a helping hand and asks her, "Why don't you at least watch her one time?" Because of that, Kiyomori falls in love with Hotokegozen. Why did Giou do that? Silly! And so, Giou leaves a poem behind and enters Giouji Temple. (The poem said something like "Even the most beautiful flower will wither away in autumn, just as Kiyomori tired of me and dumped me.")

But one night someone comes knocking on the door of Giouji Temple... It turns out to be Hotokegozen, who had come to visit Giou. She too wanted to become a priestess.

See! It's such a nice story! (Although I'm sure other people have other opinions.) Giouji Temple is also famous for its moss garden. It was a very lovely place. I recommend you visit it! A white cat lives there, and that makes the temple even better!

After that we went to a café called "Saganoyu," located near Saga-Arashiyama station, to have lunch. ♪ The café used to be a public bathhouse, and they have done a wonderful job of keeping the original atmosphere! We shared a plate of pasta and pancakes there. ♥ The plates and cutlery were very nice, and the food tasted great too!

That night we stayed at a hot springs inn in Arashiyama...

Continues →

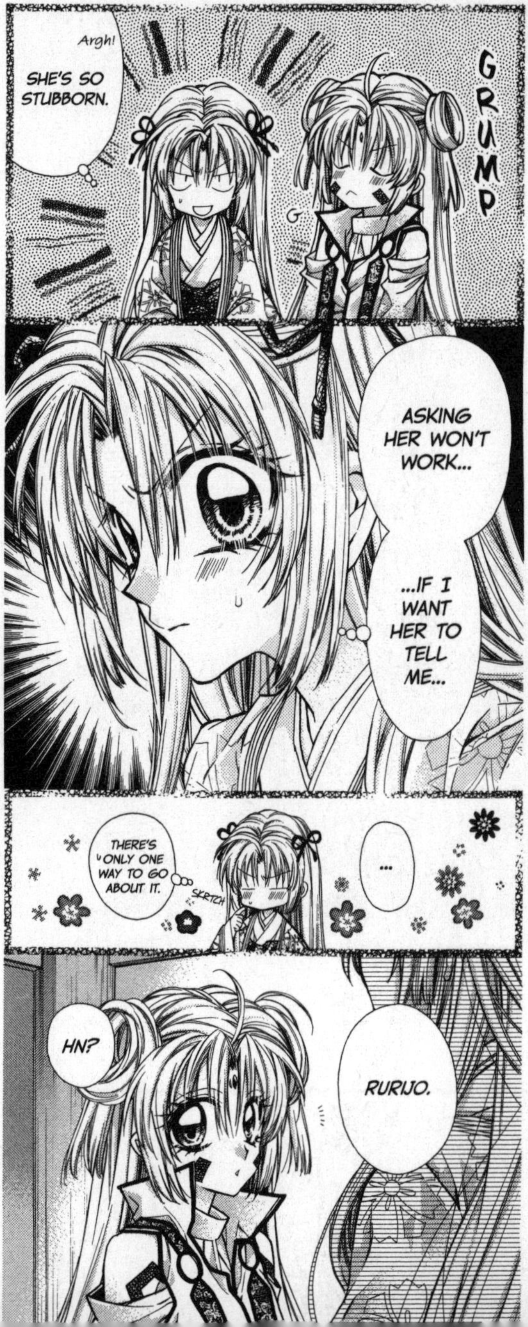
GRUMP
Argh!
SHE'S SO STUBBORN.
ASKING HER WON'T WORK...
...IF I WANT HER TO TELL ME...
...
THERE'S ONLY ONE WAY TO GO ABOUT IT.
SKRTCH
RURIJO.
HN?

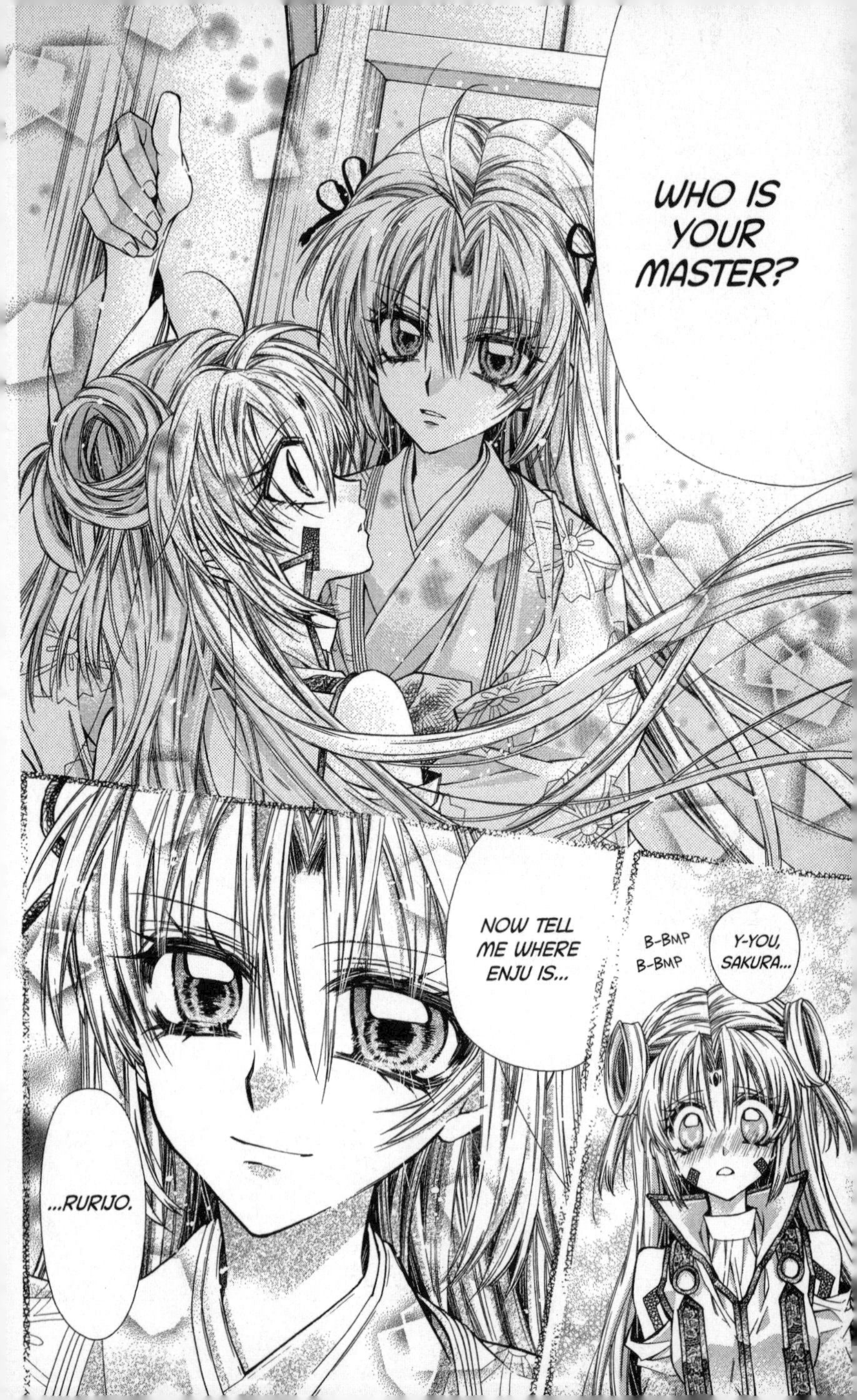
WHO IS YOUR MASTER?
Y-YOU, SAKURA...
B-BMP B-BMP
NOW TELL ME WHERE ENJU IS...
...RURIJO.

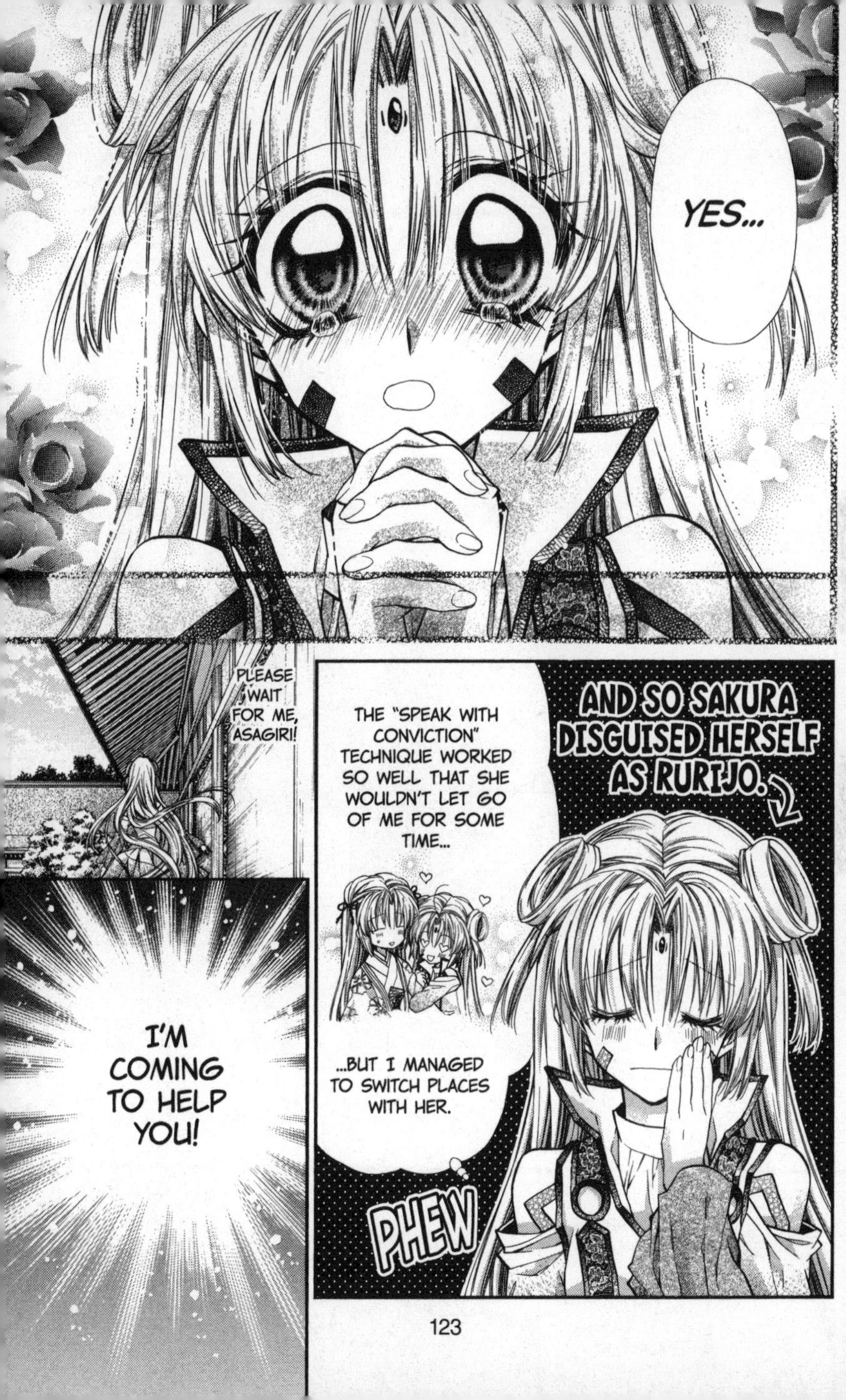
YES...
AND SO SAKURA DISGUISED HERSELF AS RURIJO.
THE "SPEAK WITH CONVICTION" TECHNIQUE WORKED SO WELL THAT SHE WOULDN'T LET GO OF ME FOR SOME TIME...
...BUT I MANAGED TO SWITCH PLACES WITH HER.
PHEW
PLEASE WAIT FOR ME, ASAGIRI!
I'M COMING TO HELP YOU!

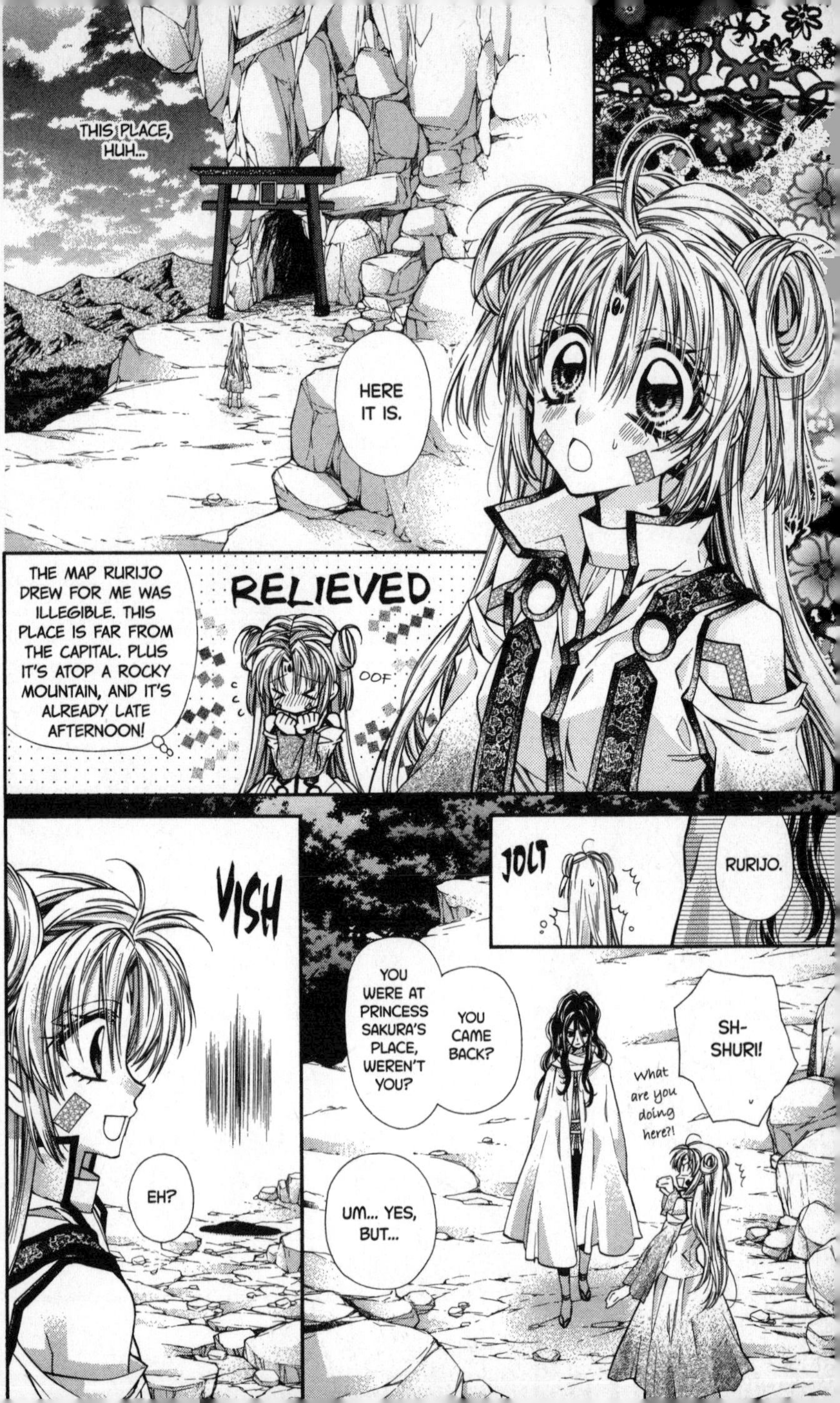
THIS PLACE, HUH...
HERE IT IS.
THE MAP RURIJO DREW FOR ME WAS ILLEGIBLE. THIS PLACE IS FAR FROM THE CAPITAL. PLUS IT'S ATOP A ROCKY MOUNTAIN, AND IT'S ALREADY LATE AFTERNOON!
RELIEVED
OOF
RURIJO.
JOLT
SH-SHURI!
What are you doing here?!
YOU CAME BACK?
YOU WERE AT PRINCESS SAKURA'S PLACE, WEREN'T YOU?
UM... YES, BUT...
VISH
EH?

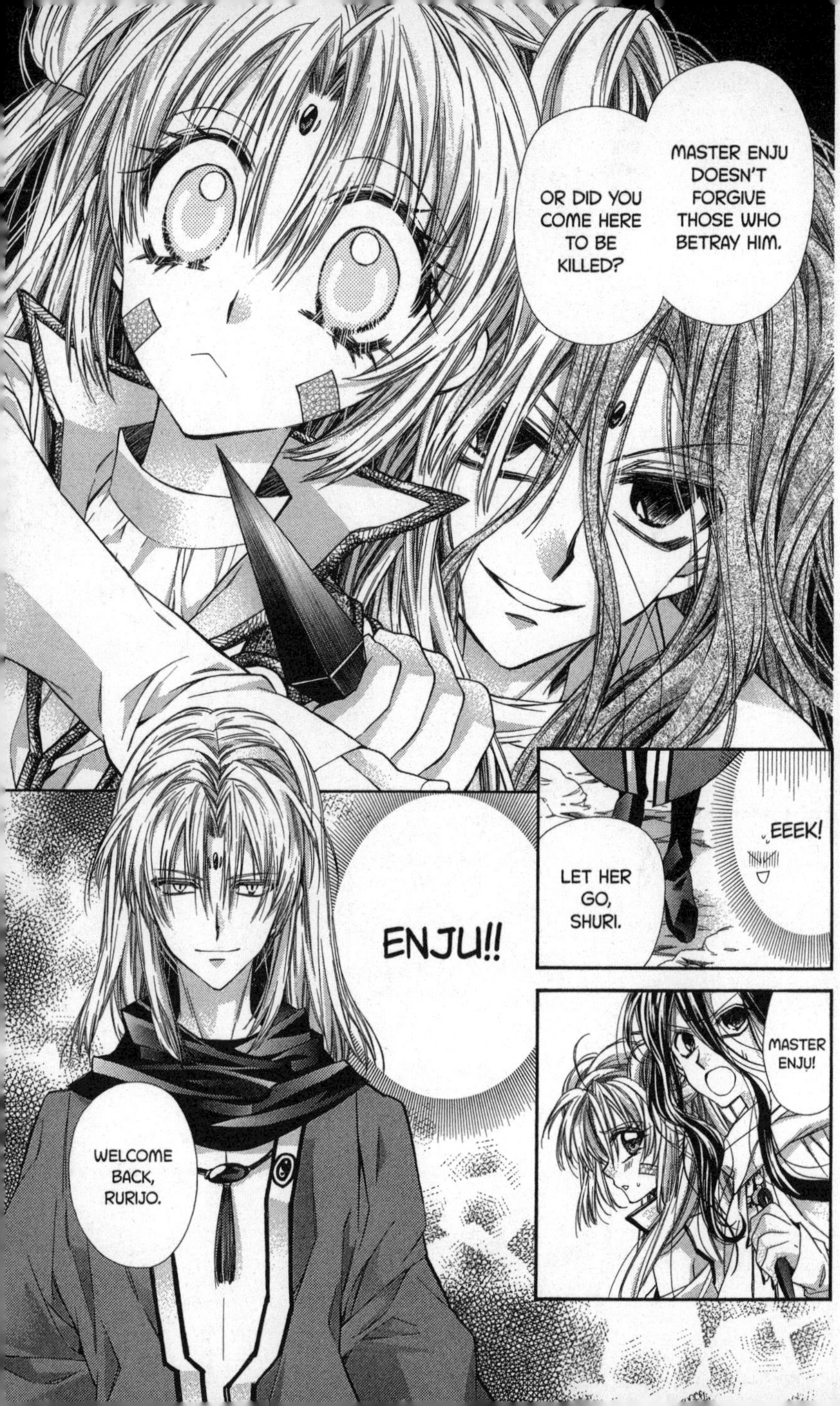
MASTER ENJU DOESN'T FORGIVE THOSE WHO BETRAY HIM.
OR DID YOU COME HERE TO BE KILLED?
EEEK!
LET HER GO, SHURI.
MASTER ENJU!
ENJU!!
WELCOME BACK, RURIJO.

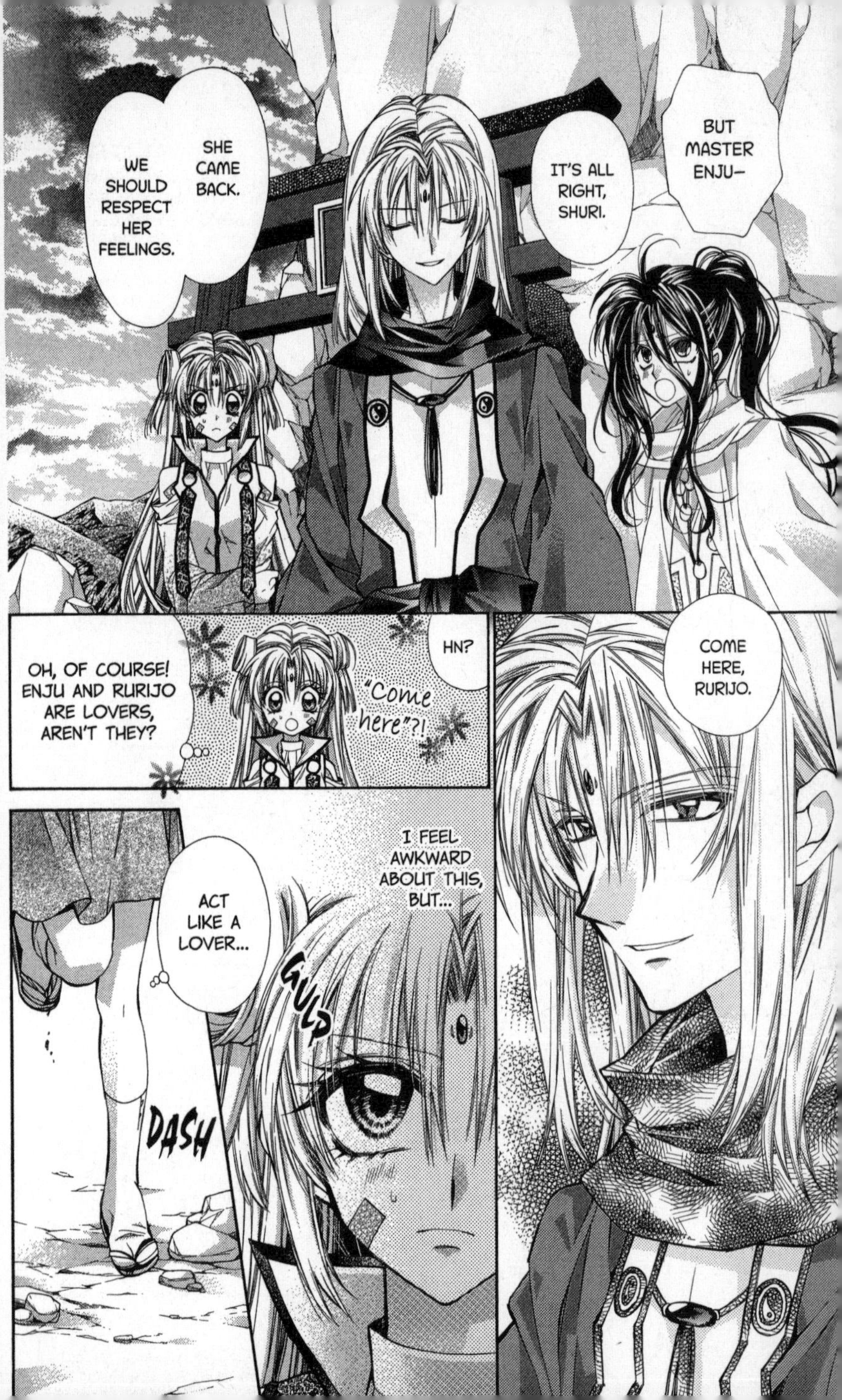
BUT MASTER ENJU–
IT'S ALL RIGHT, SHURI.
SHE CAME BACK.
WE SHOULD RESPECT HER FEELINGS.
COME HERE, RURIJO.
HN?
"Come here"?!
OH, OF COURSE! ENJU AND RURIJO ARE LOVERS, AREN'T THEY?
I FEEL AWKWARD ABOUT THIS, BUT...
ACT LIKE A LOVER...
GULP
DASH

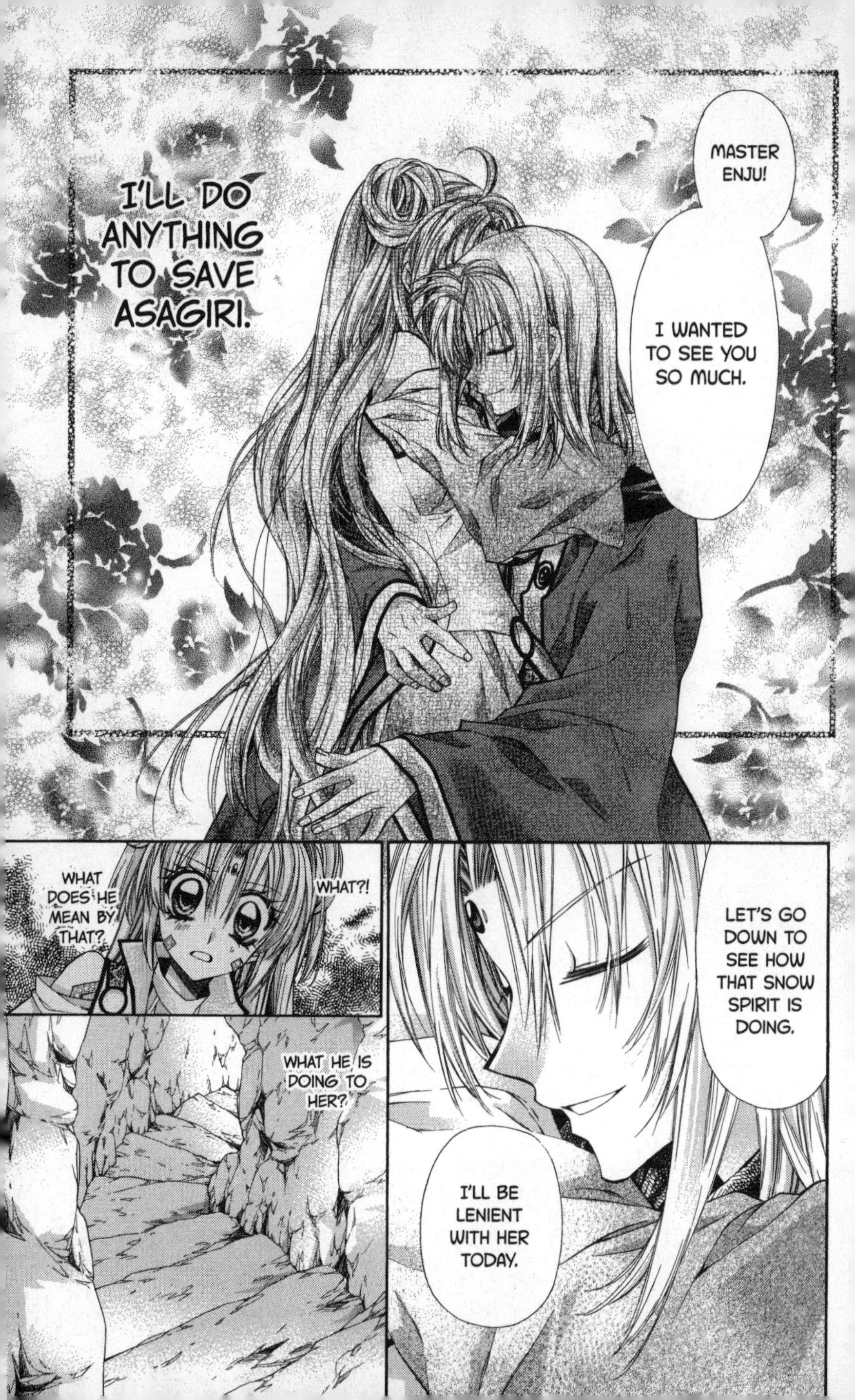
MASTER ENJU!
I WANTED TO SEE YOU SO MUCH.
I'LL DO ANYTHING TO SAVE ASAGIRI.
LET'S GO DOWN TO SEE HOW THAT SNOW SPIRIT IS DOING.
I'LL BE LENIENT WITH HER TODAY.
WHAT?!
WHAT DOES HE MEAN BY THAT?
WHAT HE IS DOING TO HER?

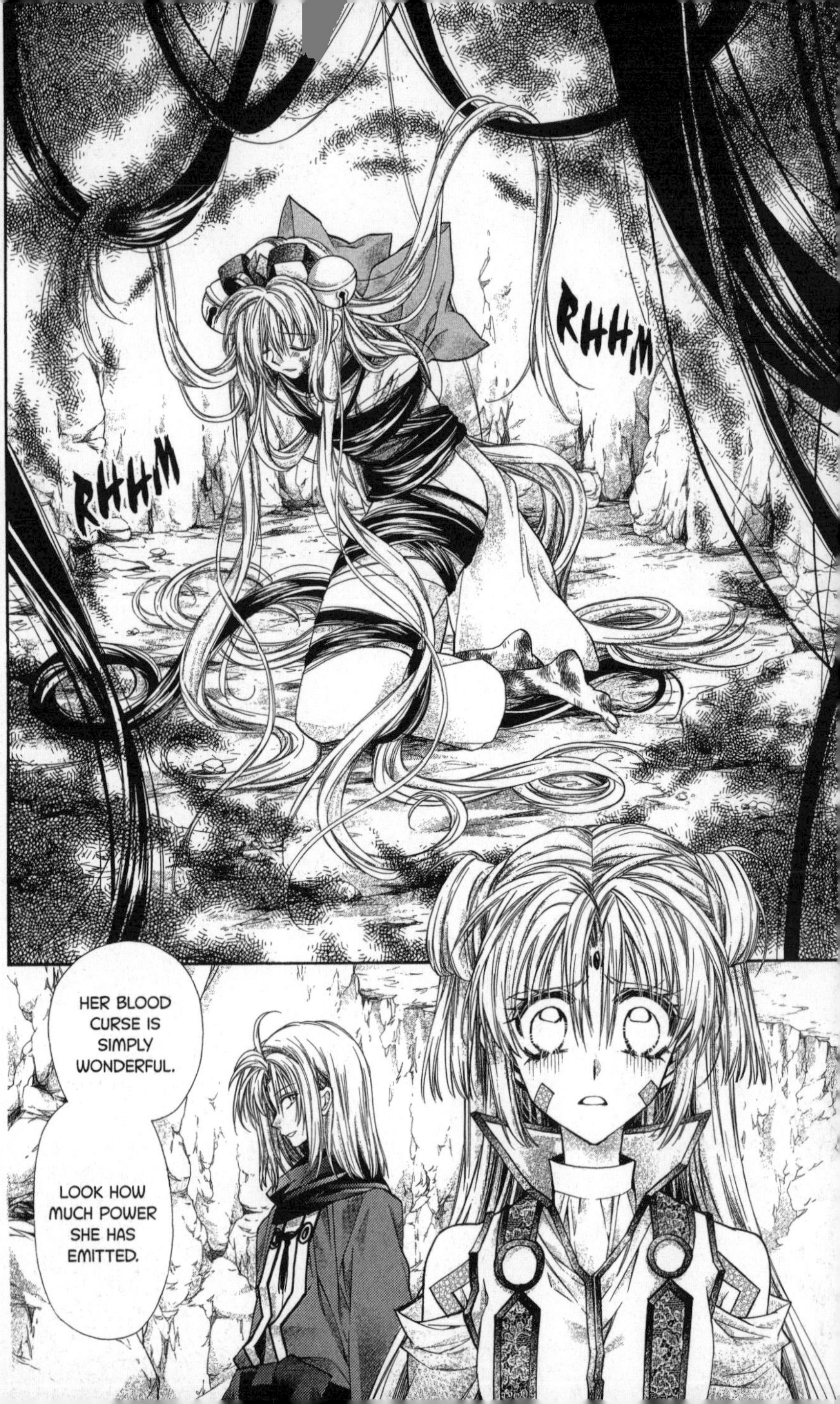
RHHM
RHHM
HER BLOOD CURSE IS SIMPLY WONDERFUL.
LOOK HOW MUCH POWER SHE HAS EMITTED.

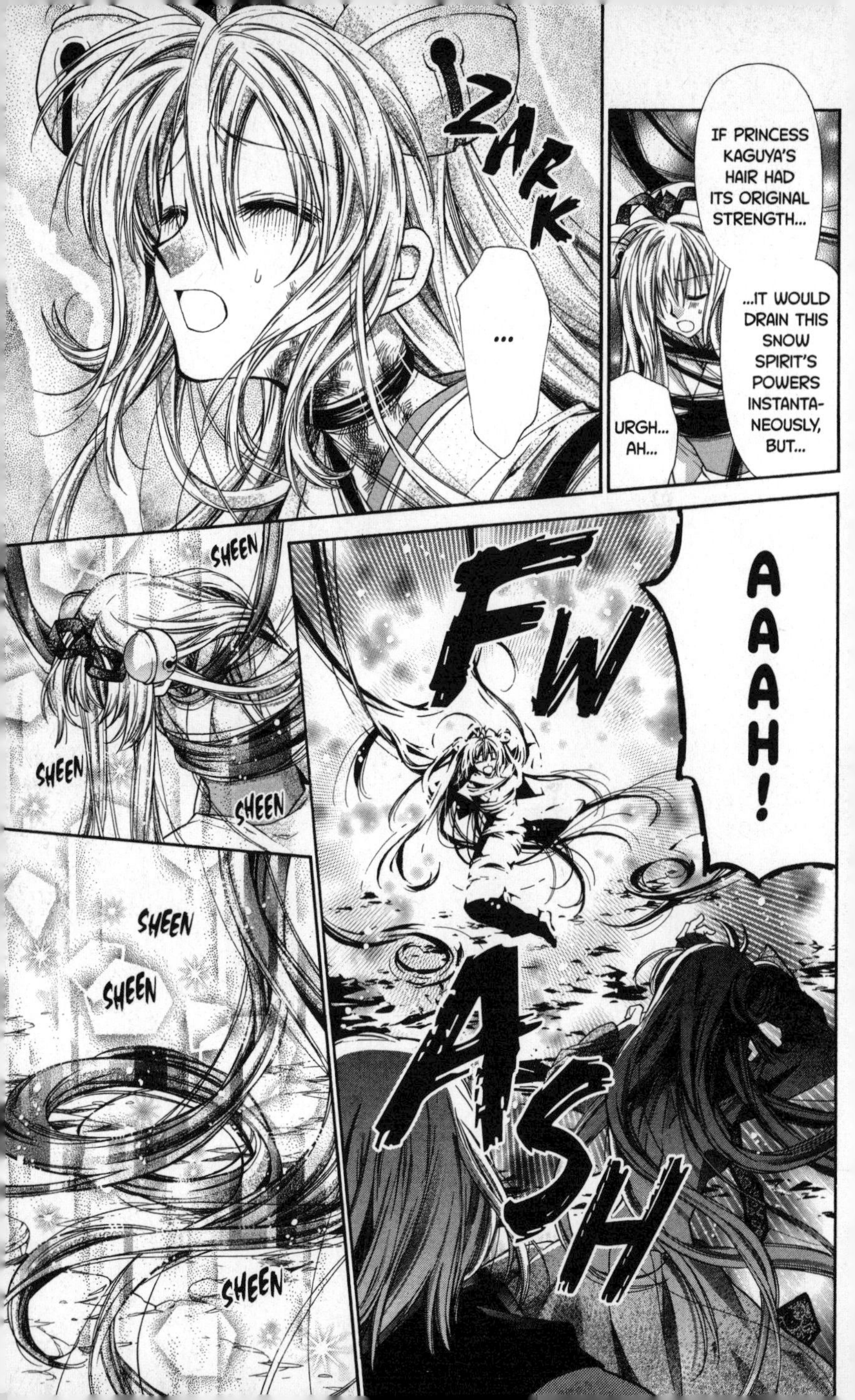
IF PRINCESS KAGUYA'S HAIR HAD ITS ORIGINAL STRENGTH...
...IT WOULD DRAIN THIS SNOW SPIRIT'S POWERS INSTANTA-NEOUSLY, BUT...
URGH... AH...
ZARK
...
AAAAH!
FWASH
SHEEN
SHEEN
SHEEN
SHEEN
SHEEN
SHEEN

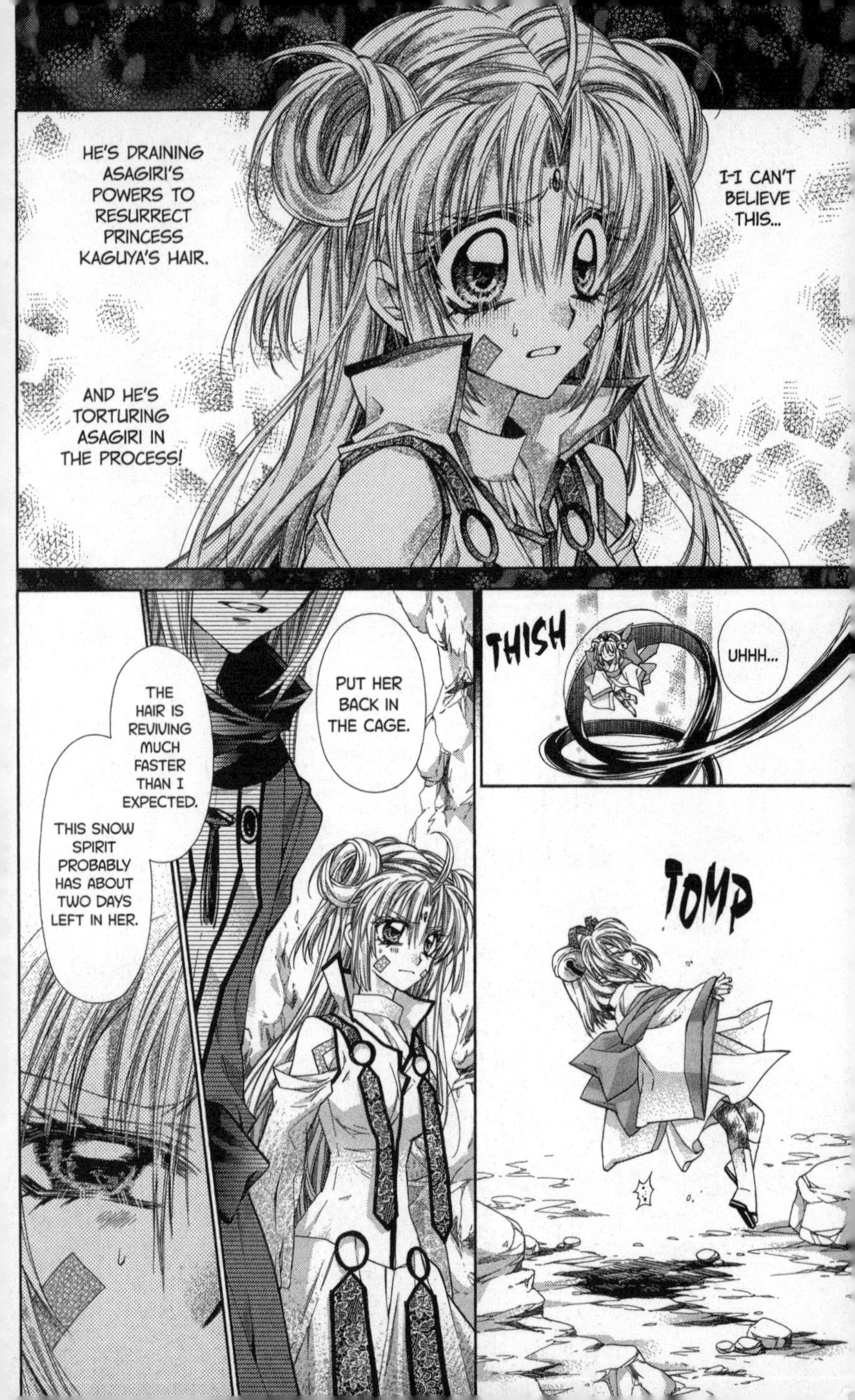
I-I CAN'T BELIEVE THIS...
HE'S DRAINING ASAGIRI'S POWERS TO RESURRECT PRINCESS KAGUYA'S HAIR.
AND HE'S TORTURING ASAGIRI IN THE PROCESS!
UHHH...
THISH
TOMP
PUT HER BACK IN THE CAGE.
THE HAIR IS REVIVING MUCH FASTER THAN I EXPECTED.
THIS SNOW SPIRIT PROBABLY HAS ABOUT TWO DAYS LEFT IN HER.

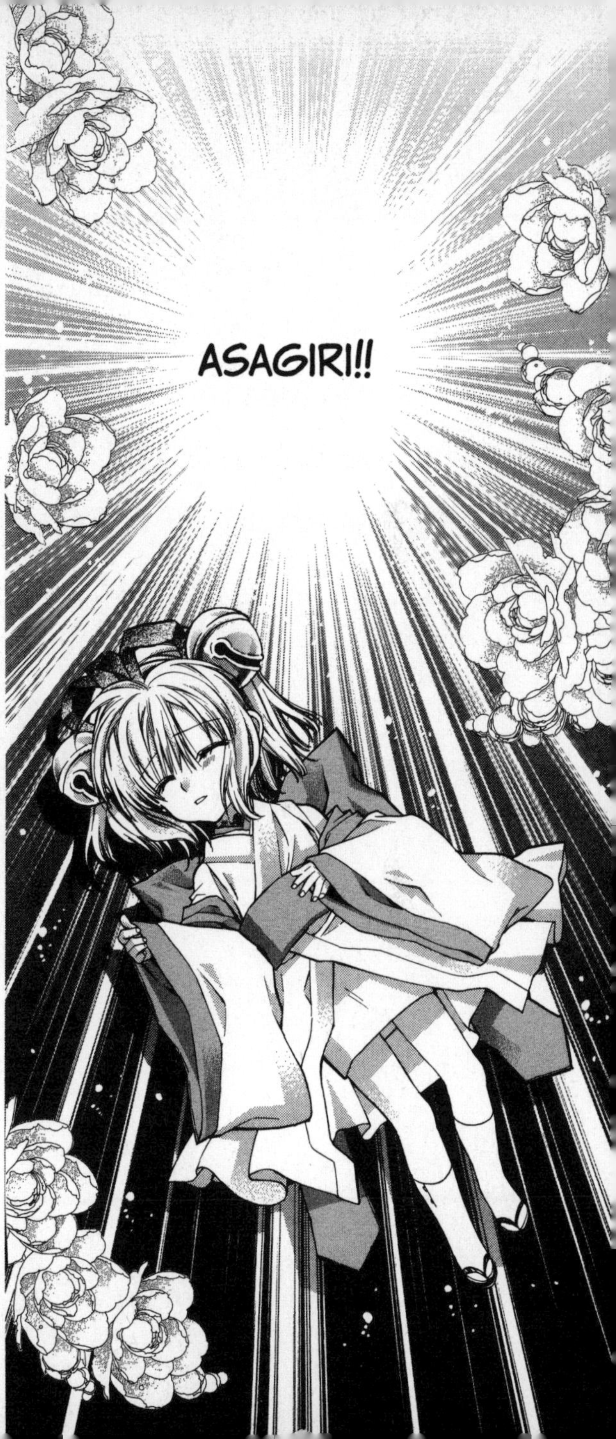
ASAGIRI!!

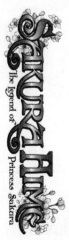

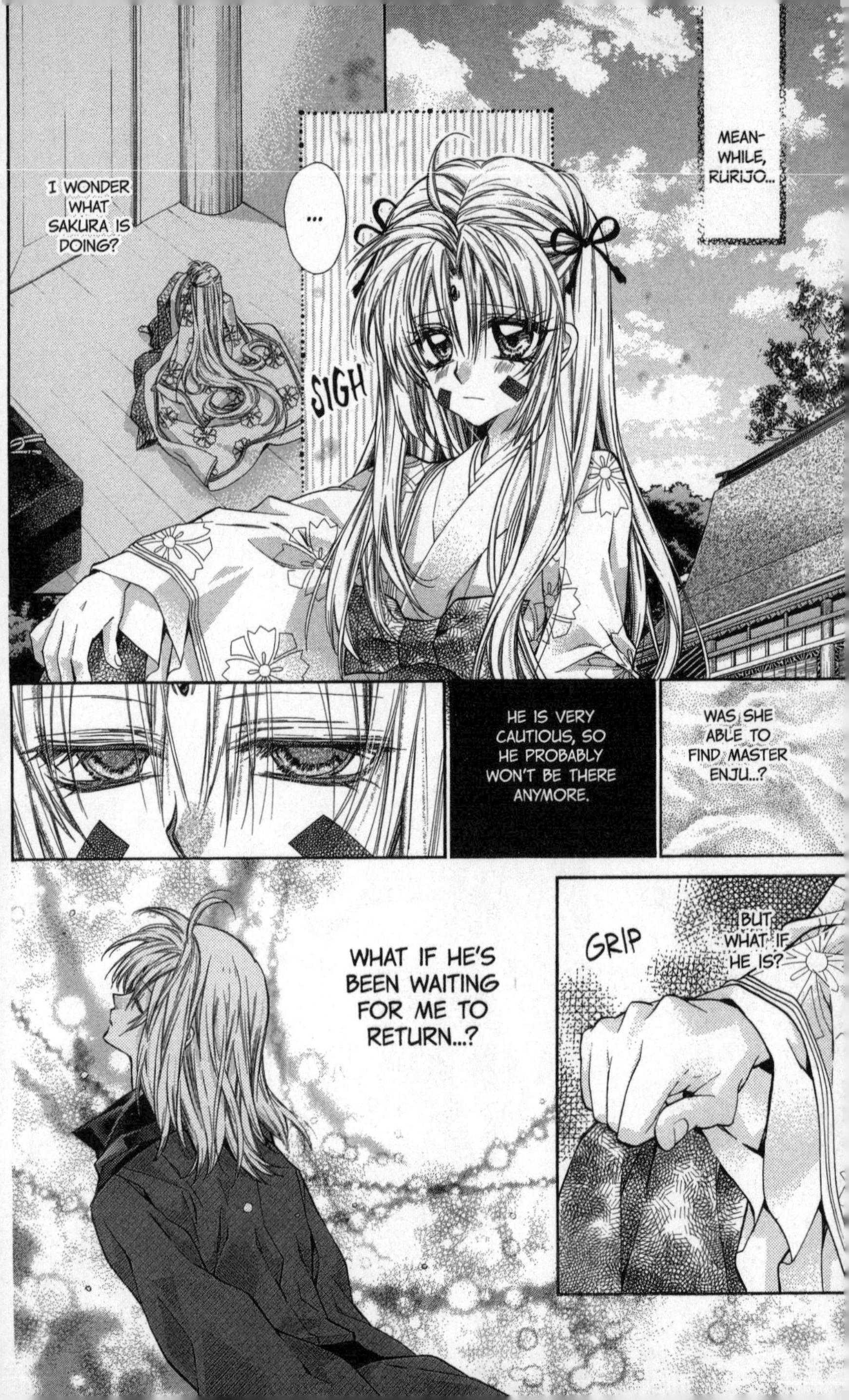
MEAN-WHILE, RURIJO...
...
SIGH
I WONDER WHAT SAKURA IS DOING?
WAS SHE ABLE TO FIND MASTER ENJU...?
HE IS VERY CAUTIOUS, SO HE PROBABLY WON'T BE THERE ANYMORE.
BUT WHAT IF HE IS?
GRIP
WHAT IF HE'S BEEN WAITING FOR ME TO RETURN...?

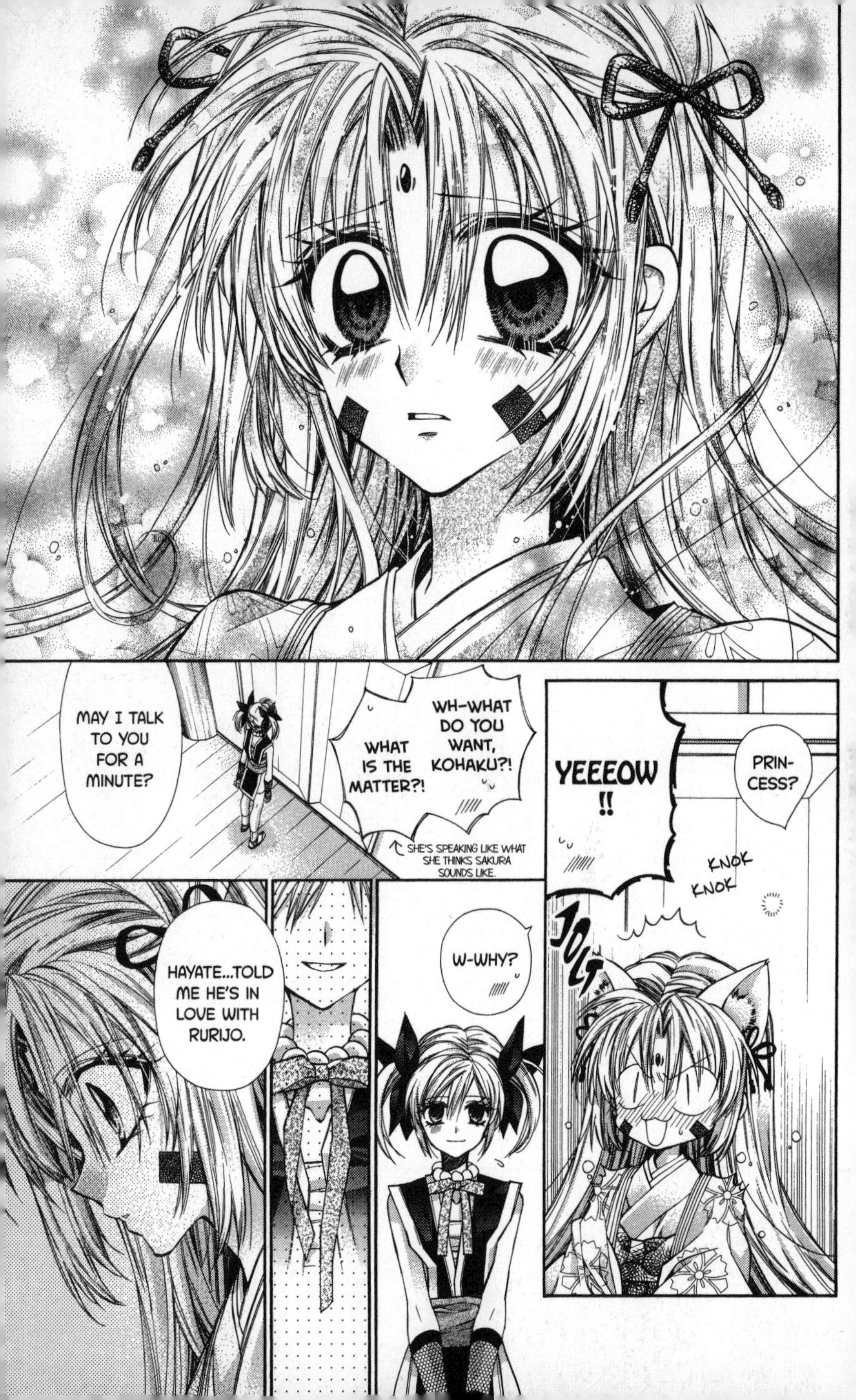
PRIN-CESS?
KNOK KNOK
YEEEOW!!
JOLT
WH-WHAT DO YOU WANT, KOHAKU?!
WHAT IS THE MATTER?!
SHE'S SPEAKING LIKE WHAT SHE THINKS SAKURA SOUNDS LIKE.
MAY I TALK TO YOU FOR A MINUTE?
W-WHY?
HAYATE...TOLD ME HE'S IN LOVE WITH RURIJO.

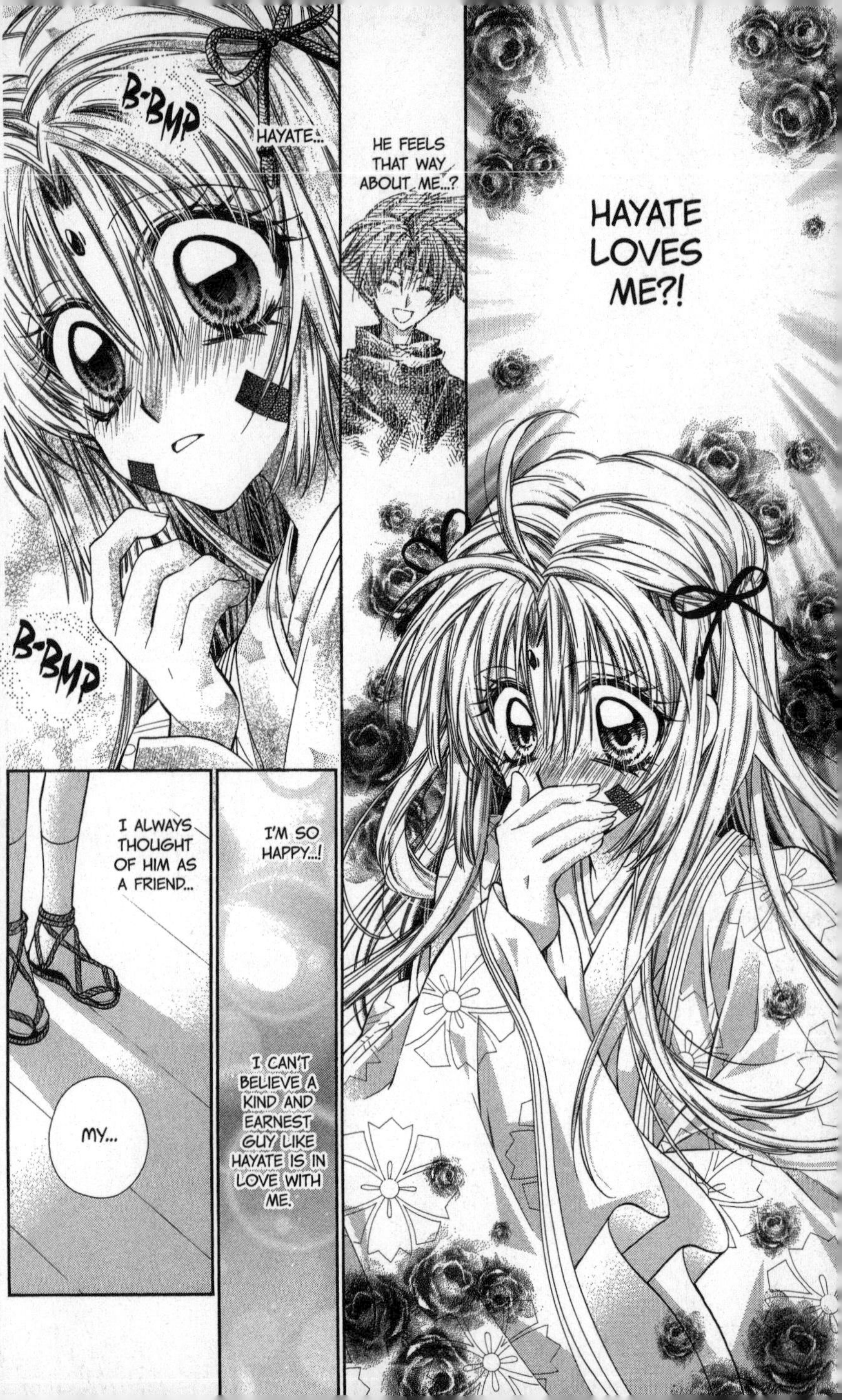
HAYATE LOVES ME?!
HE FEELS THAT WAY ABOUT ME...?
B-BMP
HAYATE...
B-BMP
I'M SO HAPPY...!
I CAN'T BELIEVE A KIND AND EARNEST GUY LIKE HAYATE IS IN LOVE WITH ME.
I ALWAYS THOUGHT OF HIM AS A FRIEND...
MY...

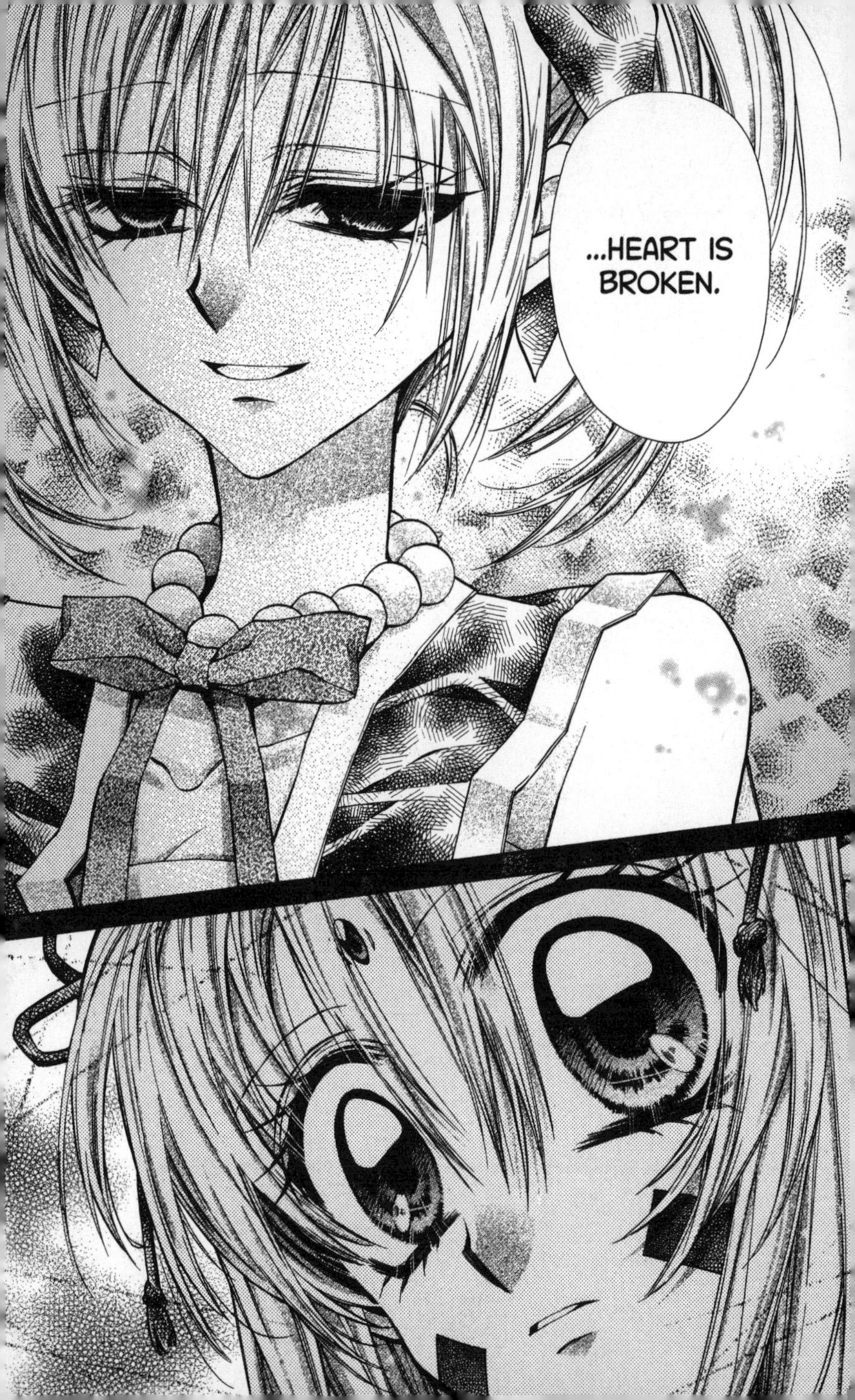
...HEART IS BROKEN.

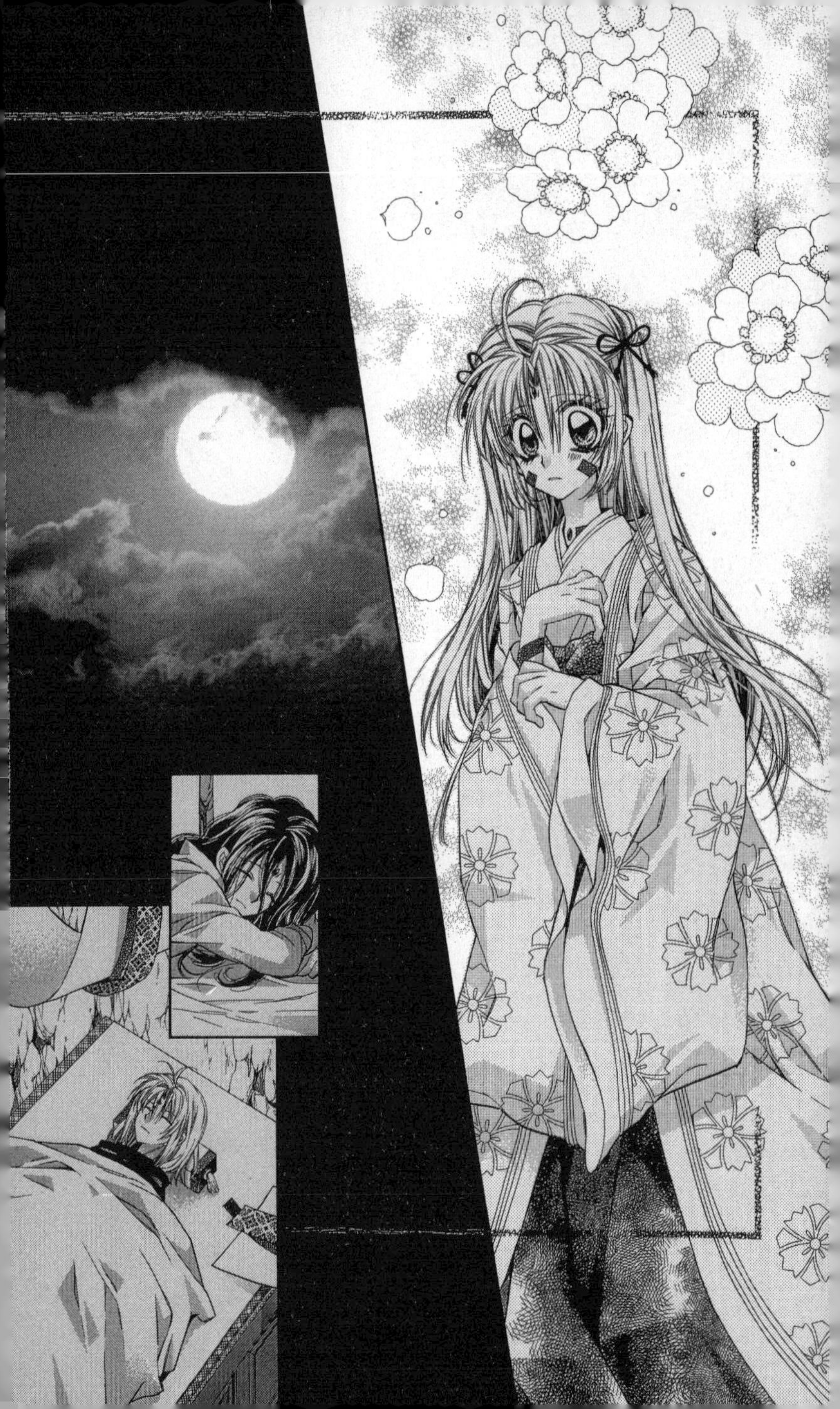

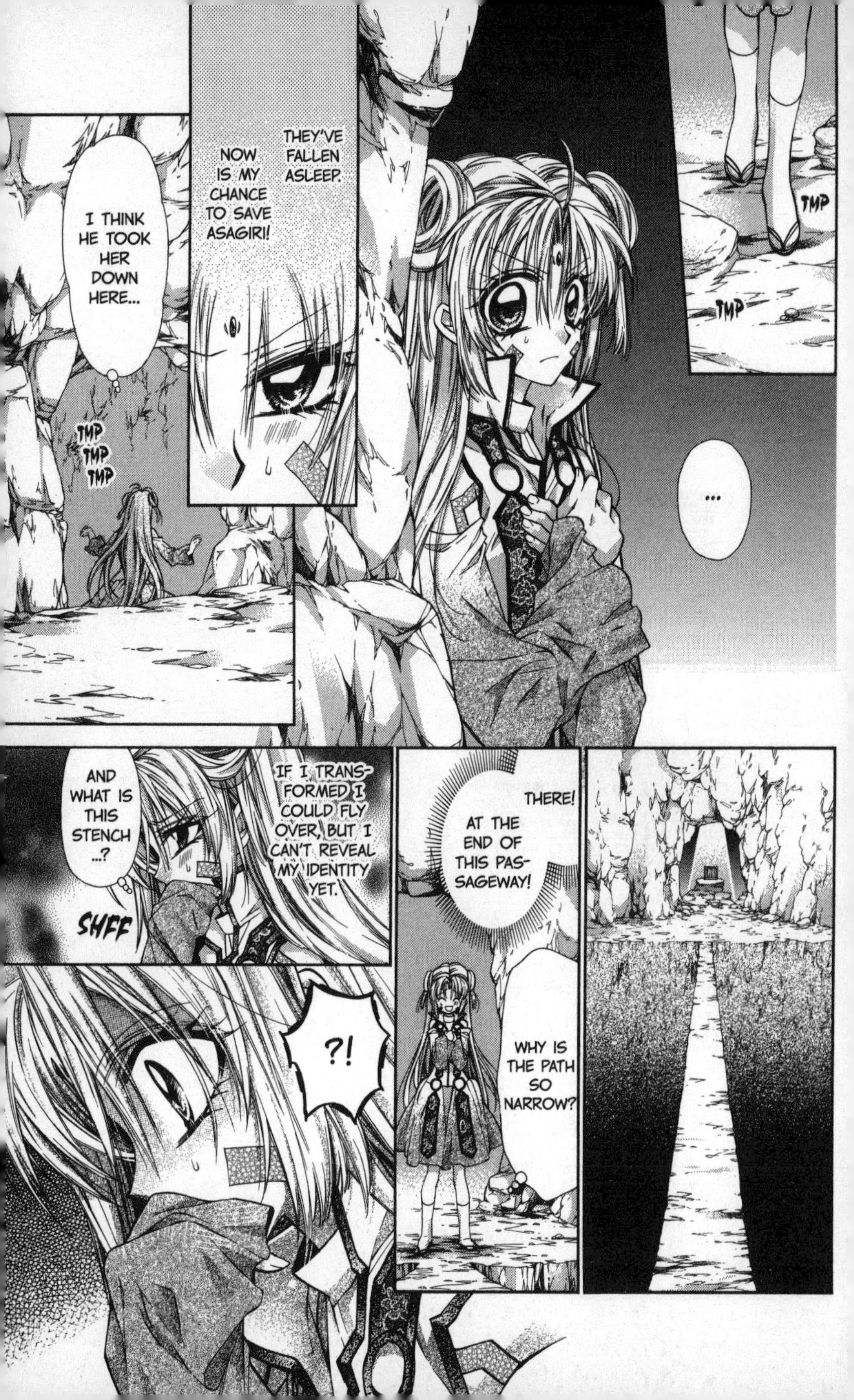
TMP
TMP
...
THEY'VE FALLEN ASLEEP.
NOW IS MY CHANCE TO SAVE ASAGIRI!
I THINK HE TOOK HER DOWN HERE...
TMP
TMP
TMP
THERE!
AT THE END OF THIS PAS-SAGEWAY!
WHY IS THE PATH SO NARROW?
IF I TRANS-FORMED I COULD FLY OVER, BUT I CAN'T REVEAL MY IDENTITY YET.
AND WHAT IS THIS STENCH ...?
SHFF
?!

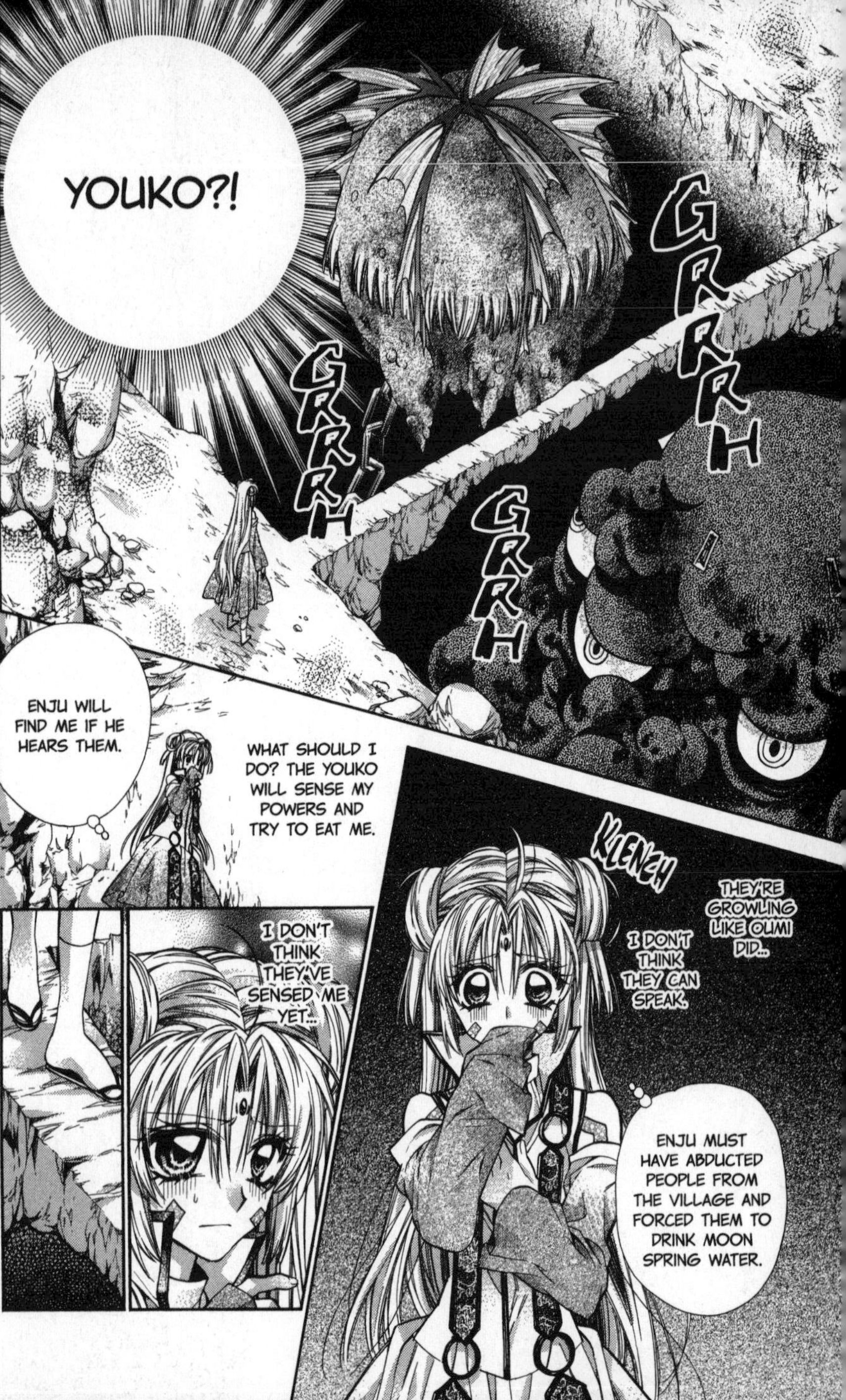
GRRRH
YOUKO?!
GRRRH
GRRRH
KLENCH
THEY'RE GROWLING LIKE OUMI DID...
I DON'T THINK THEY CAN SPEAK.
ENJU MUST HAVE ABDUCTED PEOPLE FROM THE VILLAGE AND FORCED THEM TO DRINK MOON SPRING WATER.
WHAT SHOULD I DO? THE YOUKO WILL SENSE MY POWERS AND TRY TO EAT ME.
ENJU WILL FIND ME IF HE HEARS THEM.
I DON'T THINK THEY'VE SENSED ME YET...

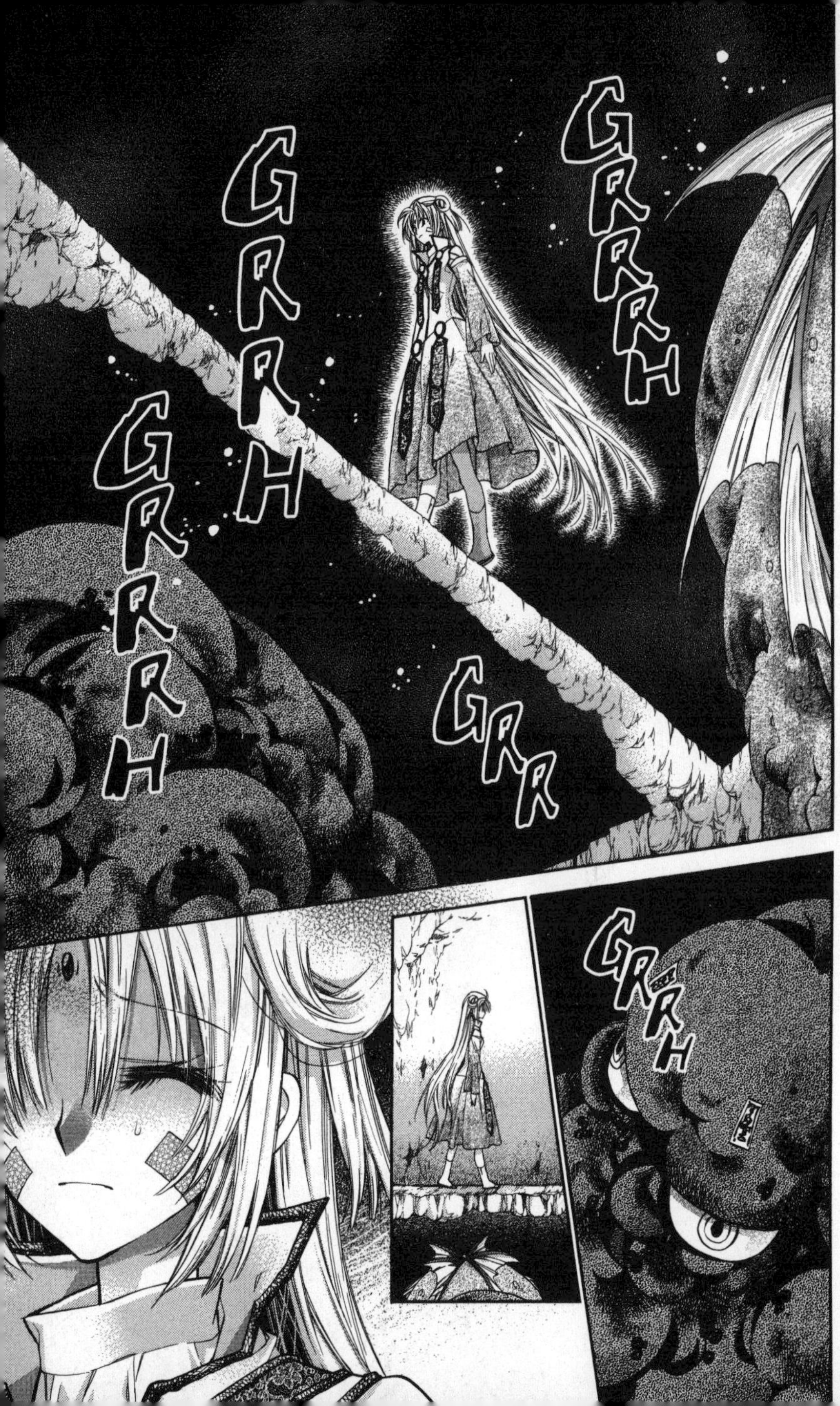
GRRRH
GRRH
GRRRRH
GRR
GRRH

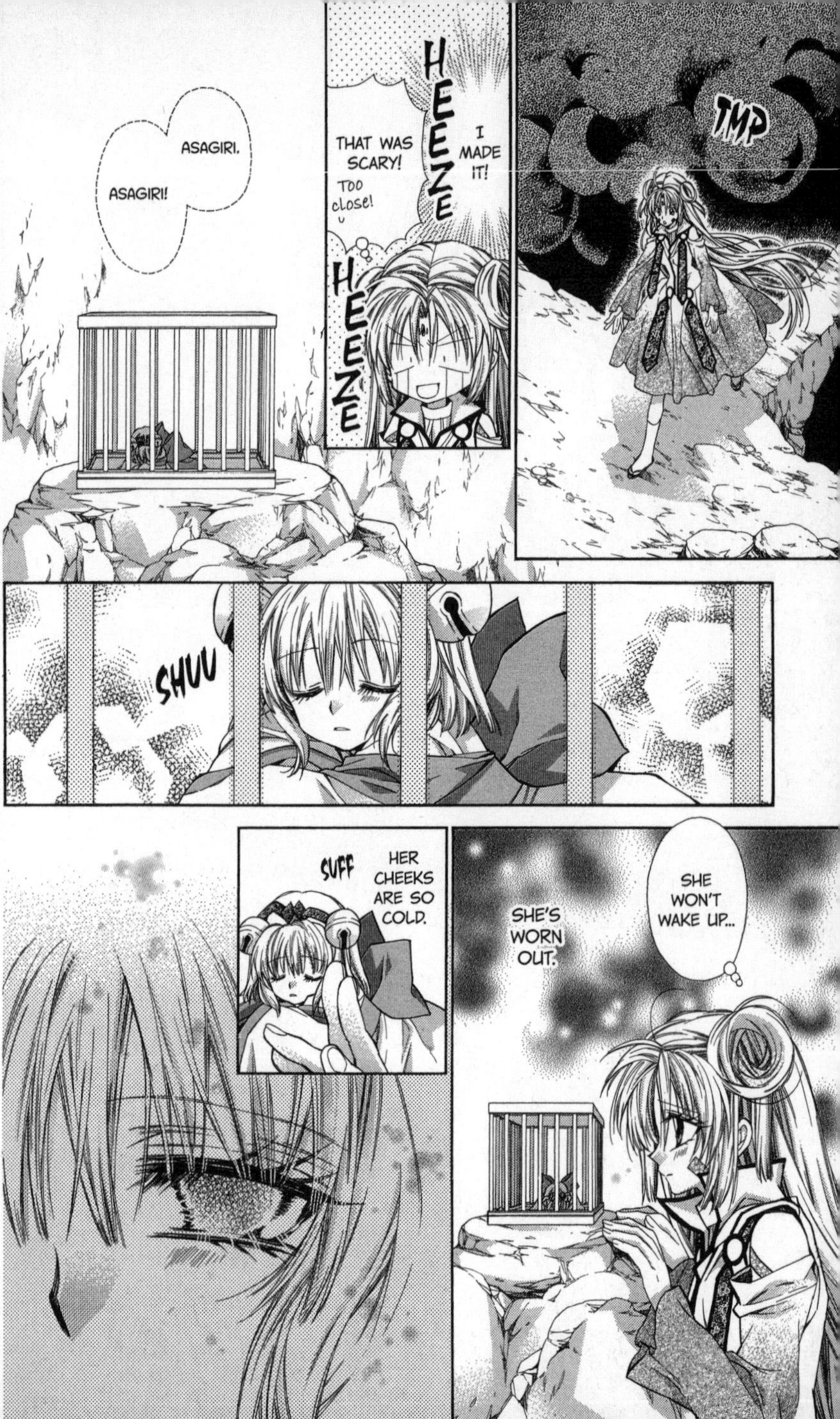
TMP
I MADE IT!
HEEZE
THAT WAS SCARY!
Too close!
HEEZE
ASAGIRI.
ASAGIRI!
SHUU
SHE WON'T WAKE UP...
SHE'S WORN OUT.
HER CHEEKS ARE SO COLD.
SUFF

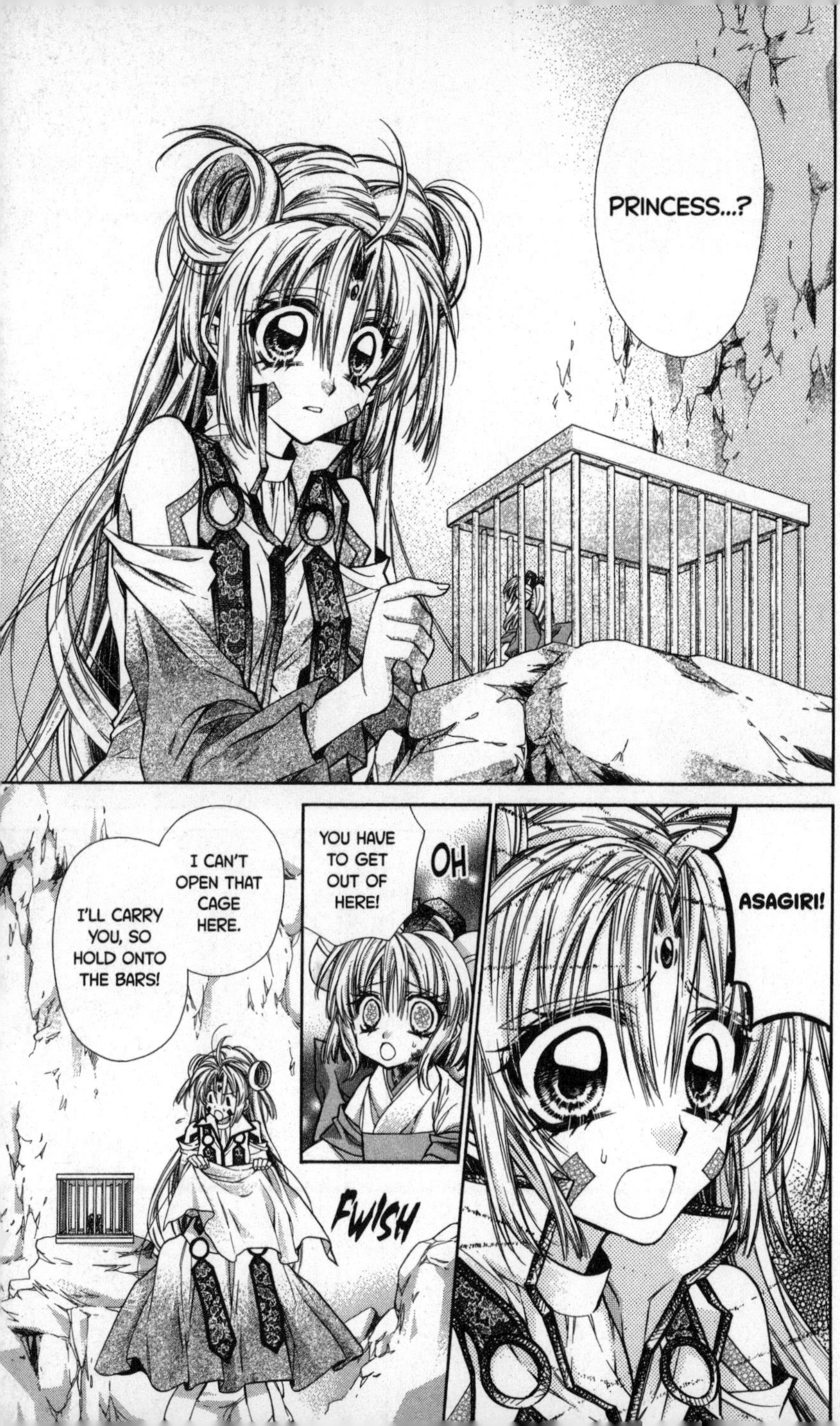
PRINCESS...?
ASAGIRI!
OH
YOU HAVE TO GET OUT OF HERE!
I CAN'T OPEN THAT CAGE HERE.
I'LL CARRY YOU, SO HOLD ONTO THE BARS!
FWISH

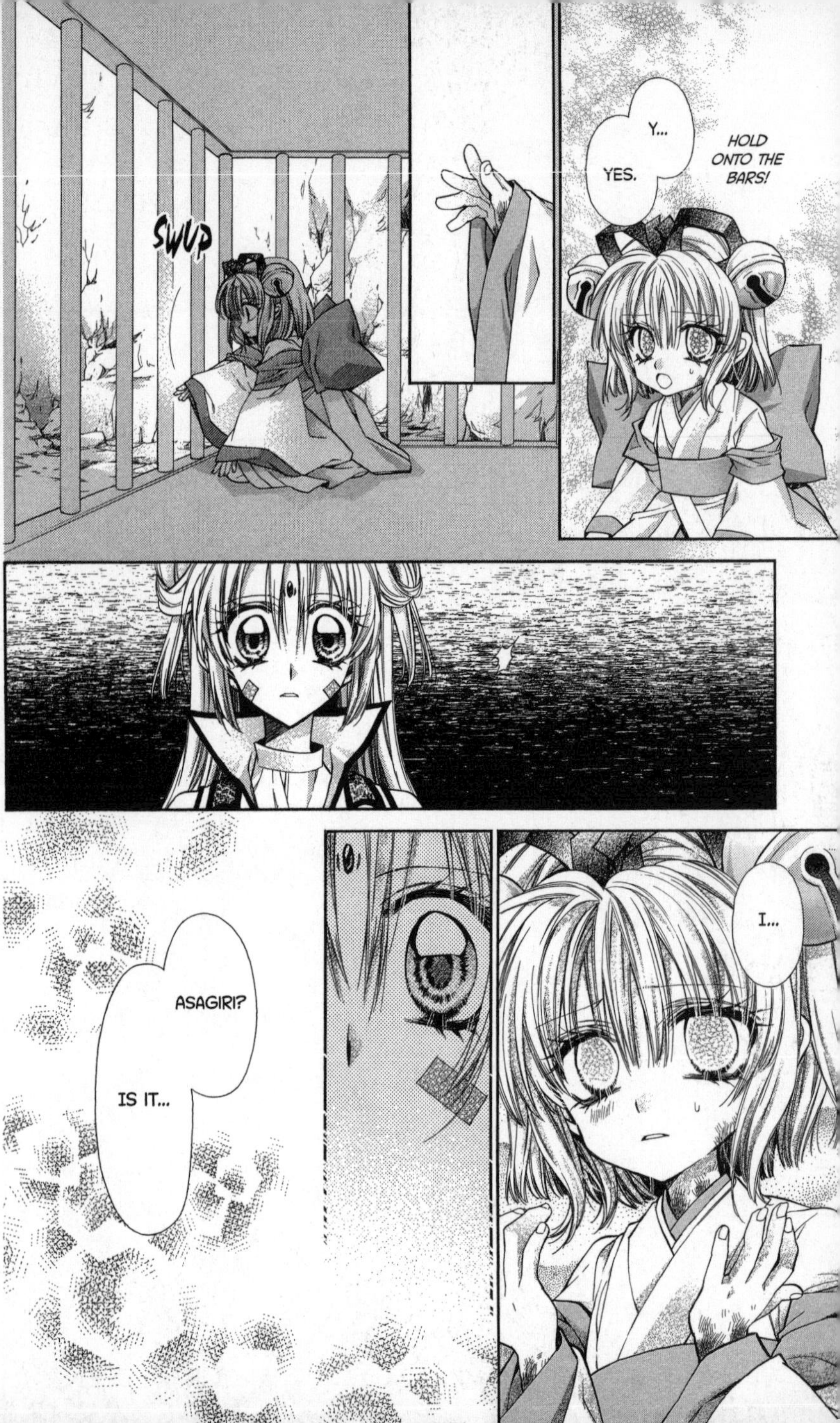
HOLD ONTO THE BARS!
Y... YES.
SWUP
I...
ASAGIRI? IS IT...

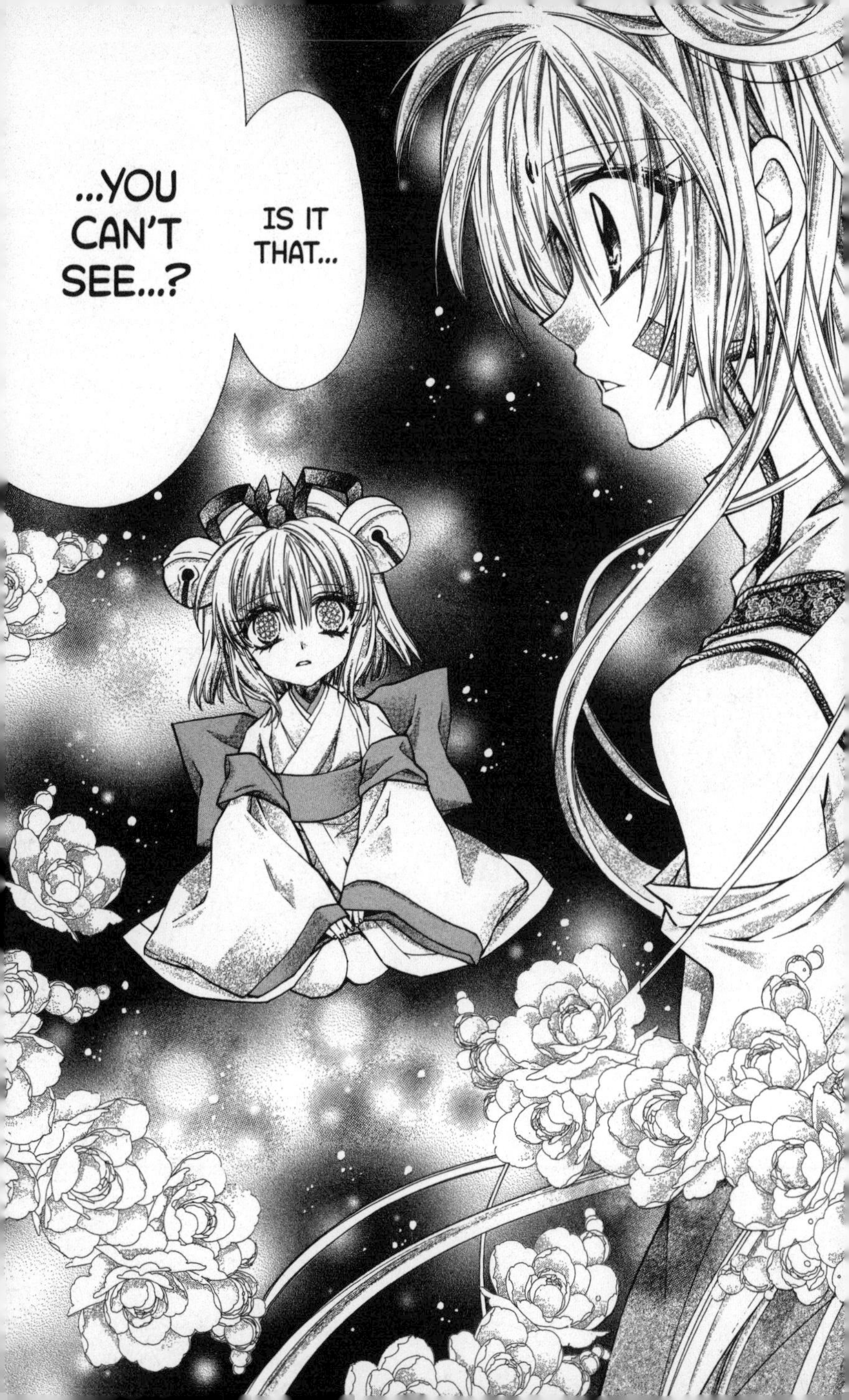
IS IT THAT...
...YOU CAN'T SEE...?

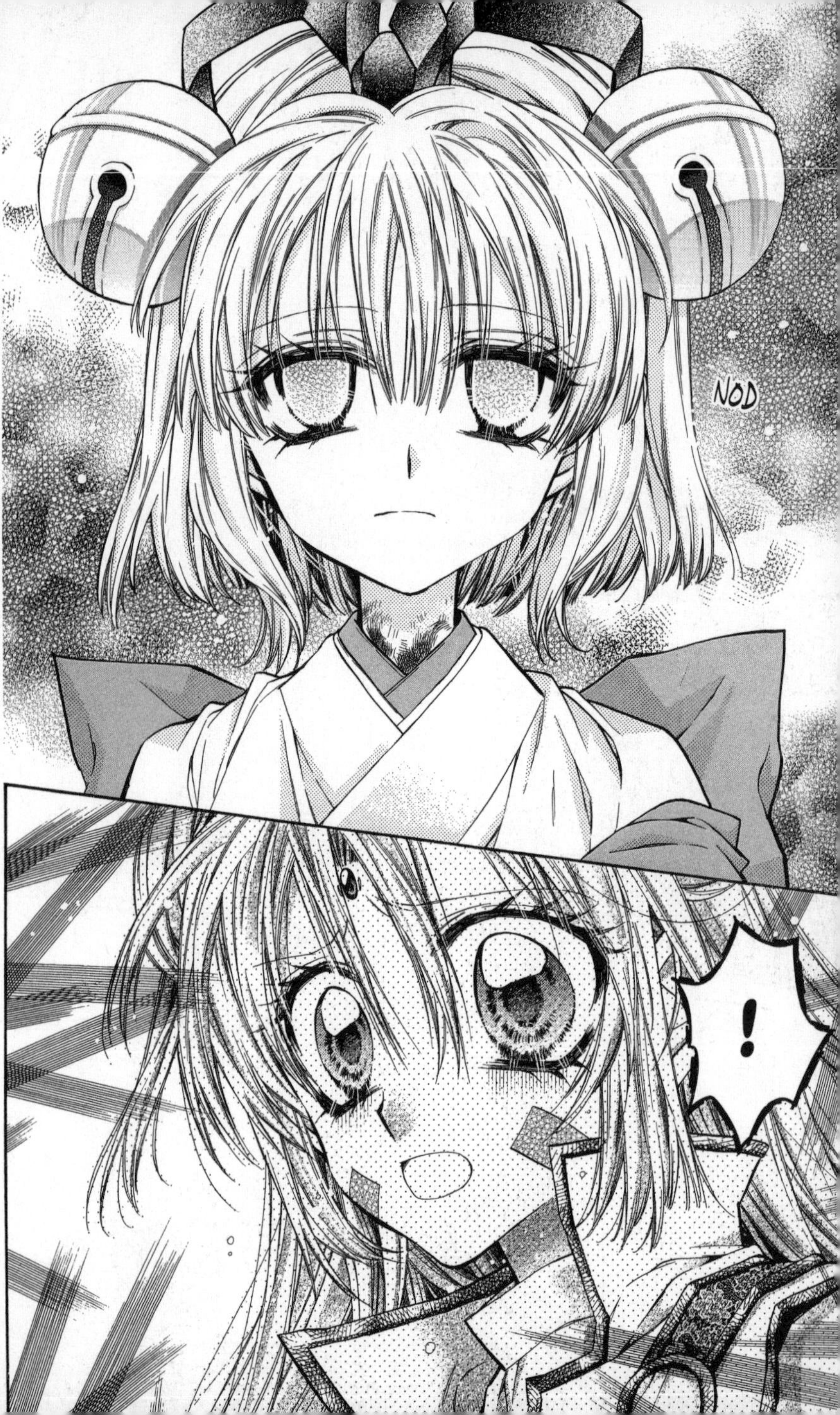
NOD
!

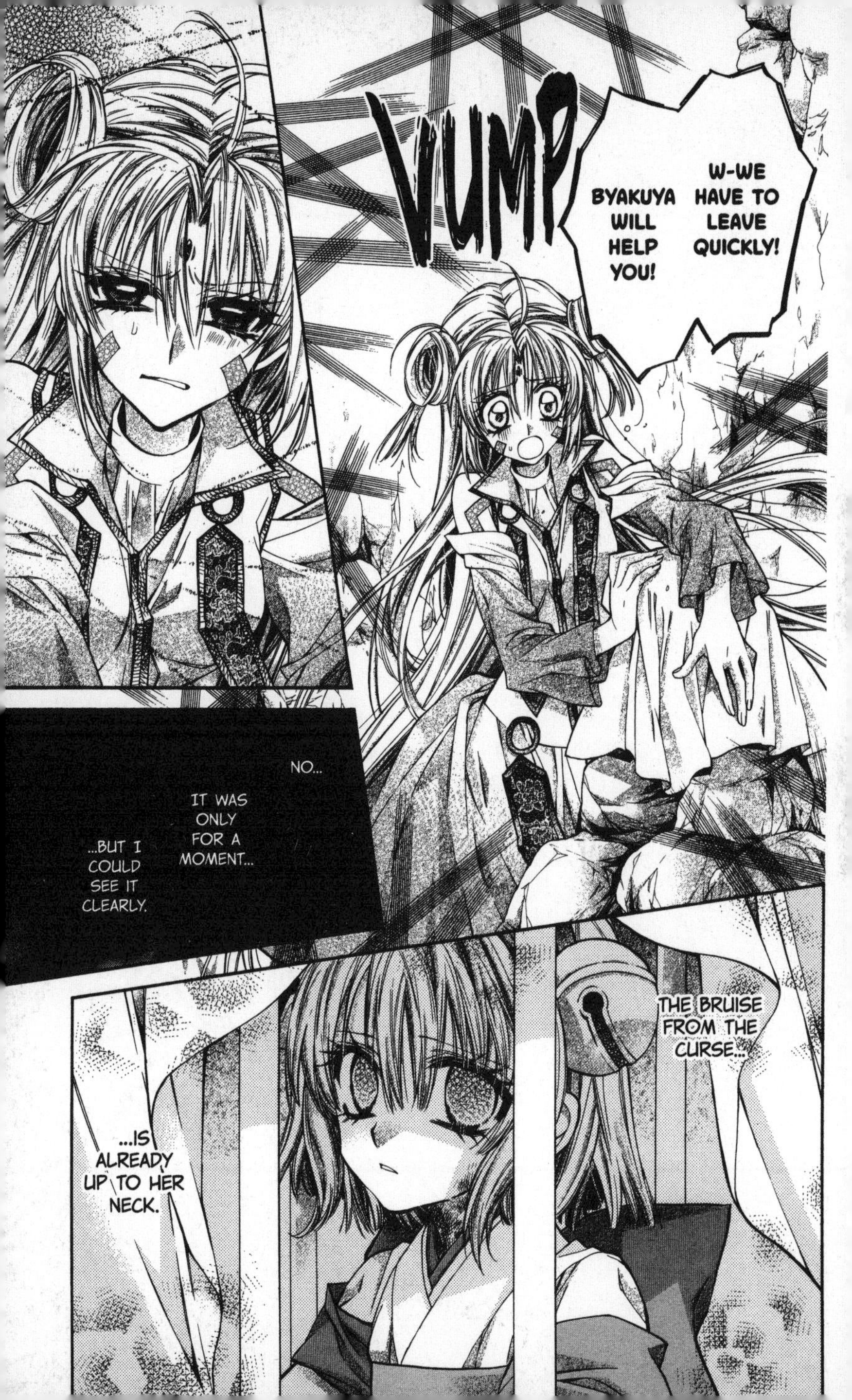
VUMP
W-WE HAVE TO LEAVE QUICKLY!
BYAKUYA WILL HELP YOU!
NO...
IT WAS ONLY FOR A MOMENT...
...BUT I COULD SEE IT CLEARLY.
THE BRUISE FROM THE CURSE...
...IS ALREADY UP TO HER NECK.

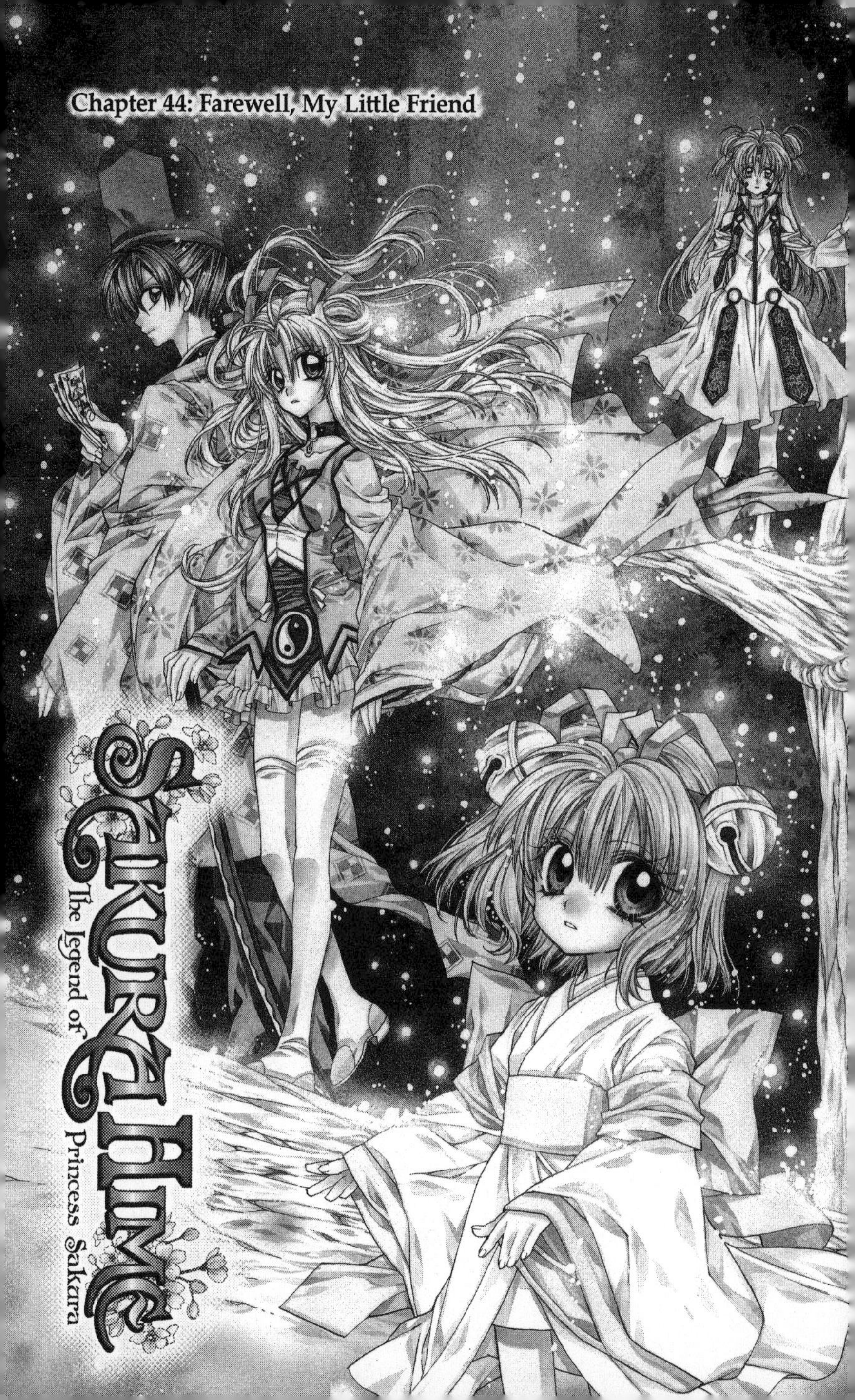
Chapter 44: Farewell, My Little Friend
Sakura Hime
The Legend of Princess Sakura

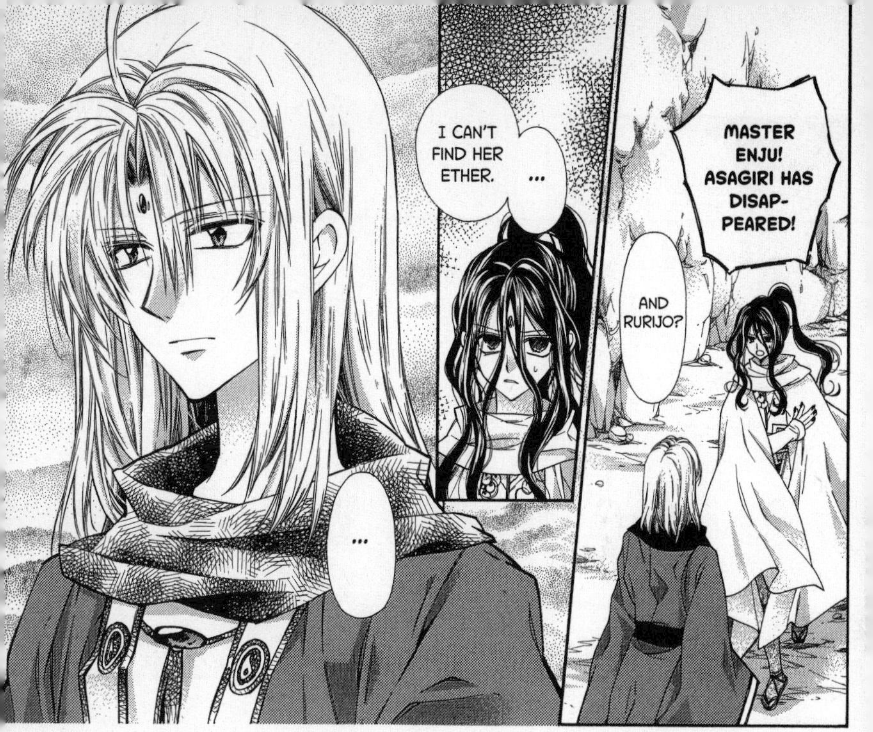
MASTER ENJU! ASAGIRI HAS DISAP-PEARED!
AND RURIJO?
I CAN'T FIND HER ETHER.
...
...

Chapter 44: Farewell, My Little Friend

(※I'm giving away the story.)

I tried something rather daring in this chapter! The chapter title is a spoiler. Well, you don't know what kind of "farewell" it is, but you can tell that something will come to an end. Asagiri has been looking for Sakura's kimono, and that is done with too. But there is more to the story, so please look forward to it. (?) As for the end, I usually would have come up with a reason for Asagiri's life, but she is such an ill-fated character that I decided not to have one ready for her. I think Asagiri is thinking too much about the whole thing... Now all that's left is for me to keep running towards the finale. And so, *Sakura Hime* will come to an end in the next volume and total 50 chapters. I hope you will continue to support this series to the end.

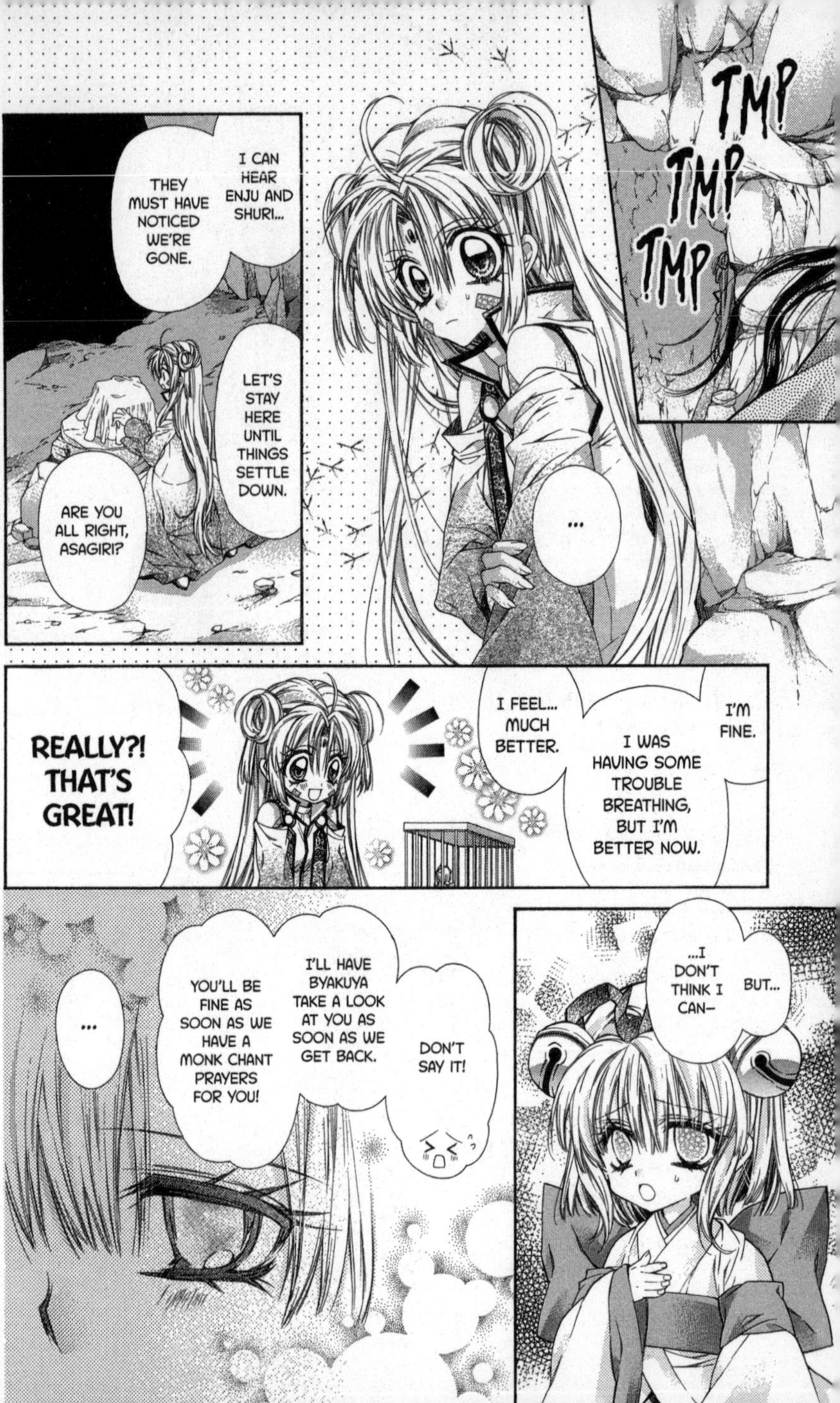
TMP TMP TMP
...
I CAN HEAR ENJU AND SHURI...
THEY MUST HAVE NOTICED WE'RE GONE.
LET'S STAY HERE UNTIL THINGS SETTLE DOWN.
ARE YOU ALL RIGHT, ASAGIRI?
I'M FINE.
I WAS HAVING SOME TROUBLE BREATHING, BUT I'M BETTER NOW.
I FEEL... MUCH BETTER.
REALLY?! THAT'S GREAT!
BUT...
...I DON'T THINK I CAN—
DON'T SAY IT!
I'LL HAVE BYAKUYA TAKE A LOOK AT YOU AS SOON AS WE GET BACK.
YOU'LL BE FINE AS SOON AS WE HAVE A MONK CHANT PRAYERS FOR YOU!
...

Continued → ④

We arrived at our second inn. Everything we ate in Kyoto tasted fabulous! The dinner at the inn had a lot of vegetables from Kyoto. It was delicious.✧

On the third day we were told that the Hozu River Cruise would take place, so we headed down to Kameoka on a train. (There is a minecart train that goes down there, but it wasn't running in time for the first cruise of the day, so we rode it the day before). The cruise is usually two hours long, but it was just an hour due to the flooding. I really recommend this cruise! We saw a deer up close that had come down to drink some water! The view was beautiful and the ride was thrilling too. It was relaxing and just great!

In the afternoon we entered the city of Kyoto and had lunch in the Chourakukan ♪ at an Italian restaurant called "Coral." We spent some quality grown-up time there.♥ Chourakukan is a Western-style building that is about 100 years old. In the past, official guests of state stayed there. There was a very pretty café too! A festival was being held in the park behind it, but we didn't have time to explore.

We headed back to Tokyo and Kyan-chi went straight to work from there. I went home and slept for about 15 hours. She has more stamina than I do! (laugh)

I'd love to go to Arashiyama again. Oh, the Kyoto Imperial Palace was open to the public at that time, so we toured that as well.♥ Thank you for a wonderful three days, Kyan-chi.~

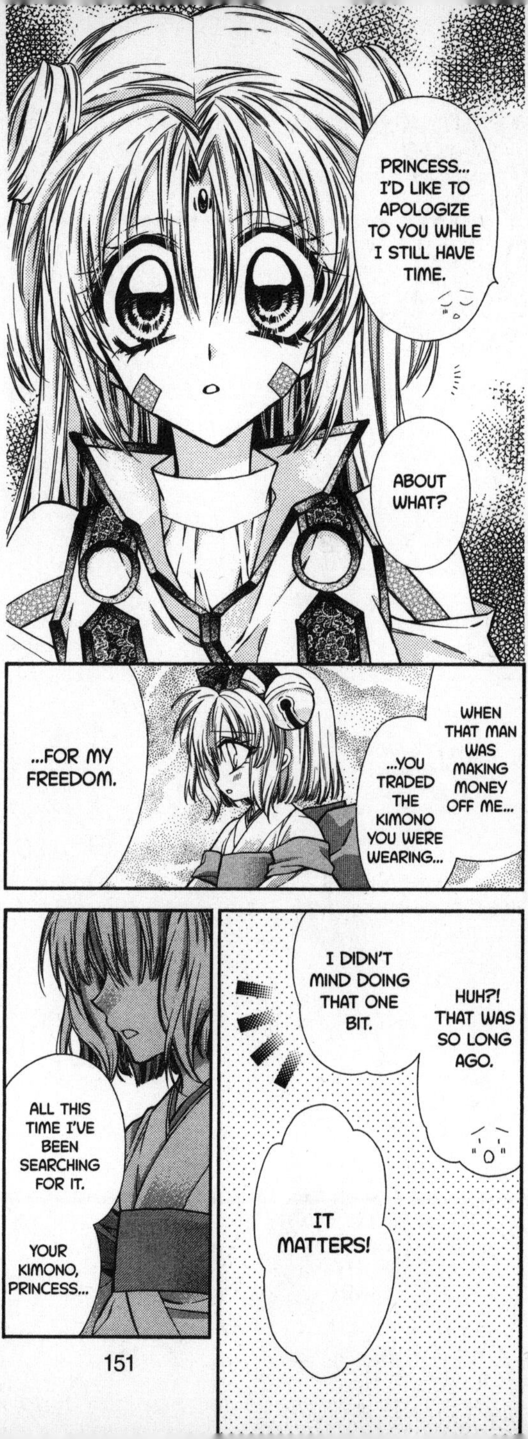
PRINCESS... I'D LIKE TO APOLOGIZE TO YOU WHILE I STILL HAVE TIME.
ABOUT WHAT?
WHEN THAT MAN WAS MAKING MONEY OFF ME...
...YOU TRADED THE KIMONO YOU WERE WEARING...
...FOR MY FREEDOM.
HUH?! THAT WAS SO LONG AGO.
I DIDN'T MIND DOING THAT ONE BIT.
IT MATTERS!
ALL THIS TIME I'VE BEEN SEARCHING FOR IT.
YOUR KIMONO, PRINCESS...

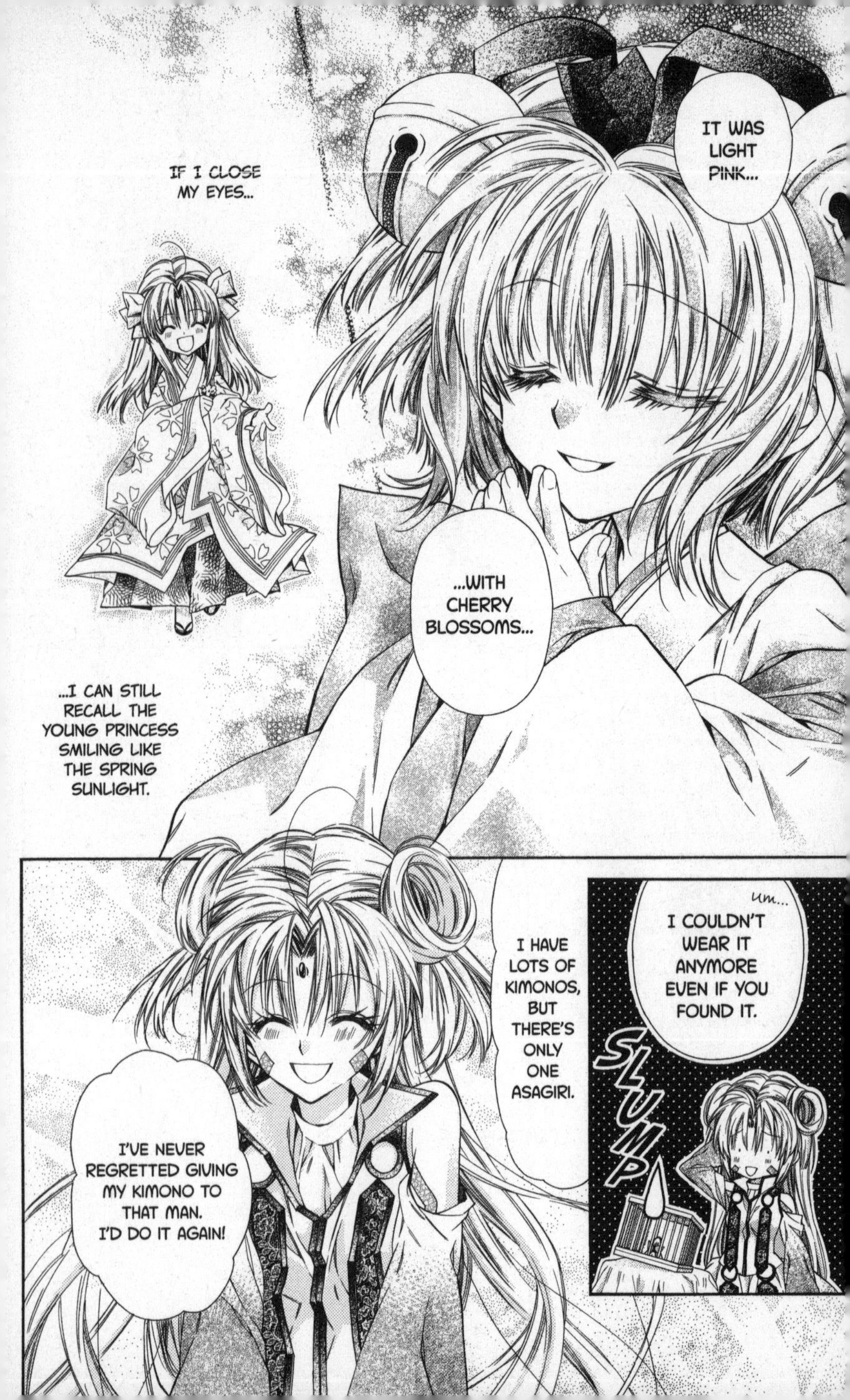
IT WAS LIGHT PINK...
IF I CLOSE MY EYES...
...WITH CHERRY BLOSSOMS...
...I CAN STILL RECALL THE YOUNG PRINCESS SMILING LIKE THE SPRING SUNLIGHT.
UM...
I COULDN'T WEAR IT ANYMORE EVEN IF YOU FOUND IT.
SLUMP
I HAVE LOTS OF KIMONOS, BUT THERE'S ONLY ONE ASAGIRI.
I'VE NEVER REGRETTED GIVING MY KIMONO TO THAT MAN. I'D DO IT AGAIN!

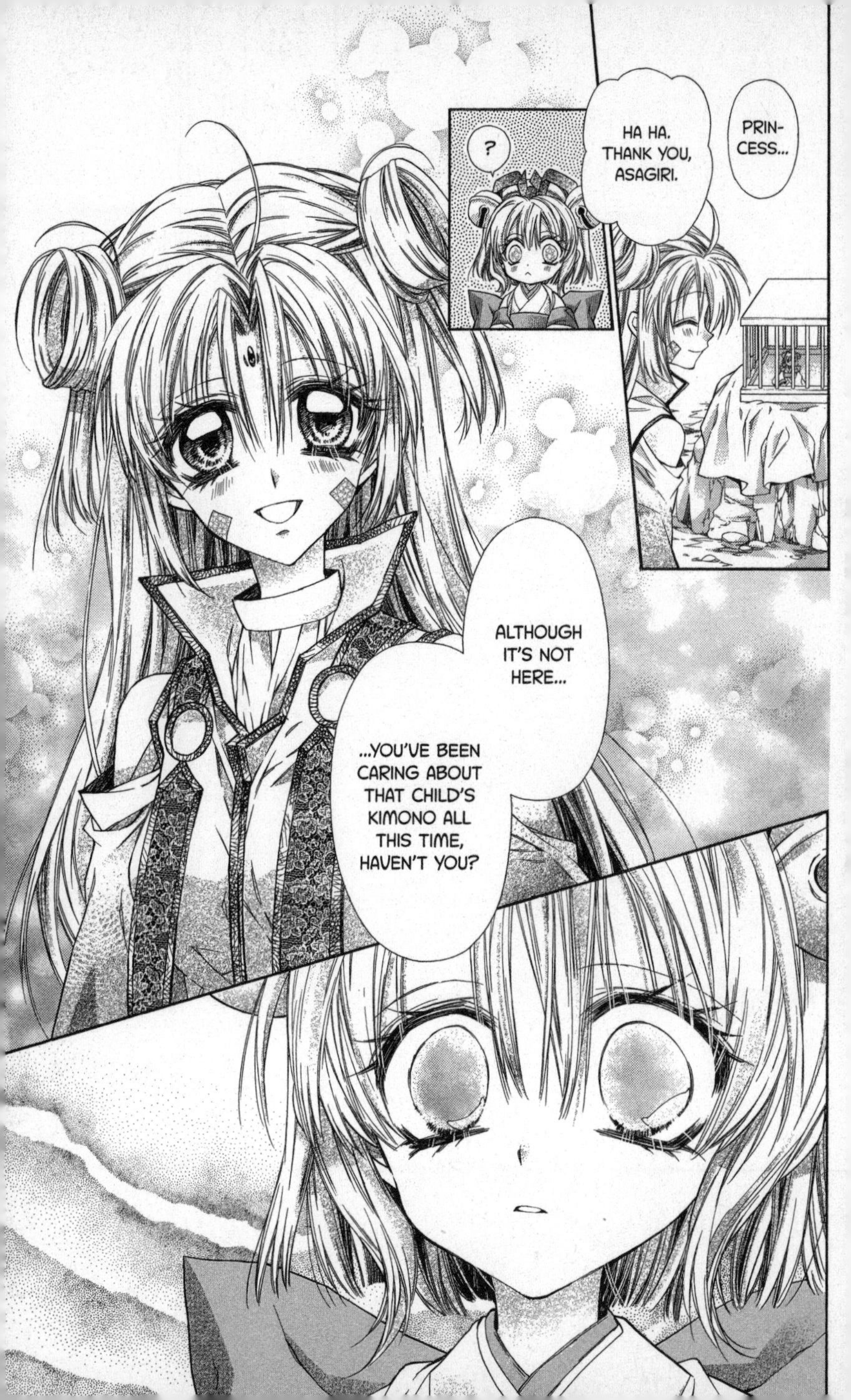
PRIN-CESS...
HA HA. THANK YOU, ASAGIRI.
?
ALTHOUGH IT'S NOT HERE...
...YOU'VE BEEN CARING ABOUT THAT CHILD'S KIMONO ALL THIS TIME, HAVEN'T YOU?

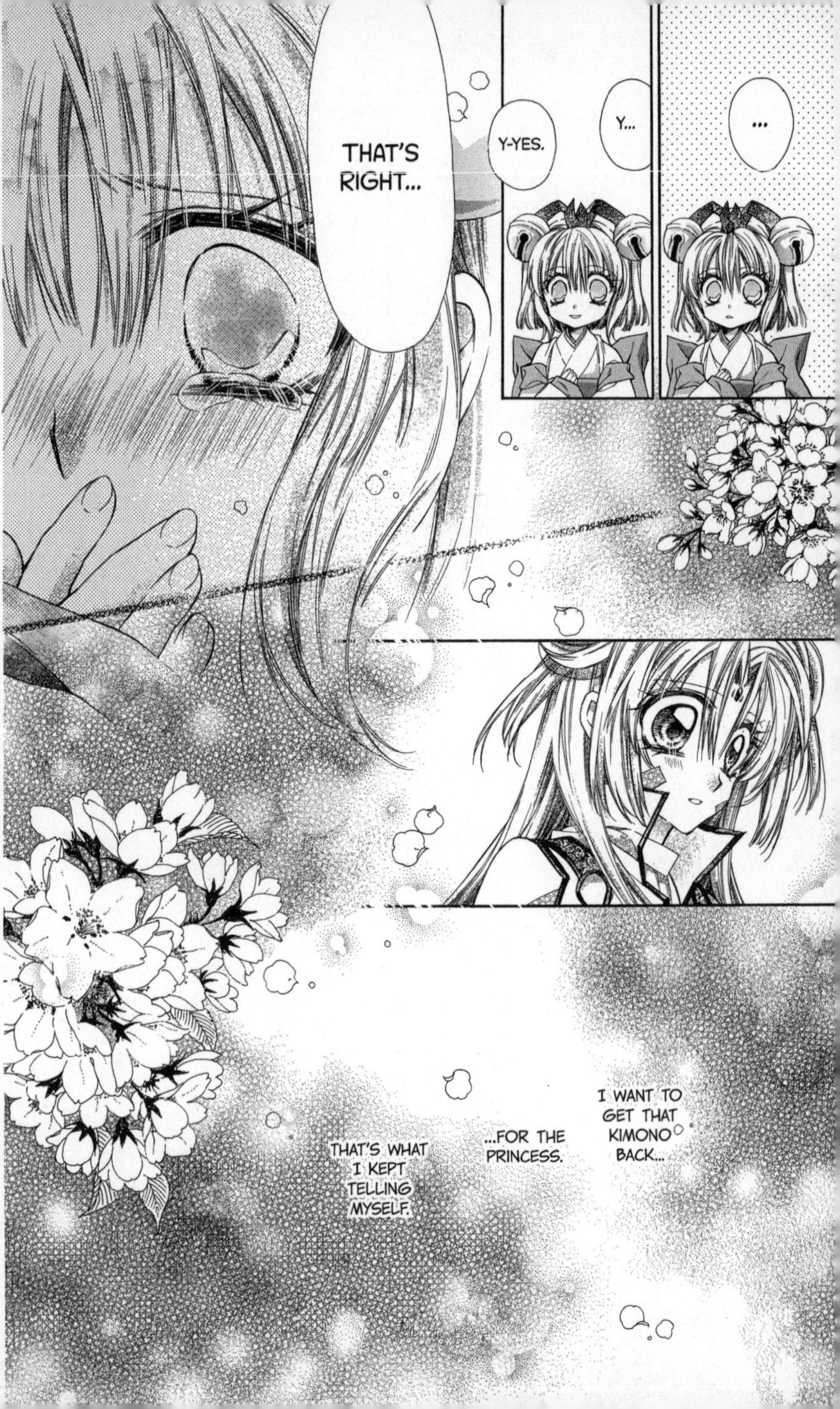
...
Y...
Y-YES.
THAT'S RIGHT...
I WANT TO GET THAT KIMONO BACK...
...FOR THE PRINCESS.
THAT'S WHAT I KEPT TELLING MYSELF.

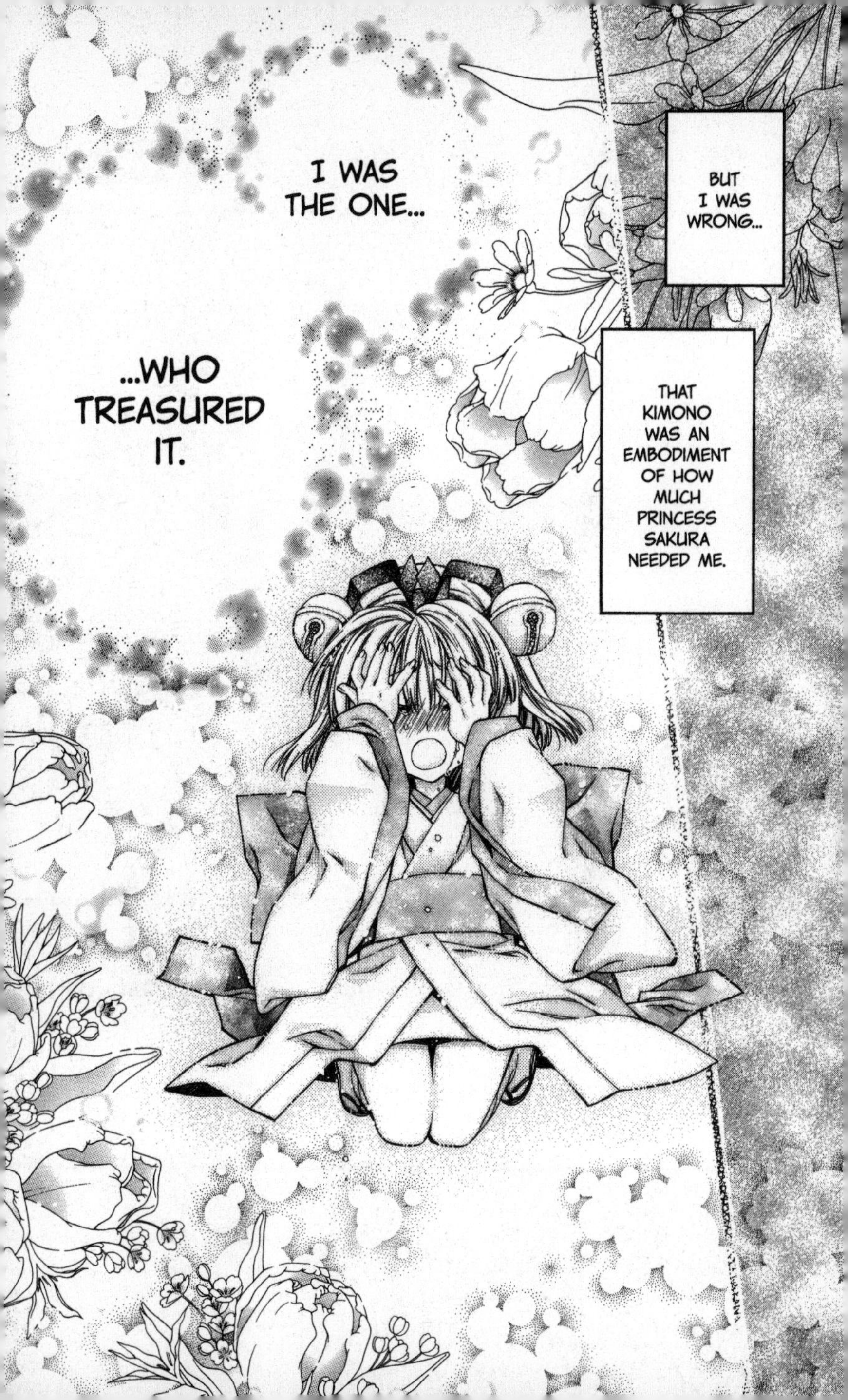
BUT I WAS WRONG...
THAT KIMONO WAS AN EMBODIMENT OF HOW MUCH PRINCESS SAKURA NEEDED ME.
I WAS THE ONE...
...WHO TREASURED IT.

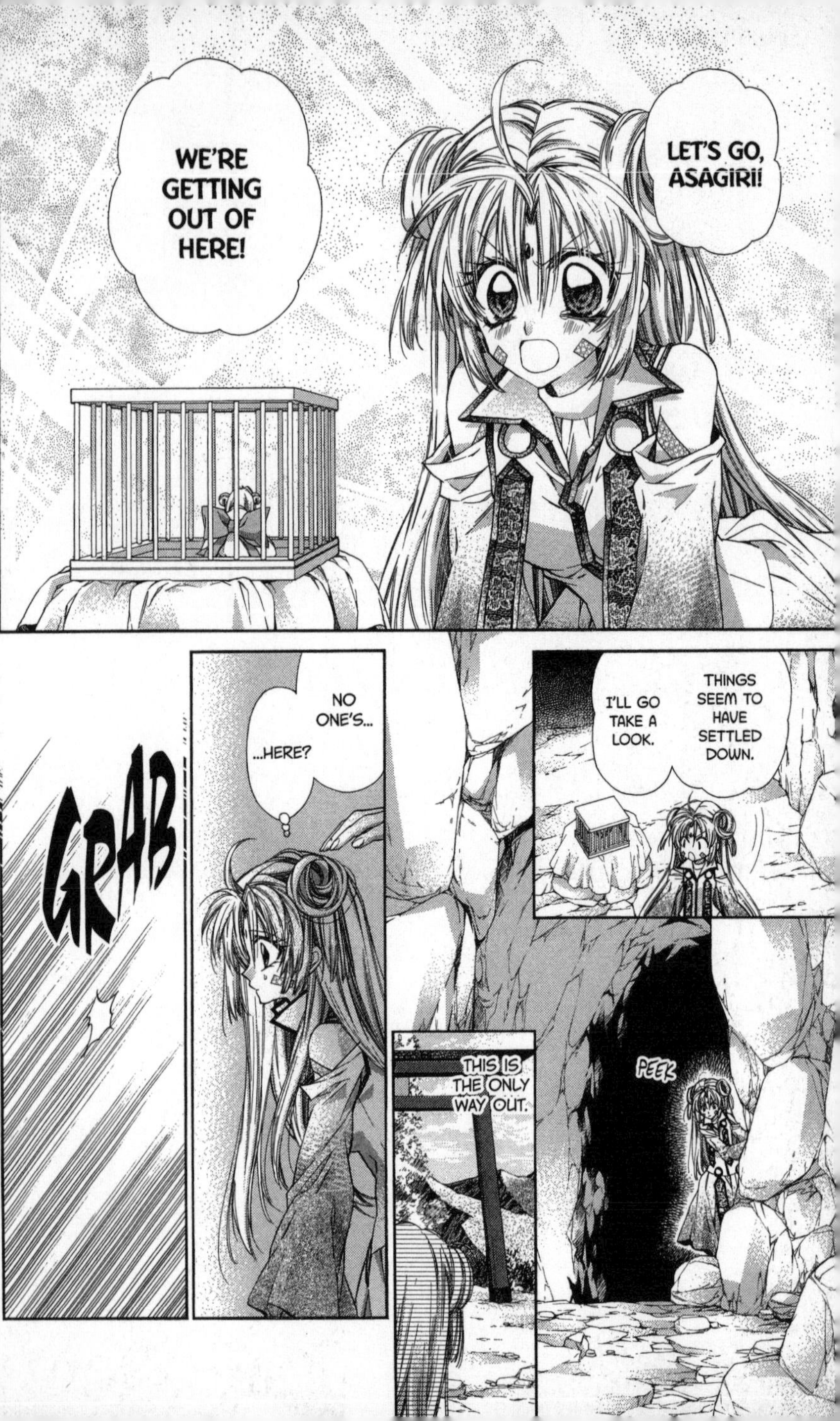
LET'S GO, ASAGIRI!
WE'RE GETTING OUT OF HERE!
THINGS SEEM TO HAVE SETTLED DOWN.
I'LL GO TAKE A LOOK.
PEEK
THIS IS THE ONLY WAY OUT.
NO ONE'S...
...HERE?
GRAB

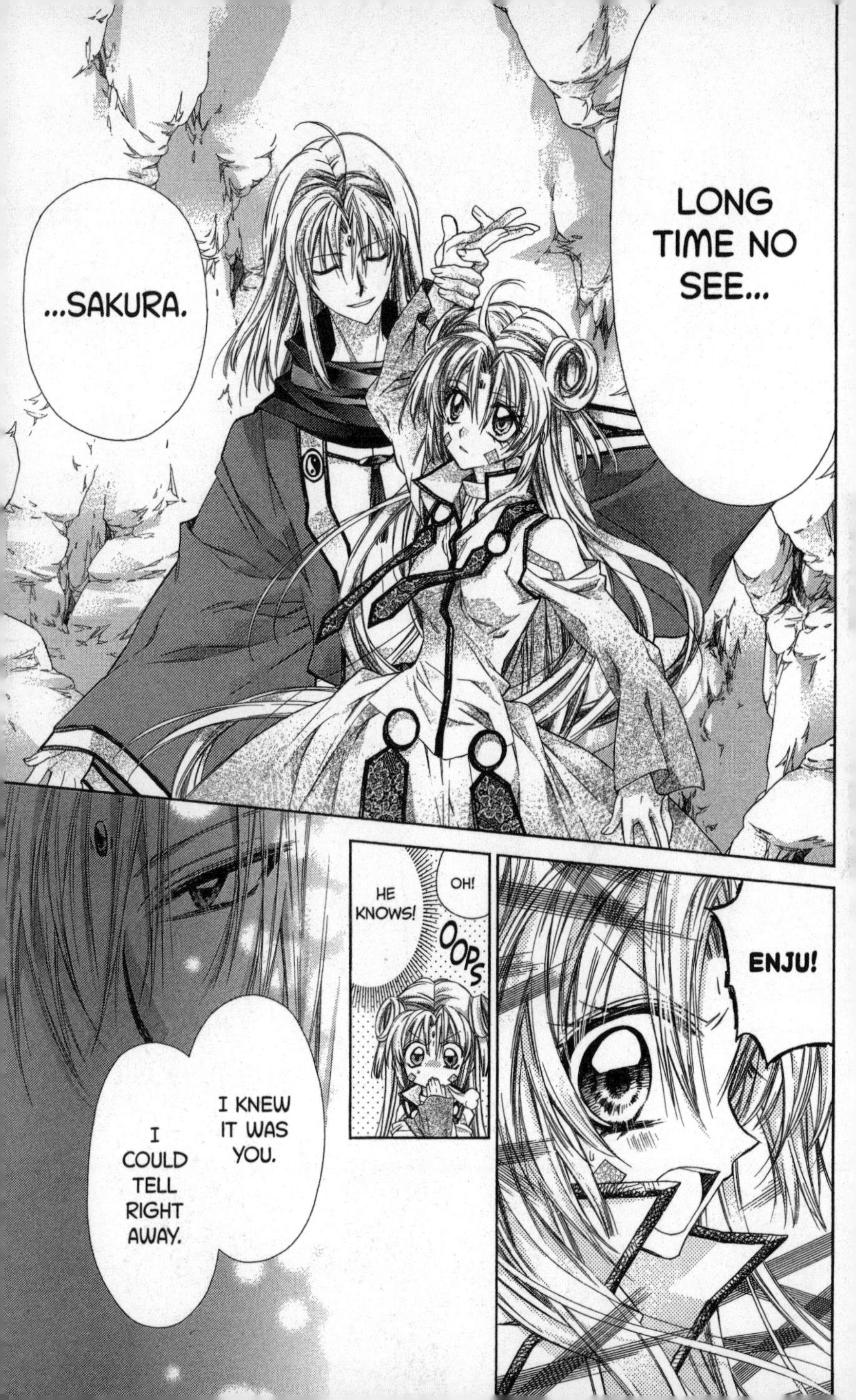
LONG TIME NO SEE...
...SAKURA.
ENJU!
OH!
HE KNOWS!
OOPS
I KNEW IT WAS YOU.
I COULD TELL RIGHT AWAY.

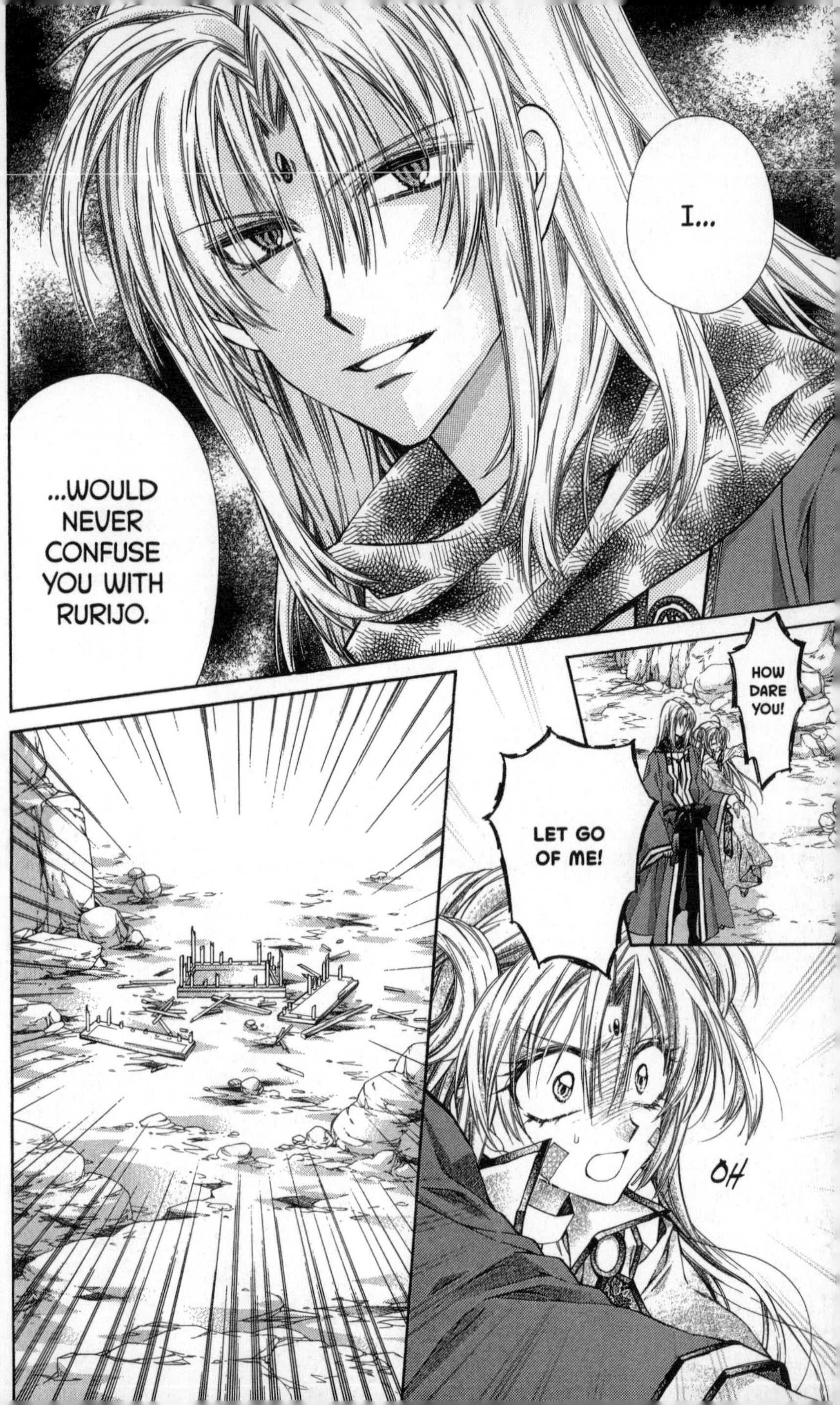
I...
...WOULD NEVER CONFUSE YOU WITH RURIJO.
HOW DARE YOU!
LET GO OF ME!
OH

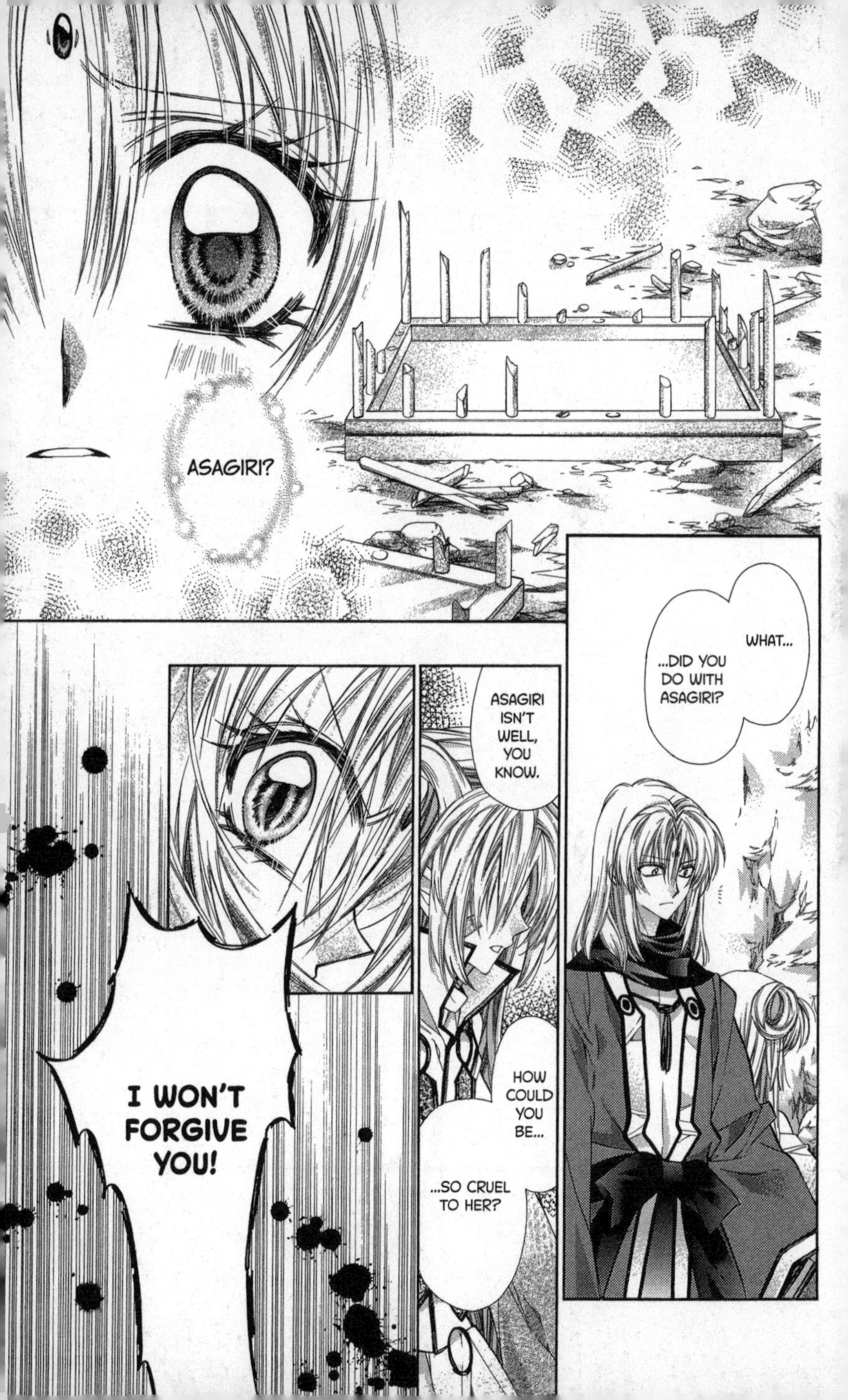
ASAGIRI?
WHAT...
...DID YOU DO WITH ASAGIRI?
ASAGIRI ISN'T WELL, YOU KNOW.
HOW COULD YOU BE...
...SO CRUEL TO HER?
I WON'T FORGIVE YOU!

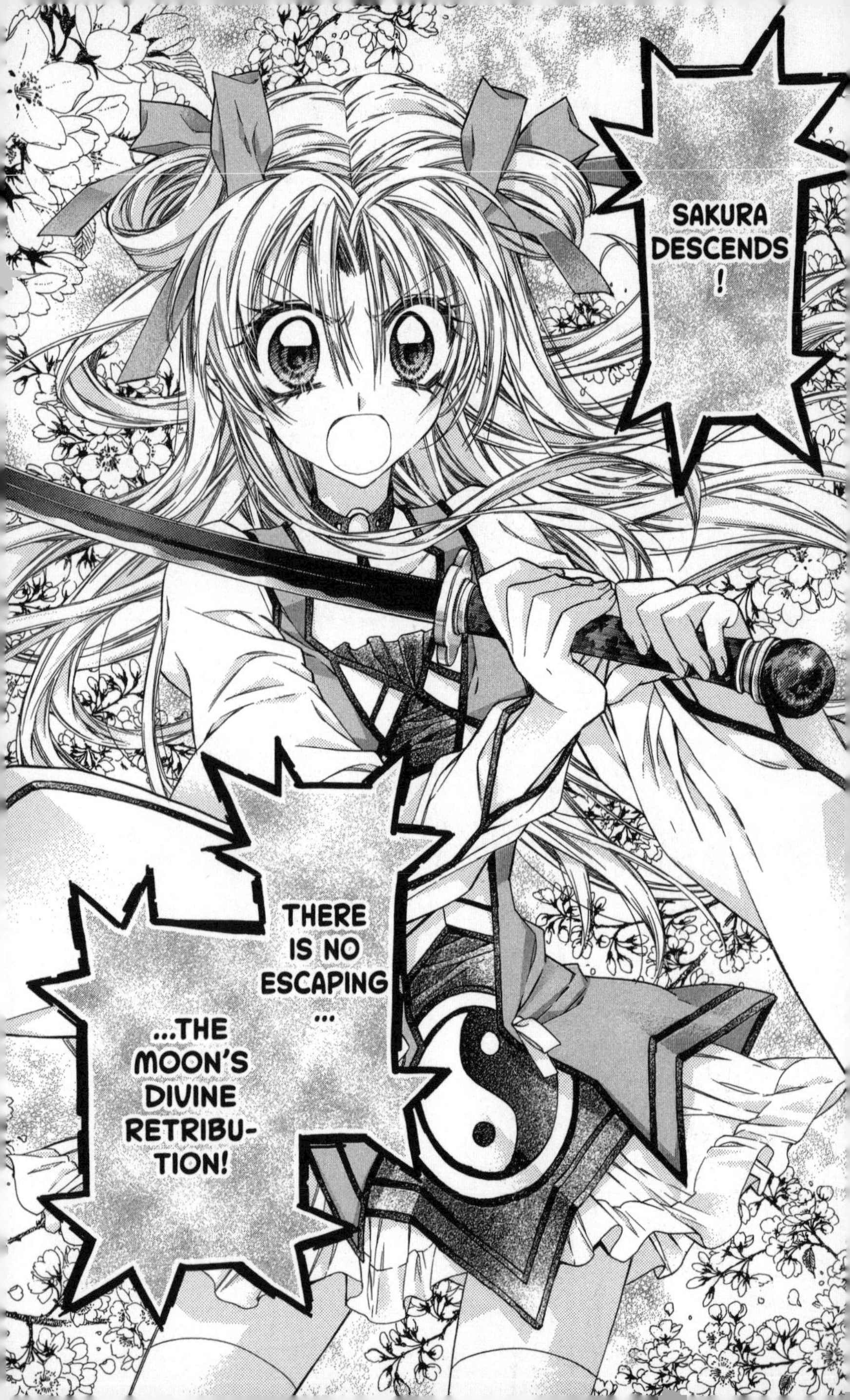
SAKURA DESCENDS!
THERE IS NO ESCAPING...
...THE MOON'S DIVINE RETRIBUTION!

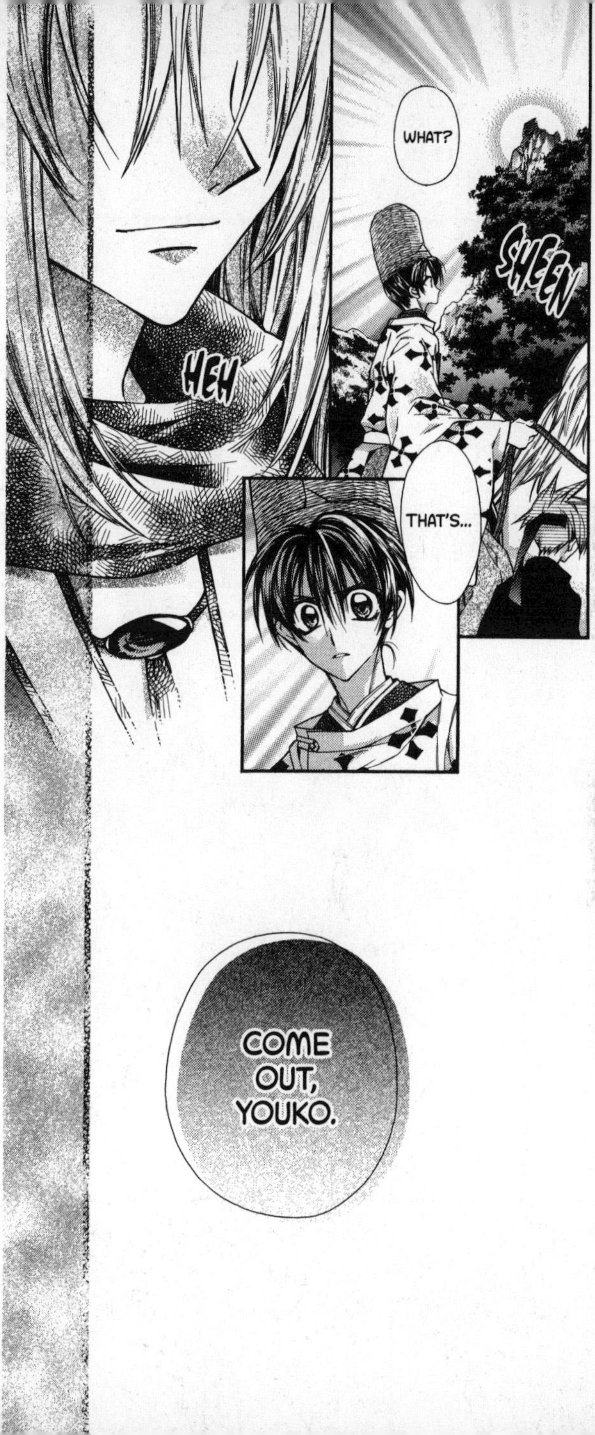
WHAT?
SHEEN
THAT'S...
HEH
COME OUT, YOUKO.

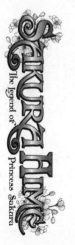

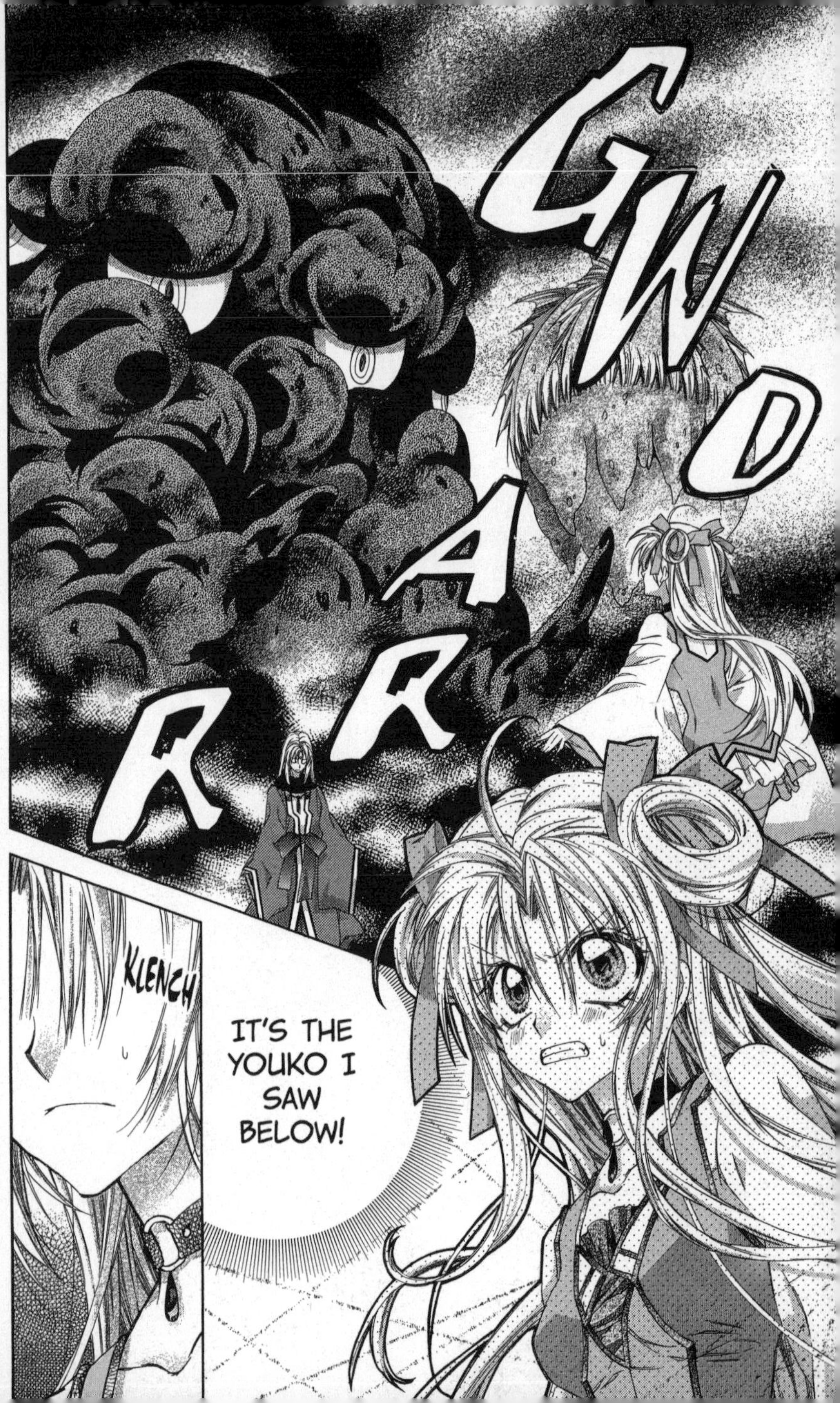
GWOARRR
KLENCH
IT'S THE YOUKO I SAW BELOW!

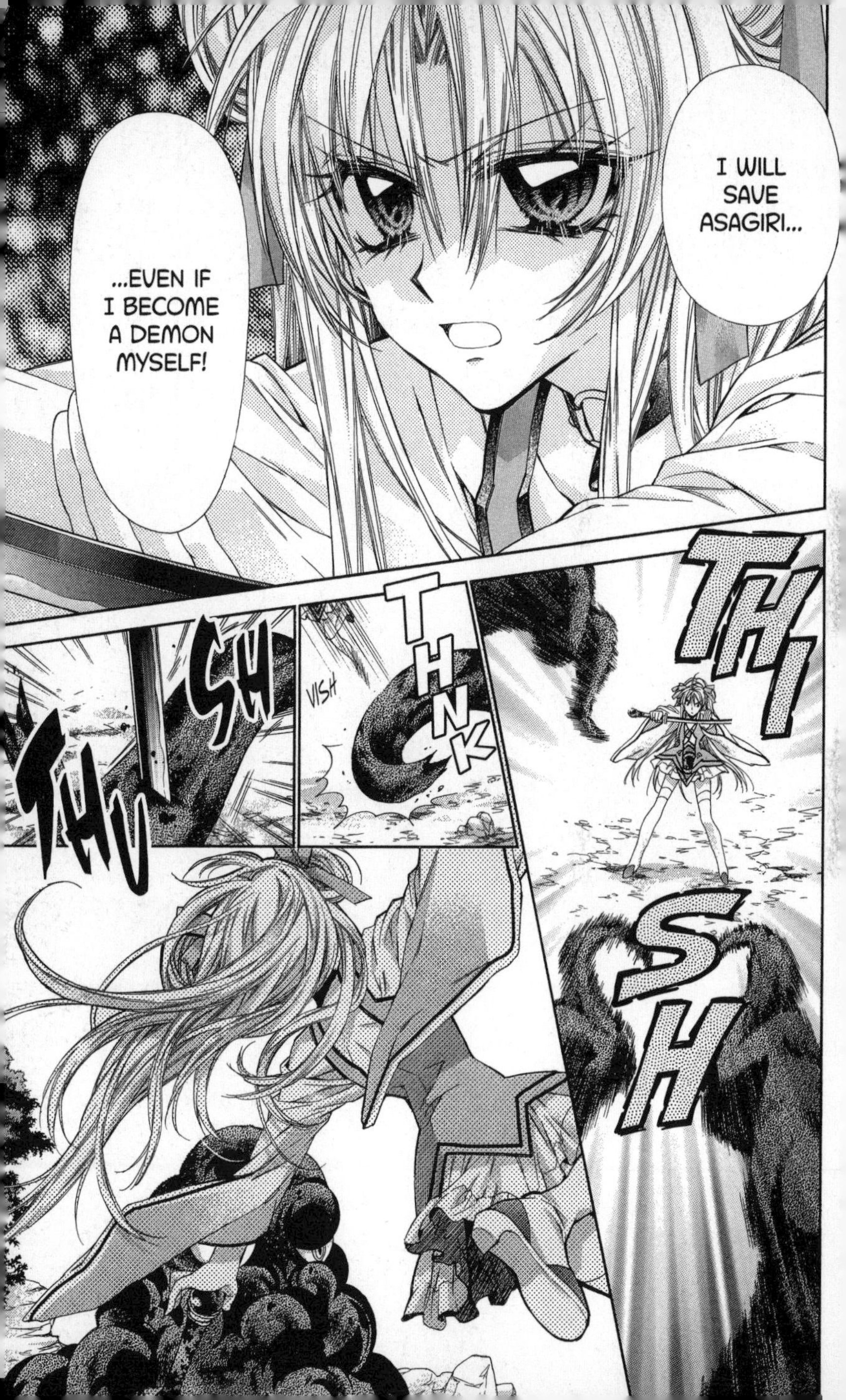
I WILL SAVE ASAGIRI...
...EVEN IF I BECOME A DEMON MYSELF!
THISH
THNK
VISH
THUSH

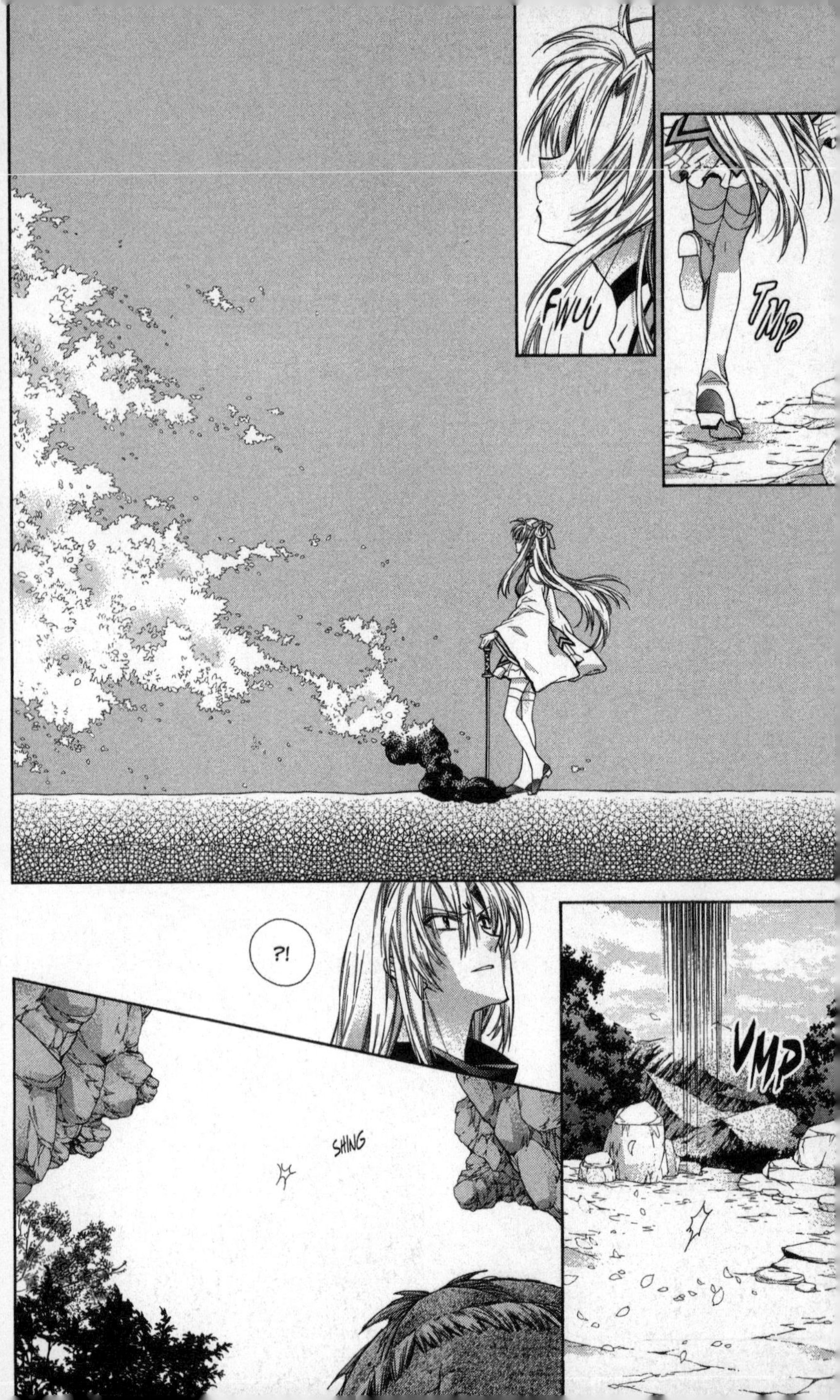
TMP
FWUU
VMP
?!
SHING

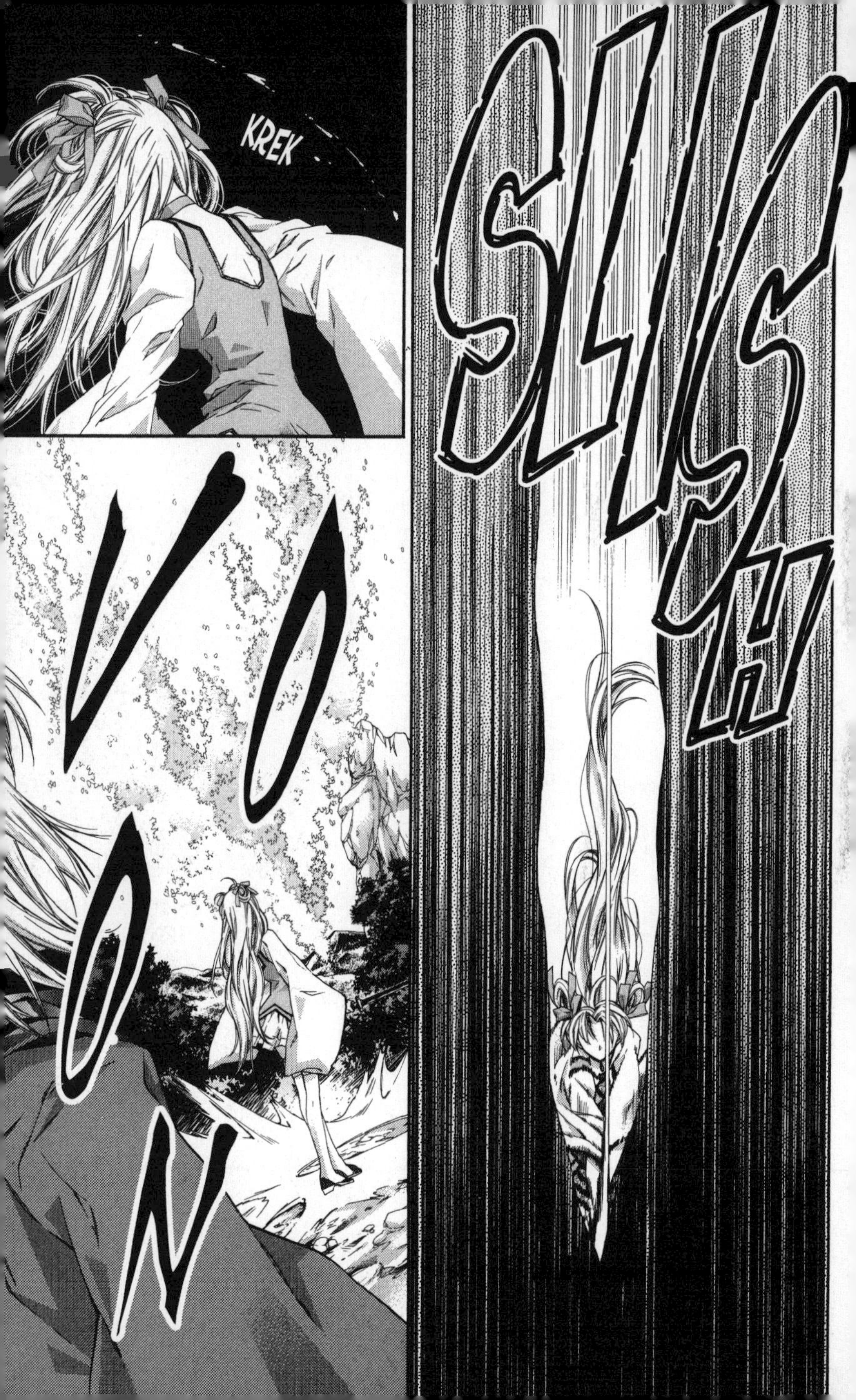
SLASH
KREK
VOON

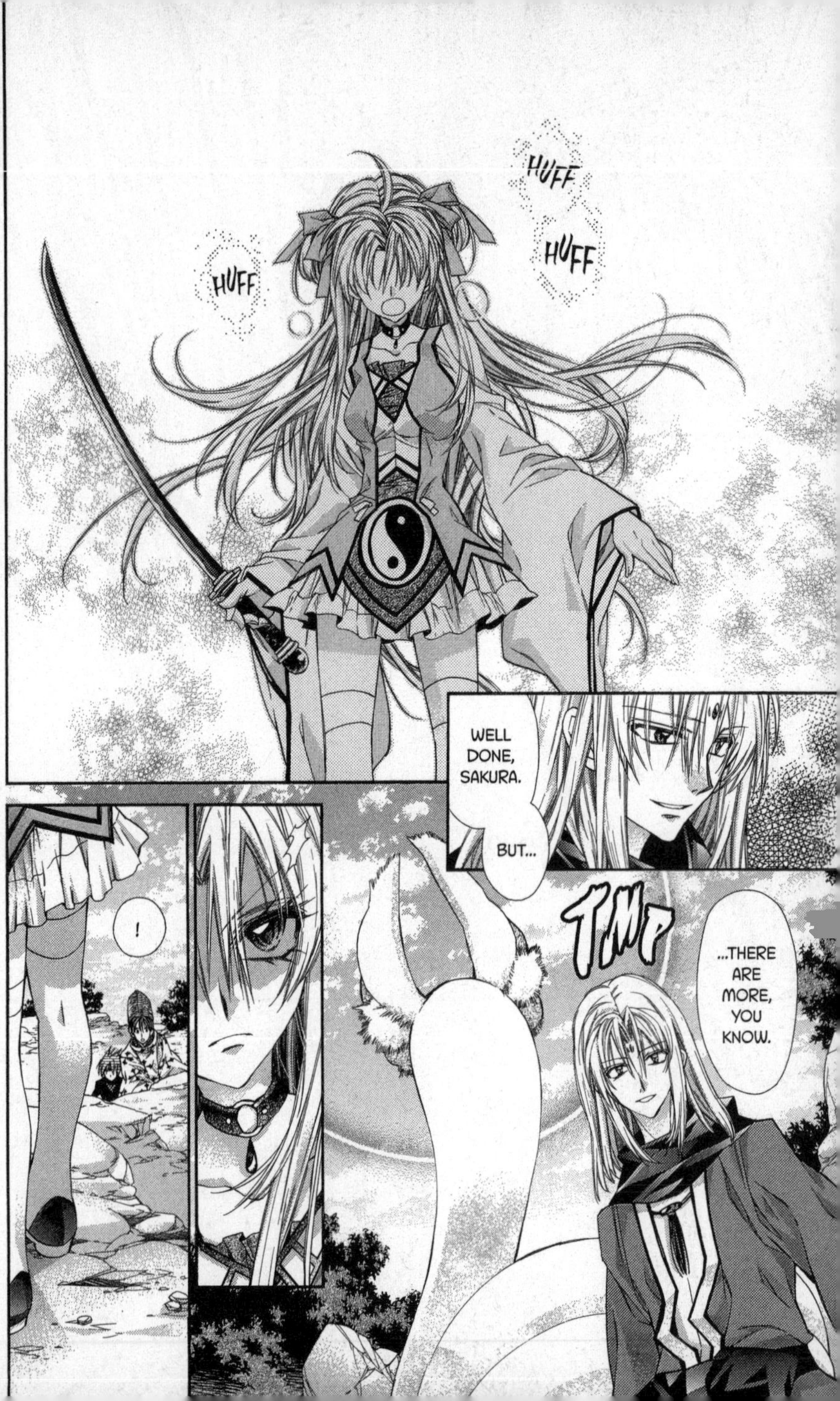
HUFF
HUFF
HUFF
WELL DONE, SAKURA.
BUT...
TMP
...THERE ARE MORE, YOU KNOW.
!

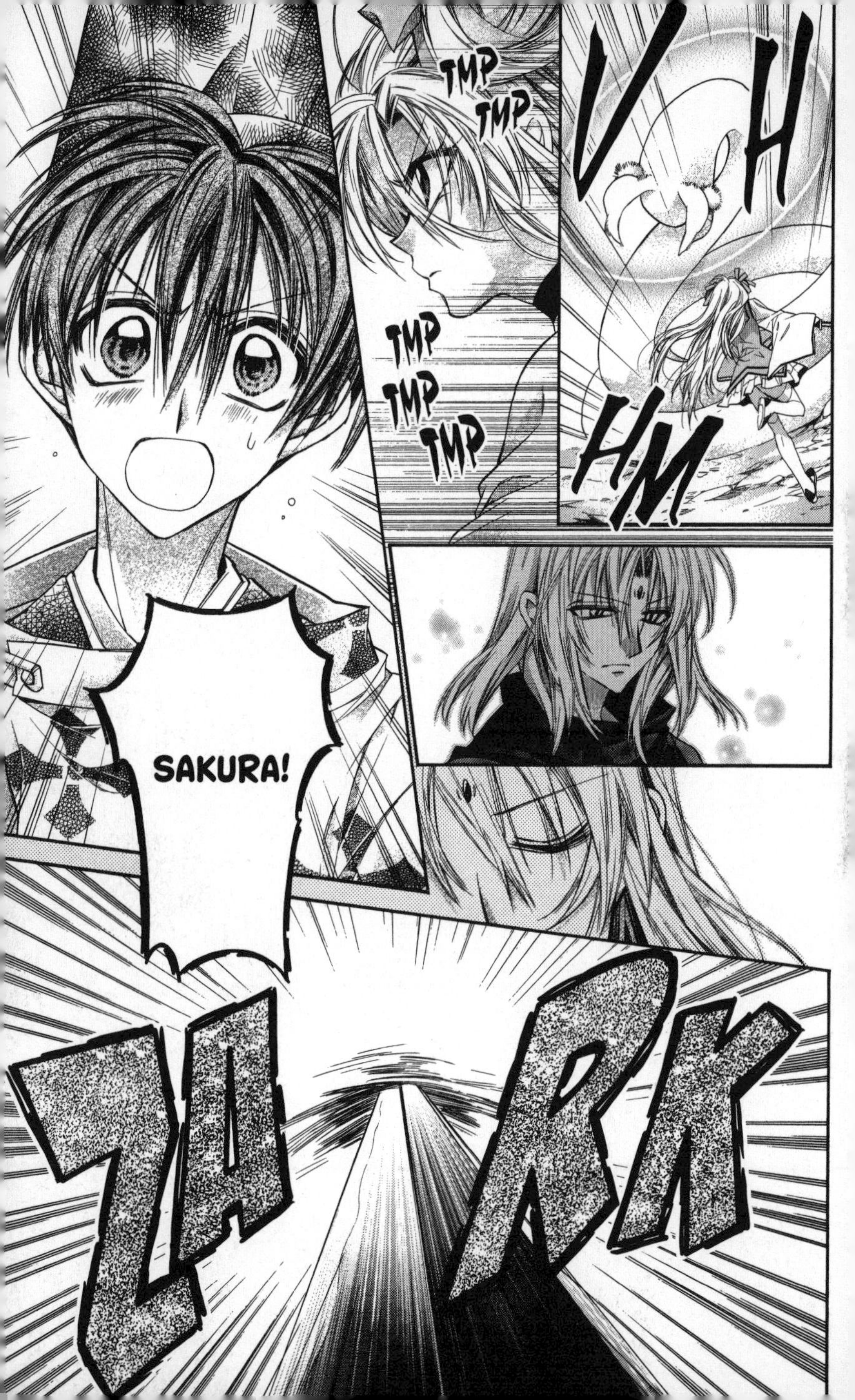
VH
HM
TMP TMP
TMP TMP TMP
SAKURA!
ZA RK

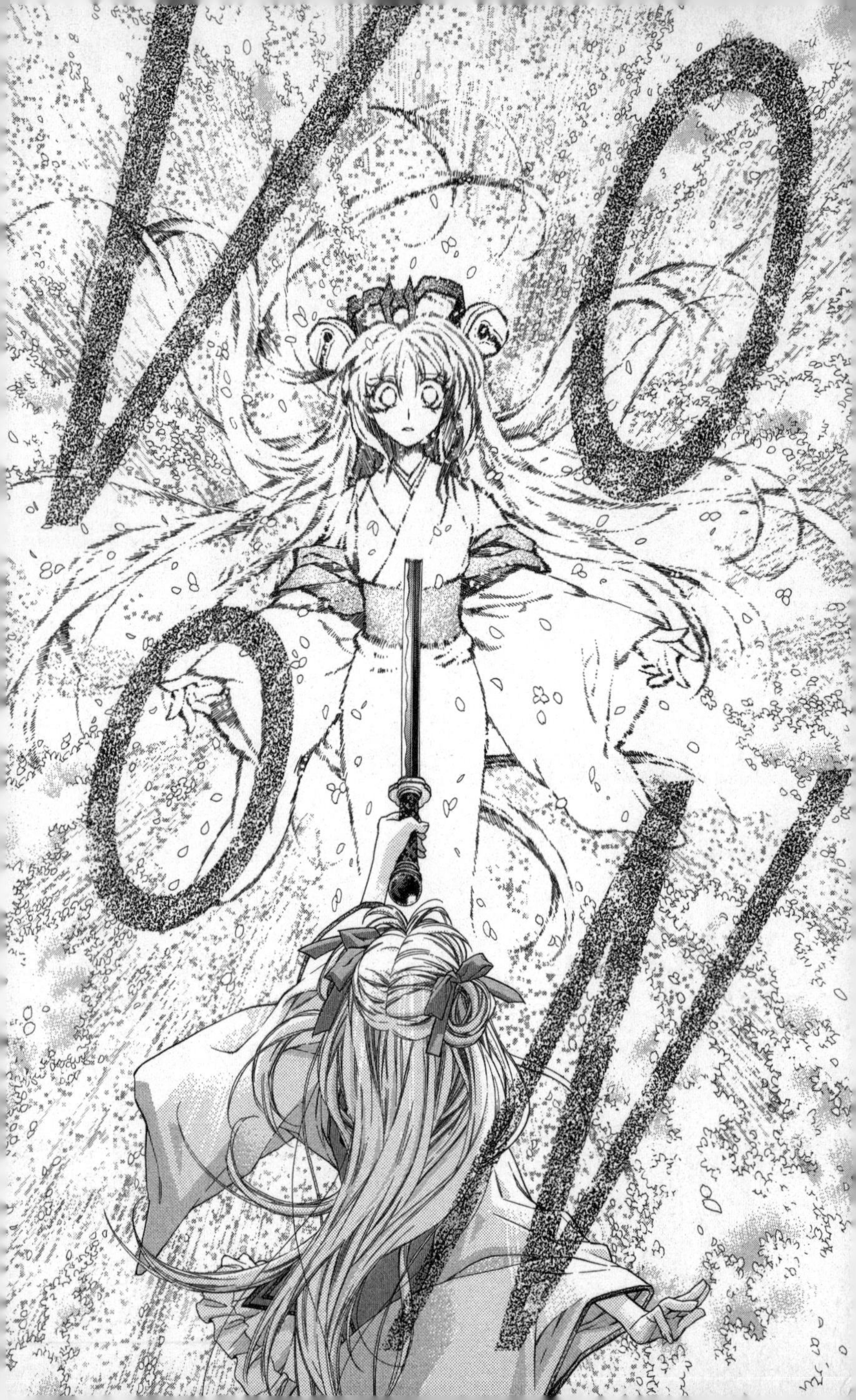

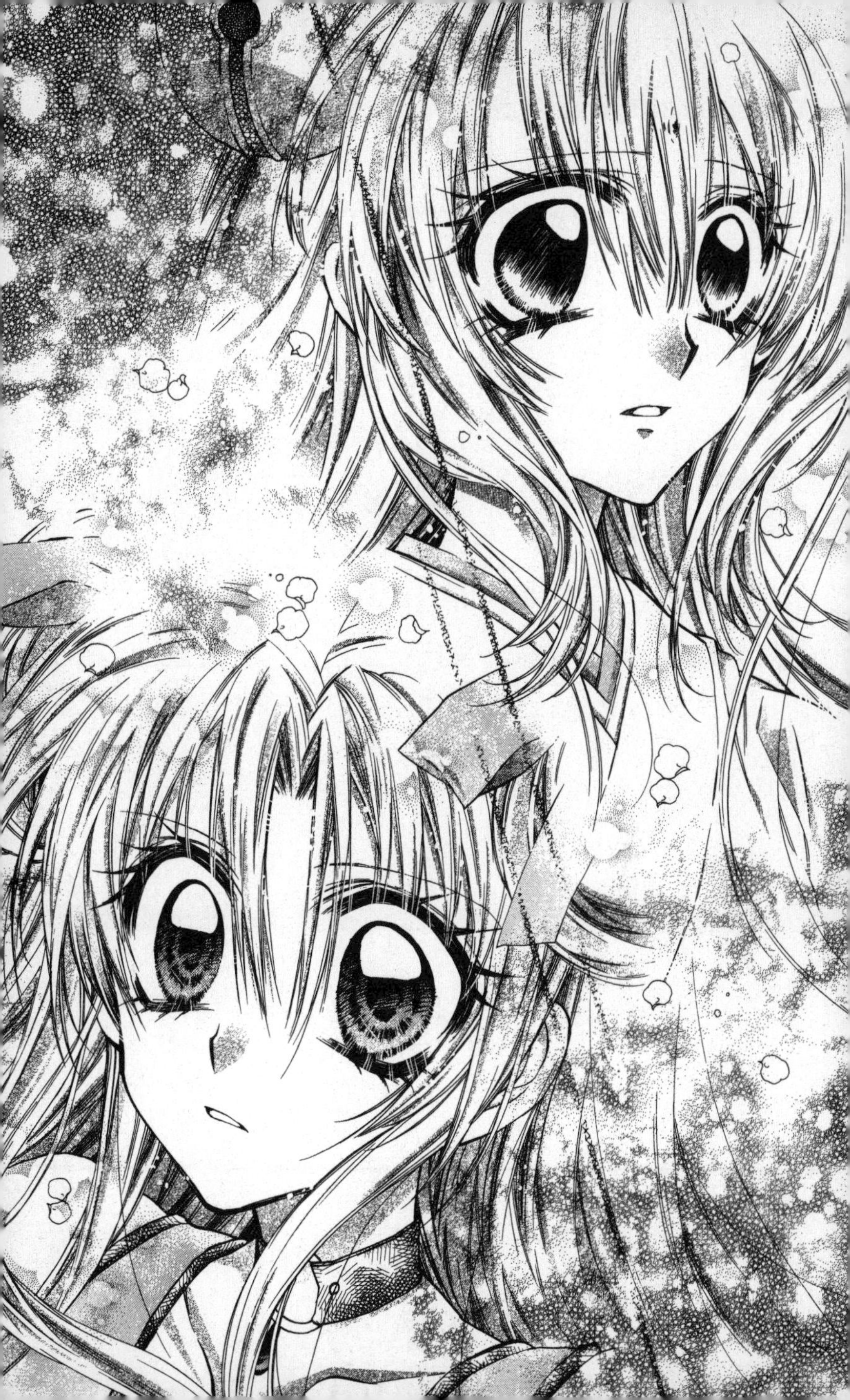

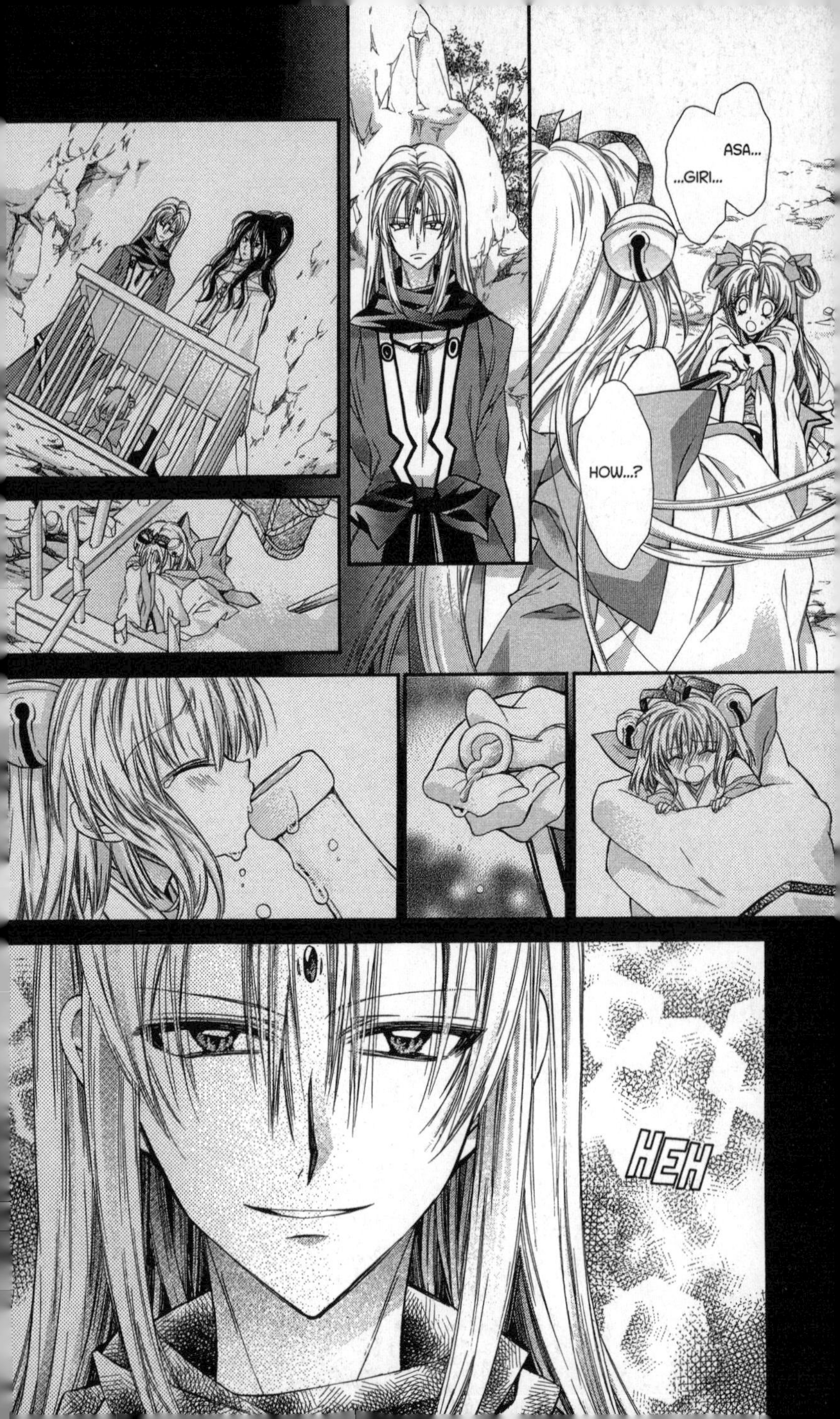
ASA...
...GIRI...
HOW...?
HEH

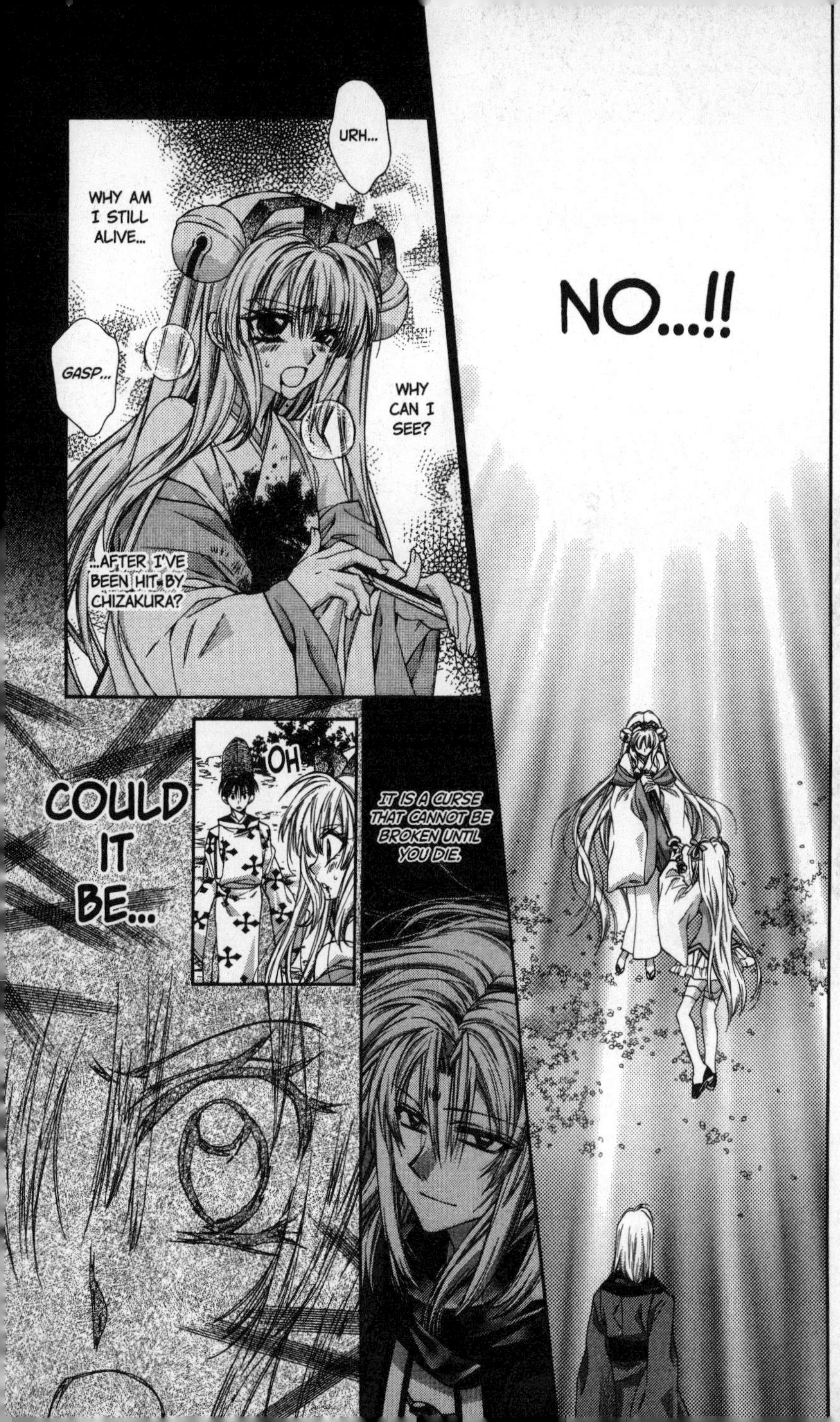
NO...!!
URH...
WHY AM I STILL ALIVE...
GASP...
WHY CAN I SEE?
...AFTER I'VE BEEN HIT BY CHIZAKURA?
IT IS A CURSE THAT CANNOT BE BROKEN UNTIL YOU DIE.
OH
COULD IT BE...

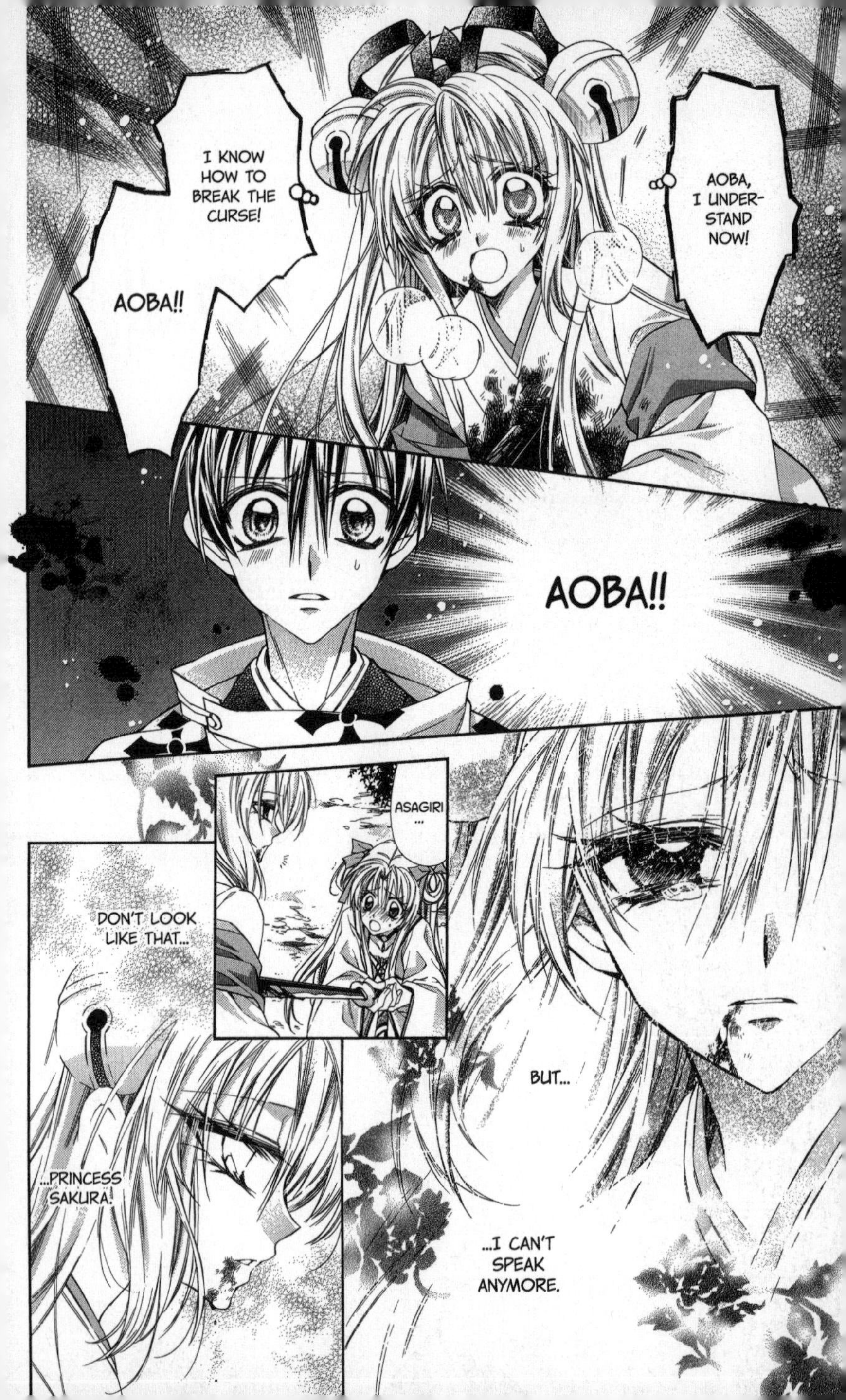
AOBA, I UNDER-STAND NOW!
I KNOW HOW TO BREAK THE CURSE!
AOBA!!
AOBA!!
ASAGIRI ...
DON'T LOOK LIKE THAT...
...PRINCESS SAKURA!
BUT...
...I CAN'T SPEAK ANYMORE.

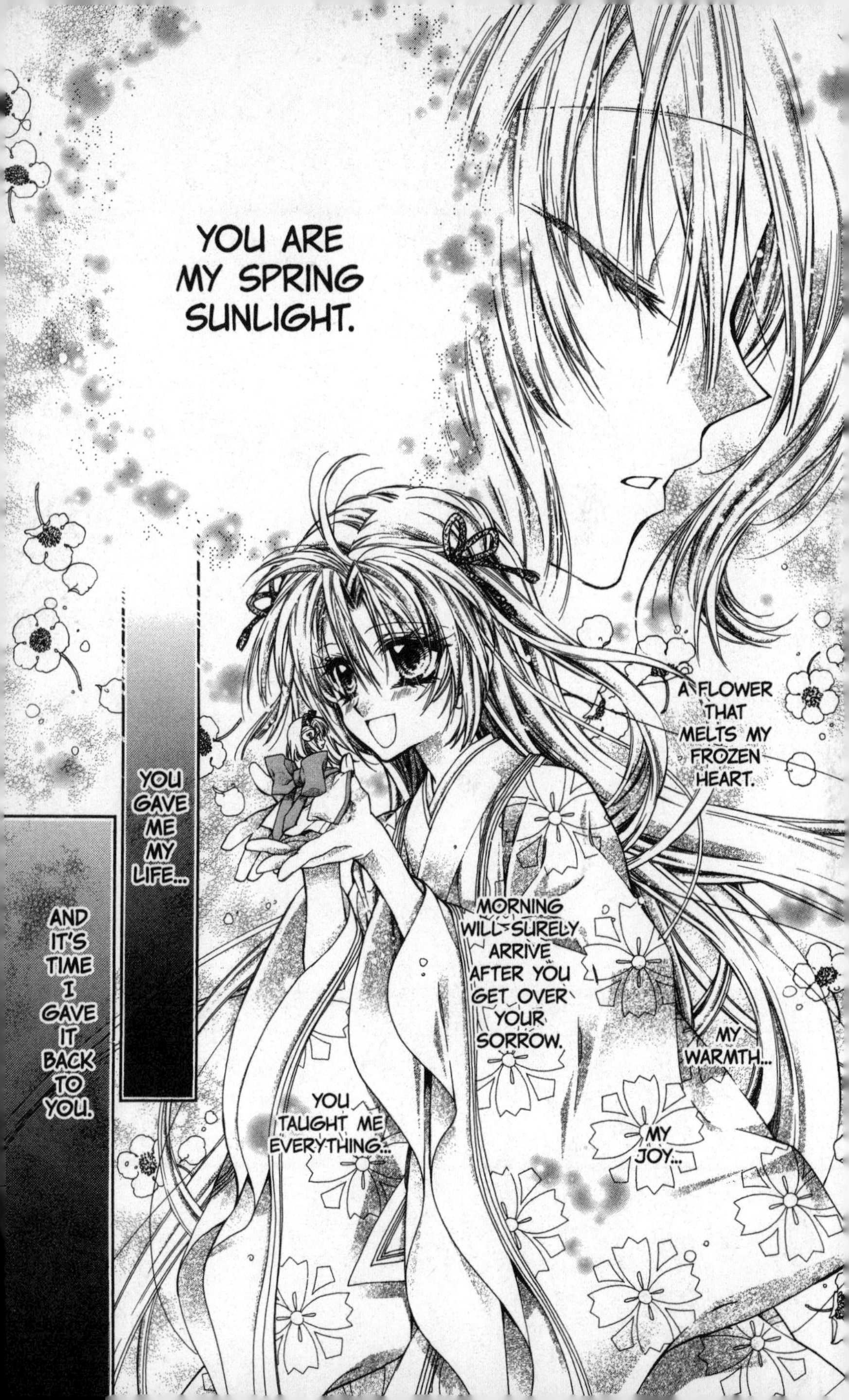
YOU ARE MY SPRING SUNLIGHT.
A FLOWER THAT MELTS MY FROZEN HEART.
MY WARMTH...
MY JOY...
MORNING WILL SURELY ARRIVE AFTER YOU GET OVER YOUR SORROW.
YOU TAUGHT ME EVERYTHING...
YOU GAVE ME MY LIFE...
AND IT'S TIME I GAVE IT BACK TO YOU.

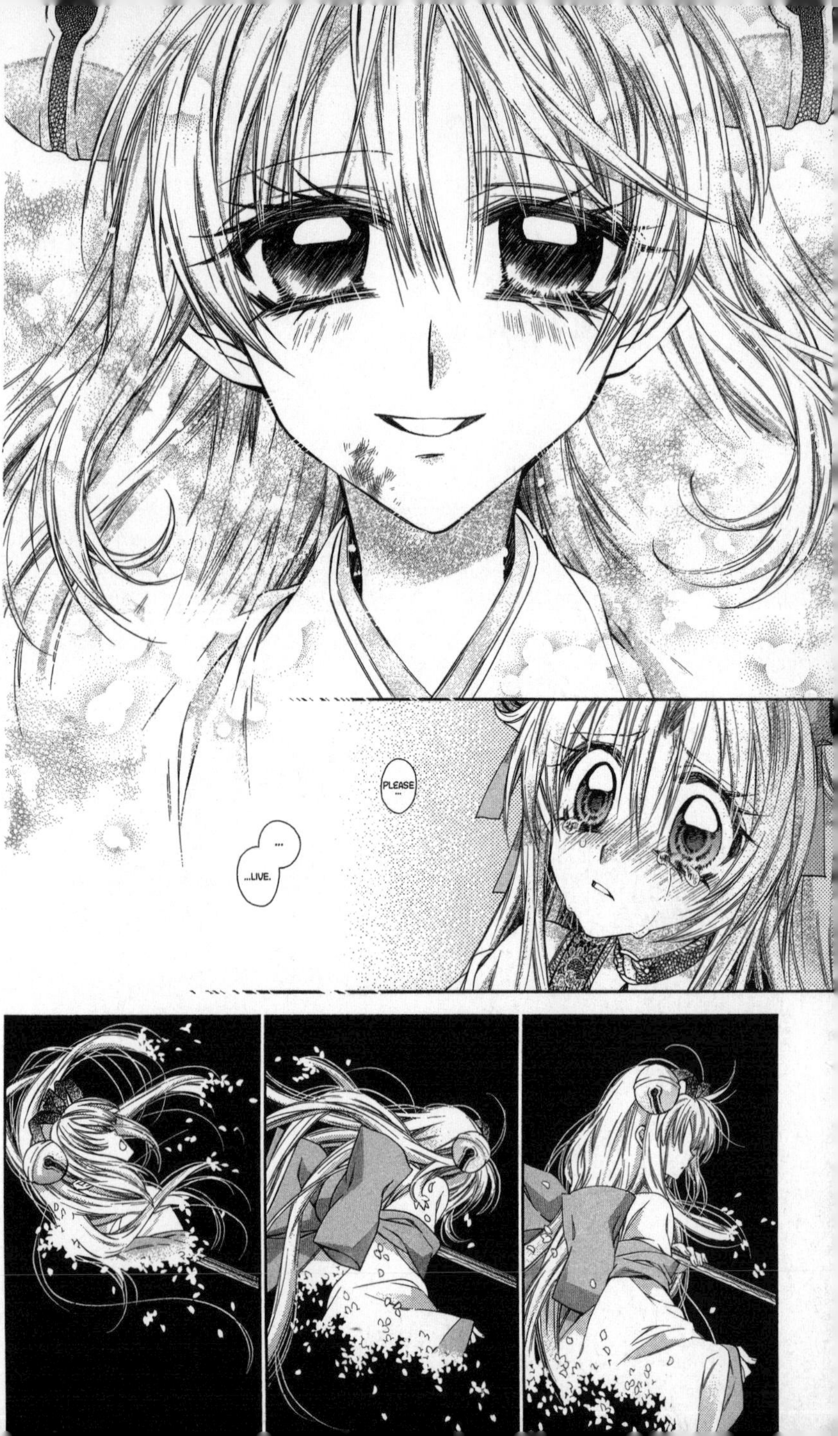
PLEASE
...
...
...LIVE.

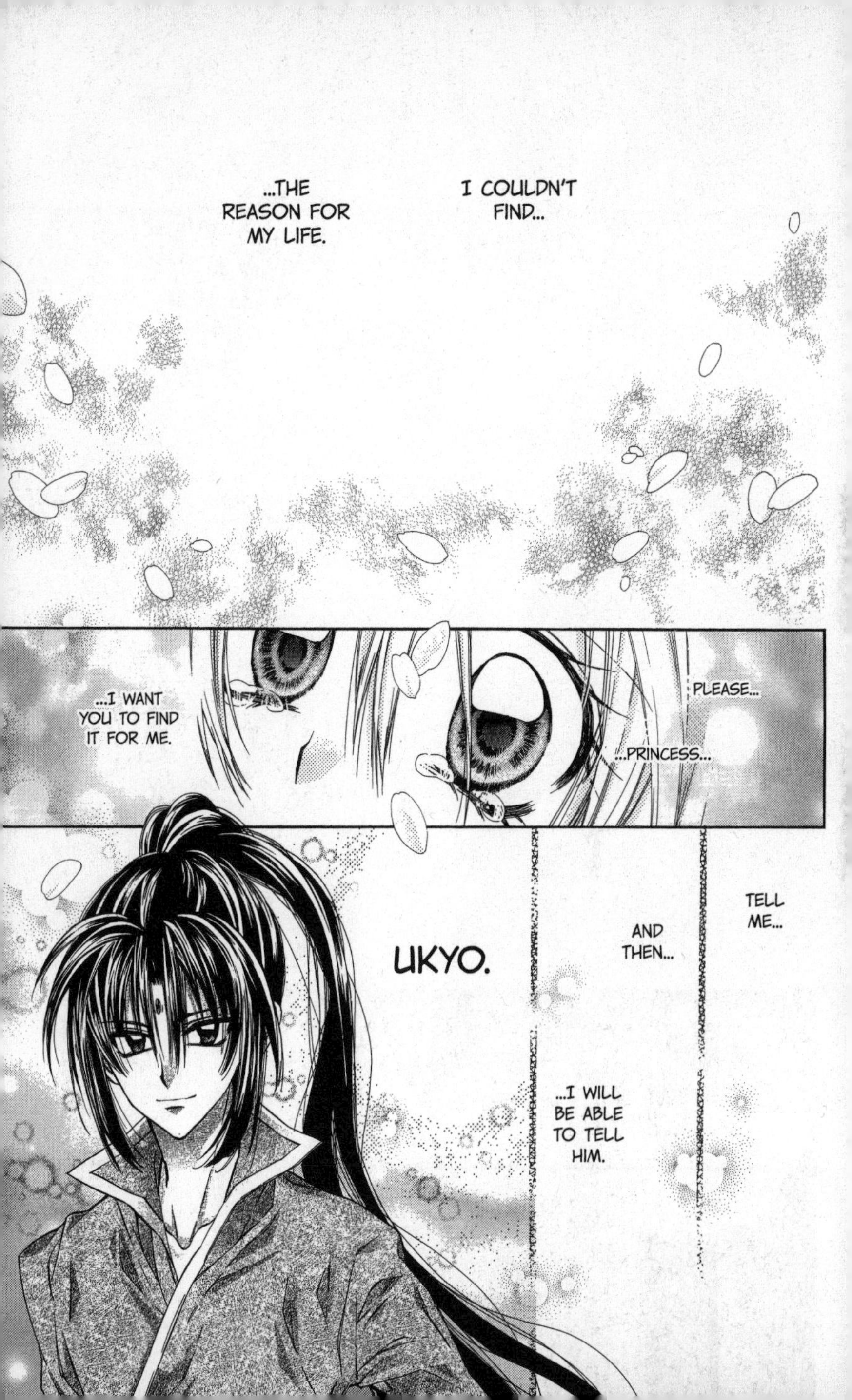
I COULDN'T FIND...
...THE REASON FOR MY LIFE.
PLEASE...
...PRINCESS...
...I WANT YOU TO FIND IT FOR ME.
TELL ME...
AND THEN...
...I WILL BE ABLE TO TELL HIM.
UKYO.

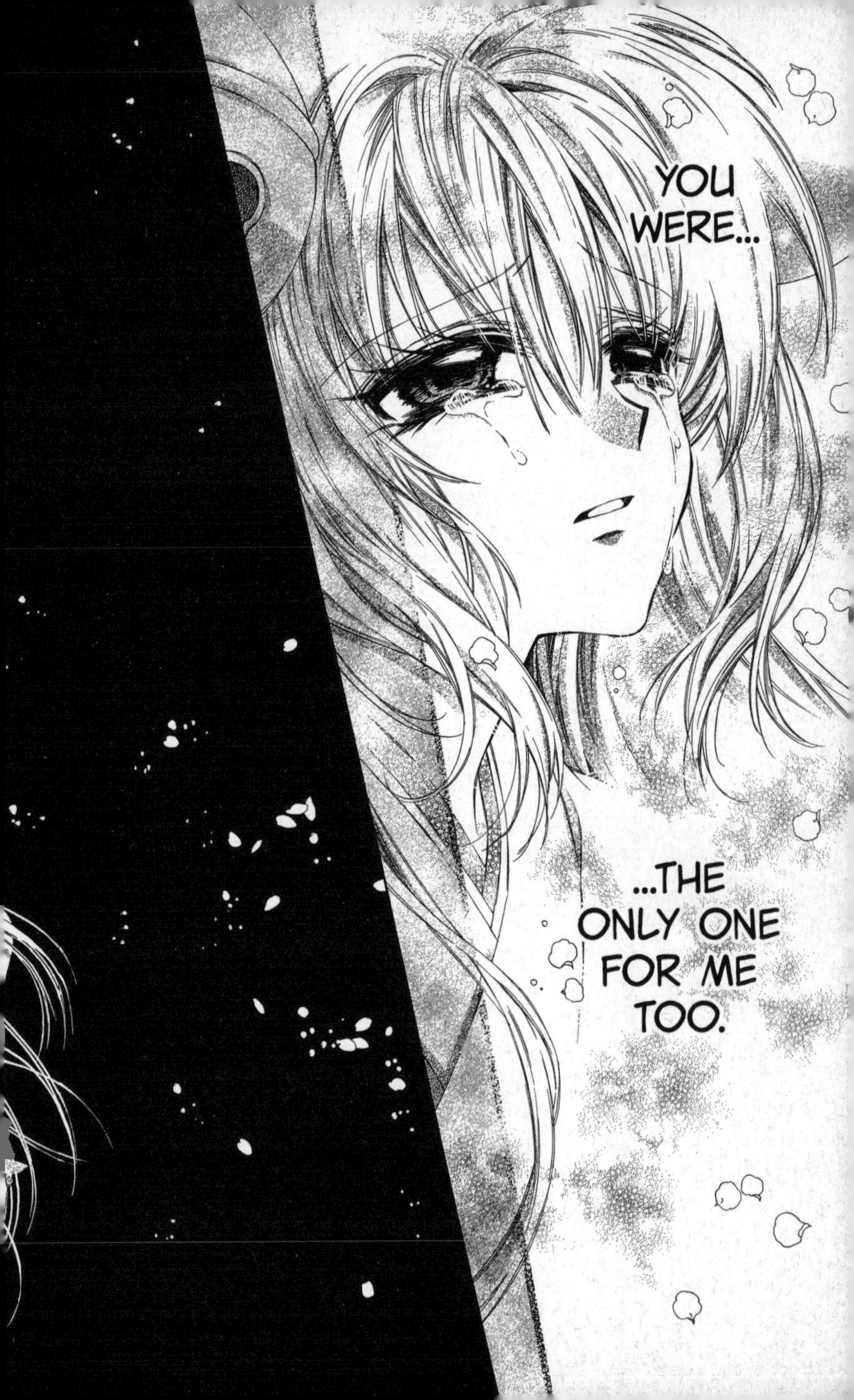
YOU WERE...
...THE ONLY ONE FOR ME TOO.

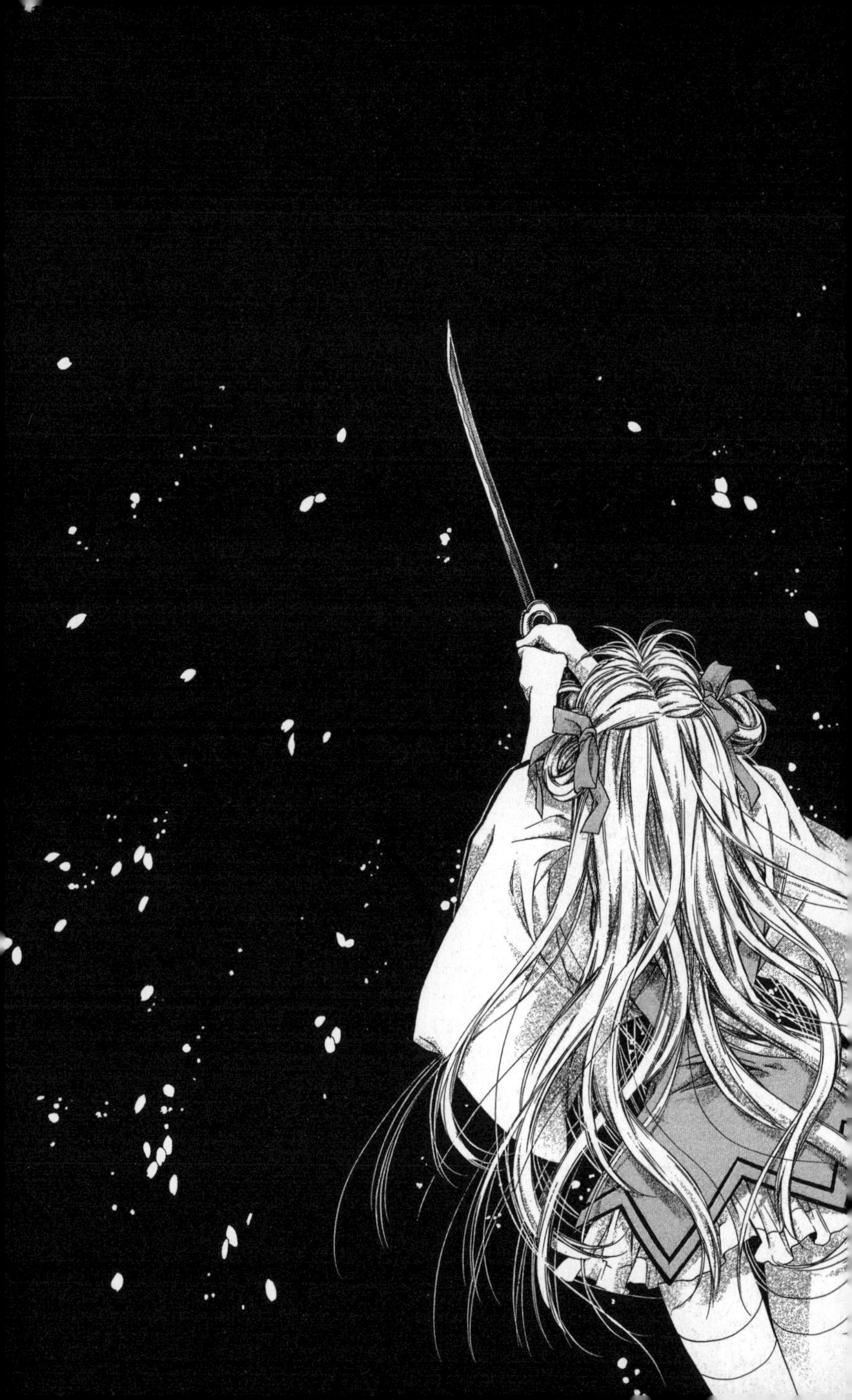

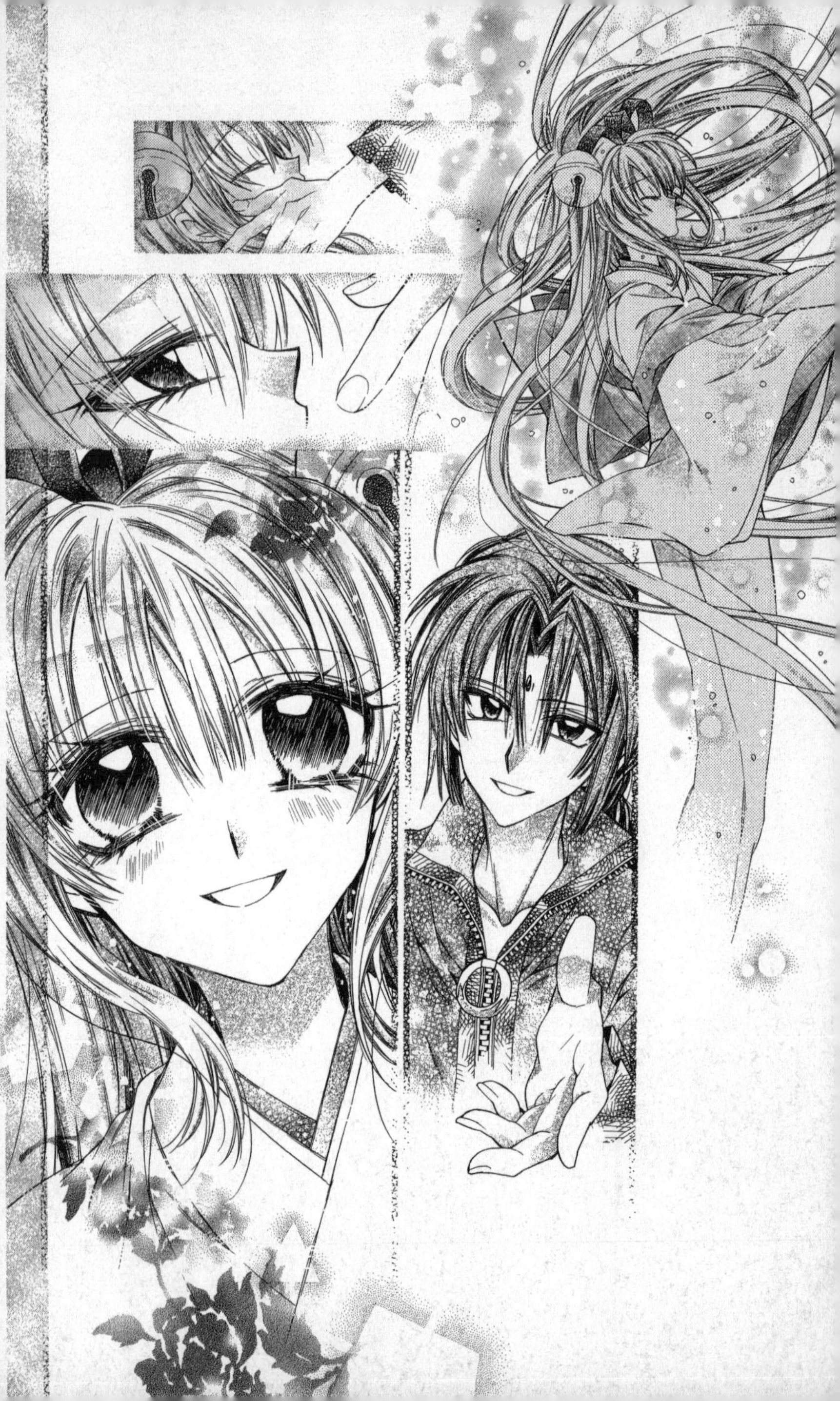

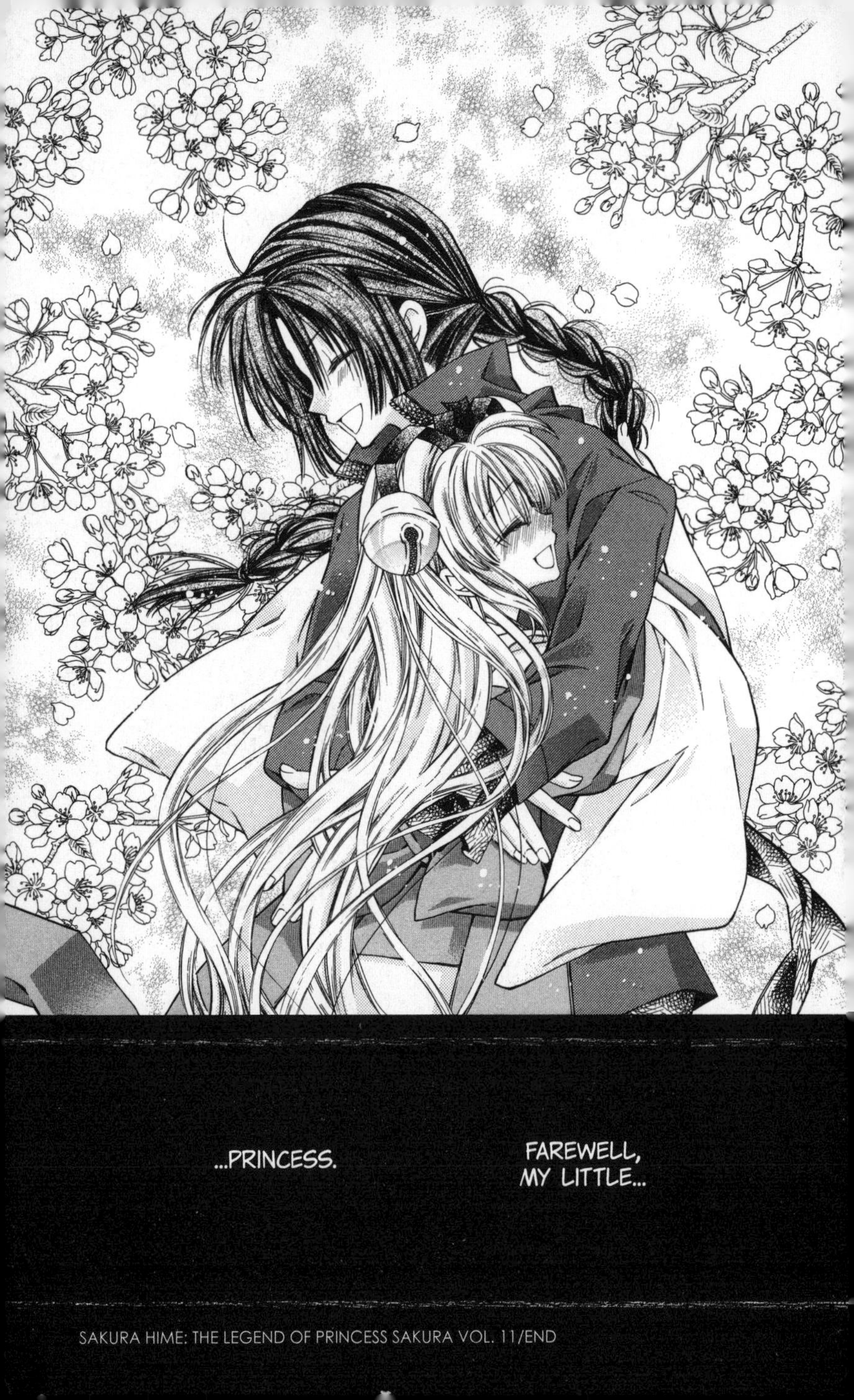

FAREWELL,
MY LITTLE...

...PRINCESS.

SAKURA HIME: THE LEGEND OF PRINCESS SAKURA VOL. 11/END

Special ★ Thanks

✿ Nakame	✿ Momoko
✿ Matsun	✿ Hii-chan
✿ Yogurt-chan	✿ Acchan
✿ Icchi	✿ Naho Minami-chan
✿ Mari	✿ Rena-san
✿ Miichi	✿ Ikurun

Acchan drew an illustration for me this time. ♥

Thanks for all your help, Acchan.

Congratulations on volume 11!

Hello. I'm Acchan, the assistant. It's great to be able to work under Arina Sensei for the *Sakura Hime* series that I love so much. ♡ I read the chapters with excitement every time. ·ᴗ·

I'm looking forward to reading more of your wonderful work!

ARINA TANEMURA

Sakura Hime: The Legend of Princess Sakura has reached its climax; it will conclude in the next volume. As I work on this series, I've been asking myself "What is life...?" Asagiri left a question for Sakura to answer, and what will fate have in store for Sakura? Please continue to watch over her until the very end.

Arina Tanemura began her manga career in 1996 when her short stories debuted in *Ribon* magazine. She gained fame with the 1997 publication of *I·O·N*, and ever since her debut Tanemura has been a major force in shojo manga with popular series *Kamikaze Kaito Jeanne*, *Time Stranger Kyoko*, *Full Moon*, and *The Gentlemen's Alliance †*. Both *Kamikaze Kaito Jeanne* and *Full Moon* have been adapted into animated TV series.

Sakura Hime: The Legend of Princess Sakura
Volume 11
Shojo Beat Edition

STORY AND ART BY
Arina Tanemura

Translation & Adaptation/Tetsuichiro Miyaki
Touch-up Art & Lettering/Inori Fukuda Trant
Design/Sam Elzway
Editor/Nancy Thistlethwaite

SAKURA-HIME KADEN © 2008 by Arina Tanemura
All rights reserved.
First published in Japan in 2008 by SHUEISHA Inc., Tokyo.
English translation rights arranged by SHUEISHA Inc.

Printed in the U.S.A.

Published by VIZ Media, LLC
P.O. Box 77010
San Francisco, CA 94107

10 9 8 7 6 5 4 3 2 1
First printing, October 2013

www.shojobeat.com   www.viz.com

RATED

PARENTAL ADVISORY
SAKURA HIME is rated T for Teen
and is recommended for ages
13 and up.
ratings.viz.com

SURPRISE!

You may be reading the wrong way!

It's true: In keeping with the original Japanese comic format, this book reads from right to left—so action, sound effects, and word balloons are completely reversed. This preserves the orientation of the original artwork—plus, it's fun! Check out the diagram shown here to get the hang of things, and then turn to the other side of the book to get started!

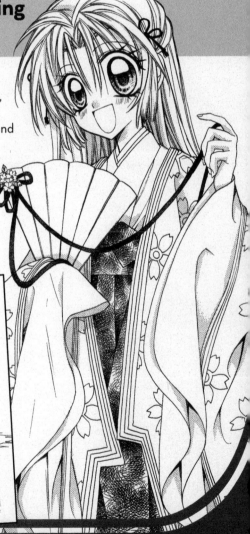

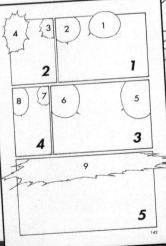